Teachers College
Studies in Education

The Scottish Enlightenment and the American College Ideal

Douglas Sloan

TEACHERS COLLEGE PRESS
Teachers College, Columbia University

© 1971 by Teachers College, Columbia University
Library of Congress Catalog Card Number: 75-132938

Manufactured in the United States of America

To Fern

Preface

As Americans in the eighteenth century strove to establish their own cultural identity and integrity, they did not rely solely upon themselves or respond only to the special needs and conditions presented by life in the new world. They were also part of a larger transatlantic cultural community, from which they never completely severed themselves, even in their most intense moments of reaction against it. Sometimes deliberately, sometimes unknowingly or by necessity, Americans drew upon the constant flow of ideas, people, and practices binding the members of this wider community together. While they were participants with England, France, even Germany, in this cultural exchange, Americans—particularly those consciously involved in the tasks of shaping a new society—turned increasingly for inspiration and example to Scotland.

This is a study of the influences exerted by the universities of Scotland and the ideas of Scottish intellectuals on eighteenth-century American higher education. Historians have become ever more insistent that the American past is not to be fully understood from a narrow national perspective alone. This spirit has been demonstrated by those historians of the American college and university who have long stressed the importance of the English antecedents of the three original colonial colleges and the impact of the German example on the emergence of the American university in the late nineteenth century. It is especially surprising, therefore, to discover that, with few exceptions, historians have tended to treat the eighteenth-century American college as an almost totally indigenous, American creation. Perhaps one explanation for this is that the close identification of the colleges of the period with the interests of the new nation as it attempted to break free from European hegemony has fostered the illusion that transatlantic educational influences during the eighteenth century were relatively inconsequential. It is my conclusion, however, that this has been a mistake, and that to complete the picture

Scotland must take its place with England and Germany as a major influence on the development of American higher education.

Important contacts between Scotland and America developed very early in the century, and by 1760 a complex network of cultural relationships—each of them directly educational or having educational relevance—drew the two countries together. Throughout the eighteenth century a continual stream of Scottish and Scotch-Irish immigrants poured into the American colonies. Outstanding individual Scotsmen, such as Cadwallader Colden in New York, Alexander Garden in Charleston, and William Douglass in Boston, made major contributions to the cultural life of the colonies. Although the bulk of the Scotch-Irish—the name given to the Scottish settlers from north Ireland—were unlettered, they brought with them their Scottish-university-educated ministers and an important educational institution, the Presbyterian academy. Moreover, Scottish educators, such as John Witherspoon at Princeton and William Smith at the College of Philadelphia, assumed important academic posts as administrators and professors in various American colleges. At the same time, increasing numbers of young Americans were sailing to Scotland for advanced studies in medicine. Finally, in almost every sphere of intellectual life—from literature to geology, mathematics to medicine, philosophy to economics—Scottish thinkers gained the respect of learned men everywhere. Americans, even more than others, turned with special interest and admiration to the achievements of the Scottish Enlightenment.

This intertwining of Scottish and American culture becomes all the more intriguing in light of the profound changes taking place in American higher education at the same time. Developments in the colleges both reflected and contributed to the new forces at work in America. Serving as an arena for the struggle between conflicting cultural ideals, and simultaneously as an active agent for realizing those ideals, higher education was itself transformed.

The most dramatic manifestation of change was the sudden surge at mid-century in the founding of new institutions. Between 1740 and 1770 scores of academies were established and six new colleges were chartered—the first in nearly half a century—and this was only the beginning of a wave of college-founding that was not to subside until the Civil War. The birth of new institutions, moreover, was accompanied by equally significant attempts to create a modern curriculum and to reconceive the social uses of the higher learning. In all of these areas, institutional and intellectual, the influence of Scotland was important and, at times, decisive. In fact, when the Scottish contribution is ignored, it also becomes much easier to overlook or to misunderstand the new movements within the colleges, as well as the light they shed upon the larger culture.

This study explores one major pattern of Scottish influences on American higher education: the appeal Scottish higher education in the eighteenth century had for many Americans; the extent and importance of the Presbyterian academy movement in America; and the thoughts and careers of representative individual educators who were related to the academy and early Princeton traditions. By focusing primarily, though not entirely, on this pattern, I have foregone any attempt at a comprehensive appraisal of Scottish influences on every aspect of American higher education or in every American college. It is my hope, however, that whatever has been sacrificed in coverage has been compensated for by a better understanding, not only of what certain Americans took from Scotland, but also of why they took what they did and how they adapted what they took to their own particular needs and circumstances.

It is with deep pleasure that I express my gratitude to those whose advice and criticisms I have relied upon. My greatest debt is to my teacher, Professor Lawrence A. Cremin of Teachers College, for his constant encouragement and always perceptive counsel. To him I owe an educational experience that has been enjoyable and valuable beyond measure. I also extend my special thanks to Professor Robert T. Handy of Union Theological Seminary and to the late Professor Richard Hofstadter of Columbia University for their careful and critical reading of the study as it progressed. My appreciation, too, goes to Professor Robert W. Lynn of Union Theological Seminary, to Professor Lefferts A. Loetscher of Princeton Theological Seminary, and to Professor Wilson Smith of the University of California at Davis for their generous assistance at various early stages of the study. Of the many others who have my gratitude, I mention particularly Dr. John Calam, who read, listened, and questioned, and Miss Judy Suratt, who astutely and unstintingly helped with all manner of practical and technical detail. Responsibility for errors and shortcomings in the study is, needless to say, totally my own.

Douglas Sloan

Contents

The Scottish Universities
in the Enlightenment

The brilliance of the Scottish Enlightenment has frequently been noted, and rightly so. From an economically and culturally depressed country at the time of the Union with England in 1707, Scotland emerged in less than seventy-five years as one of the leading centers of the larger European Enlightenment. What has not been so well recognized, however, is the special influence the Scottish Enlightenment exerted upon American cultural life. At no point was its impact felt with more dramatic and transforming effect than in the newer American colleges of the late eighteenth century. That this should be, owed much not only to a deep American admiration of Scottish cultural achievements generally, but also to the unique and commanding position traditionally held by the universities in Scottish society.

I

Benjamin Franklin provides a ready illustration of the American awareness of the Scottish intellectual renaissance. In February 1759, as agent in London for the province of Pennsylvania, Franklin was awarded an honorary Doctor of Laws degree by the University of St. Andrews in recognition of his electrical experiments and discoveries. That summer Franklin made the first of two visits to Scotland, but by that time he had already formed, over the course of nearly two decades, close personal and intellectual friendships with Scotsmen.[1]

---

[1] Franklin's second trip to Scotland was in 1771. Both visits have been chronicled in detail in J. Bennett Nolan, *Benjamin Franklin in Scotland and Ireland* (Philadelphia: University of Pennsylvania Press, 1938). Nolan's account illustrates Franklin's many-sided relationships with Scottish intellectuals.

Franklin had first learned of "electrical fire" from a Scots physician and graduate of Edinburgh medical school, Adam Spencer. In 1743 Spencer delivered a course of demonstration lectures on the subject in Boston, which Franklin attended. The following year, when Spencer repeated his lectures in Philadelphia, Franklin, with the help of other scientific-minded gentlemen, purchased Spencer's equipment, and began his own celebrated experiments in electricity.[2] William Strahan, the famous printer from Edinburgh, was Franklin's London publisher and, for forty years after 1750, was his correspondent, friend—"Scotch Straney"—and business adviser. It was from Strahan's London office that David Hall of Glasgow went to Pennsylvania in 1748 to become Franklin's business partner. Strahan and Hall appear to have spoken often to Franklin in glowing terms of Scotland. Also among Franklin's close friends in London were the Quaker physicians John Pringle, for a time Professor of Moral Philosophy at the University of Edinburgh and later President of the Royal Society in London, John Coakley Lettsom, and John Fothergill, all one-time students at the Edinburgh medical school.[3]

A few years after his first visit to Scotland Franklin wrote to Jonathan Potts, a young Philadelphia medical student en route to Edinburgh. "You have great advantages," Franklin wrote, "in going to study at Edinburgh at this time where there happen to be collected a set of as truly great men, Professors of the Several Branches of Knowledge, as have ever appeared in any age or country." Among those Franklin was referring to were several personal acquaintances and correspondents: Sir Alexander Dick, President of the College of Physicians; Adam Ferguson, the philosopher; William Cullen, Joseph Black, and the Munros (father and son), physicians; and William Robertson, the historian and Principal of Edinburgh University. On his trip to Scotland in 1759 Franklin had also met Adam Smith and David Hume, with whom he corresponded in the years that followed.[4] Franklin was perhaps somewhat carried away with admiration in his letter to Potts, though understandably so.[5]

[2] Carl Bridenbaugh, *Cities in Revolt* (New York: Alfred A. Knopf, 1959), p. 206.
[3] Nolan, *Franklin in Scotland and Ireland*, pp. 15–17.
[4] Letter from Franklin to Potts quoted in *ibid.*, p. 50; also see p. 60. For other information on the Scottish acquaintances Franklin made during his 1759 journey, see C. R. Fay, *Adam Smith and the Scotland of His Day* (Cambridge: At the University Press, 1956), pp. 124 ff.
[5] Franklin was no less enthusiastic about the intellectual wealth of Scotland in the eighteenth century than the modern historian William Law Mathieson. The eighteenth century in Scotland, Mathieson writes, was "the most brilliant epoch in

The Scottish renaissance in learning and letters was from one perspective only another manifestation of the general eighteenth-century Enlightenment, in which America, Britain, and the Continent all participated. Yet the social and cultural transformation of Scotland in the eighteenth century also makes it possible to speak of a distinctive Scottish Enlightenment with its own characteristic features. Although the intellectual achievements of the Scots cannot be explained completely in terms of the economic and political changes in the life of the country—or vice versa—their interrelationship must be considered. It will become evident that Americans certainly tended to view the intellectual advancement of Scotland as intimately connected with her material progress.

Opportunities for making headway against the chronic poverty and backwardness that had been Scotland's lot for centuries came with the Union of Scotland and England in 1707. Union meant that Scotland would no longer be excluded by the Navigation Acts from the profitable overseas trade or hampered by tariff barriers from trade with England. At first the Union did not fulfill expectations, and, in fact, actually set Scottish trade and industry back; but by the second quarter of the century Scottish economic expansion was well under way.[6]

The success of the Scots in the tobacco trade with America was perhaps the most dramatic evidence that new forces were at work. Glasgow merchants, taking advantage of their location on the Clyde and establishing resident agents in the American colonies, were able to become the major importers of tobacco in the entire United King-

---

the history of her literature and science. Nowhere but in France was there so rich and varied an efflorescence of genius. The England of that day produced no such philosopher as Hume; no such opponent of his scepticism as Campbell; no such historians—to adopt the contemporary verdict—as Hume and Robertson; no such tragic dramatist as Home; no poet of such European reputation as Macpherson; no such novelist as Smollett; no such biographer as Boswell; no such preacher as Blair; no such economist as Adam Smith; no such geologist as Hutton; no such surgeon as Hunter; no such engineer as Watt; . . ." William Law Mathieson, *The Awakening of Scotland* (Glasgow: James Maclehose and Son, 1910), p. 203. For a more judicious appraisal of this list of names, and a caution against lumping them all together as a manifestation of a unified national culture, see David Daiches, *The Paradox of Scottish Culture: The Eighteenth-Century Experience* (London: Oxford University Press, 1964), pp. 74–75. One does not have to reject Daiches's reservations to agree that Scotland was extraordinarily blessed with persons of intellectual renown.

[6] On the economic consequences of the Union of 1707, see Henry Hamilton, *An Economic History of Scotland in the Eighteenth Century* (Oxford: Clarendon Press, 1963), pp. 88–89, 132, 255; also see R. H. Campbell, *Scotland Since 1707* (New York: Barnes & Noble, Inc., 1965), pp. 1–8.

dom. Imports of tobacco into Glasgow in 1715 totaled 2½ million pounds; grew to 33 million pounds in 1765; and by 1771 topped 47 million pounds, equaling more than half of the trade of all the other British ports taken together. The growth in linen manufacturing was nearly as spectacular, and provided the basis for Scottish economic success later in the eighteenth century. Linen had become a major industry by 1760. The annual output of cloth stamped for sale by the Board of Trustees for Improving Fisheries and Manufactures set up in 1727 rose from approximately 2,200,000 yards in 1728 to 11,750,000 yards in 1760, and to 13,000,000 yards in 1770. The founding of the great Carron Iron Works in 1759, the building of new roads and turnpikes, and the expansion of banking and credit facilities also attested to the economic revival of Scotland.[7]

Great improvements also took place in agriculture, still the basis of the economy throughout the eighteenth century. The famine of 1696–1703 tragically underlined the notoriously backward and unproductive nature of Scottish agriculture at the time of the Union. The initiative for improvement came from landowners, whose social and political power made it possible for them to act effectively. Eager to improve their own economic situation, and to show themselves to be men of learning and science, Scottish landowners in increasing numbers began to introduce on their own estates methods of advanced agriculture they had observed in Holland and England. The formation of the Honourable Society of Improvers in the Knowledge of Agriculture in Scotland in 1728 at Edinburgh gave an important boost to the spread of scientific farming, and was the first of many similar agricultural societies.[8]

Improvement was slow and uneven throughout the country, but by 1790 in the lowlands and parts of the highlands Scottish agriculture had been transformed. The old runrig system of ownership, with its narrow, separated strips of land, was abolished, holdings were consolidated, and long-term leases were instituted. Along with new land policies came the practice of crop rotation and afforestation, the

[7] See Hamilton, *Economic History*, pp. 256, 404; also see Jacob M. Price, "The Rise of Glasgow in the Chesapeake Tobacco Trade, 1707–1775," *William and Mary Quarterly*, 3rd ser., XI (April 1954), 179–199; Campbell, *Scotland Since 1707*, pp. 63 ff. For another assessment of Scotland's economic progress, see Agnes Mure Mackenzie, *Scotland in Modern Times, 1720–1939* (London: W. and R. Chambers, Ltd., 1941). Also useful is Henry Hamilton, *The Economic Evolution of Scotland in the 18th and 19th Centuries*, Historical Association Leaflet, No. 91 (London, 1933).

[8] Hamilton, *Economic History*, pp. 61–62, 67–68.

introduction of new crops, the modernization of the plow and other implements, and the development of more vigorous breeds of live-stock. In the process, although it was originally imitative of the Dutch and English examples, Scottish agriculture achieved a fame of its own. Even by mid-century many individual farmers were recognized as among the most progressive in Europe; Scottish agricultural specialists and gardeners were eagerly sought after; and the published writings of Lord Kames, Andrew Wight, and other Scottish spokesmen for the new "agricultural sciences" were widely read.[9] It is important, however, to bear in mind that Scotland's economic progress was gradual, and that for long periods its fruits were not shared by many segments of society. Rural areas, especially, continued to be afflicted by poverty, and late in the century emigrants were still leaving Scotland because of high prices and high rents, dislocation and famine. Scotland's economic development was nevertheless real and its effects perceptible in the growth of cities, the increase of national wealth, and the development of an urbane culture.[10]

The transformation of Scotland was not a haphazard process; nor did it spring from any wide popular demands. Political and economic affairs, and intellectual affairs as well, were controlled and, as far as possible, directed by a relatively small and cohesive group of people. The Union of 1707 had eliminated the Scottish parliament and privy council, thus depriving Scotland of its central administrative organization. In response, however, the chief Scottish landowners moved into the power vacuum created by the Union and assumed leadership. The terms of the political settlement were, in fact, such as to allow Scotland's leading groups to tighten and consolidate their control.

By operating as a united body in Parliament, Scottish leaders were able to retain the positions they had enjoyed before the Union, and to exploit British politics for their own purposes. Throughout the eighteenth century, Scottish politicians traded their support of the English party in power in London for laws and policies advantageous to themselves and Scotland. The forty-five representatives allowed Scotland in the House of Commons by the terms of the Union constituted a large enough block that by acting unanimously,

[9] Hamilton, *Economic History*, pp. 67–70; Mackenzie, *Scotland in Modern Times*, pp. 10–13; Campbell, *Scotland Since 1707*, pp. 32–33.
[10] A brief description of the effects of economic development upon the social and cultural life of eighteenth-century Scotland may be found in George S. Pryde, *Social Life in Scotland Since 1707*, Historical Association Pamphlet, No. 98 (London, 1934), especially pp. 3–15.

as they usually did, they could tip the scales of power, and they were willing to do so in return for concessions and privileges from the ruling party. This non-ideological and opportunistic, almost cynical, political strategy was made possible by an electoral system which guaranteed that political power in Scotland would remain in the hands of a few persons with wealth and land. Control of both local government and parliamentary representation was largely determined by land ownership.[11]

Although families successful in industry, banking, and law were allowed entrance into the landed gentry from below, the social structure of Scotland remained well defined and control by the landed interests intact. At the end of the century there were still fewer than eight thousand proprietors of Scottish land.[12] While symptomatic of underlying nationalist feelings ignored by the groups in control, the Jacobite rebellions—the "Fifteen" and the "Forty-five"—actually served to consolidate and further strengthen the strategy of the ruling leadership by eliminating from its ranks potential adventurers and discontents.

[11] At the parish level, heritors, the proprietors of heritable property, together with the minister and the kirk session, were the responsible authorities. Heritors, however, were always well represented in the church session, so that even at the smallest local unit the power of the landed gentry was predominant. Most higher local authorities, such as justices of the peace, were also recruited from the landed gentry, who, though unpaid for their services, reaped benefits of prestige and control. G. D. Henderson, *The Scottish Ruling Elder* (London: James Clarke and Co., 1935), pp. 170–172; Laurence James Saunders, *Scottish Democracy 1815–1840: The Social and Economic Background* (Edinburgh: Oliver and Boyd, 1950); pp. 18–20.

The electoral system further enhanced and ensured control by the gentry. The fifteen burgh representatives to the House of Commons were chosen by the town councils, one by Edinburgh and the fourteen others by delegates from groups of the other burghs. The town councils were, however, self-elected, and the burgh electors tended to be the instruments of a powerful few. In the counties the electoral system was even more firmly controlled by the gentry and landed nobility. The exercise of the county franchise was limited to those who owned lands of a certain value or who possessed a bare title, or "superiority," of land of the required value. The latter provision made it possible to create "paper votes" by merely conferring a superiority without actually transferring the land. The result of these stipulations was that there were few persons qualified to vote, and of these many were manipulable "paper votes." Elections were, then, controlled by small groups of similar status, origin, and interest. The national average, for example, was 71 voters per county, and in 1788 in all of Scotland there were only 2,624 voters, half of them "paper" or "parchment barons." Mathieson, *The Awakening of Scotland*, pp. 17–20; Saunders, *Scottish Democracy*, p. 21; G. S. Pryde, *Scotland from 1603 to the Present Day* (London: T. Nelson, 1962), p. 120; David Kettler, *The Social and Political Thought of Adam Ferguson* (Columbus: Ohio State University Press, 1965), pp. 20–22.

[12] Saunders, *Scottish Democracy*, p. 14.

It was to this phenomenon—the maintenance of leadership by the few—that Adam Smith indirectly gave witness later in the century when discussing alternatives for British-American relationships. At the height of the American Revolution, Smith said that one conceivable outcome could be a union between Great Britain and America. Such a solution, he suggested, might have an appeal to certain groups in America because it would mean that the leading men of America would continue in power "in the same manner as the leading men of Scotland continue to be the principal men of their own country, after the union with England." [13] Whatever merit his analysis of the American situation may have had, Smith had accurately described the social realities of Scotland.

The Society of Improvers illustrates how thoroughly Scottish affairs were in the hands of the landowning and wealthy few. The membership of the Society numbered about three hundred and comprised most of the peerage, the landed gentry, and the outstanding professional men of Scotland. The concerns of the Society extended beyond agriculture alone, and for several years it worked closely with the Convention of Royal Burghs to bring pressure on the government to encourage manufacturing in Scotland. Similar organizations—and they were many—were formed throughout the country during the whole of the eighteenth century to encourage and improve Scottish economic development.[14]

The Scottish intellectual leaders—the professors, liberal-minded clergymen, lawyers, and other men of letters—were closely associated with the political and economic leadership of the country. They shared the goal of guiding and shaping Scotland's material and cultural progress. They addressed themselves self-consciously to the task of spreading enlightened ideas and ideals through the masses and of representing Scotland before the rest of the world as a center of enlightenment.

The legal profession presented one of the clearest and most extreme examples of the interpenetration of the intellectuals and the ruling interests. Lawyers had immense political influence in Scotland, which after the Union maintained its own national legal system. Many

[13] Quoted in Fay, *Adam Smith*, p. 113.
[14] Campbell, *Scotland Since 1707*, p. 33; Hamilton, *Economic History*, 298. In addition to many local societies, among the most important organizations were the Board of Trustees for Improving Fisheries and Manufactures in Scotland, established in 1727, and the Edinburgh Society for Encouraging Arts, Sciences, Manufactures, and Agriculture, established in 1754.

Lords of Session and Advocates held estates, including some of the most important of the progressive farmers—men such as John Cockburn of Ormistead in East Lothian, Sir Archibald Grant of Monymusk in Aberdeenshire, and Lord Kames, one of the most active "improvers" among several in the High Court of Justiciary itself.[15] Kames provides an excellent example of one who attempted to fulfill the ideal of combining political, literary, and scientific pursuits. "Indeed," wrote Ramsay of Ochtertyre, "farming was one of the sciences in which he wished to be thought as learned as in jurisprudence or ethics." [16] Most lawyers, like Kames, took much pride in being counted as men of letters and reflection. Lord Kames and Lord Monboddo vied with each other for honors from the Scottish literati, and like many others of the profession wrote and published without inhibition on the major philosophical, historical, and literary questions of the day.

The other members of the literati besides the lawyers—professional men, ministers, and university professors—were usually persons of more humble background, without estates or great wealth. They nevertheless enjoyed the same alliance with the dominant social groups as did their lawyer friends. Their social leadership was ensured by their undeniable intellectual accomplishments and by their positions in the church and university, the two other chief institutions of the country in addition to the legal.

If these two venerable institutions of Scottish culture did not provide direct access to levers of political and economic power, they did furnish a vantage from which the intellectuals could perform the role of cultural guides. The relationship between the Scottish intellectuals and Scotland's political-social leadership undoubtedly helped to determine many of the central themes of Scottish philosophical thought in the eighteenth century. As the Scottish philosophers sought to spread enlightenment, to influence national policy, to guide and account for Scotland's growing prosperity—and to justify their own involvement with the governing order—they devoted considerable attention to subjects bearing on the progress of civilization, the relationships and institutions of society, the rationalization of power, and the ethics and religion of rational man. Scottish moral philosophy in

[15] Campbell, *Scotland Since 1707*, pp. 28–29. Also, on the lawyers as members of the upper classes and leaders in the intellectual life of Scotland, see Daiches, *The Paradox of Scottish Culture*, especially pp. 56–60, *passim*.
[16] Quoted in Daiches, *The Paradox of Scottish Culture*, p. 8.

the hands of such men as Hume, Smith, and Ferguson was distinguished for its treatment of just such subjects.[17] From their positions within the church and university the outstanding Scottish thinkers and writers attempted to set intellectual and literary standards, and actually to instruct the nation's leaders in their social duties and responsibilities.

II

The church had always been an influential force in Scottish life, and it came to play an important and unusual role in the Scottish Enlightenment.[18] Since the days of the Reformation, Scotsmen of all classes had demonstrated their zeal and interest in religious affairs. The strength of the church was further reinforced by the special character of presbyterian church government, which provided an institutional structure extending from the local to the highest level of national life.

Under presbyterianism the church was governed by a graded, or hierarchical, system of courts. These were of four types and included the kirk session, the presbytery, the synod, and the General Assembly. The kirk session, consisting of the minister and the elected representatives of the congregation, the elders and deacons, was responsible for the supervision of the local parish and the spiritual and moral life of its members. The presbytery, comprising the minister and one elder from each congregation in a given area, examined, ordained, and watched over the conduct and discipline of the ministers in its jurisdiction. The synods, made up of ministers and representative elders from several presbyteries, handled church affairs for a still larger district. Responsibility for all matters concerning the national church resided in the General Assembly, which possessed the power to over-

[17] A definitive analysis of the main themes of Scottish thought in the eighteenth century is provided by Gladys Bryson, *Man and Society: The Scottish Inquiry of the Eighteenth Century* (Princeton: Princeton University Press, 1945). Two recent biographies of Adam Ferguson and David Hume examine their careers and the central themes of their writings in the context of Scottish culture, and their roles as members of the intelligentsia allied with the ruling groups of Scotland. See Kettler, *The Social and Political Thought of Adam Ferguson*, and John B. Stewart, *The Moral and Political Philosophy of David Hume* (New York: Columbia University Press, 1963).

[18] Extremely helpful in understanding Scottish religion and church history is G. D. Henderson, *Religious Life in Seventeenth-Century Scotland* (Cambridge: At the University Press, 1937). Other useful works by the same author are *The Church of Scotland, A Short History* (Edinburgh: Church of Scotland Youth Committee, 1939); *The Kirk Through the Centuries* (Edinburgh: Church of Scotland Committee on Publication, 1937); *The Scottish Ruling Elder*. Also see J. H. S. Burleigh, *A Church History of Scotland* (London: Oxford University Press, 1960).

rule the lower church courts. Meeting annually and drawing its membership from the ministers and important elders of the church, including nobles, lairds, burgesses, and university professors, the General Assembly was extremely representative of the leading groups in Scottish society.

The presbyterian system was first acknowledged and ratified by the king and Parliament in 1592; but it soon came under attack by the king, who much preferred the rule of his own bishops to that of the independent presbyteries. Throughout the seventeenth century, control of the church alternated between episcopacy and presbyterianism. Despite the vehemence shown by partisans of each side to the other, however, the differences between Scottish Episcopalianism and Scottish Presbyterianism during this period should not be exaggerated. The Scottish church historian, G. D. Henderson, has shown that even after the Restoration, Episcopalianism in Scotland was of a very moderate kind. Under Charles II the church courts, the presbyteries and kirk sessions, continued their work; ministers were still examined and licensed by the presbyteries; and even worship and preaching did not alter radically, since the Westminster Confession and Shorter Catechism remained the recognized doctrinal standards. At bottom the major struggles of the century turned on the issue of whether ultimate church control should rest with the king and his bishops or with the church and its presbyteries. For most people the quality of religious life changed surprisingly little. The essential unity of the church, moreover, remained unbroken by schism. Whether under episcopacy or under presbyterianism all Scotsmen belonged to the one national church.[19]

At the beginning of the eighteenth century appearances suggested the possibility of still greater unity in the church. With the Revolution Settlement of 1690 Parliament restored Scottish Presbyterianism as the Church by Law Established. By giving its reluctant support to the Union of Scotland and England in 1707, the General Assembly secured further guarantees that the national church would remain Presbyterian. If anything, the church in 1707 was more strict in its doctrine and discipline than it had been in 1690. The hope, however, that only one "face of Kirk" would prevail in Scotland was soon to be disappointed.

The Church of Scotland in the eighteenth century was to reflect on a small scale, but with great intensity, the ideological and power

[19] Henderson, *Religious Life in Seventeenth-Century Scotland*, p. 141.

struggles that were transforming the country as a whole. Discontent was increasingly voiced on the one side by those who felt the church was too strict and narrow, and on the other by those who were persuaded the church was too lax, too worldly. By the third decade of the century two major parties had formed within the church, and were contending for its control.

The Moderate party in general consisted of those ministers who wished to see themselves and the church ranged on the side of high culture and the new thought of the time. Although they formally acknowledged the church's official doctrinal standards, the Moderates espoused toleration and avoided fine points of religious controversy. They approved highly of their members who contributed to the world of letters; stressed ethics as the essence of the religious life; and were eager to apply to preaching and theology the canons of taste and judgment being enunciated by the eighteenth-century philosophers and literati. Against the Moderates, and closer to the actual life and thinking of the majority of congregations, stood the Evangelical, or Popular party. The Evangelicals demanded doctrinal purity and close adherence to the austerity and personal discipline of traditional Presbyterianism.[20]

In order to secure their own position the Moderates began to support the exercise of "patronage," which had been revived in 1712, transferring the power of appointing ministers from the congregation to the crown and heritors. Because landowners were traditionally responsible for the protection of their tenants and for providing them with a church and a minister, patronage had from time to time been an accepted practice. Patronage, however, could be exercised without regard for the feelings of the congregations, and it came in the course of events to be associated with the centralized directiveness of episcopal rule. Abolished by Presbyterians in 1649, and restored by Charles II in 1662, it was only natural that patronage was abolished again when Presbyterians returned to power in 1690 under William. The revival of patronage once more in 1712, viewed by many as a violation of the Act of Union, had, in fact, been intended to favor episcopal landowners, and it aroused much resentment in Scotland. Although the Patronage Act of 1712 was initially passed in the face of strong

[20] For an excellent treatment of the controversies between the Moderates and Evangelicals, see Mathieson, *The Awakening of Scotland*, Chapter IV, "Ecclesiastical Politics," and Chapter V, "The Noontide of Moderation." For other good but more brief accounts see Henderson, *The Church of Scotland*, pp. 101–116, and Burleigh, *A Church History of Scotland*, pp. 286–308.

opposition in the church, the Moderates began to view patronage favorably as a weapon they could wield to their advantage.

Acting in collusion with the gentry, Moderate party leaders were enabled under patronage to impose a minister upon a congregation even against the people's wishes. Thus arose the somewhat paradoxical picture of the self-appointed spokesmen for liberality and progress resorting to oligarchic control, and at times out-and-out authoritarian measures, to gain their own way. The result was major schism in the church, as large groups of radical Evangelicals, first in 1733 and again in 1752, seceded in order to establish their own church bodies. The Moderates were willing to pay this high price for control.

It may be conjectured that, had the outlook of the social and political elite been more congenial to the Evangelical party, they would not have hesitated any more than did the Moderates to make use of the powers at hand. As it happened, however, the Moderates were the ones who emphasized the need for order and authority in the church and sought to enhance the power and prestige of the clergy, while the Evangelical party claimed to speak for the rights of the local congregations and of the laity to have a voice in church affairs.

In this respect the struggle in the church reflected the course of change in the country itself. Everywhere the schemes for implementing the new ideas of progress tended to be imposed and directed from above, and did not always proceed smoothly. Just as the agricultural improvers often saw their new-fangled implements wrecked and their newly-planted hedges and forests uprooted by suspicious tenants, so, too, the Moderates in the church frequently found their own congregations pitted against them. Yet under the astute leadership of William Robertson, Principal of Edinburgh University, the Moderates emerged from the struggle in the 1750's firmly in control of the General Assembly and the church government, but not without having seen the life of the church seriously disrupted in the process.[21]

The Moderate clergy, nevertheless, rendered indispensable services to the Scottish Enlightenment. The historian William Robertson, the philosopher Thomas Reid, the rhetorician Hugh Blair, the playwright John Home, the mathematician and popularizer of James Hutton's revolutionary geological theories, John Playfair, and the philosopher and social analyst, Adam Ferguson, all were Moderate

---

[21] Some of the major conflicts in the church between the Moderates and Evangelicals will be examined in greater detail in Chapter IV.

clergymen of the Church of Scotland. The extent of the cultural leadership provided by Moderate ministers is indicated by their participation in the Philosophical Society of Edinburgh. The Philosophical Society began as a medical society in 1731, was expanded eight years later to include those interested in literature and philosophy, and finally, in 1782, at the proposal of William Robertson, was reorganized as the Royal Society. In 1787, according to one recent count, of a total of 215 members, including nonresidents of Edinburgh, there were 37 clergymen, 38 medical men, 26 lawyers, 34 university professors of subjects other than theology and medicine, and 24 of the peerage. Over half of the clergymen in the Society were also university professors.[22] Without the readiness of the Moderate clergy to assist "the progress of civilization" in Scotland—and that meant, also, their willingness to impose culture when necessary—Scottish intellectual life would have suffered a severe loss.

The victory of the Moderates was highly significant in shaping the expression and determining the direction of Enlightenment thought in Scotland. The Moderates were determined to show that the cause of science, progress, and genteel culture and the interests of religion were not only compatible, but also necessary to one another. The result was that in Scotland the potential for conflict between the forces of enlightenment and of religion was greatly lessened.

The suspicion and enmity that sometimes characterized the attitudes of the French philosophies toward religion, for example, were seldom to be observed in Scotland. *Écrasez l'enfâme* was never a Scottish slogan, even among those who, like David Hume and Adam Smith, held the most tenuous relationship with the church and were

[22] Ten of the minister-professors taught divinity, four taught other subjects, and five held principalships. William Nelson Hawley, "The Intellectual Development of the Scottish Clergy in the Eighteenth Century" (master's thesis, University of Chicago Divinity School, 1937). Clergymen were also prominent members of the Edinburgh Select Society, founded in 1754, and its successor, the Poker Club.

Mathieson quotes with approval Alexander Carlyle's panegyric to Scotland's Moderate clergy: "Who have wrote the best histories, ancient and modern? It has been clergymen of this Church. Who has wrote the clearest delineation of the human understanding and all its powers?—a clergyman of this Church. Who wrote a tragedy that has been deemed perfect?—a clergyman of this Church. Who was the most profound mathematician of the age he lived in?—a clergyman of this Church. Who is his successor in reputation as in office? Who wrote the best treatise on agriculture? Let us not complain of poverty; for it is a splendid poverty indeed! It is *paupertas fecunda vivorum*." Mathieson, *The Awakening of Scotland*, p. 205. Mathieson is sympathetic to the Moderate cause, and Carlyle was himself a Moderate of the Moderates. After their biases have been taken into account, however, the fact remains: the Moderate clergy supplied one vital nucleus of Scotland's intelligentsia.

close friends of such persons as Voltaire, d'Holbach, Rousseau, and other fairly radical continentals.[23] To be sure, David Hume, the most brilliant and penetrating of all the Scotsmen, was often seen as a threat to morality and faith, and he dominated the intellectual scene. Hume disturbed many of the Scottish intellectuals, who were constantly stimulated to further wrestling with the issues and doubts his work posed for them; but Hume took pains to see that his servants were always provided with church pews, and his opponents remained on friendly terms with him. Moderate clergymen counted it a high personal privilege, as well as a mark of their liberality, to be able to number "le bon David" among their intimate friends.[24] The radical Enlightenment was in a real sense tamed and domesticated by the Moderate clergy of Scotland. Although the Moderate cause in its early years was a source of offense to many of the orthodox, its ultimate effect was to help legitimate Enlightenment thought and interests in the eyes of many of religious persuasion, and to broaden the appeal of distinctively Scottish expressions of the Enlightenment.

III

The Scottish Enlightenment was unique also in that the university was at its center. The leaders of the Enlightenment in England were not noted for their connections with English universities. In fact most English scientists and literary figures were to be found outside the universities in various kinds of learned societies and associations.[25] By contrast the intellectual leaders of Scotland were almost to a man university professors or involved in university affairs. Even David Hume had twice sought a university appointment, once to the Chair of Moral Philosophy in Edinburgh, and once to that of Logic

---

[23] For information on the continental friendships and correspondence of Smith and Hume, see Fay, *Adam Smith*, pp. 146 ff.; Henry Grey Graham, *Scottish Men of Letters in the Eighteenth Century* (London: Adam and Charles Black, 1908), pp. 45–50, 158–160; and John Hermann Randall, Jr., *The Career of Philosophy* (New York: Columbia University Press, 1962), I, 790 ff.

[24] See, for example, Alexander Carlyle, *Autobiography* (Boston: Ticknor and Fields, 1861), pp. 222 ff. Graham presents some touching examples of Hume's reticence to offend the sensibilities of those who believed more firmly than he. See, for example, Graham, *Scottish Men of Letters*, pp. 40, 56.

[25] See Bryson, *Man and Society*, p. 8; also, on the fact that English intellectuals operated outside the two English universities, see J. Bronowski and Bruce Mazlish, *The Western Intellectual Tradition* (New York: Harper & Brothers, 1960), pp. 323–324.

in Glasgow, but was unsuccessful.[26] In a real sense, the Scottish Enlightenment was a university movement.

The Scottish universities were themselves unique. Indeed, one reason for their importance in Scotland was that the universities were part of an educational system and tradition whose ideal was to reach all classes of society and not merely the privileged. Through the universities sons of lower-class and middle-class parents could enter the church and other professions, and take their place among the cultural leadership of the country. Any boy who could do the work was welcome; the money necessary for the relatively small tuition fees and lodgings in town could usually be scraped together somehow. Thus, the universities served as the main channel for supplying the nation's need for talent and ability.

The five universities of Scotland in the eighteenth century were part of a distinctive educational tradition that extended back to the Scottish Reformation, the Renaissance, and, beyond, to the medieval church and university. The three oldest universities—St. Andrews, Glasgow, and Aberdeen—were created by papal bull in the fifteenth century, and were modeled after the great universities of Europe, to which students from Scotland flocked during the Middle Ages. The founding of the colleges at Edinburgh in 1582 and at New Aberdeen in 1593 did not take place until after the main struggles of the Reformation.[27] A brief glance at the course of higher education in Scotland following the Reformation will help to highlight the noteworthy characteristics of the eighteenth-century Scottish university.

The Scottish Reformation itself brought new forces to bear upon the development of education in Scotland. In producing the *First Book of Discipline* (1560), which formulated policy for church and state and aimed at a total "Reformation of Religion in the whole Realm," John Knox and his fellow reformers drew the most intimate connection between reformation and education. Within the church itself educational standards were set high. Ministers were to be examined in scriptural exposition and theology in order to qualify for

---

[26] John Kerr, *Scottish Education, School and University* (Cambridge: At the University Press, 1910), p. 240.
[27] The strongest influence upon the founding of the older Scottish universities came, perhaps, from the University of Paris, which had its own Scots College in the fourteenth century and where the numbers of Scottish students were so great as to be of concern to the authorities. Papal recognition was accorded the University of St. Andrews in 1413, the University of Glasgow in 1451, and the University of Aberdeen in 1495.

election, and every local church was to have a Bible in English, which was to be read and interpreted to the people regularly. Knox refused to make "the raritie of godlie and learned men" a reason for lowering the standards of ministerial education, and in 1574 Regent Morton went beyond Knox by demanding that no one should be admitted to the ministry who had not studied philosophy and graduated with a bachelor's degree in theology from one of the universities of the realm.[28]

The plan of national education proposed for the country as a whole, however, was one of the most remarkable features of the *Book of Discipline*. The stated aim of the plan was to instill wisdom, learning, and virtue into the youth of the country and thus provide both church and state with qualified leaders. The scheme called for a school in every kirk or parish in which the "rudiments" and the catechism would be taught; a grammar school in every town, and a higher school or college, capable of instructing in Latin and Greek and "of the Arts at least Logic and Rhetoric," in the notable towns or cities; and university instruction for those with capacities for the higher learning. Qualifications for each stage were carefully specified, and those who did qualify were to be compelled to move on up the educational ladder, even against their parents' will, the rich paying for their own children and the church supporting the poor.[29] Youth of all classes would, therefore, enter the colleges, where they would remain "until the commonwealth have profit of them," at which time they would either proceed to the university and a profession, or enter a trade.[30]

Although the *First Book of Discipline* did not receive the approval of Parliament, the educational ideals expressed in Knox's plan were never lost slight of.[31] The church insisted upon its right of

[28] John Knox, *History of the Reformation*, edited by W. Croft Dickinson (2 vols.; London: T. Nelson and Sons, 1949). *The First Book of Discipline* is contained in the appendices. Also see the discussions in Kerr, *Scottish Education*, pp. 76 ff.; and in Burleigh, *A Church History of Scotland*, pp. 163 ff.

[29] Parents who could pay, but who still refused to send their children to school, were required to make full payment, even if they continued to keep their children at home, and to pay a fine as well. Kerr, *Scottish Education*, p. 97.

[30] Although the plan did not call for the founding of new universities, thoroughgoing reforms in organization and curricula for the three existing universities, St. Andrews, Glasgow, and Aberdeen, were demanded. At age twenty-four students in the universities would be ready, it was thought, to enter the professions—law, medicine, or the ministry, as they chose—or to be retained as teachers. Knox, *The First Book of Discipline;* Kerr, *Scottish Education*, pp. 77 ff., 105 ff.; Alexander Morgan, *Rise and Progress of Scottish Education* (London: Oxford University Press, 1933), pp. 42 ff.

[31] *The First Book of Discipline* failed to receive parliamentary approval because some

supervision and visitation, and continually prodded Parliament and the town councils to provide schools with qualified teachers. The church frequently took the lead in demanding better educational facilities, but close cooperation existed between church and state to try to provide schools and schoolmasters in every local unit.[32] Success was greatest in the burghs, where more funds for education were available than in the rural districts. Despite the general poverty of the country, scarcely a burgh or important town throughout the seventeenth century lacked provision for Latin instruction for both rich and poor (some even provided Greek).[33] These schools enabled youth from all classes who could qualify academically to enter the universities and professions.

Knox had called for thoroughgoing reform in the three existing universities, but their life was so seriously disrupted by the discord and turmoil accompanying the Reformation that no changes were undertaken according to his plan. Only when the young Calvinist scholar Andrew Melville returned from his study and teaching on the Continent to become Principal of Glasgow University in 1574 did the outlook for the universities begin to improve. In a new charter, called the *Nova Erectio*, and secured in 1577, Melville initiated a complete reform and reorganization of the University of Glasgow.[34]

---

thought it to be the impractical work of "devout imaginings," and because few of the nobility, into whose hands had fallen most of the church property confiscated in the Reformation, were prepared to release the kinds of funds required for such an ambitious reform plan.

[32] Church and state joined in a series of Education Acts, notably those passed in 1646 and 1696, to improve and advance the nation's educational facilities.

[33] Kerr, *Scottish Education*, p. 97; Morgan, *Rise of Scottish Education*, pp. 56–62. In the country parishes the educational picture was much darker. There the heritors were responsible for supporting schools, and they often found abundant ways of avoiding or even neglecting this duty altogether. For long periods many parishes had no provisions whatsoever, and the Society for Propagating Christian Knowledge in Scotland (S.P.C.K.), when it began its work in 1709, discovered numerous areas in which its schoolmasters were needed. An excellent brief discussion of parish education that describes the situation in numerous specific parishes is in Henderson, *The Scottish Ruling Elder*, pp. 146 ff. One recent study maintains that in the eighteenth century there was much more schooling available than has been commonly thought, and that by 1758 only a limited number of parishes were without public schools. See D. J. Withrington, "The S.P.C.K. and Highland Schools in Mid-Eighteenth Century," *The Scottish Historical Review*, XLI (1962), 89–99. For discussions of the pre-Reformation church and burgh schools, see Morgan, *Rise of Scottish Education*, Chapter 2; and James Grant, *History of the Burgh Schools of Scotland* (London and Glasgow: W. Collins and Sons, Co., 1876).

[34] Melville, who combined a background of solid scholarship, firm Presbyterian convictions, and a willingness to enter the fray of Reformation power politics, was singularly equipped for his task of rebuilding the universities. Good, brief discussions of Melville's educational work and the humanist influence he helped to introduce into Scottish higher education may be found in Alexander Morgan,

Melville introduced the specialized professorship in place of the old practice of "regenting," whereby one regent, or tutor, had guided the same class through the entire college course. Each regent now was to teach only in his own particular fields of competence.[35] Melville also strove to liberalize the arts curriculum by including such subjects as history, geography, and chronology, and he broke the monopoly of Aristotle in logic by introducing the *Dialectica* of Petrus Ramus, his old teacher in Paris. Finally, Melville reorganized the government of the university, making clear the responsibilities of the various officers and strengthening the hand of the principal.

When Melville left Glasgow in 1579 to become Principal of St. Mary's College at St. Andrews, similar reforms along the lines of the *Nova Erectio* were introduced there. The so-called *Nova Fundatio* of King's College, Aberdeen, recorded in 1597 after thirteen years of debate and delay, was also based on Melville's *Nova Erectio*, but the extent to which the revisions were carried out at King's College is not clear. It was in the founding of Marischal College at New Aberdeen in 1593 that Melville's educational ideas were most fully extended beyond Glasgow.

The new colleges founded at Edinburgh in 1582 and at Aberdeen in 1593 were a departure from the three older medieval universities. The immediate pressures that gave rise to the new colleges came largely from the need of the church for an educated ministry and the desires of the towns to rival the other university centers and to have institutions responsive to their own educational needs. The models for the new establishments were probably, in addition to the colleges of the medieval universities, the academies that had sprung up throughout Europe in the wake of the Reformation, such as those in France

---

Makers of Scottish Education (London: Longmans, Green and Co., 1929), pp. 65–82; J. D. Mackie, *The University of Glasgow, 1451–1951* (Glasgow: Jackson, Son, and Co., 1954), pp. 63 ff; and G. D. Henderson, *The Founding of Marischal College Aberdeen* (Aberdeen: The University Press, 1947), pp. 12–18.

[35] The first regent was to teach rhetoric and classical languages and literature; the second, dialectic and logic, as well as the elements of arithmetic and geometry; the third, natural philosophy, geography, astronomy, and chronology. Melville attempted to introduce the specialized professorship at St. Andrews, but the opposition was too great. At Edinburgh the new method was never proposed during his time. It is not clear how long specialized teaching persisted at Glasgow and at King's College, Aberdeen, but Marischal College, Aberdeen, did not revert to the old regenting system again until the middle of the century. Henderson, *Marischal College*, pp. 19–20. The *Nova Erectio* is thoroughly discussed in Mackie, *University of Glasgow*, pp. 57–77; Alexander Morgan, *Scottish Universities Studies* (London: Oxford University Press, 1933), pp. 63–69, 133–144; Kerr, *Scottish Education*, pp. 116–120.

and the Geneva Academy, with which many of the Scottish reformers had been personally involved.[36] The two new colleges both had close connections with their respective town governments. The Town Council of New Aberdeen was active with the Earl of Marischal in founding the college, and the town's interest and involvement continued. The College of Edinburgh, moreover, was almost entirely "the Town College," as it was often called. The first charter placed the college under the complete control of the Town Council. The Act of 1621 further elaborated the council's authority, which it had already been exercising without legal recognition, to appoint and dismiss faculty members and to set regulations for the course of study and for the granting of degrees. Unlike the three older universities, which had been created by papal authority as independent medieval corporations, the Colleges of Edinburgh and Marischal were children of their local communities and closely tied to the needs and expectations of their towns.[37]

The determination of the Edinburgh Town Council from the beginning to gain all the benefits of a university from what was initially a mere academy, or college at best, may perhaps be evident in the degree-granting prerogatives that the college assumed. By all legal precedent only a true university could grant degrees. The original charter said nothing about a university, about university officers, or about university degrees, and yet, from the first graduating class in 1585 on, the college conferred degrees as if it were a university. Not until the Act of 1621 ratifying the original charter were the Edinburgh degrees also recognized officially as valid.[38]

By the middle of the seventeenth century, then, Scotland had developed certain distinctive educational traditions and emphases that had special significance for the universities. There was, first, a deeply embedded appreciation of learning and a high regard for standards of excellence. The presence of this ideal was manifest, as will be seen, in

[36] Henderson, *Marischal College*, pp. 83 ff.; see Alexander Grant, *The Story of the University of Edinburgh* (2 vols.; London: Longmans, Green and Co., 1884), I, 99, 143.

[37] Henderson quotes an act of Parliament in 1662 which required the Masters of Marischal College and the College of Aberdeen "to have the approbation of the respective patrons, the Earle of Marischal and Magistrates of Edinburgh and Aberdeen." Henderson, *Marischal College*, pp. 89–90; Grant, *University of Edinburgh*, I, 122–123, 204.

[38] Grant argues that the College of Edinburgh was modeled explicitly after the Academy in Geneva, and that in assuming the right to grant degrees the college was following the example set by the Municipal Council of Geneva. Grant, *University of Edinburgh*, I, 143, 122–123, 204.

the relatively quick recovery of the universities from the difficulties into which they fell in the political and religious confusion of the seventeenth century. Second, a system of schools, imperfect as it was, provided a substructure for the higher institutions which helped to keep the universities integrally related to the whole of Scottish society. Third, the universities' potential for responsiveness to the larger society was heightened by the close connection that existed at nearly every level between the institutions of education and those of church and state. There was, finally, from the days of Knox, Melville, and Marischal onward, a strong drive toward continual educational reform and modernization. However much these ideals weakened or faltered in the turmoil of the seventeenth century, they remained, and in the eighteenth century emerged with new vigor.[39]

[39] The founding of Harvard College in Massachusetts by English Puritans in 1636, less than fifteen years after the ratification of Edinburgh's charter, raises the question whether Harvard was in any significant way influenced by the Scottish educational reforms and the new Protestant colleges at Aberdeen and Edinburgh. The founders of Harvard had much in common with the religious orientation of their Calvinist brethren in Scotland, including for some of them similar experiences on the Continent, and they may have followed events in Scotland with a good deal of interest. The question becomes all the more intriguing in light of the surface similarities between Harvard College and the College of Edinburgh, especially the confusion in status between college and university; the strong college president or principal teaching divinity, as at Edinburgh, with tutors conducting other classes on the regenting system; the attempt, as in Scotland, to undergird the college with a network of feeder schools; and, perhaps most striking, the similarity between the control of the College of Edinburgh by the Town Council and the control of Harvard by the Board of Overseers, consisting of ministers and magistrates.

Professor Morison has examined the origins of Harvard College with much thoroughness and warns against the pitfall of ignoring the common medieval origins of all seventeenth century universities and exalting "what is at best a remote cousinage into direct parentage." Morison's own well-documented conclusion is that the most influential model for Harvard was Emmanuel College at Cambridge, which many of the Massachusetts founders had attended. The only evidence of a direct link between Harvard and Edinburgh is the preservation of the Harvard graduation thesis sheets from the early 1640's, which in form and content are near replicas of those used at Edinburgh. These sheets were printed broadside listing the theses, or propositions, to be debated by graduating students in the public disputations held at commencement time. Although Morison identifies the persons probably responsible for bringing the Edinburgh theses to Cambridge, he does not really inquire into why the Harvard authorities might have been persuaded to print them as their own. For his discussion of relationships between early Harvard and the Scottish universities, see Samuel Eliot Morison, *The Founding of Harvard University* (Cambridge, Mass.: Harvard University Press, 1935), pp. 126–139. One explanation, beyond the obvious suggestion that Harvard found the Edinburgh thesis sheets congenial to their own academic purposes, indicates that perhaps the founders of Harvard were fully cognizant of the similarities between their own institution and the College of Edinburgh. Harvard College from the beginning granted degrees, but without royal authorization to do so. Since the Americans

The universities of Scotland suffered greatly during the political
and religious strife of the seventeenth century; yet Scotland continued

---

were circulating appeals in Europe for funds, they may have felt it advisable to
establish in every possible way that their college was no radical departure from
precedent, that in conferring degrees without specific authorization by charter
from the crown they were only doing what Edinburgh, which they resembled in
this and many other ways, had done without objection from the king for more
than twenty-five years after its founding.

Decisive Scottish influences may also be detected in the founding of the second
colonial college, William and Mary. The college owed its birth and form to James
Blair, Commissary of the Bishop of London in Virginia. A Scotsman, born in
Aberdeenshire, Blair was educated at Marischal College and, for a time, at Edinburgh, where he received an M.A. in 1673. Blair drafted a plan for a college in
Virginia, went to London under an appointment from the General Assembly of
Virginia to present his scheme, and in 1693 received a royal charter establishing
the college and naming Blair himself President for life. For nearly half a century
the college was under his guidance and domination, as were many other Virginia
affairs. On the life and career of Blair, see Daniel Estes Motley, *Life of Commissary
James Blair, Founder of William and Mary College*, Johns Hopkins University
Studies in Historical and Political Science, Vol. XIX, no. 10 (Baltimore, 1901);
and Samuel Roop Mohler, "Commissary Blair, Churchman, Educator, and Politician
of Colonial Virginia" (unpublished Ph.D. dissertation, University of Chicago, 1940).

A. Bailey Cutts has argued that the form of lay government which emerged at
William and Mary was influenced by Scottish examples; and George Pryde has
asserted that in titles and institutions, and in the curriculum and graduating regulations, "the Scottish impact is unmistakable." See A. Bailey Cutts, "The Educational
Influence of Aberdeen in Seventeenth Century Virginia," *William and Mary
Quarterly*, 2nd ser. XV (July 1935), 229–249; George S. Pryde, *The Scottish Universities and the Colleges of Colonial America* (Glasgow: Jackson, Son and Co.,
1957), pp. 10–16; also P. J. Anderson, "Aberdeen Influence on American Universities," *Aberdeen University Review*, V (1917–18), 28–29. Pryde's discussion, however, is too vague to be of much help, and the issue of lay government is more
problematic than Cutts indicates since Oxford influences were apparently also
strong at William and Mary. See Courtlandt Canby, "A Note on the Influence of
Oxford upon William and Mary College in the Eighteenth Century," *William and
Mary Quarterly*, 2nd ser., XXI (July 1941), 243–247.

At one point in particular, however, the similarity between William and Mary
and Marischal College, which Blair attended, is striking. Blair introduced the
specialized professorship at William and Mary, the same system which had prevailed at Marischal till the middle of the seventeenth century. By 1724 there was
a full faculty of six: the master of the grammar school, also called the professor
of humanity, the master of the Indian school, two professors of theology, one of
philosophy, and one of mathematics and natural philosophy. Pryde mentions that
this was the system of teaching at the college, and also points out that, while not
unusual, "the conjunction of the 'profession' of humanity with the mastership of
the grammar school . . . is particularly reminiscent of the practice at Aberdeen's
two colleges." Pryde, *The Scottish Universities*, p. 14. However, Pryde's omission
of the Marischal precedent of the specialized professor is difficult to understand,
especially since the practice at William and Mary appears as a complete innovation
in contrast with Harvard where regenting was the accepted system.

The destruction of documents in the 1705 fire at William and Mary makes it
impossible to reconstruct the early history of the college. "Time and again,"
Mohler writes, "the trail runs out, and only conjecture is possible." Mohler,
"Commissary Blair," pp. ii–iii. It is only later in the eighteenth century that the trail
of Scottish influence at William and Mary picks up again.

to produce men of exceptional ability and commitment to learning, men who kept the universities surprisingly in touch with the intellectual currents in Europe. The Anglican "Aberdeen Doctors," before they were overwhelmed by the opposition of the radical Presbyterian Covenanters, made their colleges famous at home and abroad as centers for the teaching of the humanities and theology. Among other outstanding seventeenth-century Scotsmen were such men as James Gregory, Professor of Mathematics at St. Andrews and later Edinburgh, a friend and in some ways a precursor of Newton himself; Robert Sibbald, Edinburgh scientist and founder of the first physic garden in Scotland; and Bishop William Carstares, Principal of Edinburgh University and one of the chief movers in the reform of the university curriculum at the beginning of the eighteenth century.

Many Scotsmen also went abroad for advanced study. A vital intellectual stimulus came to Scotland from the universities of Holland —Utrecht, Franeker, Groningen, and particularly Leyden. Following the Truce of 1609, Holland became for a time one of the cultural and commercial powers of Europe. Her universities, with men like Boerhaave in medicine, Grotius in political science, and Gronovius in classical philology, were leaders in the promotion of the new learning, and were especially famous for their strong professional faculties of law, medicine, and theology. Literally hundreds of Scottish students had attended the University of Leyden by the end of the seventeenth century. These students returned from Holland eager to introduce into their own universities the advanced subject matter of the Dutch universities, as well as Dutch teaching methods, with emphasis upon lectures by specialists, classroom use of the vernacular, scientific experimentation, and clinical instruction in medicine.[40] In the last quarter of the seventeenth century it was evident that new life was stirring in the Scottish universities.

[40] Isabel Kenrick has reprinted the names of Scottish students on the matriculation lists of the University of Leyden between 1615 and 1715. Her tally of Scottish students at Leyden during this period shows over 80 Scots there between 1620 and 1650, over 350 between 1660 and 1690, and over 750 between 1660 and 1715. Kenrick also provides an excellent detailed discussion of the influence of the Dutch institutions upon the University of Edinburgh. Isabel Kenrick, "The University of Edinburgh 1660–1715; A Study in the Transformation of Teaching Methods and Curriculum" (unpublished Ph.D. dissertation, Bryn Mawr College, 1956). Also see H. W. Meikle, *Some Aspects of Later 17th Century Scotland* (Glasgow: Jackson, Son, and Company, 1947). Meikle effectively refutes Henry Grey Graham's view that "from 1690 to about 1725 there was a dreary stagnation of all intellectual life and destitution of scholarship in Scotland." See Henry Grey Graham, *The Social Life of Scotland in the Eighteenth Century* (London: A & C Black, 1928), p. 449.

By the middle of the eighteenth century the Scottish universities were distinguished among the institutions of higher education in Europe by their strong commitment to utilitarian social service and their concern for educational progress and reform. These utilitarian and reform emphases were clearly manifest in three areas: first, the attention devoted by the universities to curricular and pedagogical reform; second, the rise of the Scottish medical schools and the introduction of a wide range of scientific subjects into the curriculum; and third, the involvement of the universities and their professors in the economic and industrial development of the country.

Indicative of an early desire to revive the state of education in Scotland was the creation by an act of Parliament in 1690 of a Visitation Commission to study and make recommendations for university reform. The specific proposals of the Commission were never carried into effect, but they did signal the increasing attention being devoted to the tasks of higher education.[41] During the eighteenth century Scottish universities were fundamentally transformed in response to demands for change. Three types of reform were especially important: first, the abandonment of the old regenting system for specialized professors teaching subjects only in their fields of competence; second, the revision of the curriculum and the introduction of new subjects and course content; and third, the adoption of new teaching methods.

The reform initiated by Andrew Melville of replacing the medieval system of regents with specialized professorships had been allowed to lapse. In 1708 Edinburgh took the lead in once again moving toward specialization when the Town Council did away with the rotating regents and put the arts curriculum under six specialized professors. The way was thus opened for the expansion of the curriculum and the conversion of the college into a genuine university. The other Scottish universities followed Edinburgh's example: Glasgow in 1727, St. Andrews in 1747, and Marischal College, Aberdeen, in 1753. Only King's College, Aberdeen, refused to abandon regenting, primarily because the regenting system was thought to give the tutors an opportunity to exert a moral influence over their students. Toward the end of the century, however, King's College also found the specialized professor necessary.[42]

---

[41] See the discussion and reprint of the enactments of the Visitation Commission in Morgan, *Scottish University Studies*, pp. 70–72.

[42] Morgan, *Scottish University Studies*, pp. 72–73; Kerr, *Scottish Education*, p. 215. Opposition to the abolition of regenting at King's College appears to have been

In every case the abolition of regenting was quickly followed by growth in the college faculties and fundamental curricular changes. Edinburgh University saw the expansion of its arts faculty, the establishment of a Faculty of Law, and in 1726 the beginnings of a medical school with five professors of medicine. Glasgow, which had only a Principal, a Professor of Divinity, and four regents when the century opened, introduced specialized professors, strengthened the Faculty of Arts, established Faculties of Law and Medicine, and entered into a period which one historian of the university has said "must rank as one of the most brilliant in the history of the University." [43] Even St. Andrews, moribund through most of the seventeenth century and much of the eighteenth, broadened its curriculum and increased the number of its students and the quality of its professors.[44]

The most deliberate full-scale reconstruction of the curriculum took place at Marischal and King's College, Aberdeen, in 1753. Although only Marischal succeeded in abolishing regenting, both colleges underwent thorough organizational and curricular reform. The most important step taken was to play down the old scholastic logic and metaphysics, and in their place to emphasize a wide range of modern subjects: natural history, geography, civil history, advanced mathematics and natural philosophy, rhetoric and *belle lettres*, and modern moral philosophy with its treatment of ethics, logic, politics, economics, and natural theology.[45] In nearly every area the Scottish universities were not only quick to recognize the importance of the

led by Professor Thomas Reid, who argued that regenting had a moral influence upon the students (Kerr, p. 241). It is also likely that Reid was concerned about his own academic position. In 1752, the year before regenting was abandoned at Marischal, Reid was appointed King's College Professor of Philosophy with the responsibility for teaching mathematics and physics, as well as logic and ethics, a wide range of duties which undoubtedly would have been narrowed considerably under a system of specialized professorships. Dugald Stewart, "Account of the Life and Writings of Thomas Reid," in *Biographical Memoir of Adam Smith*, edited by William Hamilton (New York: Augustus M. Kelley, 1966), p. 253. This is a reprint of the original work by Dugald Stewart, *Biographical Memoirs of Adam Smith, William Robertson, Thomas Reid* (Edinburgh: Thomas Constable and Co., 1858).

43 Mackie, *University of Glasgow*, pp. 157, 185.

44 R. G. Cant, *The University of St. Andrews* (Edinburgh: Oliver and Boyd, 1946), p. 93.

45 See *Notes on the Evolution of the Arts Curriculum in the Universities of Aberdeen*, prepared for the General Council (Aberdeen: Aberdeen University Press, 1908), especially p. 809. Also see Morgan, *Scottish University Studies*, pp. 72–74. Morgan points out about King's College that "it is difficult to see how a course so encyclopedic could be carried out with the regenting system still in force there."

new science and philosophy, but also to reorganize their entire teaching and curricula accordingly.

Finally, the Scottish professors were early aware of the need for pedagogical reforms and the adoption of new teaching methods. The Scottish universities, for example, led in making English respectable as a language of instruction in the classroom. Early in the eighteenth century John Stevenson at Edinburgh and Gerschom Carmichal, James Wodrow, John Simson, and Andrew Ross at Glasgow used English on occasion; and George Turnbull and David Fordyce at Aberdeen may also have done so.[46] English as a language of instruction really came into its own, however, when Francis Hutcheson was appointed Professor of Moral Philosophy at Glasgow in 1730 and began to deliver his philosophy lectures in English rather than Latin.[47]

Scottish professors of medicine and other scientific subjects were also quick to adopt the demonstration lecture as a teaching device. Before 1727 the professors of natural philosophy at Glasgow were illustrating their lectures with demonstrations, and in 1730 a separate course in Experimental Philosophy was created with a regularly appointed "assistant" or "demonstrator" to help with the classroom experiments.[48] Professors Cullen, Black, and Robison at Edinburgh and Glasgow were famed for the demonstrations which they conducted as a regular feature of their classroom instruction.[49] One American student, Samuel Bard of New York, writing to his father from Edinburgh in 1762, penned an admiring description of Cullen's teaching. "As he goes along," wrote Bard, "he explains his Theory by a variety of experiments, his two last Lectures were upon the Instruments made use of to assist Solution;—his Intention in this part of his Course, is not only to give us some account of the method of operating in Chemistry, but likewise to instruct us in the Language of that Science, and enable us to prefix proper & clear ideas to the Terms made use of in it." [50] An early and active interest in improving teach-

[46] Mackie, *University of Glasgow*, pp. 159–160; H. M. B. Reid, *The Divinity Professors in the University of Glasgow, 1640–1903* (Glasgow: Maclehose, Jackson and Co., 1923), p. 253.

[47] James McCosh, *The Scottish Philosophy* (New York: Robert Carter and Buthen, 1875), pp. 60–62; Carlyle, *Autobiography*, p. 59.

[48] Mackie, *University of Glasgow*, p. 218.

[49] *Ibid.*, pp. 230–231.

[50] Quoted in Whitfield J. Bell, Jr., "Some American Students of 'That Shining Oracle of Physic,' Dr. William Cullen of Edinburgh, 1755–1766," *Proceedings of the American Philosophical Society*, XCIV (June 1950), 275.

ing can also be seen at the University of Glasgow in the demand made by university authorities in 1712 that each professor give a written account of his methods and that regulations be followed for the correct use and care of the natural philosophy instruments.[51]

The medical schools, the one at Glasgow and especially the one at Edinburgh, gained international renown and stood as the most dramatic instances of the new educational forces at work in the universities. Not all of the Scottish universities, however, succeeded in establishing strong medical faculties. Perhaps such success was a reflection of the vigor of the different universities and of the towns in which they were located. St. Andrews, for example, had a chair of medicine and conferred M.D. degrees, but never succeeded in creating a medical school. The two colleges at Aberdeen had "mediciners," as the teaching post was called, but also failed to develop an adequate medical school until as late as 1789. Glasgow, on the other hand, with a long tradition of organized medical instruction outside the university, dating from the formation of the Joint Faculty of Physicians and Surgeons in the late sixteenth century, had more success. By 1755 the university had absorbed Glasgow's extramural medical chairs and had a flourishing medical school with nearly 200 students in attendance. The moving spirit in the rise of the Glasgow medical school was Dr. William Cullen, who in 1746 began to lecture within the university in English on the theory and practice of medicine. He soon added other lectures on chemistry, materia medica, and botany, and built around himself an active medical faculty. When Cullen went to the University of Edinburgh in 1755, he was succeeded at Glasgow by Joseph Black, whose work in chemistry brought further fame to Glasgow before Black, too, followed Cullen to Edinburgh.

The most famous of all the Scottish medical schools, and the first to be organized by a university in the British Isles, was that founded in 1726 at the University of Edinburgh. The establishment of a medical faculty within the university was the final outcome of a long tradition of extramural medical instruction in the city carried out under the encouragement and sponsorship of the Town Council.[52] The first organized medical instruction in Edinburgh may be dated from 1505 when the Incorporation of Barber-Surgeons received a charter from the Town Council. By far the most important event

[51] Mackie, *University of Glasgow*, p. 160.
[52] On the role of extramural medical education, see Douglas Guthrie, *Extramural Medical Education in Edinburgh* (Edinburgh: E. & S. Livingstone Ltd., 1965).

leading to the creation of the medical school itself, however, was the chartering of the College of Physicians in 1681. The Town Council, with the sole right under the Charter of King James VI to make all professorial appointments in Edinburgh, took an active role in university affairs, and supported educational ventures outside the university as well. Between 1670 and 1720 the Town Council established several chairs of medicine; however, these were all extramural positions. Not until 1726 did the Town Council, responding to the petition of Alexander Munro, the professor of anatomy, and four of his colleagues in the College of Physicians, appoint them to be professors "in the College." [53] Edinburgh's medical school gradually eclipsed Leyden's as the leading one in Europe. Edinburgh's fame is reflected in the number of men who came there to study from outside Scotland. A total of 1,143 graduated with M.D.'s from Edinburgh from 1726 to 1799 inclusive. Of these 237 were Scots, 254 English, 280 Irish, 195 from the West Indies and North America, 26 Europeans, 8 Welsh, 3 Latin Americans and East Indians, and 140 loosely designated "British." [54]

The rise of the medical schools helped to stimulate the development of a many-sided scientific curriculum with a strong utilitarian orientation. Opportunities for clinical instruction and the application of classroom lectures were soon made available with the opening of the Royal Infirmary in 1741 in connection with the new medical faculty. In the Infirmary in 1746 John Rutherford, Professor of the Practice of Physic, began giving the first clinical lectures in Great Britain.[55] Medicine was, moreover, a carrier of subject matters which eventually evolved into specialized disciplines in their own right. For example, among the eight chairs of medicine which were instituted between 1720 and 1770 in the Edinburgh medical faculty were those devoted to botany, materia medica, chemistry, and natural history.[56]

The utilitarian and practical orientation of the Scottish universities was not confined, however, to matters of course content and teaching method. A close relationship had always existed in Scotland

---

[53] Guthrie, *Extramural Medical Education*, pp. 9–10. H. P. Tait, "Medical Education at the Scottish Universities to the Close of the Eighteenth Century," *The Evolution of Medical Education in Britain*, edited by F. N. L. Poynter (London: Pitman Medical Publishing Company, 1966), pp. 62–63.
[54] Tait, "Medical Education at the Scottish Universities," p. 65.
[55] J. Gordon Wilson, "The Influence of Edinburgh on American Medicine in the Eighteenth Century," *Institute of Medicine of Chicago*, VII (January 1929), 133.
[56] Grant, *The University of Edinburgh*, I, 320.

between the universities, the church, and the towns in which they were located. The influence of the town government was, of course, the strongest at Edinburgh, where the Town Council often looked upon the college as its own. In Edinburgh, as has been seen in the case of medicine, the practice of the Town Council was to support extramural teaching, and when it proved of value, to bring it officially into the university. The same pattern was also followed by the Edinburgh Town Council in the teaching of law, and the creation of the Faculty of Advocates.[57] This close interaction between the university and other institutions of society could not help but influence the curriculum and do much to encourage the responsiveness of the university to many of the practical needs of the larger community.

In the eighteenth century this orientation of the universities toward utility and service to society increased. Scottish professors made important theoretical discoveries and distinguished themselves for their contributions to scientific progress. Every Scottish university in the eighteenth century, for example, could boast of having an outstanding mathematician on its faculty. From the days of John Napier of Merchistoun (1550–1617), usually known as the inventor of logarithms, Scotland had produced mathematicians of note. Later, David Gregory (1661–1708) and his successor at Edinburgh, Colin Maclaurin (1698–1746), were among the most able mathematicians anywhere. Both were friends of Newton and had been appointed to their positions at Edinburgh upon Newton's personal recommendation.[58] David Gregory and his uncle, James (1638–1675), at St. Andrews, had publicly taught Newton's system before it had received wide acceptance, even at Cambridge where Newton himself was on the faculty.[59] Among the accomplished mathematicians of the eighteenth century were Robert Simson and John Playfair at Glasgow, and Alexander Rait at Aberdeen. Matthew Stewart, Maclaurin's pupil and successor, has likewise been described by an eminent modern historian as "a mathematician of considerable power." [60] The importance attached in the Scottish universities to pedagogical concerns was also reflected in the classroom reputations attained by such mathematicians

---

[57] Ibid., 283–286; Morgan, Scottish University Studies, pp. 104–5.
[58] W. W. Rouse Ball, A Short Account of the History of Mathematics (New York: Dover, 1960; reprint of the 4th ed. of 1908), pp. 313–314, 388.
[59] Bryson, Man and Society, pp. 7–8. Bryson also points out that the reputation of Maclaurin, who shared with Bernoulli a prize of the French Academy for his Essay on Tides, was not merely local.
[60] Ball, History of Mathematics, p. 388.

as Maclaurin, Rait, and Simson, who were singled out by their students at various times "with great approbation" for their inspired teaching.[61] In chemistry, botany, and natural history—those subjects associated with the medical faculties—men such as Joseph Black, discoverer of carbon dioxide, and John Hope, often credited with having introduced the Linnaean system to Scotland, similarly did important work extending the theoretical reach of their fields.

Most significant, the Scottish university professors took the lead in applying their scientific investigations to Scottish agriculture and industry. This marked one of the sharpest differences between the Scottish and English universities. As already noted, in England men of science, particularly those engaged in technological undertakings, were most likely to be found in scientific clubs and societies unconnected with the universities. In Scotland, on the other hand, the closest articulation existed between the universities, the special scientific societies, and the actual financiers of industrial ventures, with the professors prominently associated with all three. The initiative in bringing about the close contact between the universities and industry and agriculture came, as R. H. Campbell has observed in his study of Scottish economic development, from both sides. The university professors offered their aid to the men of industry, but, when necessary, the industrialists themselves did not hesitate to take the first steps in tapping the resources of the universities.[62]

A few examples will make clear how close the collaboration was. William Cullen, cited by medical historians most frequently as a systematizer of disease symptoms, reformed pharmacopoeia and pioneered in the study of agricultural science. In addition, in 1755 the Board of Trustees for Improving Fisheries and Manufactures in Scotland presented Cullen with a prize for "his ingenious experiments and observations on the art of bleaching." [63] Francis Home, Professor of Materia Medica at Edinburgh, at the request of the Board also applied his knowledge of chemistry to bleaching, conducted experiments in crop fertilization, and gave thought to problems of urban sanitation.[64] At Glasgow a young mathematical engineer from Greenoch, James Watt, received important encouragement and assistance from Joseph

---

[61] See Carlyle, *Autobiography*, p. 28; Mackie, *University of Glasgow*, p. 216; Arthur H. DeRosier, Jr. "William Dunbar: A Product of the Eighteenth Century Scottish Renaissance," *The Journal of Mississippi History*, XXVIII (August 1966), 216.
[62] Campbell, *Scotland Since 1707*, p. 2.
[63] Hamilton, *Economic History of Scotland*, p. 140.
[64] *Ibid.*, p. 141; Campbell, *Scotland Since 1707*, p. 2.

Black, Adam Smith, John Robison, and other professors, who provided him with working space in the university. Watt was introduced to the Newcomen steam engine by Robert Dick, first Professor of Physics at Glasgow; and it was under the influence of Black, discoverer of the principle of latent heat, that Watt began to develop his conception of the separate steam condenser.[65] The Glasgow printers Robert and Andrew Foulis were also given rooms by the college for their bookstore and printing press, and in another part of the college maintained their Academy of Design.[66]

Also at Glasgow the Chemical Society, founded in 1785 as one of the earliest of its kind anywhere, met regularly within the university with the permission, and perhaps under the direction, of the professors. The membership of the Society included university professors, students, and leading Glasgow industrialists.[67] At Aberdeen, Principal Chalmers and other professors were members of Gordon's Mill Farming Club, founded in 1758, which devoted much of its time to the discussion of the principles of husbandry and their application to agricultural improvement in the northeast.[68]

In the latter half of the eighteenth century the ideal originally expressed in the *First Book of Discipline* that intellectual pursuits in Scotland should be undergirded by strong national educational structures seems to have been realized at least in higher education. Furthermore, in living up to the eighteenth-century ideal of utility the Scottish universities were manifestly successful.

Foreign observers recognized the Scottish universities as unique and commented with admiration on the achievements of their professors. The Italian historian Carlo Deanina, in *An Essay on the Progress of Learning Among the Scots* (1763), extolled the Scottish accomplishments. "Taking the English alone into account," wrote Deanina,

the number of good writers in our days would be found much less than it was about thirty years ago, if the part wanting in London and the

---

[65] Fay, *Adam Smith*, p. 4; McKenzie, *Scotland in Modern Times*, pp. 25–26. While at Glasgow, Watt installed and repaired the scientific equipment used by John Anderson in his natural philosophy class. Anderson later made several bequests to encourage scientific education. Campbell, *Scotland Since 1707*, p. 2; Mackie, *University of Glasgow*, p. 219.

[66] Graham, *Scottish Men of Letters*, p. 155.

[67] J. A. V. Butler, *Early Scientific Links Between Scotland and America* (offprint from eighteenth century Lectureship in Chemistry, n.d.), pp. 153–154.

[68] Hamilton, *Economic History of Scotland*, p. 75.

British provinces on this side of the Tweed were not supplied by a prosperous growth in the country of Scotland; whose people forming one nation with the proper English, and writing in the same language, suffer not to appear, if we may so express it, to the eyes of other nations, any diminution or decay in the studies of the fine arts.

Although Deanina was mainly concerned with Scottish learning in general, he made special mention of the universities and of such academics as Hutcheson, Simson, Maclaurin, Ferguson, and Cullen.[69] Scotsmen themselves took pride in pointing to the services rendered by their universities in furthering the economic and industrial development of Scotland. In doing so they were seldom able to refrain from indulging in some invidious comparisons between their own universities and those to the south. For example, John Millar, Professor of Civil Law at Glasgow, wrote:

The same circumstances which tended in Scotland to multiply seminaries of education, contributed also to model those institutions according to utility and the conveniency of the inhabitants. While the principal schools and universities of England, from the remains of ancient prejudice, confined their attention, in a great measure, to the teaching of what are called the learned languages, those of Scotland extended their views in proportion to the changes which took place in the state of society, and comprehended, more or less, in their plan of instruction, the principles of those different sciences which came to be of use in the world.[70]

Millar's statement cannot be totally dismissed as a product of national pride since he was himself an outspoken and politically active critic of Scottish society. Adam Smith, while indicating his own awareness of the shortcomings of the Scottish universities, nevertheless expressed

[69] H. W. Meikle reprints a British copy of extracts from Deanina. See H. W. Meikle, "The Learning of the Scots in the Eighteenth Century," *The Scottish Historical Review*, VII (1910), 289–293. Another example of similar sentiments comes from a letter written by a Hungarian in Paris to Henry MacKenzie: "Toutes les fois que les anglais m'ont parlé de Scotchmen avec un ton de mépris qu'ils affectant quelque fois, je leur ai conseillé d'aller à Edimbourg pour appendre à vivre et à être hommes. Vos savans Robertson, Black, et Hume sont regardés ici comme des génies du premier rang, il n'y a que deux jours que j'ai vu M. le Comte de Buffon qui me les a tous nommés au bout de doigt, comme on nomme Newton et Locke. . . . Pour les Sciences exactes Edimbourg vaut mieux qu'Oxford et Cambridge ensemble." Quoted in Harold W. Thompson, *A Scottish Man of Feeling* (London: Oxford University Press, 1931), p. 184.
[70] Quoted in William C. Lehmann, *John Millar of Glasgow, 1735–1801, His Life and Thought and his Contribution to Sociological Analysis* (Cambridge: At the University Press: 1960), p. 78.

in a private letter an attitude similar to that of Millar, his colleague:

In the present state of the Scotch universities, I do most sincerely look upon them as, in spite of all their faults, without exception the best seminaries of learning that are to be found anywhere in Europe. They are perhaps, on the whole, as unexceptionable as any public institutions of that kind, which all contain in their very nature the seeds and causes of negligency and corruption, have ever been or are ever likely to be.[71]

Allowance can be made for the bias of nationalistic feelings in comments such as these; yet still, by the weight of available evidence, the essential correctness of their assessments stands: the relationship of the Scottish universities to society was unique for European institutions of higher education, and their role in the Scottish Enlightenment was decisive.

Of course, a complete description of the Scottish universities in the eighteenth century would require far more attention to their shortcomings than has been given in this discussion.[72] King's College, for example, was slow in getting rid of the regenting system; St. Andrews had great difficulty recovering from the depressed state into which it had fallen in the previous century; the quality of instruction varied within all of the universities and was not always high, despite the outstanding faculty members of which each university could boast; and, finally, even Edinburgh and Glasgow continued to be plagued by financial difficulties and recurring internecine faculty struggles. They may not have been as unexceptionable as Adam Smith thought, but the important point is that the Scottish universities did evoke the admiration of contemporary observers.

IV

If the picture that has been drawn of Scottish cultural life in the eighteenth century is at all accurate, then clearly Americans, too, would have found much in Scotland, and particularly in Scottish

---

[71] This passage appears in a letter in which Smith is arguing against a proposal by Dr. William Cullen that the universities regulate the licensing of physicians to practice. Smith to Cullen, September 20, 1774, reprinted in John Rae, *Life of Adam Smith*, edited with introduction by Jacob Viner (New York: Augustus M. Kelley, 1965; first published 1895), pp. 273–280.

[72] By the same token, a closer examination of eighteenth-century Oxford and Cambridge might demand a revision of the usual unflattering picture often presented of them by non-Englishmen at the time. Again, the important point is not so much the realities of instruction in the English institution, as that Scotsmen—and Americans, as will become clear—tended to compare them unfavorably with those of Scotland.

education, to admire, to take inspiration from, and perhaps to copy. In the first place, the intellectual life of Scotland exhibited a degree of unity and a sense of direction that would have given the outside observer the impression that Scotland was somehow special. This apparent unity, although in ways illusory, drew attention to Scotland's intellectual life.

Second, the Scottish universities had much about them to attract Americans concerned with their own national advancement. Here were educational institutions devoted to national progress, and, to all appearances, producing remarkable results. More specifically, the modern courses and subject matter and the emphasis on progressive teaching methods in the Scottish universities provided concrete examples for imitation. Furthermore, Americans who desired to study abroad probably found it fairly easy to feel at home in the Scottish universities, with their students drawn from all classes of society. Nor did the pragmatic character of the Scottish universities fail to appeal to Americans who were themselves enamored of "the good and the useful." [73]

Third, relationships between Scottish and American Calvinism provided an important point of possible contact between American and Scottish education. Diversity within the Scottish Presbyterian church itself made it possible for the church to encompass the educational concerns of both traditional Scottish Calvinism and the Enlightenment.

Finally, there is the elemental fact that Scotsmen wrote and taught in English. The intellectual achievements of the French, and the Germans too, for that matter, were at least as impressive as those of the Scots; yet the absence of a language problem made Scottish learning more easily accessible to Americans—a recommendation Americans did not overlook. Thomas Jefferson himself indicated that Americans weighed this consideration carefully in deciding where to study abroad. Writing to Thomas Mann Randolph, Jr., in Edinburgh in 1785, Jefferson expressed his regrets that Randolph's poor health was forcing him to leave Scotland for the Continent. "Edinburgh," Jefferson added to his commiserations,

had the two advantages of possessing science in as high a degree as any place in the world, and of conveying it in your native tongue. Places may be found on the continent which may rival it in some branches of science,

[73] For an estimation of the pervasiveness of the ideal of utility in colonial American intellectual life and in the colonial colleges, see Howard Mumford Jones, *O Strange New World* (New York: The Viking Press, 1964), pp. 210–213.

and perhaps in those most interesting to you: but you will lose from the imperfect comprehension of what is delivered in a language not familiar to you.[74]

The attraction of Scottish intellectual and educational accomplishments for such Americans as Franklin and Jefferson may well have been undergirded by the affinities that existed between Scotland and America. Two American historians, John Clive and Bernard Bailyn, have suggested that similar political and social conditions may help to explain parallel developments in the intellectual life of the two countries in the eighteenth century. They maintain that, as political and cultural provinces of England, both Scotland and America looked to London for standards and styles; but, at the same time, they resented this dependence and tried hard to establish their own cultural integrity and originality over against the capital. The tensions engendered by the ambiguities of this provincial-cosmopolitan relationship, Clive and Bailyn think, were essentially creative:

The complexity of the provincial's image of the world and of himself made demands upon him unlike those felt by the equivalent Englishman. It tended to shake the mind from the roots of habit and tradition. It led men to the interstices of common thought where were found new views and new approaches to the old.[75]

In the view of Clive and Bailyn, the flowering of intellectual life in eighteenth-century Scotland and America can be understood in large part as having been stimulated by the provincials' combined sense of pride and insecurity.

This hypothesis, however, points to still another possible relationship between Scotland and America that Clive and Bailyn themselves do not explore. The cultural affinities between the two countries may not only help to explain parallel developments, but may also have given Americans good reasons for being especially interested in Scotland. If Scottish cultural leaders were demonstrating that, although provincials, they were indeed capable of competing with London as equals, Americans would have found it natural to look to Scotland for the secret of her success.

[74] Jefferson to Thomas Mann Randolph, Jr., November 25, 1785, *The Papers of Thomas Jefferson*, edited by Julian P. Boyd (Princeton, N.J.: Princeton University Press, 1954), IX, 59–60.
[75] John Clive and Bernard Bailyn, "England's Cultural Provinces: Scotland and America," *The William and Mary Quarterly*, 3rd ser., XI (April 1954), 213.

It is true that the Scots were often pathetically attentive to English opinion. Hume and Robertson, the equals of any in their fields, worried obsessively about the persistence of Scotticisms in their written work; and the entire Select Society of Edinburgh turned out to hear Thomas Sheridan instruct them in his Irish brogue on the correct pronunciation of English. Sometimes the desire even to outdo the English could lead them to make grandiose claims for themselves, as when, for example, John Home, the author of *Douglas*, was hailed by his countrymen as the Scottish Shakespeare.[76]

What Americans would have noticed, however, was that, as a matter of fact, the Scottish intellectuals and literati *were* able to rival London's best. The sermons of Hugh Blair and his lectures in rhetoric *were* considered models that Englishmen could copy to their profit— none other than that arch-critic of the Scots, Samuel Johnson himself, admitted as much.[77] In the judgment of the age the works of Hume and Robertson *did rank* among the best of any produced in England or France. Thus Scottish achievements would have stood as examples to Americans who also wanted to make their way as equals among the learned of Europe. Provincials did not have to remain provincial in all things: Scotland was proof of that. The following chapters explore important ways in which the Scottish example affected American higher education.

[76] David Daiches, in *Paradox of Scottish Culture,* discusses the tension which existed between the indigenous folk culture of eighteenth-century Scotland and the anglicizing gentility of the establishment literati. The humorous picture of the Select Society trying to follow Sheridan's rules for correct pronunciation of English—"tǐ-tùm or tùm-tǐ-tùm-tǐ, or . . . as tǎ-tǎ-tum, or . . . tùm-tǐ-tǐ, tùm-tǐ-tǐ"—is described in Mathieson, *The Awakening of Scotland,* pp. 201–202.

[77] On the success of Blair's sermons and his acceptance into the London literary circles presided over by Samuel Johnson, see Graham, *Scottish Men of Letters,* pp. 128–129.

Log Colleges, Revivals, and the Mother Church of Scotland: The Presbyterian Academy

Beginning as a trickle in the seventeenth century, immigration to the American colonies from Scotland and the Great Plantation of Ulster in Northern Ireland grew to a stream of sizable proportions by the outbreak of the War of Independence. There were in actuality two streams, clearly distinct, one Scottish and the other "Scotch-Irish," as the Ulster immigrants were called.[1] In numbers the Scotch-Irish were by far the more important of the two immigrant groups. It has been estimated that during the eighteenth century about two hundred thousand persons immigrated to America from Ulster.[2] By contrast there was no large-scale immigration of Scots to America until the period from 1763 to 1775. Even for these later years the total number of Scots coming to America has been calculated at no more than twenty-five thousand persons—in population a serious loss to Scotland, but no significant gain to the colonies.[3]

[1] Strictly speaking, there were three groups from Scotland and Ulster: the Scotch-Irish, the Lowland Scots, and the Highland and Island Scots. Each had different social and ethnic backgrounds, emigrated for different reasons, and, generally, settled in different areas, held different ideals and goals, and pursued different vocations. Whereas the Scotch-Irish settled the inland frontier, the Scots tended to scatter along the seaboard, the Lowlanders settling as individuals, and the Highlanders tending to found farming communities. George Shepperson discusses these distinctions in "Writings in Scottish-American History: A Brief Survey," *William and Mary Quarterly*, 3rd ser., XI (April 1954), 163–178, especially pp. 167 ff.

[2] James G. Leyburn, *The Scotch-Irish* (Chapel Hill: The University of North Carolina Press, 1962), p. 180. This may be a conservative estimate. Dunaway concludes that 250,000 is more nearly correct. Wayland F. Dunaway, *The Scotch-Irish of Colonial Pennsylvania* (Chapel Hill: University of North Carolina Press, 1944), p. 41.

[3] Ian Graham, *Colonists from Scotland* (Ithaca, N.Y.: Cornell University Press, 1956), p. 189.

Economic hardship was the major cause of immigration from Ulster—not religious persecution, which was relatively mild and only sporadic, despite complaints to the contrary by some Ulster Presbyterians at the time. Most persons left Ulster for America to escape rising prices, high land rents, and the severe famines that periodically afflicted the country during the eighteenth century. In response to changing conditions in Ulster, the Scotch-Irish came to America in several great waves between 1717 and 1775.[4]

Although some Scotch-Irish attempted early in the century to settle in New England, they found the close-knit New England communities inhospitable and opportunities for acquiring land scarce. After 1730, while many landed in New York and a few in the Carolinas, the majority of immigrants from Ulster disembarked at Philadelphia. From there they pushed out to the edges of Pennsylvania, and eventually moved down the Appalachian valleys into the frontier regions of Virginia and the Carolina Piedmont.[5]

An energetic, aggressive people, the Scotch-Irish were well suited for the task of settling and taming the frontier, but most were unlettered and their numbers included few professional men. Had they not brought with them their Presbyterian ministers, the contributions of the Scotch-Irish to American higher education in the colonial period would doubtless have been slight. However, the Scots and Scotch-Irish ministers who filled the pulpits of the Scotch-Irish churches in the middle and southern colonies embodied the traditional Presbyterian concern for education, and usually were graduates of Scottish universities.[6]

---

[4] Dickson presents the best discussion of the reasons for emigration from Ulster. R. J. Dickson, *Ulster Emigration to Colonial America, 1718–1775* (London: Routledge and Kegan Paul, 1966), pp. 24–31, 41, 47, 53, 69. Leyburn describes five waves of immigration: 1717–18, 1725–29, 1740–41, 1754–55, and 1771–75. Leyburn, *Scotch-Irish*, p. 169. Dickson, whose analysis of living conditions in Ulster and passenger lists of ships leaving Ireland is more searching, breaks the movement of immigration into four phases: 1718–20, 1721–30, 1731–69, 1770–75, but his peak years generally parallel those of Leyburn.
[5] See Leyburn, *Scotch-Irish*, pp. 154 ff., 184 ff.
[6] Dickson points out that in the total emigration from Ulster the number of Presbyterian ministers was disproportionately high, since in addition to those who accompanied their own congregations, many also went as individuals in response to calls from Scots and Scotch-Irish Presbyterian settlers. Dickson, *Ulster Emigration*, p. 20. Richard Webster traces the nativity of 200 Presbyterian ministers in America before 1760; of these he lists 55 Ulster Scots, 26 Scots, 6 English, 5 Welsh, 73 native born, and 33 unknown. Richard Webster, *History of the Presbyterian Church in America* (Philadelphia: Joseph Wilson, 1857), pp. 679 ff.

I

Much of the formal higher education available in the southern and western settlements of the eighteenth century took place in academies founded by Presbyterian ministers. These academies differed from the common practice, followed by many ministers of every denomination, of giving advanced theological instruction in their homes to young college graduates who were entering the ministry.[7] While a primary purpose of the academies was to provide for ministerial education, they also accepted young men preparing for all the learned professions, and focused on college preparatory and when possible college level instruction. It was not unusual, however, for a minister to have under him, in addition to his academy pupils, one or more advanced students or college graduates reading divinity. Although the academies were often little more than high-quality grammar schools, many did acquire outstanding reputations, and a significant number were actually granted college charters. Academies were established both at the initiative of individual ministers and with the encouragement of official church policy; often a flourishing academy first started by an interested minister would be taken under the care of the presbytery or synod, sometimes with the cooperation of local civic leaders, to be nourished as a fledgling college.

The first Presbyterian academies were founded by men who had come directly from Ulster or Scotland, but after mid-century most of the academies were established by graduates of the College of New Jersey, and the pattern was repeated as these academies in turn sent out their students. Precise figures will probably never be available since many academies may have been short-lived and lost to record; however, it is possible to get some idea of the extent of the academy movement in the eighteenth century. In the seventy-five years between 1727 and 1802—from the founding of William Tennent's Log College at Neshaminy, Pennsylvania, to the chartering of John McMillan's academy in western Pennsylvania as Jefferson College—more than sixty-five academies are known to have been maintained by

---

[7] For discussions of the practice of acquiring professional theological training in the home of a minister, see Mary L. Gambrell, *Ministerial Training in Eighteenth Century New England* (New York: Columbia University Press, 1937); and William O. Shewmaker, "The Training of the Protestant Ministry in the United States of America, before the Establishment of Theological Seminaries," *Papers of the American Society of Church History*, 2nd ser., VI (1921), 177–197.

Presbyterian ministers in the southern and western settlements served by the church. In all probability there were others as well, but that these more than sixty-five can be definitely identified by location, and in most instances by the names of their minister-teachers, would seem to indicate that they achieved some degree of permanence and a local reputation.[8]

The tradition of the Presbyterian academy can be traced most directly to policies followed by the church in Ulster in the latter half of the seventeenth century, as well as to the Presbyterians' long-standing sense of responsibility for the education of their ministers and parishioners. The Scots immigrants to the Great Plantation of Ulster during the seventeenth century succeeded in carrying with them the full system of Presbyterian church government. Operating as an extension of the Church of Scotland, the General Synod of Ulster claimed jurisdiction over the entire country and set up presbyteries and congregations on a territorial basis.[9]

The original plan adopted under James I in 1607 for the Great Plantation of Ulster had as one of its chief aims to place northern Ireland under Protestant control by displacing its Catholic population with English and Scots settlers. It has been estimated that by 1740 100,000 Scots and 20,000 English had immigrated to Ulster. After the Cromwellian settlement and during the Restoration, immigrants from the lowlands of Scotland had streamed into Ulster. Presbyterians, however, were never a numerical majority as is sometimes supposed. It has been calculated that by 1715 Ulster's total population of approximately 600,000 included about 200,000 Presbyterians. Yet in the counties of Down, Tyrone, Antrim, and eastern Donegal—the last three served by the port cities of Londonderry, Portrush, Larne, and Belfast—Presbyterians predominated, and in addition they were spread throughout the rest of Ulster, so that their numbers do not adequately reflect the extent of their influence and control.[10]

Every effort was made to enforce church discipline, and with it to maintain the educational standards demanded of candidates for the ministry.[11] Since the nonconforming Presbyterians were excluded by

---

[8] See Appendix for a list of Presbyterian academies.

[9] J. C. Beckett, *Protestant Dissent in Ireland, 1687–1780* (London: Faber and Faber Ltd., 1948), pp. 14–15; Dunaway, *Scotch-Irish of Colonial Pennsylvania*, p. 26.

[10] See Dunaway, *Scotch-Irish of Colonial Pennsylvania*, pp. 24–25; Dickson, *Ulster Emigration*, pp. 3–4.

[11] See James Seaton Reid, *History of the Presbyterian Church in Ireland* (3 vols.; London: Whittaker and Co., 1853), especially III, 12–13.

law from the university in Dublin, their ministers were forced to obtain their liberal arts degrees and theological training at the universities in Scotland. Because the journey to Scotland was inconvenient and could be hazardous, the church in Ulster attempted to found academies to provide ministers with their liberal arts training. The Ulster academies, thus, were similar in origin to the dissenting academies in England, but the close ties maintained by the Presbyterians in Ireland with the Scottish church and universities probably helped to preclude the development of strong independent academies in Ulster such as were arising in England.

In Antrim a "Philosophical and Theological School" was maintained by the Reverend Thomas Gowan during the reign of Charles II. This may have been the same school which the church tried to put on an official footing in 1685, only to have the scheme fail because of a lack of students. Other academies were attempted at Stepney, Newtownards, and Comber, and in 1697 the General Synod meeting in Antrim remarked on the flourishing condition of the "philosophy school" in Killyleagh. In spite of some religious harassment, it was possible for the synod in 1708 to establish by act of Parliament a privately endowed Presbyterian school.[12] At this time the teacher at Killyleagh was the Reverend James McAlpin, who held classes in the classics, scholastic philosophy, and theology. Though McAlpin does appear to have enjoyed an outstanding reputation in the area, his was probably a fairly typical course of study, and it indicates that these academies offered instruction at a level somewhat higher than a grammar school yet lower than a university.[13] Another academy was set up during 1721 and 1722 in Dublin by Francis Hutcheson, then a young Presbyterian minister, who had studied under McAlpin and at the University of Glasgow.[14] Many, if not most, of the Ulster-born ministerial candidates probably followed the path taken by Hutcheson of spending some years in a local academy, then finally securing a degree from a Scottish university.

The relatively high academic standards of the church made the minister the intellectual and cultural leader among the new settlers from Ireland. Of the twenty-six men known to have been received

12 Thomas Witherow, *Historical and Literary Memorials of Presbyterianism in Ireland, 1623–1731* (London: William Mullan and Son, 1879), pp. 53, 149, 345; Beckett, *Protestant Dissent in Ireland*, p. 22.
13 W. R. Scott, *Francis Hutcheson* (Cambridge: At the University Press, 1900), p. 8.
14 *Ibid.*, pp. 23–24.

into the Presbytery of Philadelphia before 1717, twelve were graduates of the University of Glasgow or had taken courses there, and four had received training at the University of Edinburgh.[15]

It was common not only for future ministers, but also for boys interested in the other learned professions, to turn to the minister for help. Thus it was, for example, that young Andrew Hamilton, later famous for his role in the Zenger case, received his first instruction in law under the guidance of the Reverend Francis Makemie and with the use of Makemie's collection of law books. Makemie, leader in the founding of the Presbytery of Philadelphia (1706), had himself attended the University of Glasgow and was accomplished in the field of law.[16] In order to uphold the standards of ministerial education the Presbytery of Philadelphia, even in its earliest years, demanded that ministerial candidates satisfy an examining committee as to their competence in the liberal arts and theology.[17]

Against this background of ministerial education and the educational activities of the church in Ulster and Scotland then, it is no surprise to find the early Scotch-Irish ministers in America setting up academies. The most famous and one of the earliest of these academies was that founded by the Reverend William Tennent in 1727 on the Little Neshaminy Creek in Bucks County, Pennsylvania. Derisively labeled the "Log College" by its enemies soon after its founding, Tennent's academy was to acquire much fame through the educational work of its alumni, particularly in the founding of the College of New Jersey, and in the leadership they provided in the Great Awakening. Many later Presbyterian academies, it is true, did spring from the Log College or reactions to it, but it should perhaps be stressed that in setting up his academy Tennent himself was merely acting within a well-established tradition.

[15] The other ten were either New England educated or their backgrounds are unknown. See Henry D. Funk, "The Influence of the Presbyterian Church in Early American History," *Journal of the Presbyterian Historical Society*, XII, 156.

[16] See Burton Alva Konkle, *The Life of Andrew Hamilton, 1676–1741* (Philadelphia: University of Pennsylvania Press, 1941), pp. 9–11. Makemie's defense at his arrest by the Governor of New York for unlicensed preaching on Long Island in 1707 has been considered a landmark in the history of religious freedom. For a discussion of Makemie's significance and excerpts from his defense, see H. Shelton Smith, Robert T. Handy, Lefferts A. Loetscher, eds., *American Christianity; An Historical Interpretation with Representative Documents* (New York: Charles Scribner's Sons, 1960), I, 256–261.

[17] See Funk, "Influence of the Presbyterian Church," p. 157; also Maurice W. Armstrong, Lefferts A. Loetscher, Charles A. Anderson, eds., *The Presbyterian Enterprise* (Philadelphia: The Westminster Press, 1956), pp. 18–19, 25.

The existence of this tradition can be seen in that ministers coming to America directly from Scotland and northern Ireland continued to establish academies upon their arrival in the colonies. The two earliest known Presbyterian academies in North Carolina, for example, were founded around 1760 by James Tate, at Wilmington, and David Ker, at Crowfield, both ministers who had come over directly from Ulster.[18] The academy at Baskingridge, Pennsylvania, also was founded by an immigrant minister from Scotland, Samuel Kennedy, whose own education had been at the University of Edinburgh. Kennedy became a firm supporter of the revivalist party in the church and his academy is said to have sent numerous students to the College of New Jersey.[19]

II

The founder of the Log College, William Tennent, was born, according to the inscription on his tombstone, in 1673, either in northern Ireland or in Scotland.[20] A graduate of the University of Edinburgh in 1695, he was first licensed by a Scottish Presbytery in Ulster, and then, in 1704, ordained in the Anglican Church in Antrim. In 1718 he immigrated to America and, declaring himself a dissenter from the Anglican Church in Ireland, was received into the Philadelphia Synod. After serving several churches in New York and on Long Island, Tennent in 1727 settled at Neshaminy, where his kinsman, James Logan, secretary to the Penns and a Scotch-Irish Quaker, had obtained a sizable grant of land for Tennent.[21] Tennent began immediately to teach his own sons and other students interested in the ministry, and in 1735 erected a log building for his school. Located about twenty miles north of Philadelphia on the main road to New York, in Bucks County, where the Scotch-Irish were actually a

---

[18] Donald R. Come, "The Influence of Princeton on Higher Education in the South Before 1825," *William and Mary Quarterly*, 3rd ser., II (1945), 378.

[19] Kennedy also had a reputation as an excellent physician, another example of the variety of tasks performed by the ministers. William B. Sprague, *Annals of the American Pulpit* (New York: R. Carter and Brothers, 1858), III, 176.

[20] Almost all his biographers claim northern Ireland. Thomas Pears has pointed out, however, that this is based only on the evidence that Tennent was living in Ireland for some years before coming to America. Thomas C. Pears and Guy Klett, comps., "A Documentary History of William Tennent and the Log College" (Mimeographed manuscript; Philadelphia: Presbyterian Historical Society, 1940), p. 163.

[21] For biographical data, see *ibid.*, especially pp. 1–5, 12–14, 62. For the relationship between Tennent and Logan, who also helped Tennent negotiate some of his debts in Ireland, see pp. 18, 57, 63b.

minority, the Log College was prominent from the beginning, both physically and as a symbol.[22]

Tennent was setting up his academy just at a time when critical divisions along theological and ethnic lines were beginning to appear in the American Presbyterian church. In its earliest years the Presbytery of Philadelphia had been fairly evenly divided between ministers of New England and of Scottish or Ulster backgrounds. After 1710, however, the influx of Scotch-Irish began to increase, and by the twenties the church was showing evidence that the theological and polity commitments of the two groups did not always agree. Fearing a degeneration of doctrine and discipline, the Scotch-Irish began to urge stricter conformity to the Westminster Confession. In 1727 John Thompson, a Scotch-Irish minister of the New Castle Presbytery, brought a proposal before the synod that all ministers in the presbyteries and synod be called upon to subscribe to the Westminster Confession. Opposition to the "subscriptionists" was led by a group of ministers born in New England and educated at Yale. The chief spokesman for the New England ministers was the Reverend Jonathan Dickinson. As early as 1722 Dickinson had spoken out against the strict subscriptionists on the grounds of his conviction that the Word of God could not be fully and adequately captured by human interpretations and that no doctrinal formulations, therefore, could be absolutely binding. Dickinson said that every man must be allowed to accept the doctrines of the faith just so far as "they appear to him just and true." Even the "essential Articles of Christianity," Dickinson argued, "may not be imposed by Civil Coercion, Temporal Penalties, or any way whatsoever." [23] In addition to rejecting their authoritarianism, Dickinson may also have opposed the subscriptionists because he feared that they might attempt to place the American church under the control of the Scottish or Irish ecclesiastical bodies.[24]

The upshot of the subscription overture was a compromise solution in the form of the Adopting Act of 1729. By its terms the Westminster Confession was accepted as basically sound "in all the essential and necessary articles of faith," but individual ministers were

---

[22] See Thomas Murphy, *The Presbytery of the Log College* (Philadelphia: Presbyterian Board of Publications and Sabbath School Work, 1889), p. 76; also see Leyburn, *Scotch-Irish*, pp. 196–197.

[23] Dickinson's *Remarks* are reprinted in Smith, Handy, Loetscher, eds., *American Christianity*, I, 262–268.

[24] See Alan Heimert, *The Great Awakening* (New York: The Bobbs-Merrill Company, Inc., 1967), p. xxxii.

permitted to voice their objections and reservations regarding particular doctrines and have them adjudicated by the church.[25]

The agreement reached in the Adopting Act was not stable, however, and the appearance of the revivalist-oriented Log College soon helped to touch off the controversy again, this time in a new and more intense form. Tennent and his students, especially his eldest son Gilbert, actively evangelized their own and other ministers' congregations, preaching repentance and stressing the need for a heartfelt experience of divine forgiveness. The 1740 preaching tour of George Whitefield forged a link between the Tennents and similar revivalist forces in New England under the leadership of Jonathan Edwards. From this time on, with Whitefield as active agent and catalyst, the revivals of the Great Awakening assumed the proportions of a genuinely intercolonial movement. Edwards, already known in America and abroad for his *Faithful Narrative of the Surprising Work of God* describing the 1734 revivals in his church at Northampton, emerged as the acknowledged intellectual leader of the revivalists in both the Congregational and Presbyterian churches. Although the New England men in the Presbyterian church, such as Dickinson and Aaron Burr, had refrained at first from commiting themselves, by 1740 they had come down firmly on the side of the Tennents and the revivalist movement.[26]

Educational attitudes and ideals quickly became a prime center of dispute between the "New Side" and the "Old Side," as the contending revivalist and anti-revivalist factions in the Presbyterian church soon came to be called. The most obvious reason was that the very existence of the Log College was an offense to the Old Side, who rightly saw it as a breeding ground of revivalist ministers. A second reason education loomed so large in the conflict was that the differing theological and social orientations of the two parties were directly reflected in their educational ideals and priorities. Finally, the command of educational standards and institutions offered to each side

[25] The Adopting Act is reprinted in Armstrong, Loetscher, Anderson, eds., *The Presbyterian Enterprise*, pp. 30–32.
[26] General information on the Great Awakening is drawn from the standard treatments. See especially Edwin Scott Gaustad, *The Great Awakening in New England* (New York: Harper and Brothers, 1957); Charles Hartshorne Maxon, *The Great Awakening in the Middle Colonies* (Chicago: University of Chicago Press, 1920); Wesley M. Gewehr, *The Great Awakening in Virginia, 1740–1790* (Gloucester, Mass.: P. Smith, 1965; first published 1930); C. C. Goen, *Revivalism and Separatism in New England, 1740–1800* (New Haven: Yale University Press, 1962).

a concrete means of gaining ecclesiastical control and of propagating their own points of view.

The revivalists appeared to the Old Side as unrestrained enthusiasts and disturbers of both God and man, and, what was worse, their itinerant preachers were emptying the pews of the churches served by Old Side ministers. The Old Side charged that the revivalists were wildly emotional, irresponsibly unconcerned with the objective order and truth of Christian doctrine, and—here was the sting—poorly educated and ill-equipped to understand and interpret the scriptures rightly. Although the synod, meeting in 1738 and under Old Side control, authorized the formation of the new Presbytery of New Brunswick which was composed largely of Log College ministers and sympathizers, at the same time it took steps to rein in the Log College influence. The synod ruled by act that all candidates for the ministry who did not possess a degree from either a New England or European university would be required to stand examination before a special commission appointed by the synod. This action was obviously aimed at the Log College and was implemented within a few months when the synod refused to admit John Rowland, a Log College alumnus already licensed by the New Brunswick Presbytery.[27]

In 1739 George Whitefield visited Neshaminy and stayed with the Tennents on his way to New England. Noting in his journal the work of William Tennent and his students, Whitefield commented, "The place wherein the young Men study now is in contempt call'd *the College*. It is a Log-House, about Twenty Feet long, and near as many broad; and to me it seemed to resemble the Schools of the old Prophets." [28] Whitefield's visit and his reception in New England breathed new spirit into the New Side, and charges and counter-charges from each party mounted.

In 1740 Gilbert Tennent preached his famous sermon on "the dangers of an unconverted ministry," which, charging that Old Side ministers were anti-evangelical, served in part as his rebuke to accusations that the revivalists were anti-intellectual.[29] Many of the Old Side

---

[27] See Leonard J. Trinterud, *The Forming of an American Tradition* (Philadelphia: The Westminster Press, 1949), pp. 74 ff., 81 ff. Also Gewehr, *The Great Awakening in Virginia*, pp. 14–15.

[28] See the reprint from George Whitefield's *Fifth Journal* in Armstrong, ed., *The Presbyterian Enterprise*, pp. 34–35.

[29] Tennent's entire sermon, "The Danger of an Unconverted Ministry," is reprinted in Heimert, *The Great Awakening*, pp. 71–99

ministers, Tennent declared, were unconverted and only "letter-learned Pharisee teachers" leading their flocks astray—"hireling, murderous, Hypocrites," he called them. Not learning or a university degree, but an "Experience of a special work of the Holy Ghost" on his soul, Tennent said, was the minister's only valid stamp of authority. "Isn't an unconverted Minister," Tennent asked, "like a Man who would learn others to swim, before he has learn'd it himself, and so is drowned in the Act, and dies like a Fool?"

Tennent proposed as one solution to the problem of a dead church and unconverted ministers that schools or "seminaries of Learning" devoted to the principles of revival theology be founded throughout the land.[30] He was calling, in other words, for a multitude of Log Colleges. It is thus understandable that the Synod of Philadelphia in 1741 excluded the Presbytery of New Brunswick from the rights of membership, although the way they went about it was somewhat high-handed. The Presbyteries of New Brunswick and New York united, thereupon, to form the New Side–dominated Synod of New York.[31]

The clamor and bitterness over ministerial education reflected differing theological positions and priorities. L. J. Trinterud has shown that from its origin Calvinism has demonstrated a continuing tension between an emphasis upon a subjective awareness of the divinity and an emphasis upon the objective existence of the divinity. According to Trinterud, English Presbyterianism historically stressed the inner and more subjective side, Scottish Presbyterianism the outer and objective. The former emphasis was represented in the anti-subscriptionist sentiments of the New England men and by the revivalist convictions of the Tennents, while the latter found expression in the rational and doctrinal concerns of the Old Side. The presence of both extreme positions side by side in the American Presbyterian church raised the tension to a critical pitch.[32]

Each emphasis had different ecclesiastical and educational implications. On the one hand, the Old Side stressed the necessity for strict subscription to the Westminster Confession as an objective standard of the faith; a thorough classical education in order to be able to explicate the creeds and scriptures; and, to safeguard doctrinal standards, order in church polity as guaranteed by a properly ordained

[30] *Ibid.*, p. 85.
[31] See Trinterud, *The Forming of an American Tradition*, pp. 102–108.
[32] *Ibid.*, especially Chapter 10.

and educated clergy. On the other hand, the New Side insisted upon the necessity of conversion—for ministers without exception; subscription to the creeds only on the basis of inner conviction; and a more flexible ecclesiastical organization in order that the clergy might be free to preach for conversion wherever needed. These differences all came to the surface in the struggle for control of the church government. The reasons given by the synod in 1741 for the exclusion of the Presbytery of New Brunswick reflected this basic difference in theological and ecclesiastical orientation.[33]

The charges of the Old Side that the revivalists were essentially anti-intellectual carried weight. Breathing the hothouse atmosphere of revival excitement, the Log College men became notorious for their fervent preaching and their impudent forays into the camps of the unconverted. In spite of an order of the synod that John Rowland, a Log College graduate, make up alleged educational deficiencies, he was licensed by the New Brunswick Presbytery in 1738, and promptly thereafter touched off a revival in the Maidenhead-Hopewell congregation marked by an outpouring of emotion. Gilbert Tennent followed George Whitefield in 1740 into New England on his own preaching tour and was denounced by critics of the revival as a stamping, braying monster who crudely thundered at sinners that they were "damned, damned, damned." Samuel Finley, twice arrested and deported from Connecticut for preaching there without authorization, inspired the Connecticut Assembly to increase the fines against itinerant preachers from outside the colony. When demented James Davenport began to accuse what he called the unconverted by name, including ministers, and set to burning books at the wharf in New London, the entire Great Awakening acquired the taint of "enthusiasm"—a term which at the time carried all the overtones of wild-eyed fanaticism. It became easy for critics to lump together all the revivalists as vulgar champions of disorder and ignorance.[34]

[33] The New Brunswick Presbytery was read out of the synod on basically five counts, for: 1) encouraging their ministers to itinerate and intrude uninvited into the congregations of regularly settled ministers; 2) condemning others who did not agree with their outlook; 3) violating the Act of the synod by ordaining men without the proper educational and licensing requirements; 4) encouraging emotional excesses by preaching "the terror of the Lord"; 5) judging the converted and the unconverted by their sense of conviction and forgiveness. The synod *Protestation* is reprinted in Armstrong, Loetscher, Anderson, eds., *The Presbyterian Enterprise*, pp. 47–48.
[34] See Trinterud, *Forming of an American Tradition*, pp. 81 ff. Also Webster, *History of the Presbyterian Church*, pp. 469 ff; Goen, *Revivalism and Separatism*, pp. 15–27, 61–62.

The issues were much more complex, however, than the opponents of the Awakening represented them to be. The New Side leadership—Tennent, Blair, Finley, and Dickinson—and those in New England who took their cues from Jonathan Edwards resisted the tendency to interpret the Awakening as a conflict between the head and the heart. This was an exceedingly difficult task, since they themselves did work upon the emotions of their hearers, and they were not blameless for the disorder and emotionalism that accompanied the revivals. Gilbert Tennent's own performance in New England and his attack upon unconverted ministers had done much to encourage extremists and dissidents of all sorts.

However, although the Log College preachers did not feel ill-at-ease with the outcries and weeping of their listeners, neither did they encourage unrestrained emotionalism for its own sake. From the very start men like Jonathan Dickinson, Gilbert Tennent's younger brother, William Tennent, Jr., Samuel Blair, and Samuel Finley attempted to help their people understand the conversion experience in rational and doctrinal terms. In describing his role in the revival which began as a result of his preaching at Fagg's Manor in 1740, Samuel Blair, for example, said that he tried to show his disturbed people that they were not "to obtain or seek peace in extraordinary ways, by visions, dreams, or immediate inspirations; but by an understanding view and believing persuasion." [35] Edwards began very early to dissociate himself from the Separate extremists, who were splitting off from the New England churches. In 1741 he published his *Distinguishing Marks of a Work of the Spirit of God*, in which he defended the revivals while attempting to establish criteria for preventing their abuse, a program he carried still further in his treatise *The Religious Affections* (1746). Also in 1741, Gilbert Tennent, Samuel Finley, and Jonathan Dickinson led the New Side in repudiating the unbridled enthusiasm, and what they considered the antinomianism, of Count Zinzendorf and his Moravians.[36]

The anti-revivalists in New England also cast themselves in the role of the champions of order, education, and civility, against rampant emotionalism and self-righteous ignorance. In his study of the

[35] Quoted in Trinterud, *Forming of an American Tradition*, pp. 79 ff. Also see Davies' account of the Log College revivalist, William Robinson, and his work among the "reading converts" in Virginia. Samuel Davies, "The State of Religion in Virginia," in Heimert, *The Great Awakening*, p. 385.

[36] Trinterud, *Forming of an American Tradition*, p. 114. Also see Heimert, *The Great Awakening*, p. liii.

New England Separates, however, C. C. Goen maintains that in spite of their emphasis on direct inspiration, the oft-repeated charge that "the Separates repudiated human learning is not exactly true; it was mainly the substitution of literary polish for the leading of the Spirit to which they objected." The moderate revivalist leadership in New England and in the middle and southern colonies, guided mainly by Edwards, agreed with this point of view in principle; namely, that the question was not one of rejecting learning, but of fixing priorities. It seems undeniable, however, that the Separates and other more radical elements did come very close to a repudiation of learning as events progressed, a tendency that was resisted and eventually condemned by the moderate revival leaders. One reason why the New England Separates moved in the direction they did was the suppression of their attempts to provide educational facilities for themselves. The Connecticut Separates in the early 1740's were having special educational difficulties. Yale College at the time was distinctly unfriendly to the revivalists, and in order to provide education for their ministers, the Separates opened an academy at New London in 1742 called "The Shepherds' Tent." It may only be coincidence—there seems to be no way of knowing for sure—that Samuel Finley was in Connecticut leading revivals at the same time the Shepherds' Tent was opened, a year after Tennent's call for schools and before the differences between the Separates and the more moderate Awakeners had become fully apparent. The Shepherds' Tent was closed down in the same year and Finley was transported out of the province, both by action of the Connecticut authorities. Finley then settled as minister at Nottingham, on the Pennsylvania-Maryland border, in 1744, where he opened his own academy.[37]

Alarmed at the schism and disturbances produced by the revivals, Tennent and Edwards attempted to keep things in check without undoing the benefits of what they saw as a work of God. In 1748 Gilbert Tennent, perhaps acknowledging his own responsibility for the division among the Presbyterians, published his sermon *Irenicum Ecclesiasticum*, calling for peace and union in the church.[38] The Log College men never softened their insistence upon the necessity of heartfelt religion, but they were a different breed of revivalist from

[37] See, for example, Goen, *Revivalism and Separatism*, pp. 62–63, 58–62; Gaustad, *The Great Awakening*, p. 67. Compare Joseph Tracy, *The Great Awakening* (Boston: Tappan & Dennet, 1842), pp. 70–72, 242, 287 ff.

[38] Gilbert Tennet, *Irenicum Ecclesiasticum, or a Humble Impartial Essay upon the Peace of Jerusalem* . . . , reprinted in Heimert, *The Great Awakening*, pp. 365–375.

many of the radical lay exhorters and schismatic ministers who appeared everywhere as the revivals spread.[39] This is an important distinction to see, if the educational implications of the New Side outlook are to be understood.

For Edwards, the Tennents, and their followers, education—and not only ministerial education—was deemed highly important. In the first place ministers were to preach for conversion, and it was felt that nothing humanly possible enhanced a preacher's effectiveness more than the rhetorical and exegetical skills acquired by a thorough classical education. God acted as he willed, but he usually willed to act through his ordained means—the chief of these being the word preached.

Since conversion was the goal, revivalist oratory was, of course, always subordinate to the preaching task and was adapted to the capacity of the listeners. Although the revivalists' sermons contained their share of classical allusions—Davies referred to Horace, Plato, Tacitus, and Cicero, among others, but also to Addison, Pope, Whitefield, and Thomas Prince—the revivalists were always prepared to abandon classical and genteel literary canons of taste when the occasion demanded. In his famous recruiting sermon preached in Hanover County, Virginia, in 1758, Davies exclaimed: "Oh for all-pervading force of Demosthenes' oratory—but I recall my wish, that I may correct it—oh for the influence of the Lord of armies, the God of battles, the Author of true courage!" The sense of priorities expressed here by Davies was only an extension of the standard that ruled his revival preaching.[40]

The revivalists, moreover, were devoted to the ideal of public

---

[39] The Great Awakening, as Trinterud and Mead point out in contrast to earlier interpretations, such as that of C. H. Maxson, had its origins in the so-called right-wing churches of Protestantism, not in the pietist and left-wing churches. The leadership of Edwards and Tennent attempted to keep the revivals within the framework of the right-wing churches, with their ordered ministry, Calvinist theology, and church polity. The limited success of their efforts becomes evident with the beginning of a new phase of the Awakening in the Methodist revivals in central Virginia, in 1775 and 1776, with their Moravian-like, if not Moravian-inspired, concept of free grace. On the frontier, church order and learning were hard to come by, much harder than free grace. See Trinterud, *Forming of an American Tradition*, p. 170; Sidney Mead, "From Coercion to Persuasion: Another Look at the Rise of Religious Liberty and the Emergence of Denominationalism," *Church History*, XXV (December 1956), 331; compare Maxson, *The Great Awakening in the Middle Colonies*, pp. 1–10.

[40] For an excellent discussion of the revivalists' rhetoric see Alan Heimert, *Religion and the American Mind* (Cambridge, Mass.: Harvard University Press, 1966), pp. 114–116, 221–224, 233–234. Also Perry Miller, "The Rhetoric of Sensation," *Errand into the Wilderness* (New York: Harper Torchbooks, 1964), pp. 167–183.

service. This commitment was voiced in its extreme by Davies in the call for militia volunteers mentioned above. "Blessed is the brave soldier," Davies cried, "blessed is the defender of his country, and the destroyer of its enemies." He expressed the same concern more moderately in his hopes for the infant College of New Jersey under President Burr, from which, he said, "both Church and State expect to be supplied with persons properly qualified for public stations." [41] To the graduating class of 1760 Davies said:

Whatever, I say, be your Place, permit me my dear Youth to inculcate upon you this important Instruction, IMBIBE AND CHERISH A PUBLICK SPIRIT. Serve your Generation. Live not for yourselves, but the Publick. Be the Servants of the Church; the Servants of your Country; the Servants of all. Extend the Arms of your Benevolence to embrace your Friends, your Neighbours, your Country, your Nation, the whole Race of Mankind, even your Enemies.[42]

It was assumed that a converted heart would express itself in works for the public good, and would look for signs of the coming millennium in the improvement of society. Alan Heimert has shown that the revivalists leaned upon conversion through the spoken word as the instrument for realizing their vision of a new social order in which the arts and sciences and useful technology would flourish.[43]

The theology and psychology of conversion developed by the key leadership of the Presbyterian and Congregational revivalists was deliberately related by them to other fields of learning. As Edwards put it, there are many useful and important subjects demanding study and respect, including those that deal with the nature of reality in general, with the natural world, with man as a social and political being, and with the problems of knowing itself. "But one science, or kind of knowledge and doctrine," added Edwards, "is above all the rest; as it treats concerning God and the great business of religion."[44] This primacy of theology in the regular curriculum was typical of the revivalists, as Whitefield made clear to Benjamin Franklin when

---

[41] William Henry Foote, Sketches of Virginia (Philadelphia: J. B. Lippincott & Co., 1850), I, 299.

[42] Samuel Davies, Religion and Public Spirit; a valedictory address to the senior class, delivered in Nassau Hall, September 21, 1760 (New York: James Parker and Company, 1761).

[43] Heimert, Religion and the American Mind, pp. 70–71, passim.

[44] Jonathan Edwards, "The Importance and Advantage of a Thorough Knowledge of Divine Truth," The Works of Jonathan Edwards (New York: Leavitt, Trow & Co., 1849), IV, 3.

he commended Franklin's academy proposals, but complained, "I think there wants *aliquid Christi* in it, to make it as useful as I would desire it might be." [45]

The usefulness of which Whitefield spoke was conceived to be twofold. Divinity—evangelical divinity—would not supplant the regular disciplines, such as natural philosophy and political philosophy, but it would determine goals and ensure that such subjects be used in the service of society. Evangelical divinity would also provide a touchstone for appraising and reshaping in accordance with the priorities of vital religion those subjects that bore directly upon ethics and theology. The New Side attitude toward worldly learning was, in short, critical but not contemptuous.

From a present-day perspective, the subordination of the curriculum to religion and theology would seem to be coercively narrow and stultifying. However, the revivalist missionary impulse and the very nature of the mainline revivalist theology contained a built-in dynamic that in a real way worked to stimulate and to broaden respect for the intellect and learning. For one thing the theology of conversion developed by the revivalists placed a high value upon the role of the understanding, and required considerable intellectual effort to grasp for oneself and to convey to others. Edwards was, of course, the leader in the formulation of this theology.

Although doctrine could not be truly understood unless the heart were changed, still, Edwards insisted, "Such is the nature of man, that no object can come at the heart but through the door of understanding: and there can be no spiritual knowledge of that of which there is not first a rational knowledge." [46] This essentially Augustinian notion that holy affections and the understanding were not opposed was expressed in almost pure Edwardsean terms by Robert Smith, New Side minister and founder of the academy at Pequea. The "principles of grace in the soul," Smith said, heighten rather than diminish the importance of rational doctrine, and enable the mind to grasp it fully and to enjoy "faith in the understanding." [47]

[45] Quoted in Thomas Montgomery, *A History of the University of Pennsylvania, 1740–1770* (Philadelphia: G.W. Jacobs & Co., 1900), p. 29.
[46] Edwards, "The Importance . . . of Divine Truth," *Works*, IV, 3. This was not a random utterance of Edwards. Elsewhere he wrote: "Holy affections are not heat without light; but evermore arise from some information of the understanding, some spiritual instruction that the mind receives, some light or actual knowledge." Jonathan Edwards, *Religious Affections*, edited by John Smith (New Haven: Yale University Press, 1957), p. 266.
[47] Robert Smith, "The Principles of Sin and Holiness," *Sermons and Essays by the*

It is easy to understand how such a manifest paradox—spiritual knowledge comes through the understanding, but can only be understood by the spirit—would infuriate the Old Side, who in their way were really demanding a religiously and intellectually simpler world, and, it must be added, a less threatening world socially. One can also see that such a theology would supply a most powerful incentive to rigorous intellectual activity for those who took it seriously. "Every sermon I think worthy of the name," wrote Samuel Davies, "cost me four days hard study." [48]

The New Side, furthermore, viewed theology democratically; that is, theology and the learning attendant upon it were not to be a clerical monopoly. Theology, as Edwards put it, was "the *trade* of a Christian," and it was the duty of every Christian to know his business. Translating the New Testament word for "disciples" as "scholars or learners," Edwards admonished everyone in his congregation to "Consider yourselves as scholars or disciples." [49] Although ministers, with their superior education, might be of great help, they were to have no monopoly on learning. Probably none exerted themselves as vigorously as did Davies in Virginia to assist his congregation in carrying out this commission. Davies did not establish an academy, probably because his many other responsibilities prevented it, but he encouraged several who did, and he constantly tried to supply the people in his churches with books and reading material. He wrote often to his friends in London and Scotland requesting donations of books for the poor whites and slaves in his congregations, and he tried to see that the little reading material that was available was passed around from church to church.

Davies felt that the farmers and common folk in his churches were fully able to enjoy the delights of literature, and were entitled to them. He was not unrealistic, however, and he recognized that the reading material of his church people must be tailored to their interests and level of education. Davies was himself a prolific writer of religious verse, which he freely acknowledged was not great poetry, but was confident would be appreciated by those for whom it was intended. In the preface to a published collection of his poems, Davies voiced his concern for persons of simple learning, saying that he felt

---

Tennents and their Contemporaries, compiled by Samuel Davies Alexander (Philadelphia: Presbyterian Board of Publication, 1855), p. 318. In its conception and terminology this sermon by Smith is Edwardsean through and through.
[48] Foote, *Sketches of Virginia*, I, 303.
[49] Edwards, "The Importance . . . of Divine Truth," *Works*, IV, 9–11.

his own particular gifts equipped him better to write for them than for those of polished and discriminating tastes. The pleasure of the latter he thought was more refined, and he was not putting himself forward as "a Homer or Virgil, a Milton or Pope" to please them. "I am convinced by a Consciousness of my Incapacity," he wrote,

that this does not belong to my Province. . . . And to consult the Advantages of such only, is as unreasonable as if the English Legislature should tolerate none but silken Manufacturers. The Generality of Mankind have neither Opportunity not perhaps Capacity for these Refinements; and yet are capable of a glorious Immortality, and the purer Joys of Paradise.—For the Sake of such I write; and to some of them my Essays will not be unacceptable. They may not accurately discern the fairest Charms of Poetry, yet they generally are pleased with the Consonance of final Syllables, proportioned Numbers, etc. So that they are more ready to receive and retain those Things which are conveyed into their Minds in their Form than in heavy and tiresome Prose.

The New Side revivalists' blend of religious and educational egalitarianism was perhaps never better expressed.[50]

One commentator some years later remarked that "Davies' churches were schools." He wrote that "households generally were furnished with a few standard works of good old times; and were expected to study them carefully." He added that almost all the people he had visited who had been members of Davies' churches had "books or remnants of books, such as Watson's Body of Divinity, Boston's Fourfold State, Luther on the Galatians, Flavels' Works, Baxter's Call to the Unconverted, and Saint's Everlasting Rest, Alleine's Alarm, and others of similar character. And these were studied with a care and attention which greatly promoted the improvement of the public." [51] The majority of these books were certainly religious, that was the first order of the day, but the assumption that a change of heart demanded improvement in the head was basic. The revivalist conviction that all persons were potential subjects for salvation, "notwithstanding the great Diversity of their Circumstances as to Situation, Education, outward Instruction, etc.," [52] implied, too, that in principle all shared in the benefits and responsibilities of the saved.

---

[50] Samuel Davies, *Miscellaneous Poems Chiefly on Divine Subjects; In Two Books; Published for the Religious Entertainment of Christians in General* (Williamsburg: Printed and sold by William Hunter, 1752), pp. vi–vii.
[51] Foote, *Sketches of Virginia*, I, 378–379; Gewehr, *The Great Awakening*, p. 225.
[52] Davies, "State of Religion," in Heimert, *The Great Awakening*, p. 381.

The extravagances of the revivalists, even those of Gilbert Tennent in the beginning, which he himself lived to regret, made it possible for both their opponents and their extreme followers to ignore the fine theological distinctions and safeguards of such men as Edwards and Davies as being too precious to bother about. It is clear, however, that as far as education was concerned the real difference between the Old Side and the New Side was not over the necessity and importance of education, but, rather, its goals and priorities.

The actual formal educational undertakings of the New Side went through two overlapping phases. The first phase was the immediate implementation of Gilbert Tennent's call for the multiplication of academies to produce a climate of learning congenial to revivalist religion. Almost every major discussion of the Great Awakening in the colonial Presbyterian church contains what might be best described as a common "core account" of the academies in the Log College tradition.[53] Sometimes, to be sure, these accounts manifest some excesses of Presbyterian hagiography, but most of the attention given to the New Side schools is well deserved.

Two of the most famous of the schools maintained by students of William Tennent were the Fagg's Manor Academy of Samuel Blair and the Nottingham Academy of Samuel Finley. It was under Blair that Samuel Davies received almost all of his formal education. Before he himself became President of the College of New Jersey, Davies had been the one person most responsible for planting the Presbyterian church in eastern Virginia. Among Davies' close associates in the formation of the Presbytery of Hanover in 1755 were James Waddell, a student of Finley's academy, and John Todd, a graduate of the College of New Jersey. Waddell assisted Todd with the latter's academy in Louisa County, and later established an academy of his own in the same county.[54] Todd's work laid the foundation for Hampden-Sydney College, established by the Presbytery of Hanover during the Revolution.

Another student from Blair's academy at Fagg's Manor was Robert Smith, who became minister at Pequea, Pennsylvania, in 1751,

---

[53] See, for example, Guy Klett, *Presbyterians in Colonial Pennsylvania* (Philadelphia: University of Pennsylvania Press, 1937), pp. 198–223; Dunaway, *Scotch-Irish in Pennsylvania*, pp. 218–232; William Warren Sweet, *The Story of Religion in America* (New York: Harper and Brothers, 1950); Henry Jones Ford, *The Scotch-Irish in America* (Princeton, N.J.: Princeton University Press, 1915), pp. 413–457.
[54] Foote, *Sketches of Virginia*, I, 378–379; Gewehr, *The Great Awakening*, p. 225.

where he also set up an academy. Robert Smith was the father of Samuel Stanhope Smith, the first President of Hampden-Sydney and later President of the College of New Jersey, and of John Blair Smith, who followed his brother as head of Hampden-Sydney and from there went on to become President of Union College in New York. Other of Smith's pupils who became noted educators after their graduation from the College of New Jersey were Frederick Beasley, President of the University of Pennsylvania, and David Caldwell, who maintained an academy in Guilford County, North Carolina, for an incredible period of over fifty years, from 1767 to 1820. Caldwell is said to have had an average of fifty to sixty pupils, representing nearly every Southern state, and to have prepared more men who entered the learned professions than any other Southern educator.[55]

Still another of Robert Smith's students was John McMillan, missionary and educator in western Pennsylvania. Around 1780 McMillan set up an academy for students at Chartiers, west of the Alleghenies, which became the nucleus of Jefferson College (later Washington and Jefferson College). According to McMillan himself, he began to gather students at the inspiration and suggestion of his old teacher, Robert Smith. "When I determined to come to this country," wrote McMillan, "Dr. Smith enjoined it upon me to look out for some pious young men, and educate them for the ministry; for, said he, though some men of piety and talents may go to a new country at first, yet if they are not careful to raise up others, the country will not be well supplied." [56] The concrete needs of the New Side ministers and the drive of their missionary theology and enthusiasm led them to perpetuate the Ulster academy tradition with new vigor.

[55] E. W. Caruthers, *A Sketch of the Life and Character of the Reverend David Caldwell, D.D.* (Greensborough, N.C.: Swaim and Sherwood, 1842), pp. 30–31.
[56] Quoted in Dwight R. Guthrie, *John McMillan, The Apostle of Presbyterianism in the West* (Pittsburgh: The University of Pittsburgh Press, 1952), p. 81. The New Side line of descent from William Tennent through Blair, Finley, and Robert Smith, down to John McMillan can be traced theologically as well as educationally. Smith's own Edwardsean theology has been noted, and it was under Smith's tutelage that McMillan was converted. McMillan's own most famous pupil was James McGready, who in 1800 led the great camp meeting revivals in Logan County, Kentucky, one of the first manifestations of the so-called Second Great Awakening. A recent study of McGready has shown how insistent this nineteenth-century revivalist was upon a thorough grounding in theology and doctrine, and how closely he adhered to an Edwardsean theological outlook. See Guthrie, *John McMillan*, pp. 66, 86–88; John Opie, Jr., "James McGready: Theologian of Frontier Revivalism," *Church History*, XXXIV (December 1965), 445–456.

By 1743 it was clear to the Old Side that they, too, would have to have schools if they were to hold their own in the struggle for control of the churches. That year the Synod of Philadelphia accordingly renewed an earlier plan to establish a synodical school, and they appealed to the General Assembly of Scotland for ministers and for assistance in erecting "a seminary or school for educating young men for these ends among ourselves." [57] Francis Alison, the most outstanding of the Old Side ministers, had conducted an academy at his home in New London, Chester County, Pennsylvania, since 1742; it was this school that the synod in 1744 elected to take under its official care.

An arrangement was made with Yale for the acceptance of New London pupils, books were collected for a library, and funds were obtained in London and Scotland. For nine years the New London Academy continued under Alison's leadership; then the original plans of the synod for the institution began to falter. The Old Side was unable to meet the expense of Alison's salary, and he departed from New London in 1752 to become Rector of the Academy of Philadelphia, and, a few years later, Vice-Provost and Professor of Logic and Moral Philosophy at the College of Philadelphia. The synod maintained its connection with the New London Academy, but the College of Philadelphia became the main interest of the Old Side leadership.[58]

Although Alison's school was the most important of the Old Side institutions, several other academies were also established by Old Side ministers. Alison's successor at the New London Academy and one of its alumni, the Reverend Alexander McDowell, maintained the academy in his manse for fifteen years, and then with the help of Alison and his Philadelphia colleagues moved the academy to Newark, Delaware, where it was chartered in 1769 with hopes of eventually converting it into a college.[59] John Craig, a staunch Old Side minister, conducted the first school in Augusta County, Virginia, even before John Todd started his academy there.[60] Sampson Smith, another Old Side minister, had an academy for several years after 1753 at Chestnut Level, Pennsylvania.[61] James Latta, a member of the strenuously Old

[57] Funk, "Influence of the Presbyterian Church," p. 175.
[58] See George H. Ryden, "The Relation of the Newark Academy of Delaware to the Presbyterian Church and to Higher Education in the American Colonies," Delaware Notes, 9th ser. (1935), pp. 7–42. Also see Trinterud, Forming of an American Tradition, p. 158.
[59] Ryden, "The Relation of the Newark Academy . . . ," p. 24.
[60] Gewehr, The Great Awakening, p. 221.
[61] Dunaway, Scotch-Irish in Pennsylvania, p. 223.

Side Second Presbytery of Philadelphia, also had an academy at Chestnut Level after 1771.[62]

The New Side, meanwhile, had moved into the second phase of its educational undertakings, which led directly to the establishment of the College of New Jersey. This phase was characterized by cooperation between New Side ministers and sympathetic community leaders to lay the foundation for a bona fide, legally chartered college. The immediate occasion for the movement for a college was the retirement of William Tennent in 1742 and the closing of the Log College. The initiative was taken by the leading Presbyterian ministers and laymen of New England background in the Synod of New York. Dickinson reported that he, Aaron Burr, Ebenezer Pemberton, John Pierson, and three laymen—William Smith, Peter Van Brough Livingston, and William Peartree Smith—"first concocted the plan and foundation of the college." [63]

The College of New Jersey did not simply grow out of the Log College, although many of the Log College alumni were to be key figures in the early years of the new institution. It is true that before the College of New Jersey was moved to its permanent location in Princeton in 1756 it existed for several years on the pattern of the Log College—as an academy headed first by Jonathan Dickinson in Elizabethtown and then by Aaron Burr in Newark, New Jersey.[64] More was involved, however, than the mere continuation and enlargement of the Log College, as can be seen most sharply perhaps in the composition of the Board of Trustees under the second and permanent college charter of 1748. Of the twenty-three members, twelve were clergymen, and, of these, all but three—Gilbert Tennent, William Tennent, Jr., and Samuel Blair—were New England men.[65]

What this something more might have been can best be suggested

---

62 The academy of Sampson Smith had undoubtedly paved the way for Latta's at Chestnut Level, but the change in leadership and the apparent lapse in time between them would make it seem more accurate to count them as two separate academies. Sprague, *Annals of the American Pulpit*, III, 199.

63 T. J. Wertenbaker, *Princeton, 1746–1896* (Princeton: Princeton University Press, 1946), p. 15.

64 For discussions of the relationship of the Log College to the College of New Jersey, see George H. Ingram, "The Story of the Log College," *Journal of the Presbyterian Historical Society*, XII (1924–27), 487–511, and E. R. Craven, "The Log College of Nashaminy and Princeton University," *Journal of the Presbyterian Historical Society*, I (1901–02), 308–314. After the college was relocated at Princeton, its name continued to be the College of New Jersey. It was sometimes, however, referred to as Princeton, and sometimes as Nassau Hall, after the name of the main college building.

65 Wertenbaker, *Princeton*, p. 26.

by a glance at the several purposes such a legally-chartered college could have been intended to serve. First of all, such a college would provide a solid institutional center for the training of committed evangelical ministers in the middle colonies. The continued increase in immigrants and the expansion of New Side churches made it imperative that future ministerial education be guaranteed. In the second place, the stability and permanence of the college would be secured if the institution had wide support from the larger community. The cooperation and support of a wide spectrum of interests would surely be forthcoming for a liberal arts college that served the general welfare and, by charter, ruled out religious tests for attendance. The ideals of public service and interdenominational religion were, furthermore, both central to the New Side evangelical outlook.

It may also be conjectured that the New England men felt a special responsibility for preventing some of the excesses of revivalism which had brought the New Side forces into disrepute. Men such as Dickinson disapproved of unbounded emotionalism fully as much as did Edwards and were concerned to strike a balance between evangelical piety and rational doctrine. Just prior to Whitefield's evangelizing tour of the colonies, the Dickinson group was being called upon to decide for or against the revivalists. After Whitefield's visit they threw in their support with the New Side, but this may have impelled them even more strongly to provide some form of ordered ministerial education, since they would thenceforth be held specially accountable if Old Side predictions of a collapse of ministerial standards proved true.[66]

In founding the College of New Jersey the church leaders were not questioning the quality of instruction or discipline in the academies. They were, rather, attempting to create one institution which would serve as a pacesetter for the church's educational standards, and to which they could devote their best resources in leadership and funds. The academies accordingly furnished models for the college in its first years, and later were indispensable in providing preparatory instruction for college-bound youth. It is important, therefore, to

[66] See Trinterud, *Forming of an American Tradition*, p. 85, on the pivotal importance of the New England men at the time of Whitefield's first visit. For an excellent analysis of the determination of men such as Edwards, Dickinson, Davies, and Gilbert Tennent to maintain an ardent revivalism without abandoning rationality and order, see John Opie, Jr., "Conversion and Revivalism" (unpublished dissertation, University of Chicago, 1962), especially pp. 57 ff., 68–69.

obtain some idea of the way of life and course of study followed in the academies and the early college.

None of the academies was limited solely to the education of ministers. The compelling motive for the founding of academies during the height of the Great Awakening was, to be sure, to provide ministerial training. Once such a school was set in operation, however, students heading for other professions besides the ministry entered as a matter of course. Ministerial education was broadly conceived as resting upon the classics and liberal arts, the same curriculum considered basic to all learned professions.

One historian has estimated that probably only half of the students taught by Robert Smith were prospective ministerial candidates, an estimate that would seem to hold for most of the academies during the second half of the century, when their primary task was preparing boys for college.[67] In the earlier period, also, few of the academies appear to have been limited only to ministerial candidates. Even the Log College itself, established in the heat of the battle over control of the church's ministry, had among its pupils individuals desiring to enter other professional fields. The earliest written account of the Log College makes the point that "Several persons who became eminent in their secular profession read their education in Arts & languages at this Academy." [68] The name of only one of the original Log College students who entered a field other than the ministry is known for certain, but, if the preceding statement is accurate, there were others.[69] The groups of alumni from the academies headed by Alison, Blair, and Finley were certainly quite remarkable, and included many who were later outstanding public figures.[70]

[67] See Jacob Newton Beam, "Dr. Robert Smith's Academy at Pequea, Pennsylvania," *Journal of the Presbyterian Historical Society*, VIII (December 1915), 150.

[68] Nathaniel Irwin, "Memoirs of the Presbyterian Church of Neshaminy," in Pears and Klett, *A Documentary History of the Log College*, pp. 194–197.

[69] See the list of known Log College students in Pears and Klett, *A Documentary History of the Log College*, p. 174. Trinterud has revised this list slightly, in *Forming of an American Tradition*, p. 332. Dr. John Redman, a leading Philadelphia physician, was the one non-ministerial student known to have attended the Log College. Dr. Geradus Clarkson, another Philadelphia medical figure of note, is identified as a Log College graduate in "Notice of Dr. Geradus Clarkson," *Transactions of the College of Physicians of Philadelphia*, 3rd ser., IX (1887), lxxv–lxxvi. However, George Corner argues convincingly that Clarkson attended Finley's academy. George W. Corner, ed. *Autobiography*, by Benjamin Rush (Princeton: Princeton University Press, 1948), pp. 189–190.

[70] A glance at the names of some of the important alumni of these academies will indicate how little they were restricted solely to the preparation of ministerial candidates:
Nottingham (Samuel Finley): James Waddell—minister; Benjamin Rush, Thomas

Benjamin Rush in his *Autobiography* described the way of life and course of study at the Nottingham Academy of his uncle, Samuel Finley.[71] Rush was placed in the Academy when about seven years old, and remained there until he proceeded to the College of New Jersey in 1757 at age thirteen. The picture of the Nottingham Academy Rush presents is probably representative of the other academies as they functioned after the creation of the College of New Jersey.

Like the other Presbyterian academies, Finley's was a boarding school. The youngsters lived in the mansion house, where their meals were served by Mrs. Finley, and attended classes in a separate schoolhouse. Boarding arrangements at the different academies varied according to the number of students under the minister's care. At the Log College some of the students lodged with William Tennent himself, and the remainder lodged with families in the neighborhood.[72] Robert Smith, who had thirty boys and a tutor at Pequea in 1769, built a dormitory to house his students, and this may have been fairly typical of the larger academies later in the century[73] Discipline under Finley was strict, but, as Rush fondly recounted, it was enforced less with the switch than with the strength of Finley's personality and the edifying moral tales the minister told at every suitable occasion.

Finley wrote in a letter that students at his academy read Latin and Greek classics, studied logic, arithmetic, geography, some geometry, and "Part of Ontology, and Natural Philosophy, in a more cursory manner, as far as Opticks in Martin's order." [74] James Waddell, Finley's pupil, advertised a similar course of study for the

Ruston, John Morgan, William Shippen, John Archer, James Tilton, Geradus Clarkson—physicians; John Bayard—businessman; Ebenezer Hazard—government official and historian; Jacob Rush—judge; Richard Stockton—Signer of the Declaration of Independence and U.S. Senator; John Henry, Alexander McWhorter, Alexander Martin—Governors of Maryland, New Jersey, and North Carolina, respectively.

Pequea (Robert Smith): Samuel Stanhope Smith, John Blair Smith, John McMillan, David Caldwell, James Dunlop, Frederick Beasley—ministers, all of whom became outstanding educators; George Duffield—minister; Robert Smith, John Miller, John Watson—physicians; Robert Jenkins—Congressman; John Smith—lawyer.

New London (Francis Alison): John Ewing—minister and President of the University of Pennsylvania; James Latta, Matthew Wilson—ministers; David Ramsay—physician and historian; Hugh Williamson—physician and educator; James Smith—lawyer; George Read—Signer of the Declaration of Independence and Chief Justice of Delaware; Thomas McKean—Governor of Pennsylvania.

[71] Rush, *Autobiography*, pp. 28–35. The description of Finley's academy, unless otherwise noted, is based upon Rush's account.
[72] Ingram, "The Story of the Log College," p. 491.
[73] Beam, "Robert Smith's Academy," pp. 150, 153.
[74] Quoted in Klett, *Presbyterians in Colonial Pennsylvania*, p. 207.

academy he opened in Virginia.[75] Rush commented that, while Finley taught "several of the Arts and Sciences usually taught in Colleges . . . he was unfortunately tied down to the principles and forms that were common in the Schools of that day." [76] Rush's intimation seems to have been that Finley's teaching of the sciences was, indeed, "in a more cursory manner."

Other parts of the curriculum under Finley were more suited to the age level of his pupils. In addition to Latin and Greek Finley put special emphasis upon the study of English, drilling the students in writing and speaking it correctly. Penmanship and letter-writing likewise received much attention. Finley lost few teaching opportunities. Boys were encouraged at meal times to engage one another and guests in conversation, with Finley guiding the talk. A weekly practice was for the boys to repeat the Sunday sermon in their own words— religious, English, and speech instruction combined. It was mandatory for each boy to share the chores of the farm, an activity which was regarded as "practical argriculture" and moral as well as physical exercise.[77] Religion was, of course, basic. The boys studied the Westminster Catechism, memorized the Scottish Shorter Catechism, and every Sunday evening gathered to hear Finley deliver a simple lecture on the evidences of the Christian religion.

The one regret Rush expressed in his later years was that he had not gained all that he might have from "the literary and moral instruction" provided by Finley. He complained that the distractions at the country school—"hunting, gunning, and the like"—had too often overpowered his "relish for learning."

The base of the curriculum was essentially the same in all of the academies: the classics, with as much of the sciences and belles lettres as the individual minister-teacher could muster. The academies, as might be expected, were strongest in the classical languages. Frederick Beasley said that at Pequea, where he studied, "It was the custom of the school to require the pupils not merely to dip into the Latin and Greek classics . . . but when once they had commenced an author, to read carefully and attentively the entire work." Latin, Beasley also said, was the "habitual" language of the school, and students were often encouraged to hold contests to try each other's skill. He commented that the emphasis on the classics in the early Presbyterian academies and the proficiency demonstrated in them by the ministers

[75] *Virginia Gazette*, November 4, 1763, n.p.
[76] Rush, *Autobiography*, p. 31.
[77] See Benjamin Rush, *Letters*, edited by L. H. Butterfield (Princeton: Princeton University Press, 1951), I, 524.

in charge were owing directly to the influence of the Ulster and Scottish traditions.[78] Smith's academy was designed to prepare boys for the College of New Jersey and to take them back after college for graduate theological study.[79] Many of the earlier academies, however, as well as those founded later in the century at a distance from Princeton attempted, often with marked success, to provide college-level instruction.

Finley's course of study in the higher subjects at Nottingham, though adapted to the younger students, was much like that introduced by Burr as second president of the College of New Jersey. Both Burr and Finley probably took Yale as their primary model for textbooks and subjects taught.

Letters from William Shippen to his father during his four years at the College of New Jersey (1751–54) show that the curriculum under Burr was quite similar to that described at Yale by President Clap.[80] During his freshman year Shippen read Xenophon in Greek, and Cicero's *de Oratore*, and studied Hebrew grammar, Watt's logic, and some geography, astronomy, and rhetoric. The ambitious nature of the program is revealed in the note of desperation that creeps into one of Shippen's letters. "I shall learn Horace in a little while," he wrote to his father, ". . . but my time is filled up in studying Virgil, Greek Testament, and Rhetoric, so that I have no time hardly to look over any French, or Algebra, or any English book for my improvement. However, I shall accomplish it soon." In his sophomore year Shippen continued his classical work and went further into rhetoric and natural philosophy. Burr himself delivered lectures in natural philosophy, emphasizing astronomy especially, and he secured for the college an orrery and an "Electrical Machine." The third year Shippen continued his natural philosophy and began the study of ethics and moral philosophy. The last year was probably taken up largely by a full program of review.[81]

The College of New Jersey continued to develop in its early

---

[78] See Frederick Beasley's "Preface" to Samuel Stanhope Smith, *Sermons* (Philadelphia: J. Maxwell, 1821), I, 3–6.

[79] Beam, "Robert Smith's Academy," p. 149.

[80] The Yale curriculum described by President Clap in his *History of Yale College* may be found in Louis F. Snow, *The College Curriculum in the United States* (New York: Privately printed, 1907), p. 41. The entrance requirements at New Jersey are reprinted in John Maclean, *History of the College of New Jersey* (Philadelphia: J. B. Lippincott, 1877), I, 132–133.

[81] Shippen's letter is quoted in Maclean, *History of the College of New Jersey*, I, 141. See Francis L. Broderick, "Pulpit, Physics, and Politics: The Curriculum of the College of New Jersey, 1746–1794," *William and Mary Quarterly*, 3rd ser., VI (1949), 50–51.

years despite the death in office of one president after another. Aaron Burr served as head of the college for nearly ten years from 1748 until his death from illness in 1757. Jonathan Edwards was chosen as the new president, only to suffer a fatal reaction to small pox inoculation a bare six weeks after moving to Princeton. Edwards' successor, Samuel Davies, was President for only two years, from 1759 to 1761, when he succumbed to a chronic condition of tuberculosis. This sad and unfortunate turnover in leadership undoubtedly impeded the growth of the college. Yet, the willingness of the most respected revivalist ministers to assume the strenuous burdens of the college presidency not only indicated the importance they attached to the new institution, but also strengthened its reputation.

When President Davies died in 1761, Samuel Finley left Nottingham for Princeton to take his place. Finley followed the basic curriculum begun under Burr, but also added the study of chronology, gave greater emphasis to English, with reading from Shakespeare, Milton, Addison, and other moderns, and required all students in their last two years to take part in public disputations in Latin and English. In addition Finley instituted a system of examinations at the end of each year. It was during Finley's administration, too, that an English and Latin grammar school was established in connection with the college. Along with his regular administrative duties Finley also taught Greek, Latin, and Hebrew to the senior class.[82] The determination of the early academy and college leaders to keep their courses of study as up-to-date as possible was evident from the very beginning, as was the weakness of the accusation that New Side ministers were uninterested in learning and less than competent.

III

Several influences shaped the College of New Jersey in its early years. The Log College and Yale were at first probably the most important: the former being emulated by Dickinson and Burr as a means of getting the college off to a start; the latter providing a final model to aim for. Wertenbaker and others have suggested that the

[82] Burr and Finley both had certain of their notes on Latin grammar included in *The New American Latin Grammar*, which, under various editors, was published in several editions. See Charles Evans, *Bibliography of American Reprints*, especially #16982 and #18758. For the curriculum under Finley, see Maclean, *History of the College of New Jersey*, I, 259, 266–272.

English dissenting academies also deeply influenced the College of New Jersey.[83]

The Presbyterian academies of Ulster and the dissenting academies of England were related as cousins in origin and form. In England the exclusion of the dissenting Protestants from Oxford and Cambridge forced them to attempt to set up academies offering the university course regarded as necessary for ministers and professional men. By the early years of the eighteenth century many of the English academies were stable, flourishing institutions of higher learning, conducted by men of impressive scholarship and teaching a wide range of modern and traditional subjects.[84]

Because the Ulster academies always operated in the shade of the Scottish universities, however, no urgent need was felt for them to provide a complete university course of instruction. Consequently, in their development the Ulster academies never became much more than highly advanced grammar schools. Only in America could the Presbyterian academies expand to college level institutions, as had the English dissenting academies.

The leaders of the infant College of New Jersey would have had at least three reasons for looking to the English dissenting academies. In the first place, the English academies by mid-eighteenth century were noted for their modern curricula and progressive teaching methods. With roots in the educational reform ideas of the Puritans Hartlib, Dury, Petty, and Milton, and with their dissenters' distrust of the traditional, many tutors of dissenting academies, even in the seventeenth century, had demonstrated a marked readiness for educational innovation. Certain of the academies in the 1680's and 1690's, for example, such as those at Shrewsbury, Sheriffhales, and Newington Green, actually preceded the Scottish universities in the use of English and experimental lectures, and in the introduction of a variety of scientific and practical subjects.[85] Contact with the Dutch universities, where many dissenting tutors, like their Scots brethren, studied in the seventeenth century, and increasingly close relationships with

---

[83] Wertenbaker, *Princeton*, pp. 81 ff. Cf. Broderick, "Pulpit, Physics, and Politics," pp. 45–46.

[84] The best studies of the English dissenting academies are J. W. Ashley Smith, *The Birth of Modern Education* (London: Independent Press Ltd., 1954); and H. Mc-Lachlan, *English Education Under the Test Acts* (Manchester: Manchester University Press, 1931). Also see the earlier work by Irene Parker, *Dissenting Academies in England* (Cambridge: At the University Press, 1914).

[85] Smith, *Birth of Modern Education*, pp. 51–62.

the Scottish universities furnished important sources of ideas and inspiration.[86] The development in the academies of a broad and modern
course of study was probably as much as anything else a matter of
necessity, stemming from the demand to prepare sons of dissenting
families for the professions, and from the expectation that dissenting
ministers be able to hold down at least one secular occupation.[87]
Although the quality of instruction and scope of the curriculum
varied widely from one academy to another, individual academy leaders in the eighteenth century, such as Philip Doddridge and later
Joseph Priestley, were well-known in America and often praised for
their original educational ideas.

In the second place, the dissenting status of the English academies
in itself would have had an appeal to the Americans. Such contacts
as are known to have existed between the American and English
educators probably originated in their similar religious concerns. The
fight by Samuel Davies to secure the same immunities for dissenters
in Virginia that English dissenters enjoyed under the Toleration Act
of 1689 brought him into touch with English ministers. Davies, Edwards, Burr, and Finley all corresponded with Philip Doddridge of
the famous Northampton Academy, and with other English academy
leaders, such as Benjamin Avery, who was associated with Kendal
Academy. The letters that passed between them, however, were not
limited to religious concerns. Aaron Burr, as Wertenbaker points out,
asked Doddridge for advice on such matters as curriculum, textbooks,
and school policies.[88]

Finally, resentment at the attempts of the Old Side to require
Scottish or New England university degrees of all Presbyterian ministers may at first have made the English academies especially attractive
as far as the New Side was concerned.

Just how important the example of the English academies was
for the College of New Jersey, however, is difficult to determine.[89]

[86] *Ibid.*, pp. 64–70.
[87] *Ibid.*, p. 4.
[88] Wertenbaker, *Princeton*, pp. 81 ff.; Broderick, "Pulpit, Physics, and Politics," pp.
45–46. Some of the correspondence between Davies, Benjamin Avery, and Philip
Doddridge can be found in Foote, *Sketches of Virginia*, I, 174–178, 206–214.
[89] An important link was established in the seventeenth century between Harvard
and the Newington Green Academy near London. In 1686, Charles Morton,
founder and teacher at Newington Green for twenty-three years, migrated to New
England. Under Harvard's new charter Morton was appointed Vice-President of
the College in 1692. A graduate of Oxford, Morton had been one of the most
original and innovative of England's early academy leaders. He excelled in mathematics, but according to his pupil, Daniel Defoe, he offered a broad and balanced

Although the variety of English academies in the eighteenth century makes it almost impossible to speak of their influence in general, it makes much sense to ask about the influence of Doddridge's Northampton Academy in particular. After tutoring at his own alma mater, Kibworth Academy, Doddridge opened the Northampton Academy in 1729, and remained its head until his death in 1751. Doddridge developed a broad course of study at Northampton, with much attention to teaching methods and with a special eye to the practicality of the subjects taught, for both the ministerial and non-ministerial students. Doddridge was particularly fond of his lectures in Christian Evidences, but he also tried to keep abreast of the latest scientific studies, and put natural science taught with experimental lectures in a prominent place in his curriculum. Doddridge led most of the other academies in lecturing in English rather than Latin, and he stressed the method of learning proper English expression through essay-writing. Homiletics and practical theology were regarded as especially important aspects of ministerial training. Doddridge felt the classics were important but should not be overemphasized, and the academy offered French as an optional language. Natural, civil, and ecclesiastical history were also included as important subjects in the curriculum. From their correspondence with Doddridge at Northampton, the leaders of the College of New Jersey could have become acquainted with a modern and utilitarian course of study taught with a religious orientation that was pervasive but not oppressive.[90]

It appears beyond doubt that, in the earliest years at least, the examples of certain English academies did influence the conception and curriculum of the College of New Jersey. What also seems evident, however, is that among the different transatlantic influences at the College of New Jersey the Scottish universities soon became the most important. If the Americans at one point looked to the dissenting academies for guidance, the focus of their attention began to shift to Scotland long before John Witherspoon arrived on the scene. The

course. At Newington Green, Morton introduced the study of modern languages, and most important, used English as the medium of instruction. His *Compendium Physicae* was adopted at Harvard in 1687, and remained the textbook in natural science at Harvard for forty years. See Smith, *Birth of Modern Education*, pp. 56–61; Samuel Eliot Morison, *Harvard in the Seventeenth Century* (Cambridge, Mass.: Harvard University Press, 1936), I, 236–249; II, 475–479.

[90] Smith, *Birth of Modern Education*, pp. 129–144; McLachlan, *English Education*, pp. 143–151. Kendal Academy, with which Americans may also have had sustained contacts, was said to have excelled in mathematics and natural philosophy. Smith, *Birth of Modern Education*, pp. 188–191.

waning influence of the English academies can be documented in part, and some explanations suggested for it.

First, it should be noted that from their beginnings, after 1662, many of the English academies themselves had maintained the most intimate connections with the Presbyterian-related universities of Edinburgh and Glasgow. When the universities of Scotland again reverted from Episcopal to Presbyterian control in the Revolution Settlement of 1690 many dissenting students went from England to Scotland for their studies and degrees. Often these English students in Scotland were supported by the Presbyterian Fund, or by other scholarship provisions such as those made available at Glasgow for future dissenting ministers under the trust of Dr. Daniel Williams, the English Presbyterian divine. Olive Griffiths observes in her study of English Presbyterianism that frequently English students who were not recipients of scholarship aid also presented Scottish degrees for their ordination in England. The number of dissenting English students at Edinburgh was so large around the turn of the century that Principal Carstares suggested, though without effect, that they maintain their own English college in the university. Glasgow probably had even more students from England than did Edinburgh.[91]

The influence of Scotland on the English academies not only continued into the eighteenth century, but actually increased with the rising prestige of the Northern universities.[92] The practical and progressive spirit of the Scottish universities was much admired by the dissenters, and in the latter half of the century Scottish thought, methods of instruction, and textbooks made their way into the English academies. In McLachlan's judgment the academies' teaching "was improved and their curricula widened by the contact of their pupils and tutors with the universities of Scotland." [93]

[91] Olive Griffiths, *Religion and Learning* (Cambridge: At the University Press, 1935), pp. 68–70; McLachlan, *English Education*, pp. 29–33. Griffiths lists the names of sixty-five English students who received help from the Presbyterian Fund between 1690 and 1754, fifty-four went to Scotland, nine to Utrecht, one to Halle, and one to Leyden. She also lists the names of thirty-eight English students holding Dr. Williams' scholarships at Glasgow from 1734 through 1778 (pp. 178–182). A similar, but much smaller, trust fund was established by Dr. Ward to enable two Protestant dissenters, preferably Baptists, to study divinity for four years at a Scottish university. McLachlan, *English Education*, p. 30.

[92] Smith, *Birth of Modern Education*, p. 67.

[93] McLachlan, *English Education*, p. 33; also see pp. 22–23. The difficulty in establishing clear antecedents and precedents when the mutual influence between the English and Scottish universities was so strong is illustrated in the case of Samuel Benion, tutor at Shrewsbury in 1706. Smith cites the example of Benion as one who anticipated the Scottish universities in the new way of lecturing extemporaneously rather than merely delivering notes on a set text. Smith, *Birth of Modern Education*,

Of special importance to the English dissenters were the degree-granting powers enjoyed by the Scottish universities. At least forty-seven academy heads and tutors, representing twenty-five different English dissenting academies in the eighteenth century, held degrees from Scottish universities. Twenty-seven of these persons had M.A. degrees from Scotland or had received their main education in Scotland. Another nineteen received honorary—and in at least one instance, earned—Doctor of Divinity degrees from Scotland, a testimony both to the dissenters' scholarly achievements and to the degree-granting service performed by the Scottish universities for the dissenters.[94]

There is evidence of strong Scottish influence at precisely the two academies with which the New Jersey leaders had strong ties, Northampton and Kendal. Caleb Rotheram, who founded the Kendal Academy and maintained it from 1733 to 1751, had received his early education at Whitehaven Academy in England. The tutors under Rotheram, however, were a Scots mathematician, John Barclay, who had an earned M.A. from Edinburgh, and Thomas Dixon, who received an honorary M.A. and an M.D. from Edinburgh. Rotheram himself was admitted M.A. at Edinburgh in 1743, and shortly thereafter received an earned Doctor of Divinity with the submission of his thesis. Among Rotheram's students who proceeded from Kendal to Scotland for their degrees, was John Seddon, later the leading founder of the famous Warrington Academy in England. Seddon received his degree from Glasgow, and became a proponent at Warrington of the ethical theories of his Glasgow teacher, Francis Hutcheson.[95]

Philip Doddridge at Northampton also received honorary doctorates from both Marischal and King's Colleges, Aberdeen, in 1736 and 1737. In the latter year Doddridge's first pupil at Kibworth, John Aiken, received his M.A. from King's College and returned from Aberdeen to Northampton as an assistant tutor. Two other tutors

---

pp. 69–70. Benion, however, was a graduate of Glasgow (M.A. 1696, M.D. 1703), and, according to a contemporary, Benion's predecessor at Shrewsbury, Charles Owen, had modeled the academy "as near as he could to the constitution of the College at Glasgow which he much admired." McLachlan, *English Education*, p. 84.

[94] Compiled from McLachlan, *English Education, passim*. These are all minimum figures, since McLachlan does not give the sources of all the degrees held by persons mentioned in his study. Neither do these figures include English Presbyterian ministers with Scottish degrees who were not teachers in academies. McLachlan counted a total of seventy-two different academies.

[95] McLachlan, *English Education*, pp. 188–191; Smith, *Birth of Modern Education*, pp. 107, 160, 163.

with Doddridge at Northampton were Thomas Brabant, who had studied for four years at Glasgow (1736–40), and James Robertson, who later became Professor of Oriental Languages at Edinburgh University.[96]

How the close connection between the dissenting academies in England and the Scottish universities could serve as a link to bring Americans into contact with the Scottish universities is evident in the case of Samuel Finley. After he succeeded Davies as President of the College of New Jersey in 1761, Finley became known in England and exchanged letters with several dissenting ministers, including Samuel Chandler. Chandler was sufficiently impressed by Finley to obtain for him a Doctor of Divinity from Glasgow University in 1763. The Scottish universities, simply by virtue of their power to confer degrees, if nothing else, possessed a certain prestige that many leaders of the English academies themselves acknowledged. Finley's acquaintances with Scotsmen continued to increase. In 1764 he wrote to William Hogg in Edinburgh thanking him for introducing him to "the Dear and Revd Mr: Witherspoon," with whom Finley said he was corresponding.[97]

The possibility that the English academies might have further influenced the College of New Jersey seems to have been dispelled as its leaders became increasingly aware of English Presbyterian tendencies toward heterodox theological views. On their trip to Great Britain in 1753–54 to raise funds for the college, Samuel Davies and Gilbert Tennent visited many of the dissenting academies. They grew ever more distressed, however, over the theological irregularities that they thought they detected among the English dissenters. "I find," Davies wrote in his journal while in England,

that though real religion, and the principles of the Reformation are better retained among the Independents, and though there be a considerable number of learned and judicious ministers among them, yet the greatest number of learned and polite men are among the Presbyterians; and sundry of them deserve the character, who Arminianize and Socinianize very much.

And, again, a short time later: "Alas! for the laxness that prevails here among the Presbyterians. *Quantum O Mutati!*" [98]

---

[96] McLachlan, *English Education*, pp. 149, 213.
[97] Sprague, *Annals of the American Pulpit*, III, 96.
[98] Davies' journal of the trip is reprinted in Foote, *Sketches of Virginia*, I, 228–281. See pp. 253, 257, 268.

In Scotland Davies and Tennent found important champions of evangelical religion, as well as great interest in the future of the infant American college. The Earl of Leven and the Marquis of Lothian helped to win support for the college in the General Assembly and from the Society in Scotland for Propagating Christian Knowl-edge. Davies and Tennent also received crucial help from the divinity professors William Leechman in Glasgow, John Lumsden in King's College, Aberdeen, and Patrick Cumming, Robert Hamilton, and James Robertson in Edinburgh.[99] The two Americans returned with a sum estimated at over £3,200, most of which had been collected in Scotland, where, as Davies put it, they had received "more Christian friendship" than anywhere else in Britain. The incentive to look toward Scotland had been given a very substantial boost.

Perhaps the most intimate and binding of the early New Side connections with Scotland were those established through Jonathan Edwards. It has already been pointed out that until the time of his death Edwards was looked to for leadership by all the revivalists. Samuel Davies even attempted once, after Edwards left Northampton, to persuade him to take a church in Hanover County, Virginia. In a letter to the Reverend Joseph Bellamy in England, Davies summarized his reasons for wanting Edwards in Virginia: ". . . we greatly need Mr. Edwards, whose character there [Great Britain], especially in Scotland, would have considerable influence. He might also, as you observe, do much good by keeping an academy; and which is of greater importance than all, might be the happy instrument of turning many to righteousness." [100]

Davies correctly estimated Edwards' influence in Scotland. Scottish churchmen had heard of Edwards' revivals in Northampton through his *Faithful Narrative of the Surprising Work of God*, which was published in London in 1737. The Great Awakening in America may have helped to stimulate the outbreak of revivals in the west of Scotland at Cambuslang in 1741, and the relationship between the revivals on both sides of the Atlantic was made concrete by the ap-pearance at Cambuslang of the omnipresent George Whitefield, fresh from his American tour. At that juncture the flow of letters between revivalist-minded ministers in both countries began in earnest.

The Scottish church historian, G. D. Henderson, has described

---

[99] *Ibid.*, I, 245, 258–261, 263–264. Davies correctly discerned that Professor Leechman was "verging towards Arminianism," but he did not let that stand in the way of the fund-raising.

[100] Davies to Bellamy, July 4, 1751, reprinted in Foote, *Sketches of Virginia*, II, 41–42.

in detail the close personal ties which were formed between Edwards and leading evangelical ministers in Scotland.[101] Dr. John Brown, John Maclaurin, John Erskine, Thomas Gillespie, William McCulloch, John Willison, and other Scottish ministers corresponded with Edwards and edited many of his works for publication in Scotland. A group of Scottish ministers sent a memorial to America regarding the Scottish Praying Societies, and in 1747 Edwards adapted their plan to his own proposal for an interdenominational and international union of prayer among evangelical Christians.[102]

When Edwards was evicted from the church at Northampton, John Erskine, then minister at Kirkintilloch, Scotland, proposed that Edwards should take a church in his country. This scheme did not prove feasible, so Erskine, John Maclaurin (brother of the famous mathematician), and several others sent money and a shipload of goods to be sold in America to help support Edwards and his family till they could be relocated. John Erskine, especially, took Edwards under his wing. Erskine wrote to Edwards until the latter's death, helped to see to it that Edwards was supplied with books during his seven years in the isolation of Stockbridge, and continued to edit a number of Edwards' works for publication in Scotland throughout the eighteenth century. It was probably owing in large part to his veneration of Edwards that John Erskine took a special interest in the College of New Jersey. Erskine was one of those who helped to give Davies and Tennent their warm reception in Scotland, and as late as 1802, when Erskine was eighty years old, he sent thirty volumes to the college to help replace the library lost in the fire that year.[103]

Attachments between the College of New Jersey and Scotland, which might otherwise have remained primarily formal and institutional, were cemented very early by the closest of personal ties between the New Side leadership and sympathetic Scottish churchmen. The way was thus opened for a long-lasting and many-faceted relationship.

[101] G. D. Henderson, "Jonathan Edwards and Scotland," *The Burning Bush, Studies in Scottish Church History* (Edinburgh: The St. Andrew Press, 1957), pp. 151–162. Also useful is Ralph G. Turnbull, "Jonathan Edwards and Great Britain," *The Evangelical Quarterly*, XXX (1958), 68–74.
[102] See Heimert, *The Great Awakening*, p. 563.
[103] Maclean, *History of the College of New Jersey*, II, 50–51.

Chapter III

Old Side Educator:
Francis Alison

In order to justify their demands that ministers have a university degree, the Old Side had naturally attempted to throw doubt upon the quality of instruction at the Log College. Explaining the 1738 action of the Synod of Philadelphia requiring university degrees of all ministers, Francis Alison wrote that "there was some Slackness in particular Presbyteries, in the Examination of Candidates, at their admission into the Ministry, and . . . some of late were admitted who were remarkably deficient in some Parts of useful Learning, particularly Messrs. Alexander Craighead, Charles Tennent, and John Rowland." The last two were Log College men.[1] Nearly thirty years later, long after the two factions had rejoined in the union of 1758, Alison still chose to interpret one of the main issues of the Awakening as a controversy between those who valued learning and those who did not.

In a letter written to Ezra Stiles in 1767 in response to a request for an account of his life Alison said:

at my arrival here [1735] there was not a College, nor even a good grammar School in four Provinces, Maryland, Pennsylvania, Jersey, & New York; but on the other hand all that made any pretensions to learning were branded as letter learned Pharisees; & this desparate cause, of promoting learning in this Province, I undertook, encouraged by our Synod, who allowed me only twenty pounds currency, per ann. & fifteen for an assistant; & obliged us to teach all gratis, that were pleased to accept learning on these terms; & in this the success was beyond our expectations;

---

[1] Thomas C. Pears and Guy Klett, comps., *A Documentary History of William Tennent and the Log College* (Mimeographed manuscript; Philadelphia: Presbyterian Historical Society, 1940), p. 161.

& it roused a spirit in Philada to erect an academy, & then a College; & since that time Learning became reputable, even amongst those that gave the nickname of Letter-learned Pharisees, brought up at the feet of Gamaliel.[2]

This statement makes remarkable claims. In the name of the Old Side Alison was here taking major credit, not only for rekindling a love of learning in the revivalists, but also for inspiring the creation of the College of Philadelphia itself. Alison's claims should not be dismissed as attempts at self-justification, which of course they also were in part, for his letter raises some very interesting questions.

First, what truth was there in the assertion that the Old Side had salvaged the cause of learning in "the four provinces"? Second, has the impressive success of the Log College tradition and the College of New Jersey tended to obscure the contributions of the Old Side educators? Did the Old Side have an educational impact that merits greater attention than has generally been given it?

A consideration of Francis Alison himself may supply some answers to these questions. As the major Old Side spokesman Alison represented attitudes toward learning that were not only a part of the academy tradition, but that also served as the counterpoint against which the New Side position developed and must be understood. When Francis Alison criticized the learning of the revivalists, he spoke with an authority that could not be entirely ignored. Ezra Stiles, President of Yale and for many years Alison's correspondent, drew what was a fairly accurate portrayal of his Scottish friend. "Dr. Alison Rector of the Academy as well as Vice Provost of the College," wrote Stiles, "is the greatest Classical Scholar in America especially in Greek. Not great in Math. & Phil. & Astronomy—but in Ethics, History, and general Reading is a great Literary Character. I have had a long & intimate Acquaintance with him." [3] If Alison was not the greatest classical scholar in America, he was probably the equal of any man in the Presbyterian church; and if the revivalists were effectively to refute the charges of anti-intellectualism leveled against them, they had to demonstrate scholarly capacities and interests at least in the same class with those of Alison.

[2] Alison to Stiles, December 12, 1767, reprinted in *Extracts from the Itineraries . . . of Ezra Stiles, 1755–1794*, edited by Franklin B. Dexter (New Haven: Yale University Press, 1916), pp. 431–432.
[3] Franklin B. Dexter, ed., *The Literary Diary of Ezra Stiles* (3 vols.; New York; Charles Scribners Sons, 1901), II, 338.

This the New Side educators were able to do; nevertheless they must have regarded Alison's learning as a formidable challenge. A very intriguing, though unanswerable, question, for instance, is to what extent Samuel Finley's early interest in English literary studies may have been spurred by the example of Alison, as well as by their obvious usefulness to the revival preacher. As early as 1742, while the Log College was still his only serious educational rival, Francis Alison was providing his students at New London, Maryland, with a full program of rather advanced instruction in English grammar, composition, and literature. A man as astute and audacious as Samuel Finley may well have been quick to take a lead from his opponents. In any case, Alison's critique of New Side learning and the example of his own abilities probably added powerful impetus to the revivalists' desire to establish their educational respectability and competence.

Alison's total life work as an educator, however, was even more significant in its own right. His opportunities for influencing American higher education were many. Not only did he found an outstanding academy of his own and help to launch the College of Philadelphia, where he was Vice Provost and member of the faculty for years, he was also a friend of other important American educators elsewhere. In all of his educational work his own background as a student under some of Scotland's most illustrious early eighteenth-century university professors was decisive. A close look at Alison will help to reveal among other things the larger pattern of Scottish influences into which the College of New Jersey itself—especially after the 1758 union of the Old and New Side parties—was increasingly drawn.

I

Alison was born in Donegal County, Ulster, in 1705. The history of his early education is somewhat cloudy. He received his early formal education in Ireland at the Royal Academy of Raphoe in Donegal County, under the direction of Nicholas Forster, future Bishop of Raphoe. He is known to have graduated from Edinburgh University in 1732, but since both Benjamin Franklin and Ezra Stiles asserted that he was educated at Glasgow, he may have attended more than one Scottish university. Alison was awarded an honorary Doctor of Divinity degree from Glasgow in 1755.[4] During the years of Ali-

[4] Biographical data on Alison is taken mainly from two treatments of his life by Thomas Pears. The *Itineraries* and *Literary Diary* of Ezra Stiles are also invaluable for source materials. See Thomas C. Pears, "Francis Alison, Colonial Educator,"

son's attendance the Scottish universities were already well into the intellectual and teaching revival that was to make them prestigious among eighteenth-century institutions of higher learning.

As a student Alison had come under the influence of two of the most outstanding early leaders in the transformation of Scottish university education, John Stevenson, Professor of Logic and Metaphysics at Edinburgh (1730–1775), and Francis Hutcheson, Professor of Moral Philosophy at Glasgow (1730–1747). Stevenson stressed Locke and Heineccius, rather than the old logic of Ramus, and has been credited with being the first to introduce Locke into the university teaching of Scotland.[5] Stevenson was most popular, however, for his lectures in rhetoric. Using Aristotle's *Poetics* and Longinus's *On the Sublime*, along with his own selections from French and English critics, Stevenson compared ancient and modern authors and introduced his students to the problems of literary taste and criticism. Of Stevenson as a person, Carlyle wrote that he "was the most popular of all the Professors on account of his civility and even kindness to his students"; and of Stevenson's course, that "our minds were more enlarged, and . . . we received greater benefit from that class than from any other." [6] William Robertson, Dugald Stewart, John Erskine, and others echoed Carlyle's testimony to Stevenson's teaching abilities and influence.[7]

Whether Alison first became acquainted with Francis Hutcheson in Ireland or at Glasgow is uncertain. He knew Hutcheson well enough, however, to write to him for advice in 1746 concerning the curriculum and books to be used in his own academy at New London.[8] Hutcheson's leadership in modernizing Scottish university teaching, particularly in making English respectable as the medium of classroom instruction, has been noted. Hutcheson was famed for the ease and eloquence of his lectures, which he delivered without notes while

Delaware Notes, 17th ser. (1944), pp. 9–22, "Francis Alison," *Journal of the Presbyterian Historical Society,* XXVII (1950), 213–225. Also see George H. Ryden, "The Relation of the Newark Academy of Delaware to the Presbyterian Church and to Higher Education in the American Colonies," *Delaware Notes,* 9th ser. (1935), pp. 7–42.

5 John Veitch, "Memoir of Dugald Stewart," in Dugald Stewart, *Biographical Memoir,* edited by William Hamilton (New York: Augustus M. Kelley, 1966; first published 1858), p. xiii.

6 Alexander Carlyle, *Autobiography* (Boston: Ticknor and Fields, 1861), pp. 36–37.

7 See John Veitch, "Memoir of Dugald Stewart," p. xv; also James McCosh, *The Scottish Philosophy* (New York: Robert Carter and Brothers, 1875), pp. 107–108.

8 See Hutcheson's comments on the request for advice he received from Alison in William Robert Scott, *Francis Hutcheson* (Cambridge: At the University Press, 1900), pp. 136–137. Alison's promise to send Ezra Stiles a copy of the letter he received from Hutcheson in answer may be found in Stiles, *Itineraries,* p. 433.

"walking backwards and forwards in the area of his room"; he fostered long-neglected classical and literary studies; he helped to reformulate and broaden the scope of moral philosophy; and he befriended his students both in and out of class. According to nearly all accounts, even from those hostile to his theological views, Hutcheson fired his students with a love for himself and his teaching.[9] It was out of this background of some of the most progressive currents in eighteenth-century higher education that Alison spoke in his critique of the revivalists.

Alison's own educational efforts at New London and at Philadelphia bear the unmistakable marks of his Scottish university education. The classical and literary course of study Alison offered in his New London Academy was probably as good as any available in any colonial college at the time. One of his earliest students, Matthew Wilson, described Alison's course of study for the readers of the *Pennsylvania Journal* in 1780. English grammar and composition were taught, according to Wilson, in conjunction with the Latin and Greek lessons, and fairly intensive instruction was given in "every part of the Belles Lettres." That Alison was also an imaginative teacher is seen in his method of helping students to develop a correct and engaging style of expression. "We received the greatest advantage," wrote Wilson, "from his critical examination every morning of our themes, English and Latin, epistles, English and Latin, descriptions in verse, and especially our abstracts or abridgements of a paper from the *Spectator* or *Guardian* (the best standards of our language), substantially contracted into one of our exercises."

After completing their basic language study, boys in the upper classes began the study of moral and natural philosophy, with Alison giving the lectures, holding examinations, and requiring the students to continue to write abridgements of the lectures and readings. The modern orientation of Alison's course of study was almost certainly derived from the example of his Scottish teachers, and his instruction in rhetoric and the belles lettres was with little doubt a direct reflection of his experience under John Stevenson. Alison's scholarship, in fact, drew Wilson's attention to the "colleges of Scotland," where he thought Alison must have been "taught by very learned and correct teachers." [10]

---

[9] McCosh, *The Scottish Philosophy*, pp. 60–62; Carlyle, *Autobiography*, p. 59; Scott, *Francis Hutcheson*, pp. 74–76.
[10] Pears has reprinted Wilson's article in its entirety in "Francis Alison," *Journal of the Presbyterian Historical Society*, XXVIII (1950).

Ezra Stiles did not rate Alison's scientific and mathematical abilities high, perhaps with good reason. Stiles, in 1758, for example, had been excited by the prospect of tracing the course of Halley's comet and comparing notes with other colonial astronomers. However, Alison's report of sighting the comet with Theophilus Grew, Professor of Mathematics at Philadelphia, was disappointing to say the least. "I got up about three, one morning to observe it with him [Grew]," wrote Alison, "but the skie was clouded, & the morning was so raw, that I almost lost my health by it, which brought me to a resolution that effectually destroyed my star-gazing." For himself, Alison concluded, such knowledge could wait until the next stage of his existence, when it might be acquired "with more certainty & less trouble" by conversing with the great astronomers of the past.[11] Such flippancy about an event so momentous that it had captured the attention of men of science in Newport, Philadelphia, Cambridge, and New Haven could not have impressed Stiles that Alison grasped the seriousness of scientific pursuits.

Testimony from other contemporaries, however, indicates that, if Alison was not accomplished himself in the subject, he certainly encouraged the study of natural science. In his *Journal* article, Matthew Wilson acclaimed Alison as "the first who introduced real learning, not only Latin and Greek . . . , but also diffused the liberal arts and sciences, which enlarge and improve the mind: not only in Pennsylvania, but in all the neighboring states. . . ." [12] William Smith, the Reverend Jacob Duché, and others also added their praise of Alison's "pious and faithful labors for the propagation of useful knowledge in these untutored parts." [13] These descriptions of Alison's educational influence were couched as eulogies, and were, therefore, understandably extravagant. The careers of Alison's leading students, Hugh Williamson, John Ewing, and Charles Thomson, indicate, however, that there was some truth in them, not least in the claims that science and mathematics received prominent emphasis in Alison's program of instruction.

Hugh Williamson studied under Alison at New London, and after that at the College of Philadelphia, where he served from 1761 to 1764 as Professor of Mathematics. Williamson then studied medi-

[11] Alison to Stiles, May 27, 1759, in Stiles, *Itineraries*, pp. 422–423.
[12] Pears, "Francis Alison, Colonial Educator," *Delaware Notes* (1944), p. 16.
[13] See the testimonials to Alison printed in Thomas Montgomery, *A History of the University of Pennsylvania, 1740–1770* (Philadelphia: G. W. Jacobs & Co., 1900), pp. 164–166.

cine for two years at Edinburgh and Utrecht. Upon his return he was appointed to the chair of mathematics and natural philosophy at the College of Philadelphia, but lack of funds prevented him from accepting the the post. As a physician in Philadelphia, Williamson continued his studies in science, and, in 1772, his astronomical observations brought him the award of an honorary Doctor of Law from the University of Utrecht. Williamson later moved to North Carolina, where he practiced medicine, became influential in politics, and eventually published a two-volume history of the state. David Hosack, in his memorial to Williamson as scientist and physician, emphasized the importance of Williamson's association with Alison at New London and Philadelphia.[14]

John Ewing completed the course of study under Alison at New London and remained with him for three years as tutor in mathematics and the classics. Then, after graduating from the College of New Jersey, he studied theology under Alison and became pastor of the First Presbyterian Church of Philadelphia. In 1779 Ewing was appointed Provost and Professor of Natural Philosophy of the University of Pennsylvania, posts which he held until his death in 1802. Ewing was a vice-president of the American Philosophical Society, and served on several boundary commissions with David Rittenhouse. He contributed articles on astronomy to the first American edition of the *Encyclopedia Britannica* (1798), edited by the Scotsman Thomas Dobson, and in 1808 he published his *Lectures on Natural Philosophy* in two volumes.[15]

Charles Thomson, famous as the Secretary of the Continental Congress, went in 1751 to the Philadelphia Academy, which became part of the College of Philadelphia, as the first tutor in Latin and Greek. Thomson's scholary métier was classical studies—in his retirement he devoted his last years to making an American translation of the Greek Septuagint—but throughout his life he evinced an active interest in the promotion of science and useful knowledge. He took a leading part in the formation of the American Philosophical Society, and he helped Jefferson prepare his manuscript copy of *Notes on the State of Virginia* (1785).[16] Thomson's comments were included in

[14] See David Hosack, "Biographical Memoirs of Hugh Williamson," *Collections of the New York Historical Society for the Year 1821*, III (New York: E. Bliss and E. White, 1821), 125–180.

[15] See the article on Ewing by Samuel Miller in William B. Sprague, *Annals of the American Pulpit* (New York: R. Carter and Brothers, 1858), III, 216–219.

[16] See James Edwin Hendricks, "Charles Thomson and the American Enlightenment" (unpublished Ph.D. dissertation, University of Virginia, 1961), pp. 50 ff., 222–224.

the first and second editions of the *Notes* as an appendix. Thomson, Williamson, and Ewing all served with William Smith and David Rittenhouse on the committee set up by the American Philosophical Society to observe the transits of Venus and Mercury in 1769. Thus, while Alison's strength was in the literary subjects, he clearly was able to provide the inducement and intellectual foundations to enable his students to excel in scientific studies.

At the same time Alison also used his position in the church to encourage the spread of learning and the practical sciences. Preaching a sermon on "Love of Country" in 1758, Alison called for the promotion of "industry, agriculture, and home manufacturers" as a prime expression of true patriotism.[17] Four years earlier Alison had written to Scotland for help in devising a way to aid the widows of ministers and to educate and provide for their children. He adopted the "Scotch Plan," and the Presbyterian Ministers Fund was incorporated in 1759.[18] Under the direction of Alison, the Fund also maintained a library, which, according to the Bridenbaughs, loaned books to ministers living far from Philadelphia and to schoolmasters in rural districts.[19]

Although Alison left New London in 1752 to take charge of the Philadelphia Academy, he continued his interest in the New London school under Alexander McDowell. When the New London Academy was moved to Newark, Delaware, and chartered in 1769, Alison was named President of the Board of Trustees. At that time, according to Alison's description, the Newark school had sixty students under McDowell and two assistants, who taught the classics, arithmetic, geometry, practical mathematics, and logic.[20]

Three years later Alison organized a fund-raising trip by John Ewing and Hugh Williamson to Great Britain on behalf of the Newark Academy. Alison composed an appeal "To all Pious and Charitable Christians in Great Britain and Ireland" to be carried by the two emissaries. In this official document, and in a letter to Stiles requesting further letters of introduction for Ewing and Williamson, Alison stated his case for supporting the Newark institution. Of special interest is the conception that Alison presents of the social

[17] Francis Alison, "Love of Country," Manuscript Sermon, Presbyterian Historical Society, MS A1 4.
[18] Alison to Stiles, December 12, 1767, in Stiles, *Itineraries*, p. 431.
[19] Carl Bridenbaugh and Jessica Bridenbaugh, *Rebels and Gentlemen* (New York: Oxford University Press, 1965; first copyright, 1942), p. 92.
[20] Alison to Stiles, May 7, 1768, in Stiles, *Itineraries*, p. 433.

function of higher education in rural and recently settled areas. The development of the frontier regions, he argued, was of utmost importance to the future of the country. The rapid rise of population in these areas, however, was making it extremely difficult to provide them with sufficient numbers of ministers and other public leaders. If their needs were to be met, leaders would have to come from the people in the new settlements themselves. "Farmers' sons must furnish ministers & magistrates for all our frontier inhabitants," Alison urged, "or they must sink into Ignorance, licentiousness, & all their hurtful consequences." Ample opportunities for education and the taming and civilizing influences of "Religion and Science . . . to soften the tempers of such wide multitudes" were absolute necessities in these areas.

Unfortunately, Alison pointed out, despite the presence of three new colleges in New York, New Jersey, and Philadelphia, few settlers were availing themselves of them. They were too few, too far removed, and too expensive; moreover, many parents feared the bad influences that city life might have on their children. The Academy at Newark, Alison wrote, clinching his argument, suited the needs of these people perfectly. Newark itself was located in open and healthy countryside; its inhabitants were "few, frugal, and Industrious," and tuition and living accommodations at the academy were inexpensive.[21]

This trip, unfortunately, could hardly have been undertaken at a less propitious moment for money-raising purposes. Williamson, who had sailed from Boston, had the unhappy task, according to one historian, of being the first to inform the British government of the Boston Tea Party.[22] John Witherspoon, by that time President of the College of New Jersey and fearful of competition from the Newark Academy, further hampered the trip by intimating in letters to friends in Britain that Ewing's and Williamson's orthodoxy was suspect. To make matters worse, Williamson fell in love in London, and Ewing had to make the trip to Scotland alone. Ewing's reception in Scotland, however, was enthusiastic. Glasgow, Montrose, Dundee, and Perth all presented him with the keys to their cities, and the University of Edinburgh conferred upon him the degree of Doctor of Divinity.

[21] See the letter from Alison to Stiles, of October 22, 1773, printed in full in Pears, "Francis Alison, Colonial Educator," *Delaware Notes* (1944), pp. 20–22. This letter does not appear in Stiles' *Itineraries*, but compare the similar letter from Alison in Stiles, *Itineraries*, p. 433.

[22] Montgomery, *History of the University of Pennsylvania*, p. 312.

Little, however, was gathered in the way of money.[23] Fortunately, the foundations of the academy had been well-laid, and except for an interval during the war years, the Academy continued in operation until 1834, when it merged with Delaware College (today the University of Delaware).

Alison's statement to Ezra Stiles that it was his New London Academy that first "roused a spirit in Philadelphia to erect an academy, and then a College," was not an empty claim.[24] Charles Thomson may have been one of the first to call Alison to the attention of Benjamin Franklin, Richard Peters, and the other trustees of the Philadelphia Academy.[25] At any rate it was mainly at the behest of Franklin that Alison left New London in 1752 to become head of the academy in Philadelphia.[26] Franklin, whose admiration for Scottish learning was considerable, was not disappointed in Alison. In 1755, when Alison and the naturalist John Bartram made a trip to New England, Benjamin Franklin sent letters of introduction to various New England leaders. To the Reverend Jared Eliot, Franklin wrote:

I wrote to you yesterday, and now I write to you again. You will say, it can't rain but it pours; for I not only send you manuscript but living letters. The former may be short, but the latter will be more longer and yet more agreeable. Mr. Bartram I believe you will find to be at least twenty folio pages, large paper well filled, on the subjects of botany, fossils, husbandry, and the first creation. This Mr. Alison is as many more on agriculture, philosophy, your own catholic divinity, and various other parts of learning equally, useful and engaging.[27]

This letter illustrates not only Franklin's high estimation of Alison, but also the latter's widening connections with influential persons throughout the colonies.

Alison was soon joined at the academy in Philadelphia by the Anglican minister William Smith. A Scotsman himself, Smith had attended King's College at Aberdeen for four years from 1743 to

---

23 See Ryden, "The Relation of the Newark Academy . . . ," pp. 31 ff.
24 The Bridenbaughs agree with Alison that the original inspiration for the Philadelphia Academy came chiefly from Alison's New London school. Carl and Jessica Bridenbaugh, *Rebels and Gentlemen*, p. 57.
25 Montgomery, *History of the University of Pennsylvania*, p. 162.
26 Ryden, "The Relation of the Newark Academy . . . ," p. 15.
27 Quoted in Pears, "Francis Alison, Colonial Educator," *Delaware Notes* (1944), p. 9. Also see Franklin's letter to Ezra Stiles, September 1, 1755, in Stiles, *Itineraries*, p. 4.

1747, although he may not have taken a degree. Together Alison and Smith proposed to the trustees that a college be established with the full right to grant degrees. Shortly thereafter, in 1755, a college charter was obtained naming Smith Provost and Alison Vice-Provost of the New College, Academy, and Charity School of Philadelphia. In this capacity Alison also taught moral philosophy, logic, classics, metaphysics, and geography until his death in 1779.[28]

Smith came to the academy after favorably impressing Franklin with his scheme for a new world college sketched in his little pamphlet *A General Idea of the College of Mirania*.[29] The course of study set forth by Smith in his description of the imaginary College of Mirania fit well with Alison's own educational emphases, and provided the basis for the curriculum they introduced at the College of Philadelphia. The underlying assumption of Smith's educational theory was the necessity for the early separation of students into "the two grand Classes" made up of those headed for the learned professions—"Divinity, Law, Physic, Agriculture, and the Chief Offices of the State" —and of those "design'd for the Mechanic Professions, and all the remaining People of the State."

Boys in the mechanics school studied English as their only language and such other subjects as would have practical application to their future work. This school, Smith carefully pointed out in *Mirania*, was "much like the English School in Philadelphia first sketched out by the very ingenious and worthy Mr. Franklin." Aristocratically inclined, however, Smith was mostly interested in his young gentlemen and men of affairs. For them he devised a course of study that he thought would equip them perfectly for their future high stations in society—a liberal arts curriculum firmly grounded in the ancient languages, but including the latest in current literary studies and the natural sciences.

In shaping his curriculum Smith probably drew on several sources in addition to his own ideas. His main inspiration appears to have come from the 1753 curricular reforms instituted at King's and Marischal Colleges at Aberdeen. Smith had attended King's College during the period when pressures for revamping the old medieval arts course had been building. These curricular and organization reforms

[28] Montgomery, *History of the University of Pennsylvania*, pp. 164, 209–210, 233, 527.
[29] I have relied upon Albert Gegenheimer's summary of and extensive quotations from *The College of Mirania*. Albert Frank Gegenheimer, *William Smith, Educator and Churchman, 1727–1803* (Philadelphia: University of Pennsylvania Press, 1943), pp. 14–42.

at the Aberdonian colleges were finally carried out in 1753, the same year Smith published *The College of Mirania*.

Both the ideal curriculum depicted by Smith in his pamphlet and the actual, less ambitious course of study introduced at Philadelphia closely resembled the reform emphases at Aberdeen. Describing the College of Mirania Smith had written, "Logic and metaphysics are in great Disrepute," mathematics being considered "a more advantageous Study" than "the sophisticated Distinctions and idle Jargon of School-Logic." Although Smith was forced to compromise his ideal plan by abandoning the five-year college course of Mirania for a more realistic three-year program at Philadelphia, he was able to follow through on many of his other ideas. The classics were studied all three years, but with comprehensive instruction in rhetoric, literary criticism, and composition. Unlike the Mirania and Aberdeen plans, logic and metaphysics were still first-year subjects, but they were taught from modern texts—the *Logic* of the Aberdonian professor William Duncan serving as "a classic." Moreover, logic and metaphysics led to the early introduction of moral philosophy in the second year under Francis Alison, whose orientation in that subject, as will be seen, was thoroughly in keeping with current Scottish thought.

The Philadelphia curriculum also provided for a progressive three-year study of mathematics, natural philosophy, natural history, astronomy, and chemistry. One historian of American colonial science has underscored Smith's "remarkably full" mathematics program and his "impressive familiarity with mathematical literature," evidenced by his many suggestions for supplementary reading. Smith's reading list included such important Scottish mathematicians as David Gregory, Colin Maclaurin, John Keil, and Robert Simson.[30]

In the Mirania plan, and at Philadelphia so far as realities would permit, Smith eliminated the regenting system that he had known at King's College. In this regard, as his biographer has pointed out, Smith's practice closely resembled the example of Marischal College under the 1753 reforms.[31] So close, in fact, was the parallel that it is worth detailing. In abolishing the regenting system the principal and masters of Marischal College agreed that in addition to the specific chairs of Greek and divinity each professor of philosophy should be

[30] Theodore Hornberger, *Scientific Thought in the American Colleges, 1638–1800* (Austin: The University of Texas Press, 1945), p. 55. The complete curriculum and Smith's recommended readings are printed in Montgomery, *History of the University of Pennsylvania*, pp. 236–239.

[31] Gegenheimer, *William Smith*, p. 28.

assigned to a particular branch of that subject, whether it be "Natural and Civil History, Natural Philosophy, or Moral and Rational Philosophy." At the same time the Marischal faculty did not completely abandon the older practice. Probably in order to compensate for the sustained personal guidance afforded under the practice of regenting, and perhaps in an effort to take account of the reasons given by King's College for not doing away with regents, the Marischal faculty assigned one teacher to have charge of each class for a year. The Professor of Greek was appointed to direct the academic course of first-year students, and three other professors were named to "constantly teach" the "semi," "tertian," and "magistrand" classes respectively. Continuity with the past was further maintained by a provision that "the meetings on Sabbath evenings" of all students should continue as before.[32]

In all three specifics Smith's program was similar to that at Marischal. Smith replaced regenting with a detailed course curriculum taught by specialized professors; at the same time, he assigned an individual teacher to each year and retained the Sunday evening meetings. Circumstances, however, forced Smith and the other teachers to restrict the college course to three years, and to double up on teaching loads.[33]

The relationship between Alison and Smith proved to be a stormy one. Almost from the day he arrived at Philadelphia, Smith began to scheme and push for the appointment of an Anglican bishop to the colonies. Alison, as a leading Presbyterian, lived in constant fear that Smith might succeed in his intrigues, and that he was attempting

[32] Details and statements from the Aberdeen plans are taken from *Notes on the Evolution of the Arts Curriculum in the Universities of Aberdeen,* Prepared for the General Council (Aberdeen: Aberdeen University Press, 1908), pp. 8–9.

[33] Theodore Hornberger has challenged the suggestion that the main influence on Smith's curriculum was the University of Aberdeen. Hornberger thinks that Samuel Johnson's preface to Robert Dodsley's *Preceptor* (1748) was a more decisive influence. Two of the most important articles in the *Preceptor,* however, were written by the Aberdeen professors, David Fordyce and William Duncan, who took a hand in the 1753 reforms. Fordyce wrote the article for the *Preceptor* on "Moral Philosophy," and Duncan the article on "Logic," which was later published separately and used by Smith at Philadelphia as the logic text. Mutual influences at this point become difficult to trace, but it would seem that the importance of the Aberdeen example is just as difficult to avoid. See Theodore Hornberger, "A Note on the Probable Source of Provost Smith's Famous Curriculum for the College of Philadelphia," *Pennsylvania Magazine of History,* LVIII (1934), 370–376. For a discussion of the importance of the articles by Fordyce and Duncan in the *Preceptor,* see Dale Randall, "Dodsley's *Perceptor*—A Window into the Eighteenth Century," *Journal of the Rutger's University Library,* XXII (December 1958), 10–27. Also see McCosh, *The Scottish Philosophy,* pp. 106–107.

to make the College of Philadelphia itself an Anglican stronghold. The Bridenbaughs have written that "a steady crescendo of religious animosity echoed through the College in the nineteen years from its founding to the outbreak of the War for Independence." [34] So bitter did Alison become toward Smith and the Anglicans that on occasion he voiced his strong temptation to leave the college. One reason for Alison's staying on was probably the fear that Smith would actually succeed in taking over the college if he left it. Despite their sectarian antagonism, however, the two men continued to work together on the faculty with no apparent detriment to the quality of instruction. The academic standards of the college remained high and its reputation increased over the years.

The ability of Smith and Alison to continue together in the teaching tasks of the college, their strained relationship notwithstanding, is in actuality no great puzzle. They shared many of the same educational ideals, they had similar educational backgrounds in the universities of Scotland, and, with Smith teaching natural philosophy and Alison moral philosophy, they complemented each other on the faculty. Alison's own emphasis on English, for example, was grounded, like Smith's, in the classics and was directed more toward literary accomplishments than was Franklin's own original, practical interest in the subject.[35] In the combined teaching of Alison and Smith the influences of the three leading institutions of higher education in Scotland—Edinburgh, Glasgow, and Aberdeen—were brought to bear on the College of Philadelphia. With the founding of the medical school at the college in 1765 other important Scottish influences were to be added.

Alison's own educational influence was not confined to the College of Philadelphia and the Newark Academy. His contacts with New England leaders, especially with Ezra Stiles, helped to nourish the growing awareness at Harvard and Yale of the Scottish universities. Alison was particularly well known at Yale, where he enjoyed friendly relationships with two successive college administrations. In 1755 he was awarded an honorary Yale doctorate signed by President

---

[34] Carl and Jessica Bridenbaugh, *Rebels and Gentlemen*, p. 62.
[35] It was Smith, however, not Alison, who was saddled by Franklin with blame for subordinating the English School—Franklin's pet—to the college, although Alison probably concurred in this development and may even have encouraged it. This may suggest that Franklin's pique with Smith was actuated as much by political and personal reasons as by strictly educational considerations. See Carl and Jessica Bridenbaugh, *Rebels and Gentlemen*, p. 45; also Gegenheimer, *William Smith*, p. 148.

Clap and the trustees; the year before, Alison had received Ezra Stiles in Philadelphia and conducted him on a tour of the academy.[36]

Stiles and Alison shared many educational and religious views and wrote to each other for years. At one point Stiles requested a copy of Alison's Glasgow diploma, and Alison promised to send it to him along with a copy of his letter from Francis Hutcheson regarding the Old Side plans for an academy.[37] Stiles, who was himself anxious for an honorary doctorate, wrote Charles Chauncy in Boston in 1761 asking for a recommendation for the Doctor of Divinity degree for two friends of his. Chauncy, also an acquaintance of Alison, replied that the best chances for easily obtaining a prestigious degree lay in Scotland. "Edinburgh-University is the highest in reputation," Chauncy counseled Stiles, "and Glasgow next. A degree from either of these universities will be honorable, the most so from the former, and it will be with most difficulty obtained." [38] In 1765 Stiles received his own honorary doctorate from Edinburgh—"Mrs. Whittelsey bids you Joy of your New Garters," wrote Chauncy Whittelsey from New Haven—and entered into correspondence with many persons in Edinburgh, among them John Erskine, who frequently sent Stiles packets of books for his library.[39]

Evidence of Stiles' continuing interest in the Scottish universities is especially strong in one long passage in his diary where extensive excerpts from Henry Marchant's description of his travels through Scotland in 1771 are copied. Marchant had graduated from the College of Philadelphia in 1759, and was later sent to England as the colonial agent for Rhode Island.[40] The longest passages from Marchant's diary copied by Stiles referred to the universities of Edinburgh and Glasgow, which Marchant and Benjamin Franklin visited together. Stiles took down in detail Marchant's favorable reports of the university lectures he and Franklin attended and of the hours they spent dining and conversing with David Hume and various faculty members. Stiles also took pains to enter Marchant's judgment of

36 The Yale degree is in the Alison papers at the Presbyterian Historical Society, Philadelphia. Bridenbaugh describes Stiles' tour in 1754; see Carl Bridenbaugh, *Mitre and Sceptre* (New York: Oxford University Press, 1962), p. 112.
37 Alison to Stiles, May 7, 1768, in Stiles, *Itineraries*, p. 433.
38 Chauncy to Stiles, February 7, 1761, in Stiles, *Itineraries*, pp. 438–439.
39 Whittelsey to Stiles, December 24, 1765, in Stiles, *Itineraries*, p. 588. References to letters and packets received from John Erskine and other Scottish correspondents are found throughout Stiles' *Literary Diary*.
40 J. Bennett Nolan, *Benjamin Franklin in Scotland and Ireland, 1759 and 1771* (Philadelphia: University of Pennsylvania Press, 1938), p. 173.

Oxford that by common accounts "one would be led to think very little Learning Religion or Morals were to be obtained at the University."[41] Thus Stiles' interest in things Scottish found confirmation and support from other sources besides his friendship with Alison.

II

Alison is of particular interest as a teacher of moral philosophy, for to him must go the major credit for introducing the thought of Francis Hutcheson to America. As Professor of Moral Philosophy at Glasgow from 1730 until his death sixteen years later, Hutcheson had immense influence upon the leading Scottish intellectuals of the eighteenth century, including Adam Smith, David Hume, and Thomas Reid. He helped to set many of the themes that were to dominate Scottish moral philosophy, which after him had its own distinct concerns, method of inquiry, and even organization and delineation of topics.[42]

Scottish moral philosophy was to have a decisive impact upon the religious and educational ideals at both the College of New Jersey and the College of Philadelphia. Although the first comprehensive introduction of Hutcheson's thought into America came through an Old Side leader, even at the very beginning the New Side was not immune to his influence. For these reasons a rather close look at certain of the central themes of Hutcheson's thought as they were transmitted by Alison will repay the effort.[43]

Alison appears to have adopted Hutcheson's moral philosophy totally and uncritically. In having his students make abridgements of important authors, Alison was following one of the teaching devices popularized by Francis Hutcheson. It was apparently Alison's practice in his moral philosophy course to have his students prepare abridgements of Hutcheson's *Short Introduction to Moral Philosophy*, usually referred to simply as the *Compend*.[44] In his metaphysics course, too, Alison drew heavily upon Hutcheson.

41 Stiles, *Literary Diary*, III, 304 ff.
42 See Gladys Bryson, *Man and Society: The Scottish Inquiry of the Eighteenth Century* (Princeton: Princeton University Press, 1945), especially pp. 176 ff.; for another assessment of Hutcheson as a germinal figure in the Scottish Enlightenment, see Scott, *Francis Hutcheson*, pp. 25 ff.
43 For an interesting discussion of Hutcheson's influence and reputation in America, see Caroline Robbins, " 'When It Is That Colonies May Turn Independent:' An Analysis of the Environment and Politics of Francis Hutcheson," *William and Mary Quarterly*, 3rd ser., XI (April 1954), 214–251.
44 A Latin version of Hutcheson's lectures was first published in 1742. Five years later it appeared in English translation under the title, *A Short Introduction to*

Although the topics covered by Alison in metaphysics under the three headings of "The Human Soul," "Being in General," and "The Being and Attributes of God" were traditional enough, his infusion of Hutcheson's thought into his treatment of these topics shows how far Alison was beginning to depart from the old rationalistic metaphysics. In one summary passage on the mind and the proper approach to knowledge, for example, Alison told his students:

Here we should remember that human Reason is but weak and incapable to discover the intimate Essences of Things . . . and that we are not induced by Arguments drawn from the Essences of Things to admit of some very important Opinions in Philosophy, but rather from our Experience and inward Feelings, & from the Bents or Instincts implanted in our Nature.[45]

This passage contains in particular two broad assumptions or emphases that, after Hutcheson, became characteristic of Scottish thought.

In the first place, Scottish philosophy came to concentrate more and more upon "inward feelings" and the "Bents or Instincts implanted in our nature"—upon the emotions and affections—and less upon a priori reason as the guide to human conduct. Hutcheson's impelling interest was ethical: he wanted to lay a solid foundation for moral judgment and action that was in keeping with the demands for clarity, order, and rationality being made by proponents of natural religion.[46] In doing so Hutcheson rejected the brand of rationalism represented by such English moralists as Samuel Clarke and William Wollaston, who believed that reason alone can guide conduct by

Moral Philosophy. Unless otherwise specified, the shorter name, *Compend,* by which this work was known, is used in this discussion. See Francis Hutcheson, *A Short Introduction to Moral Philosophy* (Glasgow: Robert Foulis, 1747).

His longer *System of Moral Philosophy* was published posthumously in 1755. See Francis Hutcheson, *A System of Moral Philosophy* (2 vols.; London: published by his son, 1755).

The extant manuscript copies at the University of Pennsylvania of notes taken by Alison's students follow the outline of Hutcheson's *Compend* topic by topic. See Jasper Yeates, "Moral Philosophy in Three Books . . . To Which is subjoined Communis Ethicae Compendium: or A Compend of Ethics, in Latin. 1759," and Samuel Jones, "His Book of Practical Philosophy, viz. Ethics and the Law of Nature: begun 7th Anno Dom. 1760, at the College of Philadelphia under the Direction and Tuition of the Rev. Mr. Francis Alison, D.D." Both are in the manuscript collection of the University of Pennsylvania Library.

45 Jasper Yeates, "Metaphysics in Three Parts . . . Read in the College of Philadelphia under the Tuition and Direction of Francis Alison, 1760," Manuscript Collection, University of Pennsylvania, p. 4.

46 Hutcheson discusses natural religion in his larger *System.* See Francis Hutcheson, *A System of Moral Philosophy* (2 vols.; London: published by his son, 1755), I, 35–36.

showing the intelligible and immutable relationships in "the nature of things," to which human action should conform. Although Hutcheson shared with them a concern to avoid the arbitrariness they all felt was inherent in purely revealed religion, he did not accept their position that reason in itself could be an adequate foundation for ethics. Hutcheson thought the a priori, essentially Cartesian rationalism of Clarke and Wollaston too abstract, complex, and hypothetical to provide sound guidance. For Hutcheson a much surer basis for ethics than logical inference was to be found in the human emotions. The emotions were givens in the experience of all men; moreover, the emotions were available to observation, and could be described, analyzed, and classified with a high degree of empirical certainty—so Hutcheson thought.[47]

Hutcheson discerned in man a number of internal or "reflex senses," which guide the affections and enable man to judge the moral and aesthetic world, just as his external senses make known the physical world. Francis Alison enumerated for his students some of the most important and interesting of Hutcheson's internal senses, including the sense of beauty; "the Common Sense or Social Bent, by which we interest ourselves in all the joys & Sufferings of Mankind"; the sense of honor; the sense of ridicule; and the moral sense.[48] Building upon the ideas of Lord Shaftesbury, Hutcheson himself thought that the true foundation of morality was to be found in benevolent affections guided by the moral sense. Like the sense of beauty or taste, with which it had much in common according to Hutcheson, the moral sense grasped the morality in a situation or person immediately and intuitively. Moral judgments were no more the products of a long chain of reasoning than were aesthetic responses to a painting or a landscape. Those who followed Hutcheson handled the same problem somewhat differently, but all were one with him in ascribing primary importance to the affections. The ultimate source of human conduct,

[47] A detailed treatment of the empiricist and rationalist schools appears in Sir Leslie Stephen, History of English Thought in the Eighteenth Century (New York: Harcourt, Brace, & World, Inc., 1962; first published 1876); II, 2–11, 39–52. For a briefer discussion of the two positions, see L. A. Selby-Bigge, ed., "Introduction," British Moralists (Oxford: Clarendon Press, 1897).

[48] Hutcheson invested his ideal man with a sense of beauty; a sense of imitation or artistic enjoyment; senses of music, of design, of novelty, and of grandeur; a sympathetic sense; a sense of honor and decorum; and a moral sense. Hutcheson's enumeration of the internal, or reflex senses, varied at different times in his writings. A convenient distillation of the main internal senses identified by Hutcheson is found in Scott, Francis Hutcheson, pp. 216 ff. Alison's presentation of the internal senses is taken from the notes of Joseph Yeates, "Metaphysics," pp. 15–16.

the bonds of social solidarity, even the possibility of human communication were for the Scots located, not in the reason, but in the emotions and feelings.[49]

This stress upon the affections and repudiation of reasoning from the essences of things went hand in hand, in the second place, with a desire on the part of the Scots philosophers to be scientific. Scottish thinkers—some before Hutcheson and certainly most after him—came to feel that they could apply to all realms of knowledge the method of study they took to be the ideal of Baconian and Newtonian science: a simple, inductive empiricism. Through the empirical method the physical world and also human nature and society were thought to be amenable to scientific study. Observation and experience, rather than metaphysics and rationalistic deduction, were, as Gladys Bryson has put it, "the lauded procedural ideal." [50]

The inductive method and its application to human nature also shifted new attention to the study of man's social environment, its structures, relationships, and institutions. Just as Hutcheson based his account of man's behavior and the good life upon an empirical investigation of human nature, he also turned to the description of society as the product and the arena of human conduct. This third element in Hutcheson's thought was not neglected by Alison. In his moral philosophy course Alison had his students summarize Hutcheson's *Compend* chapter by chapter under each of its three major headings: "The Elements of Ethics," "The Elements of the Law of Nature," and "The Principles of Economics and Politics." The last two introduced the students to questions touching on natural rights, religious duties, property, contracts and oaths, family life, the origins of society, and government, politics, and civil and international law. Through the teaching of Francis Alison the full sweep of the reconstruction of moral philosophy, in which Hutcheson played such an important initial role, entered the American college at a very early date.

Hutcheson was concerned to provide his students with guidelines applicable to the concrete problems of life. This practical interest—characteristic of so much in eighteenth-century Scotland—can be seen in Hutcheson's desire to avoid empty abstractions that had no

---

[49] Gladys Bryson has shown the resemblance of Hutcheson's emphasis on the emotions to Hume's conviction that reason does not govern action, to Smith's and Hume's emphasis on sympathy, and to Ferguson's idea that it is the affections that bind men together in social solidarity. Bryson, *Man and Society*, pp. 48, 129, 156–160.

[50] Bryson, *Man and Society*, p. 17.

relevance to actual life situations. In the preface to his *Compend*, Hutcheson stated explicitly that it was not being published for the learned, but rather "for those who study at universities" in order that they might grasp at the outset the importance for their own lives of the subjects discussed in moral philosophy. Hutcheson urged his readers not to allow philosophy "to rest in speculation" or to regard the study of philosophy as "a matter of ostentation, or shew of knowledge, but as the most sacred law of life and conduct." [51] Alison's own Calvinist concern with right conduct probably found strong support in such sentiments—Hutcheson and Alison were, after all, both Presbyterian ministers. In the two areas of politics and education, especially, Alison drew upon specific themes in Hutcheson's thought that had significant consequences for his own influence as an educator at the College of Philadelphia and elsewhere.

As Caroline Robbins has demonstrated, Hutcheson made major contributions to eighteenth-century political theory.[52] Hutcheson can be seen as a leading eighteenth-century representative of the tradition of "political Calvinism" and its ideas of natural rights, government by contract and consent, popular sovereignty, and the right of resistance. This body of ideas had been championed during the Reformation by followers of Calvin in Scotland, England, and on the Continent.[53] Scottish Reformers had played a special part in enunciating and acting upon the doctrine of the right of the people to resist tyranny. One need only mention Knox's struggle with Queen Mary, Andrew Melville's confrontation with James VI—"God's sillie Vassal"—and later Samuel Rutherford and his treatise *Lex Rex*.[54] Calvinist political thought was further refined and developed in the seventeenth century by Grotius, Pufendorf, and other representatives of the natural rights school, and in England by such theorists of the Commonwealth tra-

---

[51] Hutcheson, *Compend*, pp. i–iv.
[52] Robbins, " 'When It Is That Colonies May Turn Independent' . . . ," pp. 243 ff., *passim*.
[53] See especially Herbert D. Foster, "International Calvinism through Locke and the Revolution of 1688," *American Historical Review*, XXXII (April 1927), 475–499. Various aspects of Calvinist political thought are explored in the essays in George Hunt, ed., *Calvinism and the Political Order* (Philadelphia: The Westminster Press, 1965); see especially the essay by Winthrop Hudson, "John Locke: Heir of Puritan Political Theorists," pp. 108–129. An incisive development of the Calvinist origins of liberal democracy is in James Hastings Nichols, *Democracy and the Churches* (Philadelphia: The Westminster Press, 1951), pp. 17–41. Nichols also has an extensive bibliography of the voluminous literature on the subject. Also see J. T. McNeill, "Natural Law in the Teachings of the Reformers," *Journal of Religion*, XXVI (1946), pp. 168–182.
[54] See Hunt, ed., *Calvinism and the Political Order*, pp. 72–73.

dition as Sidney, Harrington, Milton, and Locke. Hutcheson drew upon all of these thinkers, as well as upon the ancients, in shaping the distinctive emphases of his own political ideas.[55]

Two of Hutcheson's most important emphases were the right of resistance to tyranny and the necessity of balanced forms of government.[56] Francis Alison not only taught these ideas, but also put them to good use long before they were to assume the roles assigned to them in Revolutionary and post-Revolutionary America. By teaching them and by acting upon them, Alison was able to make his own presence at the College of Philadelphia a primary source of resistance —against Anglicanism and, eventually, against the British government.

In a paraphrase of Chapter VII of Hutcheson's *Compend*, entitled "Of the Rights of the Supreme Power, & the Methods of Acquiring It," Alison wrote:

While the Publick interests are tolerably secured and consulted it is unjustifiable in any people to have recourse to civil wars & force for lighter causes: but when the publick liberty & safety cannot be otherwise secured it is lawful and honourable to make strong efforts for a change of Government.[57]

Alison was no more content than Hutcheson to allow philosophy "to rest in speculation." As his fears of Anglican encroachment mounted, Alison led the Presbyterians in the middle colonies in efforts to thwart the appointment of an Anglican bishop. From 1766 to 1768 Francis Alison and Ezra Stiles together were the chief organizers of

[55] For a detailed study of the Commonwealth tradition, see Caroline Robbins, *The Eighteenth-Century Commonwealthman* (Cambridge, Mass.: Harvard University Press, 1961). G. D. Henderson documents the influence of Hugo Grotius on all schools of political thought in seventeenth-century Scotland, and shows that the influence of Grotius continued unabated in the teaching of all the Scottish universities in the eighteenth century. Henderson writes of Hutcheson: "At Glasgow University early in the eighteenth century Francis Hutcheson was in the habit of conducting a special class on the *de Veritate*, which he threw open to students of all Faculties free of charge and which created wide interest." G. D. Henderson, *Religious Life in Seventeenth-Century Scotland* (Cambridge: At the University Press, 1937), pp. 75–76, 260.
[56] Hutcheson, *Compend*, pp. 255–278, 304–305.
[57] Alison continued: "The divine right of governors is a dream of court flatterers. In one sense every right is divine & is constitutedly the law of God & nature. The rights of the people are divine as well as those of Princes. Nay more divine, as princes were constituted for the good of the people." Francis Alison, Manuscript Fragment, Presbyterian Historical Society, Philadelphia. Compare Hutcheson, *Compend*, p. 302.

the drive to form a union of the Congregationalists in New England and the Presbyterians in the middle colonies against the Anglicans.[58] With the publication in 1768 of a series of essays in the *Pennsylvania Journal* entitled "Centinel," Alison emerged in this struggle as the outstanding propagandist against the Anglicans. In one of these essays he made direct use of Hutcheson's notion of balanced government to explain his opposition to the power which would be vested in a bishopric. "The abuse of power," he wrote,

has in all ages, furnished the most copious fund of materials to the moralist, and to the historian, and has ever given the greatest perplexity to the Legislator. . . . The passions and prejudices of men are constantly leading them into one mistake or another; and the remonstrances of reason and duty alone, are but feeble restraints. In order therefore to curb the licentiousness of leading men, it hath been found expedient to distribute the powers of government among the different sorts and orders of which the community is composed, so as to excite, and employ those of one rank and interest, to correct the irregularities of another.[59]

Nearly twenty years before the Constitutional Convention, Alison was applying the principle of balanced government to lay bare the dangers he saw in episcopacy.

The determination of the non-Anglican churches to maintain their freedom from an episcopate and the larger colonial quarrel with England were in Alison's mind clearly two sides of the same struggle. Alison worked to mobilize Presbyterians against the Stamp Act, and in 1766 presented an overture to the synod "that an address should be made to our Sovereign, on the joyful occasion of the repeal of the Stamp Act, and thereby a confirmation of our liberties." [60] Although Alison was not especially prominent in the Revolution itself—he was an old man by then and declining in health—many of his students were. Charles Thomson's service as perpetual secretary of the Continental Congress has already been noted, and two other of Alison's students, George Read and Thomas McKean, were signers of the Declaration of Independence. Hugh Williamson, Alison's student and

---

[58] Bridenbaugh, *Mitre and Sceptre*, pp. 271–274.
[59] Quoted in Thomas Pears, Jr., "Presbyterians and American Freedom," *Journal of the Presbyterian Historical Society*, XXIX (June 1951), 87.
[60] Quoted in *ibid*. For Alison's full sentiments on the Stamp Act as "an insult to Common Sense," see the letter from Alison to Stiles, June 13, 1765, in Stiles, *Itineraries*, pp. 426–427.

long-time friend, was a member from North Carolina of the Constitutional Convention.

Alison perceived a close relationship between his classroom teachings and the political and religious issues in which he and the College of Philadelphia were embroiled. As he expressed it in a letter to Stiles, the promotion of "the kingdom of Christ, or the cause of Liberty, virtue, or Learning" was for him one and the same task.[61] When General Howe occupied Philadelphia, Alison was forced to flee for a time. In a letter written while he was taking refuge at the home of Thomas McKean in Delaware, Alison said:

I have three different times changed my place of residence to avoid the enemy, & was almost as often within a few miles of these unmerciful plunderers. Dr. Smith & Mr. McCannon & I shut up the College for this reason, because all our tuition money would not be sufficient to buy firewood for our Schools this winter, & it is uncertain when we shall meet again; & whether we shall receive any sallary henceforth. If the English keep the City I expect none. Dr. Smith has made his peace with Howe, but on what terms I know not. But he sent me word to come in, & open the College, & I would be safe; but I am not willing to trust them.[62]

This passage makes quite plain Alison's suspicions of Smith and his fear that he might be singled out by the British because of his influence and activities at the college.

In summary, the significance of Francis Alison's teaching career at the College of Philadelphia deserves to be retrieved from the shadow of William Smith's colorful personality, in which it has often been allowed to stand. Alison's educational outlook and activities helped to reinforce and complement the progressive college curriculum instituted under Smith, and broadened the Scottish influences at Philadelphia still further. He introduced the moral philosophy of Francis Hutcheson, with its attempt to apply eighteenth-century scientific method to the study of human nature and society. And, by making use of Hutcheson's political theory for his own religious and social purposes, he provided one very early demonstration of the relevance of Scottish academic philosophy to certain pressing American problems.

A pertinent question is whether Alison was essentially a theologi-

[61] Alison to Stiles, May 27, 1759, in Stiles, *Itineraries*, p. 424.
[62] Quoted in Pears, "Presbyterians and American Freedom," p. 90.

cal Moderate like his mentor, Francis Hutcheson.[63] As Professor of
Moral Philosophy at Glasgow, Hutcheson not only strove with much
success to reform the university; he was also one of the most influential
of the early leaders of the Moderate party in the Church of Scotland.
The Moderates, it will be recalled, wanted to free the churches of
what they considered narrow and bigoted views, and to equip the
clergy to feel at home among the polite and cultured classes of Scotland. In Hutcheson's own description of his efforts and those of his
protégé, the Professor of Divinity at Glasgow, William Leechman,
they desired to "put a new face upon Theology in Scotland." [64]

One of the consequences of Hutcheson's theological views was
that he was charged with heresy by the Presbytery of Glasgow on
two counts: for teaching "first that the standard of moral goodness
was the promotion of the happiness of others"—benevolence; "and
second that we could have a knowledge of good and evil without,
and prior to a knowledge of God"—the moral sense.[65] After this
Hutcheson redoubled his efforts to influence the theology of the
church, and as one of his master strokes succeeded in having his
friend Leechman appointed to the chair of divinity in 1743. In the
not unbiased words of Alexander Carlyle, a student and admirer of
both men, it was through Hutcheson and Leechman "that a better
taste and greater liberality of sentiment were introduced among the
clergy in the western provinces of Scotland." [66]

Although similarities did exist between certain of Alison's views
and the Moderate orientation, Alison cannot really be said to have
been a Moderate. The truly Moderate spirit was exhibited by Leechman, who in a controversial sermon on prayer said that the chief
benefits of prayer were its effects on the mind of the person praying.[67]
Little of this ultra-liberal theological spirit can be found in Alison's
preaching, and an examination of his manuscript sermons shows just

[63] Trinterud, calling attention to the link between Alison and Hutcheson, says that
"No category fits Alison so well as that of a 'Moderate.'" Leonard J. Trinterud,
The Forming of an American Tradition (Philadelphia: The Westminster Press,
1949), p. 333, n. 14. I have tried to indicate why I think Trinterud's conclusion
about Alison is misleading.

[64] Extracts from letters of Hutcheson describing his work and aims in the church and
college are reprinted in McCosh, *The Scottish Philosophy*, Appendix, pp. 465 ff.

[65] Scott, *Francis Hutcheson*, p. 184.

[66] Carlyle, *Autobiography*, p. 58.

[67] It was none other than Hume who commented on Leechman's sermon with the
observation that prayer was useless if the person praying did not think he could
have a direct influence on God and have his prayers answered. See, Scott, *Francis
Hutcheson*, p. 87; John Hill Burton, *Life and Correspondence of David Hume*
(Edinburgh: W. Tait, 1846), I, 164.

what a firm Calvinist he was. In one passage which could have been delivered by Gilbert Tennent, Alison asked,

What Real comfort can a hypocrite or formalist have, who knows as often as he reflects & examins his heart & conduct that God sees the unsoundness of his heart & abhors his varnish & pretense, what comfort can that man have in any of his approaches to God who regards him in his heart; his conscience reproaches him—he knows he is still in his sins & his religion is in vain.

One of Alison's favorite texts was "Seek the Lord while he may be found." "O Sinner," Alison said, "When you read or hear such calls from the Sacred Scripture believe that when God your father calls you, that it is dangerous, it is presumtion to disobey his heavenly calls." [68]

Such declarations may have reflected some desire on Alison's part to counter revivalist charges that the Old Side was religiously cold and lax, but even this motive would probably not have swayed a genuine Moderate too far. Without this strain of concern for a solid and orthodox religious commitment, it would be difficult to understand how the 1758 union of the Old Side and New Side could have been effected, shaky as it was, or why Tennent in his *Irenicum* and Alison in his response could have harbored hopes for reconciliation.[69] It would also be difficult to explain the theological and confessional strictness that later characterized the outlook of Alison's students who succeeded him to posts of leadership in the church—men such as John Ewing and Samuel Miller.

Together with his background in the Scottish universities, aspects of Alison's Old Side Presbyterianism itself are sufficient to explain the appeal Hutcheson's moral philosophy had for him. The Old Side repulsion at the emotional excesses of the revivals led Alison as a matter of course to seek help from his friend, Hutcheson, who in his own program to improve the polish and learning of Scottish ministers was an avowed opponent of zealotry and enthusiasm of all sorts. That

[68] Francis Alison, Manuscript Sermons, Presbyterian Historical Society, Philadelphia, Pennsylvania, MS Al 4.

[69] Alison's only published sermon was the one calling for reunion, in which he made peace overtures to the New Side by commending the efforts to heal the church divisions that had been made by Dickinson, Burr, Blair, and Gilbert Tennent—singling out Tennent especially. Francis Alison, *Peace and Union Recommended, A Sermon Preached before the Reverend Synod of Philadelphia and the Reverend Commission of the Synod of New York at Philadelphia, May 24, 1758* (Philadelphia: W. Dunlap, 1758).

Hutcheson's analysis of the affections offered resources for the development of a conversion psychology was not missed by Jonathan Edwards, but Hutcheson's emphatic distinction between the calm and the violent passions may have seemed to Alison to rule out the philosophical validity of the revivalist position.[70] The strong awareness of the larger social world intrinsic in the broad classical outlook common to Hutcheson and Alison, and the Old Side tendency toward a form of clerical elitism emphasizing church order—both fit naturally with the attention given by Hutcheson to social structures and institutions, and with Alison's own easy movement into William Smith's program of studies at the College of Philadelphia, with its underlying educational and social elitism.

Finally, the Old Side concern, which appears repeatedly in Alison's preaching, with obedience to the moral law rather than conversion as the essence of true religion could find support in Hutcheson's stress upon virtue and the moral sense. Writing to Stiles in 1759, Alison explained why he thought moral philosophy "should be a business of greater care & closer application than is now the common practice." "Without this branch of knowledge," he said, "we shall be ill able to defend our holy christian religion; to understand the rights of mankind; or to explain & enforce the duties which we owe to God, our neighbors, & our selves." [71]

Although the Old Side outlook was not that of Scottish Moderatism, it was vulnerable to a drift in that direction, as Alison himself learned to his dismay when Presbyterian students at the College of Philadelphia began to enter the more latitudinarian Anglican Church. "Young men educated here," Alison complained to Stiles in 1766, asserting his readiness to quit the college because of what he saw happening, "get a taste for high life & many of them do not like to bear the poverty & dependence of our ministers." Several of them, he reported, had already been enticed by their Anglican friends to sail to London for their orders. They, not Alison, were the genuine Moderates in the American Presbyterian church.[72]

---

[70] "But beside the calm motions or affections of the soul," Hutcheson had written, ". . . there are also others of a very different nature; certain vehement turbulent Impulses, which upon certain occurences naturally agitate the soul, and hurry it on with a blind inconsiderate force to certain actions, pursuits, or efforts to avoid, exerted about such things as we have never deliberately determined to be of consequence to happiness or misery." Hutcheson, *Compend*, pp. 8–9.

[71] Alison to Stiles, May 27, 1759, in Stiles, *Itineraries*, p. 423.

[72] Alison to Stiles, October 30, 1766, in Stiles, *Itineraries*, p. 428. If one were to categorize Alison, the term "Old Calvinist Presbyterian" would be more accurate than

After the union of 1758, difficulties persisted between the Old Side and New Side that eventually culminated in an unsuccessful attempt in 1766, led by Alison and his student John Ewing, to gain control of the College of New Jersey. Part of the continued friction between the two parties was simply partisan politics, part of it was theological and social. Throughout the entire period the differences between the two parties were reflected in their attitudes toward learning. Despite many similarities in the actual courses of study in their respective academies, the conception of the religious and social function of learning and the educational priorities of the two groups were significantly different.

In one area of learning—philosophy—these differences were especially apparent, as a brief comparative glance at Jonathan Edwards' treatment of Hutcheson will indicate. Edwards' reaction to Hutcheson should also help to illustrate how early and widespread was the acquaintance with Scottish thought, and how seriously it was taken on all sides. In his important essay *The Nature of True Virtue* (written, 1755; published, 1765), Edwards undertook a dialogue with Francis Hutcheson and Lord Shaftesbury.[73] He accepted the central terms and concepts of their analysis of the nature and foundation of virtue. Hutcheson and Shaftesbury had argued that virtue consists in benevolence or disinterested affections toward others. Edwards agreed

"Moderate." As Gaustad has shown in his treatment of the Great Awakening in New England, two major groups opposed the revivalists: the theological liberals and the so-called Old Calvinists who distrusted the emotionalism of the revivalists, but who valued doctrinal orthodoxy more highly than did the liberals. If parallels were to be drawn, the New England liberals and the Scottish Moderates would be the corresponding groups. Trinterud himself has pointed out that the Old Side preaching was fully orthodox. The element of truth in Trinterud's ascription of "Moderate" to Alison was that the Old Calvinist legalistic stress on discipline and the moral law sometimes facilitated a movement by Old Calvinists to the Moderate position, with its emphasis upon the social code and refined conduct. See Edwin Scott Gaustad, *The Great Awakening in New England* (New York: Harper & Brothers, 1957); compare Trinterud, *The Forming of an American Tradition*, p. 184. On the tendency of the Scottish legalists, or "Neo-Nomians," as they were called, to move toward Moderatism, see John McLeod, *Scottish Theology in Relation to Church History Since the Reformation* (Edinburgh: The Free Church of Scotland, 1943), pp. 198–205.

73 Jonathan Edwards, *The Nature of True Virtue*, in *The Works of Jonathan Edwards*, edited by Sereno E. Dwight (10 vols.; New York: G. & C. & H. Carvill, 1829–1830) III, 93–157. Aldridge correctly notes that Edwards' essay can be considered as an extended commentary on Hutcheson's *An Inquiry into the Original of Our Ideas of Beauty and Virtue* (1725). Aldridge analyzes Edwards' argument in detail. A. O. Aldridge, "Edwards and Hutcheson," *The Harvard Theological Review*, XLIV (1951), 40 ff. For an analysis slightly different from that of Aldridge, see Clarence Faust and Thomas Johnson, eds., *Jonathan Edwards, Selections* (New York: Hill and Wang, 1962), pp. lxxc–xciii.

with this definition, and he also concurred that the recognition of virtuous affections and actions is akin to a sense of taste or beauty. To this extent Edwards was very much on the side of Hutcheson and the ethical empiricists who regarded the emotions as more important than reason or the will in governing human actions. Edwards had already found in the empirical analysis of the affections an indispensable conceptual tool for spelling out his doctrine of conversion.[74]

Edwards' concern in the essay on virtue, however, was not to explore the dynamics of conversion as such, but to demonstrate that true benevolence has its ultimate ground only in conversion. Accepting Hutcheson's and Shaftesbury's definition of virtue and utilizing their terminology, Edwards' tactic in the essay was then to attempt to subvert their argument for his own purposes by pushing it to the extreme. He did this by simply permitting no compromise in what his opponents' definition of true benevolence entailed. Hutcheson had written that "the most useful action imaginable loses all appearance of Benevolence as soon as we discover that it only flows from Self-love or Interest." [75] This was all that Edwards needed. Having taken Shaftesbury and Hutcheson on their own terms, he proceeded to argue that everything they had described as benevolence could be explained as a manifestation of interest. In a devastating analysis of pity, family love, moral conscience, charity, patriotism, and sympathy, Edwards showed that all could be attributed to self-love, natural instinct, or an appreciation of natural beauty, which Edwards had been careful to distinguish from the higher beauty of virtue.[76]

In Edwards' view the reason that men are incapable of true benevolence is that they live out of a narrow circle of experience as if it were the whole. This was the nature of sin: erecting from one's own interest "a private system" without regard for other beings or for being in general. Benevolence is possible only when the private system is broken and the individual sees himself as a participant in the whole of reality and is thus enabled to act accordingly.[77] For

---

[74] See Jonathan Edwards, *Religious Affections*, edited by John E. Smith (New Haven: Yale University Press, 1959).

[75] Francis Hutcheson, *An Inquiry into the Original of Our Ideas of Beauty and Virtue; In Two Treatises*, 2nd ed. (London: Printed for J. Darby, A. Bettesworth, 1726), Treatise II, p. 140.

[76] Edwards, *True Virtue*, pp. 118 ff.

[77] "True benevolence," Edwards wrote, "most essentially consists in benevolence to Being in general. Or perhaps to speak more accurately, it is that consent, propensity, and union of heart to Being in general, that is immediately exercised in a general good will." *Ibid.*, p. 94.

Edwards the private system could only be broken from without by the onslaught of universal being. The crumbling of the private system he called "conversion."

Compressing Edwards' argument as severely as this does not do justice to him or to his antagonists, but the main point of interest here is his critical appropriation of Hutcheson's thought. In a way Edwards, in *True Virtue*, was offering a case study in the application of the revivalists' dictum that divinity should be the capstone of the curriculum. Edwards was illustrating in practice how evangelical divinity supplied criteria for testing and reshaping points of view in those areas of the curriculum that touched upon ethics and religion. The method of the critique was selective and did not necessarily involve wholesale rejection of the opposing position.

What is of special interest in *True Virtue* is that while Edwards worked to undermine Hutcheson's main assumption—the possibility of true benevolence in natural man—he also adopted and preserved much in Hutcheson that he deemed valuable, including Hutcheson's terminology and a good portion of his empirical psychology. Experiential religion and empirical ethics both focused on the emotions as the center of the human personality.

It would be some time before the New Side would again encounter the thought of Francis Hutcheson and his Scottish followers in their own midst, but it is clear that even in philosophy both Old Side and New Side had very early discovered important common resources in Scotland, although their interpretations diverged radically. A recognition of this will help to make many later developments at the College of New Jersey much more understandable.

The most stubbornly recurring tensions in the church after the union of 1758 would continue to concern the standards of ministerial education and the question of conversion. Never again, however, would the issues be framed as starkly as they had been before 1758, for they were being blurred by the sweep of larger events. The College of New Jersey was becoming more cosmopolitan, more involved with other educational institutions, as its alumni went to Philadelphia and Europe for graduate professional studies. Resurgent Scotch-Irish immigration, which reached its peak in the eighteenth century between 1771 and 1773, posed new problems for the church and upset old balances of control. As the quarrel with England intensified, issues of national politics encompassed all parties and eclipsed the importance of their earlier disagreements. And, finally, as the first generation of church leaders began to die off, the church took the occasion to look for someone who could wrest genuine unity out of the agreement of 1758. In John Witherspoon of Scotland the church found its man.

The Scottish Enlightenment Comes to Princeton: John Witherspoon

The untimely death of Samuel Finley in the summer of 1766 left the College of New Jersey once again without a president. For a brief moment the Old Side leadership in Philadelphia saw the vacancy at Princeton as an unexpected opportunity for themselves. Alarmed and discouraged by the strength of Anglican influence at the College of Philadelphia, the Old Side concocted a plan to take over the New Jersey institution. The Old Side scheme was to propose to the trustees of the College of New Jersey, when they met in November to choose a successor to Finley, that Francis Alison be appointed president and John Ewing professor; or, if they were unacceptable, to name Alexander McDowell and Matthew Wilson to the posts. The plan, however, became known to the trustees, who kept the Old Side delegation waiting while they proceeded to elect John Witherspoon of Scotland president. When the delegation of prominent Old Side laymen from Philadelphia was finally admitted to the meeting, they found themselves confronted with a fait accompli, and could do nothing but return home empty-handed.[1]

By choosing John Witherspoon, a man who had not been party to either faction, the trustees of the college were taking a step patently intended to transcend the bitterness that had divided the church for more than a quarter of a century. Despite his chagrin, Francis Alison himself acknowledged, grudgingly to be sure, the conciliatory possibilities in the choice of Witherspoon. "They the trustees," Alison wrote to Stiles,

---

[1] Leonard J. Trinterud, *The Forming of an American Tradition* (Philadelphia: The Westminster Press, 1949), pp. 216–220.

have chosen one Wetherspoone, a minister in Paisley in Scotland; he is esteemed as a keen satirical writer, but they know nothing of his academical abilities, nor whether he will accept their offer; . . . whether he can teach anything but Divinity is hard to say. Should he accept the invitation and undertake this Province, this would be a likely way to unite us, but in the meantime the College is sinking in its reputation for the want of a head.[2]

Witherspoon almost did not accept. Two years of confusing negotiations passed before the Doctor and his wife were persuaded to leave Paisley for Princeton.[3]

I

To understand Witherspoon's life and work in America, it is important to realize that when he came to America he was forty-five years old and already at the height of his career as a respected and leading minister in the Church of Scotland. Witherspoon may first have come to the serious attention of American Presbyterians through Gilbert Tennent and Samuel Davies as a result of their money-raising trip to Great Britain in 1753 for the College of New Jersey.[4]

When Tennent and Davies arrived in Scotland they had already spent many hours visiting leaders of the dissenting churches of England. There they had been disturbed to discover that their English Presbyterian brothers did not all hold to strict Calvinist principles.[5] Davies was even more deeply distressed to find a similar erosion of the faith among many powerful figures in the Church of Scotland who were using their positions in the church government to enforce their opinions.

It was encouraging to Davies to note, however, that strong opposition was being mounted by such men as John Witherspoon. "I find," Davies wrote in his Journal,

[2] Alison to Stiles, December 4, 1766, in *Extracts from the Itineraries of Ezra Stiles,* edited by Franklin B. Dexter (New Haven: Yale University Press, 1916), p. 430.
[3] A documentary account of the negotiations between Witherspoon and the trustees, with many of the letters exchanged, is presented by L. H. Butterfield, *John Witherspoon Comes to America* (Princeton: Princeton University Press, 1953).
[4] In the same year Witherspoon published an essay on Lord Kames in the *Scots Magazine* which was sent by John Erskine of Edinburgh to Joseph Bellamy of New England. Collins says this was Witherspoon's introduction to American readers. Varnum Lansing Collins, *President Witherspoon* (2 vols.; Princeton: Princeton University Press, 1925), I, 41.
[5] See Davies' Journal in W. H. Foote, *Sketches of Virginia* (2 vols.; Philadelphia: J. B. Lippincott & Co., 1850), I, 253, 257, 268.

a great number of the clergy and laity have of late carried church-power to an extravagant height, deny to individuals the right of judging for themselves, and insist upon absolute universal obedience to all the determinations of the General Assembly. I heard sundry speeches in the House on this head, which really surprised me. The nobility and gentry who are lay-elders, are generally high-flyers: and have encroached upon the rights of the people, especially as to the choice of their own ministers. Violent settlements are enjoined by the authority of the General Assembly, and there is no prospect of a redress.—There is a piece published under the title of the Ecclesiastical Characteristics, ascribed to one Mr. Wetherspoon, a young minister. It is burlesque upon the high-flyers under the ironical name of moderate men: and I think the humour is nothing inferior to Dean Swift.[6]

Although Davies had completely muddled his labels, he had correctly identified many of the main issues and chief protagonists of the struggle.[7]

Tennent and Davies were in Scotland at a time when the conflict between the Moderate and Evangelical parties in the Scottish Church had entered its most virulent and critical phase. Theological and social differences in the church had intensified during the first half of the century, and on occasion had already resulted in actual schism. With the formation of the Associate Presbytery under Ebenezer Erskine in 1733, in opposition to the General Assembly's exercise of patronage, and with the final expulsion of Erskine and his followers seven years later, the splintering of the church body had begun in earnest. The first secession of the Associate Presbytery was followed by a second in 1752. That year in another patronage dispute the Moderates, under the astute leadership of William Robertson, successfully demanded that the General Assembly depose Thomas Gillespie of Carnock. This victory was decisive for the Moderates in their rise to control over the established church, although some of the most bitter invective was yet to come.

Angered by a pamphlet personally attacking certain Evangelical ministers who had opposed Moderate policies, John Witherspoon retaliated in 1753 with an anonymous work entitled *Ecclesiastical Characteristics; or the Arcana of Church Policy—being a humble attempt to open up the Mystery of Moderation*. Witherspoon had spoken out before in the General Assembly against the Moderates on

[6] Quoted in Foote, *Sketches of Virginia*, I, 262.
[7] Actually, the epithet "high-flyers" was the name fastened in derision upon Witherspoon's own party by their opponents.

specific issues, but in the *Ecclesiastical Characteristics* he leveled a full-scale satiric assault against the whole character and outlook of the Moderate minister. Witherspoon sketched the guidelines by which the successful Moderate minister conducted himself. Maxim I stated that "All moderate men have a kind of fellow-feeling with heresy." Maxim III required that the subjects of his sermons "be confined to social duties" and that he avoid "the mysteries of grace, which the common people are so fond of." Maxim V held that he must "catch as much of the air and manner of a fine gentleman, as possibly he can." The other requirements, elaborated by Witherspoon in detail, were all variations of these.[8] The work immediately became a sensation, arousing consternation among the Moderates and delighting their enemies. Witherspoon's authorship of the *Ecclesiastical Characteristics* soon became known, and made him one of the major recognized spokesmen for the Evangelical party.

Witherspoon engaged in further pamphlet warfare against the Moderates, but never with quite the devastating effect he had achieved with the *Ecclesiastical Characteristics*. Perhaps one of the most important controversies in which he became involved was over the stage play *Douglas* in 1757. Written by John Home, minister of Athelstaneford, this play was performed in Edinburgh, and among those attending were ministers of the Moderate party, who were also seen fraternizing with the actresses during rehearsals. The theater had always been suspect in Calvinist Scotland, and reaction from the stricter Presbyterians to *Douglas* and the conduct of their ministers was prompt and vigorous. Witherspoon led the attack with *A Serious Inquiry into the Nature and Effects of the Stage*, showing the moral corruption of the theater and the unchristian character of ministers who attended it.[9] However, when charges were brought before the General Assembly against the ministers involved, especially against Alexander Carlyle, the Popular, or Evangelical, party succeeded in exacting only mild penalties.[10] The Moderate persuasion was becoming well entrenched.

Many accounts of Witherspoon which take notice of the Church

---

[8] John Witherspoon, *The Works of John Witherspoon* (9 vols.; Edinburgh: John Turnbull, 1805), VI, 153–222. Unless otherwise noted all references to Witherspoon's writings will be from this nine-volume Edinburgh edition of his works.
[9] Witherspoon, *Works*, VI, 34–128.
[10] William Law Mathieson, *The Awakening of Scotland* (Glasgow: James Maclehose and Sons, 1910), pp. 160–168.

of Scotland controversies in which he participated look only at the split between the Moderates and the Evangelicals. The result is an oversimplified picture which contrasts liberal Moderates with conservative Evangelicals. From this perspective Witherspoon then emerges as the leader of the conservatives in the Church of Scotland. While there is much truth in this interpretation, it is also misleading, for it does not do justice to the complexity of Witherspoon's peculiar relationship to either the Evangelicals on the one hand or the Moderates on the other. Consequently, the real significance of Witherspoon's role in the Scottish Church is obscured, and the first key to an understanding of his American involvement is lost.

John Witherspoon resisted the control of the Moderates in the General Assembly at every opportunity, in print and in church debate, but he never joined the Secession movement. The really radical Evangelicals were leaving the Church of Scotland for the Associate Presbytery of Erskine and his men, or for the Relief Church formally organized by Thomas Gillespie in 1761. Although comparative figures are difficult to obtain, it was said in 1765 that over 120 churches and more than 100,000 persons had joined the Secessionists.[11] The schism had reached alarming proportions and was growing.

Witherspoon had given strong support to the Evangelical manifesto against the exclusion of Gillespie, if he did not, in fact, actually help write it.[12] Nevertheless, the overriding significance of Witherspoon's position in the struggle was that he served as leader of those Evangelicals who chose to remain within the Church of Scotland even though they were a minority group. Witherspoon constantly defended the traditional doctrines of Calvinism, as he understood them, against their neglect and secularization by the Moderates. He was increasingly concerned, however, to make some room for basic agreement without sacrificing the fundamentals.

Two of Witherspoon's most important religious tracts were his *Essay on Justification* (1756) and *Treatise on Regeneration* (1764), written to educate the general church member in the essential doctrines of the church. Both stressed the authority of scripture, the sovereignty of God, the sinfulness of man, and justification of the sinner through "the imputed righteousness of Christ." The *Essay* was unsparing in its criticism of Moderate ministers who avoided these

[11] *Ibid.*, p. 176.
[12] Collins, *President Witherspoon*, I, 33.

hard doctrines in exchange for popularity.[13] By 1764, however, having seen the failure of his efforts to check the Moderate influence, Witherspoon struck a conciliatory note with the publication of his *Treatise on Regeneration*. Here, rather than launching another frontal attack, Witherspoon presented the doctrine of regeneration as one which all sides could accept as central. "The subject I have made choice of," he wrote,

and intend to handle in the ensuing treatise, immediately regards the substance of religion, and is happily as little entangled in controversy as any that could be named. We are told, that 'except a man be born again, he cannot see the kingdom of God.' In this all parties, every profession and denomination of Christians do or ought to agree.[14]

In the conclusion to the *Treatise* he returned again to the same theme:

This may teach us, what judgment Christians ought to form of the many parties and factions which divide the visible Church. There may be many differences, which keep them asunder on earth, while, in faith and in love to an unseen Savior, they are, perfectly united.[15]

Even in the earlier *Essay* Witherspoon had explicity stated his desire to treat controversial doctrines in a way that would minimize differences as much as possible. "The reason of my doing so," he said, "is that I would willingly rather reconcile, than widen these differences. . . ."[16]

In relation to the Moderates, Witherspoon was a religious conservative, and his defense of traditional doctrine never wavered. Yet in comparison with those sizable elements within the Evangelical fold that were deserting the establishment Witherspoon was in a genuine sense, if not a Moderate, at least moderate. Schism was repugnant to him, and while he did battle with his opponents, he remained with them in the national church. A recognition of this will help to explain much about Witherspoon's activity in America that always seems to defy description in terms of "liberal" or "conservative."

The mediating position taken by Witherspoon, manifest in his

---

[13] Witherspoon, *Essay on the Connection between the Doctrine of Justification by the Imputed Righteousness of Christ, Works*, I, 36–104, especially 38.
[14] Witherspoon, *A Practical Treatise on Regeneration, Works*, I, 109–110.
[15] *Ibid.*, pp. 314–315
[16] Witherspoon, *Works*, I, 49.

refusal to join the Seceders despite his sympathy with them, may very well have helped to inspire hopes among American Presbyterians that he would try to reconcile both sides of their church. Certainly the Americans had other good reasons for hoping that he could effect a meaningful reconciliation. In the first place, Witherspoon brought with him the prestige of being one of the most respected leaders of the Evangelical party in the Church of Scotland. Although he had suffered ultimate defeat in the General Assembly, he had held high posts in the church, having been elected Moderator of the Synod of Glasgow and Ayr (1759), and his published writings were widely read and admired. In the second place, his outlook in theology and church polity appeared to meet the demands of both Old Side and New Side. He was an orthodox Presbyterian, insistent upon church order and authority, but as an Evangelical he also favored a strong laity and an active congregational life. Like the New Side, Witherspoon spoke of the need for conversion; but, like the Old Side, he staunchly insisted on sound doctrine. After years of ill-suppressed distrust and hostility both Old Side and New Side must have found Witherspoon's concern for the unity of the church extremely attractive.

II

On an August Sunday in 1768 the Reverend Doctor and Mrs. Witherspoon disembarked from the brig *Peggy* in Philadelphia. They were met at the docks by leading gentlemen of the city who entertained the new arrivals in their homes for several days. On August 12 they set out by carriage for Princeton. At Trenton they were greeted by a delegation of citizens and college trustees living in the neighborhood, and at the province line, about a mile from Princeton, they found the faculty, undergraduates, and townspeople assembled to conduct them to their new home. That night candles burned in all the windows of Nassau Hall. "Our reception," wrote Witherspoon to Benjamin Rush, an American medical student in Edinburgh who had played a crucial role in convincing the Witherspoons to leave Scotland, "has even exceeded Your own hyperbolical promises. God grant that I may be in any respect worthy of it. . . ." [17] The arrival of John Witherspoon in 1768 signaled the beginning of a new period

[17] Butterfield, *Witherspoon Comes to America*, pp. 76–78.

in the intellectual and religious life of the church and the College of New Jersey.

Witherspoon lost no time in making needed contacts and rounding up support for himself and the college. Immediately after his arrival he made his first visit to New York and New England with the Reverend John Rodgers.[18] After this visit the Reverend Charles Chauncy in Boston wrote to Ezra Stiles describing Witherspoon as:

a gentleman of good learning, strong powers, and a catholic, charitable Spirit. We are highly pleased he has come over to be president of the Jersey-College. We are persuaded he will do better than any who have gone before him. He is no friend to the grand and distinguishing Tenets of Mr. Edwards which have been almost universally imbibed in that part of the Country.[19]

Had it become known to them, New Side ministers would have found this testimony from the chief New England critic of revivalism most disquieting. It is clear from the impression he made on Chauncy, however, that John Witherspoon was determined to be his own man, and not to allow past disputes in which he had had no part to stand in his way.

Again, just after the college commencement of 1769, Witherspoon departed for Virginia to raise funds and to publicize the college. On this and a second trip to Virginia the following February, he preached, collected funds, and made the acquaintance of prominent Virginia families, including the Madisons, Lees, and Washingtons. Within little more than a year Witherspoon had made himself a nationally known figure, and had given notice that the college had a leader.

John Witherspoon strengthened the course of study at the College of New Jersey in at least three important ways. He gave attention to improving teaching methods and materials and to raising academic standards; he broadened and enriched the curriculum; and he brought to his students the stimulus of his own vigorous mind and personality. One of Witherspoon's first projects was to improve the instructional materials at the college. Before sailing he had visited London and Holland and arranged for the purchase of books and apparatus. He brought over three hundred volumes with him, and

[18] These trips are described in detail by Collins, *Witherspoon*, I, 113 f., 125 f.
[19] Chauncy to Stiles, November 19, 1768, quoted in Collins, *Witherspoon*, I, 114.

informed the trustees that "another considerable benefaction in Books" was on its way.[20] The acquisitions to the library contained theological, political, and educational treatises, including works by French Calvinists and almost all the modern Scottish authors—Robertson, Hume, Hutcheson, Kames, Adam Smith, Ferguson, and others.

Always shrewd, always prudent, but seldom indecisive, Witherspoon, immediately after his arrival at the college, purchased the famous Rittenhouse orrery literally out from under William Smith at Philadelphia. Smith had coveted the orrery for his own college, and was incensed that Rittenhouse would consent to let his noble invention go "to a village." Witherspoon had also acquired a "terrestrial Globe," and upon purchasing the orrery he appointed the tutor William Churchhill Houston as Curator of the Philosophical Equipment.[21]

A week after his inauguration Witherspoon advertised in the papers that he was taking the college grammar school under his own personal direction. The next spring he ran another advertisement for the grammar school depicting the advances that had been made. Latin was being taught according to the methods of the grammar school in Glasgow, "the seat of one of the universities in Scotland"; maps and the terrestrial globe were in use for geography; and arithmetic and the mastery of English were stressed.[22] The same year Witherspoon announced his intention to maintain high academic standards in the college. The entrance requirements were to be strictly enforced; and any boy applying for admission to any class above the freshman would be required to take the commencement examination of the next lower class, or, if this was impossible, he would be tested in comparison with three boys chosen by ballot from the class he desired to enter.[23]

Witherspoon chose to build upon and extend the basic pattern of the curriculum as he found it. Presidents Dickinson, Burr, Davies, and Finley had successively striven to provide as modern a course of study as possible and to include the same subjects as those taught in European universities, "save only such," they said, "as may be

---

[20] John Maclean, *History of the College of New Jersey* (2 vols.; Philadelphia: J. B. Lippincott & Co., 1877), I, 301–302; Collins, *Witherspoon*, I, 90.

[21] Howard Crosby Rice, *The Rittenhouse Orrery; Princeton's Eighteen-Century Planetarium, 1767–1954* (Princeton: Princeton University Library, 1954), pp. 32–36; Francis L. Broderick, "Pulpit, Physics, and Politics: The Curriculum of the College of New Jersey, 1746–1794," *William and Mary Quarterly*, 3rd ser., VI (1949), 60.

[22] The advertisement is reprinted in full in Collins, *Witherspoon*, I, 121–122.

[23] *Ibid.*, I, 125.

occasioned by the infancy of this institution."²⁴ The curriculum
Witherspoon found at the college was essentially that begun under
Burr and filled out by those who followed him according to their
own individual gifts and interests: first year—classics and logic; second
year—more classics and some geography and astronomy; third year—
natural and moral philosophy; fourth year—review. To this Finley
had added chronology and his English studies.

Witherspoon described the curriculum at the college in 1772 in
a pamphlet originally written as an appeal for students and funds in
the West Indies. When plans for the West Indies trip collapsed, however, the article was published in several American papers. It is clear
that under Witherspoon the curriculum was broadened and more
sharply delineated, while at the same time continuity with the past
was maintained. "The regular course of instruction is in four classes,"
Witherspoon wrote,

exactly after the manner, and bearing the names of the classes in the
English universities: Freshman, Sophomore, Junior, and Senior. In the
first year they read Latin and Greek, with Roman and Grecian antiquities,
and rhetoric. In the second, continuing the study of the languages, they
learn a complete system of geography, with the use of the globes, the
first principles of philosophy, and the elements of mathematical knowledge. The third, though the languages are not wholly omitted, is chiefly
employed in mathematics and natural philosophy. And the senior year is
employed in reading the higher classics, proceeding in the mathematics
and natural philosophy, and going through a course of moral philosophy.
In addition to these, the President gives lectures to the juniors and seniors,
which consequently every student hears twice over in his course, first
upon chronology and history, and afterwards upon composition and
criticism. He has also taught the French language last winter, and it will
continue to be taught to those who desire to learn it.²⁵

The names of the classes were, indeed, those of the English
universities, but the course of study now displayed almost the exact
pattern of the Aberdeen reform curriculum. This resemblance to the
Scottish program appears to have been more than accidental. In his
pamphlet Witherspoon cited as one of his chief qualifications his

²⁴ The development of the early curriculum at Princeton has been sketched by
Broderick, in "Pulpit, Physics, and Politics," pp. 42–60. Also see Maclean, *History
of the College of New Jersey*, I, 132–133, 140–142, 165, 174–177, 207, 216–217, 266–267.
²⁵ Witherspoon, "Address to the Inhabitants of Jamaica, and other West-India
Islands, in behalf of the College of New Jersey," *Works*, VIII, 318–319.

thorough knowledge of Scottish university practices acquired through his own education at Edinburgh and his "constant intercourse and great intimacy with the members of the university of Glasgow." The professor of moral philosophy at Glasgow since 1763 had, incidentally, been none other than Thomas Reid, formerly professor of the same subject at King's College, Aberdeen. Any young gentleman "has all possible advantages, particularly in North Britain, for improving himself" in all the classic and modern subjects, said Witherspoon, while strongly implying that young gentlemen at the College of New Jersey now enjoyed many of the same opportunities.[26]

Witherspoon frankly acknowledged to his readers that the curriculum he had described was still something of an ideal since lack of funds and personnel had handicapped its full development. "The whole branches of mathematics and natural philosophy are now taught by one professor; and the president is obliged to teach divinity and moral philosophy, as well as chronology, history, and rhetoric, besides the superintendence and government of the whole." The donations being requested would, therefore, be expressly for the creation of new professorships.[27]

Witherspoon himself was not accomplished in mathematics or astronomy, but he was fully aware of their importance in the modern college curriculum. The first professorship of mathematics and natural philosophy was established under Witherspoon in 1771. Initially filled by William Churchhill Houston, this post was assumed in 1787 by Walter Minto, a mathematician from Edinburgh.[28] In his own lectures Witherspoon underlined the importance of scientific studies whenever the opportunity presented itself. He devoted entire sections in his lectures on history and chronology, for example, to science and industry, and pointed out to his students the value of "good astronomical memoirs" in fixing the accuracy of historical events.[29]

As a teacher Witherspoon was noted for his lectures in divinity, eloquence, history, and moral philosophy, which were required of all college graduates. In his lecture method Witherspoon introduced the Scottish university practice of requiring each student to make his own personal copy of a syllabus, or full course outline, that he himself had first prepared. This syllabus then served as a basic text to be elaborated

26 *Ibid.*, p. 312.
27 *Ibid.*, p. 330
28 Maclean, *History of the College of New Jersey*, I, 347.
29 John Witherspoon, *Lectures on History*, Manuscript, Princeton University Library, see especially, Lectures II and IV.

upon in the actual classroom session.[30] The impact of Witherspoon's lectures inspired his colleague in the church, John Rodgers, to remark, "The stile of learning, if you will allow me the phrase, has been changed by him."

Witherspoon conducted the college with a firm hand. Strict study hours were set and students were not allowed to leave their rooms without permission. Witherspoon's own maxim was, "Govern always, but beware of governing too much." The many anecdotes which attest to his ability to maintain discipline at the college suggest that the force of his personality was enough to inspire order in most situations.[31] Ashbel Green said of Witherspoon that "he had more of the quality called *presence*" than any other man of his time except General Washington.[32] The unruly students of Robert Finley, a young tutor at the college who later set up an academy at Baskingridge, discovered in a typical incident how awesome Witherspoon's presence could be. When Finley found himself unable to control his pupils, he appealed to Witherspoon for help. Witherspoon not only quickly restored order, but also found it unnecessary ever to appear before Finley's students on a similar mission again.[33]

During the first years of his administration Witherspoon worked indefatigably to promote the College of New Jersey. He also took steps to ensure that he was recognized as its undisputed head by undercutting threats to his leadership from both the Old Side and New Side factions of the church. He tried to sabotage the efforts of Ewing and Williamson to raise funds in Britain for the Newark Academy, and he appears to have led the opposition to Alison's attempt to place an Old Side minister in the Third Church of Philadelphia.[34] The more radical New Side disciples of Edwardsean theology, however, could gain slight comfort from the friction between Witherspoon and Alison. When Witherspoon had first arrived at the college he had found the three tutors, Joseph Periam, John Blair, and Jonathan Edwards, Jr., vigorously propounding the Berkeleian metaphysics so dear to the Edwardseans. Witherspoon's response was

---

[30] See John Witherspoon, *Lectures on Moral Philosophy*, edited by Varnum Lansing Collins (Princeton: Princeton University Press, 1912), Introduction, p. xxii.

[31] See Thomas Jefferson Wertenbaker, *Princeton, 1746–1896* (Princeton: Princeton University Press, 1946), pp. 104–106.

[32] William Sprague, *Annals of the American Pulpit* (New York: R. Carter and Brothers, 1858), III, 297.

[33] Recounted by Isaac V. Brown, in *Memoirs of the Reverend Robert Finley, D.D.* (New Brunswick, N.J.: Terhune & Letson, 1812), p. 14 ff.

[34] Trinterud, *Forming of an American Tradition*, pp. 222–223.

prompt. "He first reasoned against the system," says Ashbel Green, "and then ridiculed it till he drove it out of the college." [35] It took him less than a year; by 1769 the three tutors he had found at the college had all resigned and were replaced by men more congenial to Witherspoon himself.[36]

Witherspoon's opposition to Periam and the other tutors was without question motivated in part by his genuine aversion to philosophical idealism of any sort. It was also a politically astute move. From that time on there was no doubt that Witherspoon would wear the mantle of intellectual leadership of the Presbyterian church that had traditionally fallen upon the shoulders of the President of the College of New Jersey. By keeping the upper hand over the Old Side as well, Witherspoon protected himself from incursions on his leadership from the other direction.

Witherspoon envisaged a prime role for the College of New Jersey in shaping the future of the new country. In the newspaper advertisement written initially for the West Indies, Witherspoon set forth what he saw as the purposes of a liberal education, the kind offered, of course, at the College of New Jersey. Education, he declared, is a promoter of arts, virtue, and industry; a "preservative" against riot and disorder; and an encouragement to public service "in offices of power or trust." [37] Witherspoon noted that already "the great utility of this seminary has been felt over an extensive country."

His recommendation of the college because of its strategic location and the number of its graduates was promotional writing with fact behind it. By the time of the Revolution the College of New Jersey was, as Trinterud has described it, "the least localized of any in America . . . both in the sources of its students and in the distribution of its alumni." [38] The training of public leaders and the promotion of the useful sciences had been goals of the college from the beginning and ones which Witherspoon was determined to keep in the forefront.

In a sense, as one writer has claimed, the College of New Jersey under Witherspoon did become "less a theological seminary, more a

[35] Quoted in E. A. Smith, *The Presbyterian Ministry in American Culture* (Philadelphia: The Westminster Press, 1962), p. 91.
[36] Maclean, *History of the College of New Jersey*, I, 307–308.
[37] Witherspoon, "Address . . . in behalf of the College," *Works*, VIII, 308–309.
[38] *Ibid.*, pp. 325–326; Trinterud, *Forming of an American Tradition*, p. 243. Trinterud's figures, taken from E. B. Greene, *Revolutionary Generation*, show that approximately one fourth of the college alumni were living in New England, one half in the middle colonies, and one fourth in the south.

school for statesmen," but this represented no abandonment of the college's original and repeatedly emphasized ideals.[39] The charter of 1748 spoke of a college erected "for the benefit of the inhabitants of the said province and others wherein youth may be instructed in the learned languages, and in the liberal arts and Sciences." [40] It is true, as Gilbert Tennent and Samuel Davies wrote in the informational pamphlet they sent ahead of their journey to Great Britain, that the "immediate Motive" to the founding of the college was the growing need for ministers; but "the two principal Objects the Trustees had in view," Tennent and Davies hastened to add, "were Science and Religion." Though this was certainly putting up the best possible front to attract potential donors of whatever religious and educational bias—Tennent and Davies were raising money—still their little tract is a fairly reliable guide to the early aims of the college and its emphasis upon a broad course of study.[41]

Illustrations of the commitment of the college leaders long before Witherspoon to modern learning and public service appear repeatedly. One of Jonathan Edwards' main doubts about accepting the presidency of the college, for example, arose from his deficiency, as he described it, "in some parts of learning, particularly in Algebra and the higher parts of Mathematics, and in the Greek classics; my Greek having been chiefly in New Testament." [42] At the 1762 commencement, morning and evening exercises closed with the singing of two hymns, "An Ode to Science" and "An Ode to Peace," composed by President Davies.[43] "Religion and Useful Learning," "Religion and Science," "Religion and Public Spirit"—these were the central rhetorical phrases describing the aims of the college from its start. That this was not mere rhetoric, however, was apparent in the constantly renewed efforts before Witherspoon to modernize the curriculum and to emphasize the goal of public service.

Witherspoon's work at the College of New Jersey was in part

[39] See James L. McAllister, "John Witherspoon: Academic Advocate for American Freedom," in Stuart C. Henry, ed., *A Miscellany of American Christianity* (Durham, N.C.: Duke University Press, 1963), pp. 219–224.
[40] Quoted in Maclean, *History of the College of New Jersey*, I, 176.
[41] The listed priorities of needs, for example, included in order: a dormitory for students, a residence for the president, books for the library, and "Apparatus for Philosophical Experiments." Princeton University, *A General Account of the Rise and State of the College Lately Established in the Province of New-Jersey in America . . . for the Information of the Friends of Learning and Piety in Great Britain* (London, 1752, reprinted, 1754), especially pp. 4, 6.
[42] Quoted by Maclean, *History of the College of New Jersey*, I, 176.
[43] *Ibid.*, I, 217.

continuous with the original college ideals. Nevertheless, enormous changes did take place in the way these ideals were conceived and expressed—changes that were subtle in their beginnings and far-reaching in their consequences. Intellectually, culturally, and politically, Witherspoon helped to give new content to the educational goals of the college. He provided a way for the Presbyterian college to come to terms with the Enlightenment; he transformed the ideal images of the minister, the public servant, and the man of learning; and he politicized the college in a new way. The remainder of this chapter will examine each of these areas of Witherspoon's influence in turn. In all of them Witherspoon's Scottish background was a decisive force.

III

As an undergraduate at the University of Edinburgh (1730–1736), where he studied under Professor John Stevenson, and as the spokesman against the forces of Moderatism, Witherspoon would not have been able to escape an encounter with the secular thought of his day had he wanted to. Although most of his published writings in Scotland were either sermons or polemic tracts, his master's thesis and his first work in print, a magazine article refuting Lord Kames' views on free will, show evidence of his early concern to work through some of the problems posed to his faith by the philosophical questions then being discussed in Scotland.[44] Called upon at the College of New Jersey to deliver formal lectures in theology and philosophy, Witherspoon was forced to develop his thought more systematically and comprehensively than he had ever done in Scotland. This time, in the lectures, Witherspoon's confrontation with the intellectual issues of the eighteenth century was no longer secondary, but was the central thread that tied the themes of his lectures together.

If Witherspoon's position among the Evangelicals of Scotland helps to explain his ecclesiastical career in America, his even more complex relationship to the Moderates determined many of his dominant intellectual concerns and shaped the manner in which he dealt with them. Witherspoon's involvement with the Moderates must not

[44] Witherspoon's Scottish background has been traced by George Eugene Rich, "John Witherspoon: His Scottish Intellectual Background" (Ph.D. dissertation, Syracuse University, 1964). Witherspoon's master's thesis, "A Philosophical Disputation: Concerning the Immortality of the Mind" (1739), and his article, "Remarks on an Essay on Human Liberty," from the *Scots Magazine*, XV (1753), are printed in their entirety in Rich, Appendix.

be viewed simply as one of opposition. At the University of Edinburgh he had been a classmate of William Robertson, Alexander Carlyle, Hugh Blair, and John Home—all of whom were later to belong to the Moderate inner circle. Witherspoon had even roomed in the same boarding house as Carlyle.[45] Although he was apparently not on intimate terms with them, Witherspoon's college relationship with Carlyle and his associates seems to have been friendly enough. Witherspoon and Hugh Blair collaborated, for example, with four others in successfully petitioning the university to renew the abandoned practice of awarding degrees to graduating arts students upon presentation of a thesis.[46] Though their careers and outlooks were to diverge, the stamp of their early years at the University of Edinburgh was to remain upon Witherspoon as well as his classmates.

With much the same background as the Moderates, it was perhaps natural that Witherspoon did not hesitate to use his opponents' own weapons in his clashes with them. The similarities between Witherspoon and the Moderates are all the more striking by virtue of their opposition. In the *Ecclesiastical Characteristics* Witherspoon expressly stated that he had adopted the method of ridicule recommended by one of the chief philosopher heroes of the Moderates, Lord Shaftesbury.[47] The title, also, was an obvious jab at Shaftesbury's own *Characteristics of Men, Manners, Opinions, Times* (1711).

Witherspoon soon discovered that, even in the age of satire, ridicule without a positive plan of action and organization was not enough. In fashioning his strategy in church politics Witherspoon again emulated his opponents. John Rodgers tells of an encounter between Robertson and Witherspoon in the General Assembly shortly after Witherspoon had outmaneuvered the Moderates on a certain issue. Robertson said to Witherspoon, "in a pleasant and easy manner, 'I think you have your men better disciplined than formerly.' 'Yes,' replied Witherspoon, 'by urging your politics too far, you have compelled us to beat you with your own weapons.' "[48] The apocryphal flavor of the story notwithstanding, it captures the spirit of the man with fine accuracy. At every point Witherspoon attempted to best his enemies on their own grounds, with the consequence that he was

---

[45] Rich, "John Witherspoon," p. vi; also see Alexander Carlyle, *Autobiography* (Boston: Ticknor and Fields, 1861), p. 26.
[46] Rich, "John Witherspoon," p. 57.
[47] Witherspoon, *Works*, VI, 251.
[48] John Rodgers, "Account of the Life of John Witherspoon," in Witherspoon, *Works*, I, xxvii.

influenced by them more than he probably knew. When Witherspoon departed for America, he carried more of the Moderate than he, his Moderate adversaries, or his American friends would have dared to suppose.

Nowhere did the influence of the Moderate outlook on Witherspoon manifest itself more transparently than in Witherspoon's lectures in philosophy and divinity. A close look at these lectures will help to identify the intellectual issues Witherspoon introduced his students to, his method of inquiry and discussion, and his attitude toward learning. Three themes dominate the lectures: Witherspoon's efforts to reconcile faith and reason, his use of the notion of the moral sense, and his appeal to experience as the test of truth.

Witherspoon's college lectures all display his concern as a believer to reconcile reason and revelation. His most extended and explicit discussion of the contending claims of reason and revelation appears in his lectures on divinity.[49] Witherspoon had two primary purposes in building his divinity lectures around this central problem. He wanted to provide his students with a rational basis for their faith that would enable them to hold to it with confidence; and he wanted to equip them to meet attacks upon the faith with the rational arguments that skeptics would respect.

Early in his lectures on divinity Witherspoon introduced his students to the struggle of the church with the forces of skepticism. He cautioned against the example of some ministers who preached as if most members of their congregations were infidels and scoffers. Nevertheless, Witherspoon said, because this controversy had become so "agitated that of late almost all other controversies have been dropped on account of it, or lost in it, a student of divinity should be well informed upon it." [50] The two chief adversaries of the church Witherspoon identified as the deists and the atheists.[51] In his view the "pretended friendship to religion" of the deists made them "worse, if possible, than infidels themselves." [52] The challenge of both was to call into question "the necessity of revelation in general." [53]

Witherspoon's own defense of revelation was threefold. First, he tried to show that there is nothing about reason that should make it inherently opposed to revelation. Drawing almost word for word upon Locke, Witherspoon distinguished between those principles and ideas that are contrary to reason, above reason, and consonant with reason. The doctrine of the trinity, for example, if it be understood that it does not express "mathematical contradiction . . . but only that there is a distinction, consistent with perfect unity of nature," is above, not contrary to reason, in that it is "beyond the power of reason to discover, and above the reach of reason to comprehend." [54]

Second, Witherspoon attempted to demonstrate the strong positive grounds for accepting revelation without sacrificing rationality. He had at his disposal a stock of arguments for the support of revealed religion, and in the lectures on divinity he called upon all of them.[55] Witherspoon had undertaken, as he himself said, the lifelong task of showing that the truths of the Gospel "are agreeable to sound reason, and founded upon the state of human nature." [56] The very demand for rationality, however, frequently led him in anti-intellectual directions.

While assuring his students that the traditional doctrines of Calvinism were ultimately reasonable, Witherspoon time and again found himself unable to render them so in words. Always his recourse was, not to explore other ways of understanding the doctrine, but merely to assert that the doctrine would in the end prove reasonable if only man had the capacity to understand, or if God were to make known all the details involved.[57] "For my own part, I freely own," he said, speaking of the difficulty of reconciling God's fixed and absolute decrees with man's moral accountability,

that I could never see any thing satisfactory in the attempts of divines or metaphysicians to reconcile these two things; but it does not appear difficult to me to believe precisely in the form of our Confession of Faith; to believe both the certainty of God's purpose, and the free agency of the creature. Nor does my being unable to explain these doctrines, form an objection against one or the other.[58]

He rejected the question of whether God might have chosen some other means of redemption than the atonement as "indecent" and assumed a pure positivism of faith. "We have an infinite concern," he

[54] *Ibid.*, pp. 85–87; John Locke, *An Essay Concerning Human Understanding*, edited by A. S. Pringle-Pattison (Oxford: Clarendon Press, 1924), p. 354.
[55] See Witherspoon, "Divinity," *Works*, VIII, 33–62.
[56] *Ibid.*, p. 60.
[57] *Ibid.*, pp. 106 ff., 113 ff., 136 f.
[58] *Ibid.*, p. 119.

said, "in what God has done, but none at all in what he might have done." [59]

There was, to be fair to Witherspoon, an element of modesty in his refusal to attempt more than he was able. Rather than simplistically dismissing doctrines not immediately amenable to reasoned exposition, his approach had the advantage of holding these doctrines in abeyance in the expectation that they would yield resources of truth and understanding in the future. Witherspoon did give expression to such a hope in continually sketching for his students the various positions held on disputed questions, with remarks to the effect that the last word had yet to be spoken. His general tendency on matters of difficult doctrine, however, was to foreclose discussion by recommending acceptance of the creed in the confidence that its affirmations were rational, but that man's limitations and God's greatness prevent full comprehension. "It will be perhaps hard or impossible for you to enter into this at once," he said, regarding the issue of God's liberty in creating the world as it is,

as I confess it was for me in early life; but I now see more of the necessity of subjecting ourselves to the divine sovereignty and making use of it to restrain and repress our rash and curious natures.[60]

Witherspoon tried, finally, to show that reason by itself is inadequate. Rationality, he thought, can carry man far in comprehending his true situation, but not far enough. Revelation is necessary to correct the distortions of unaided reason and to bring it to completion. He held that a knowledge of God is common to all men, but warned against thinking that it could be maintained uncorrupted without the stabilizing and refining influence of revelation. The examples of heathen nations and their fantastic notions of religion offered prime evidence, Witherspoon believed, of the weaknesses of reason alone.[61]

[59] *Ibid.*, p. 136.
[60] *Ibid.*, p. 113.
[61] One of Witherspoon's basic criticisms of the deists' core of rational beliefs, such as that set forth by Lord Herbert of Cherbury, was that these beliefs were in actuality abstracted from the concrete revelation of orthodox Christianity. Such doctrines as propounded by the deists, once they had been discovered in the corpus of orthodox belief and drawn from it, Witherspoon said, "can easily be shewn to be rational . . . and boasted of as the productions of unbiased reason." *Ibid.*, p. 30. This was one of the stock arguments with which Witherspoon's writings are rife. Edwards, for example, also employed it. See Jonathan Edwards, "Man's Natural Blindness in the Things of Religion," *The Works of Jonathan Edwards* (4 vols.; New York: Leavitt, Trow & Co., 1849), IV, 30–31.

Above all, unaided reason could not give the knowledge of God's forgiveness of sin. Divine mercy was to be had only in its actually being granted.[62] Here, it would appear was where Witherspoon drew an absolute line against reason, but before he had reached this point much ground had been yielded.

In all of this there was little new; Witherspoon was not an original thinker. The three main positions taken on religion in the eighteenth century have often been described as rationalism, supernatural rationalism, and skepticism.[63] Witherspoon fits so neatly into this oversimplified schema as a Presbyterian supernatural rationalist that, were it not for his own words on the subject, one might suspect the accuracy of so typing him. It was not in his originality, however, that Witherspoon's significance lay. Rather, it was in his capacity, par excellence, to absorb and re-present certain major trends in eighteenth-century thought.

Witherspoon's blending of faith and reason stood him in good stead in his dual role of churchman and educator. He could commend religion for its rationality and social utility. He could reply with confidence to charges that religion was superstition and a drag on human progress. He could make use of a growing body of philosophical and sociological works without worrying too much whether they issued from the hands of believers or nonbelievers. And, he could introduce his students to a wide range of contemporary literature in the assurance that they would not be corrupted.

In his lectures on moral philosophy Witherspoon did all of these things. His lectures followed the pattern set as the norm in Scotland by Francis Hutcheson, although in the *Ecclesiastical Characteristics*, Witherspoon had scored the Moderates for believing as an article of faith in "the perpetual duration of Mr. Hutcheson's works, notwithstanding their present tendency to oblivion." In a nice twist of irony it was Witherspoon, as much as Francis Alison, who helped to rescue Mr. Hutcheson's works from oblivion, on American soil at least. In organization, in content, and even in formulation of ideas, the similarity between the lectures of Witherspoon and those of Hutcheson is unmistakable.[64] Of course Hutcheson's published treatments of moral

[62] Witherspoon, "Divinity," *Works*, VIII, 30; see Witherspoon, *Moral Philosophy*, pp. 30, 45.
[63] See, for example, John Herman Randall, Jr., *The Role of Knowledge in Western Religion* (Boston: Starr King Press, 1958), pp. 67–68.
[64] Many writers have observed that Witherspoon frequently cited Hutcheson in his lectures, often favorably, though sometimes in disagreement. None, however, have pointed out the extent to which Witherspoon's lectures resemble those of Hutcheson, both in organization and content.

philosophy, including his *Short Introduction to Moral Philosophy*, are more complete than John Witherspoon's syllabus. Witherspoon had never intended his classroom syllabus to be published without thorough elaboration and refinement, and would have been horrified had he known that this was exactly what was to occur after his death.[65]

Witherspoon handled many of the same concerns in moral philosophy that occupied him in divinity with the certainty that he was being modern and progressive. He began by assuring his students that the study of moral philosophy was in no way damaging to the interests of religion. The danger some sensed in moral philosophy, because it is an inquiry into the grounds of morality "by reason alone, distinct from revelation," was not serious. The truth of the scriptures, he maintained, drawing upon the principles sketched in his divinity lectures, will not be contrary to reason. In fact, since natural philosophy had proved a benefit to religion, presumably because it had disclosed the divine order of the universe, the same could be expected of moral philosophy. Besides, he continued, the best way to defend religion was to meet its detractors "upon their own ground, and to show them from reason itself, the fallacy of their principles." [66]

Witherspoon shared with the Scottish philosophers the belief that empirical method could be applied to all fields of knowledge. With almost naive optimism, he appraised for his students the progress made in raising moral philosophy to the status of a science:

At first sight it appears that authors differ much more, and more essentially on the principles of moral than natural philosophy. Yet perhaps a time may come when men, treating moral philosophy as Newton and his successors have done natural, may arrive at greater precision. It is always safer in our reasonings to trace facts upwards than to reason downwards upon metaphysical principles.[67]

Here Witherspoon had placed himself directly in the company of Francis Hutcheson and those Scottish writers who attempted to follow him in his method of empirical philosophy.

From this point of view, a scientific moral philosophy would not

---

[65] Samuel Stanhope Smith, writing to William Woodward, a bookseller in Philadelphia, said that Witherspoon's lectures were "so hastily and imperfectly drawnup that [Witherspoon] would never suffer them to be printed during his life." Smith to Woodward, August 1, 1810, S. S. Smith Collection, Princeton University Library, AM 10856.
[66] Witherspoon, *Moral Philosophy*, p. 4.
[67] *Ibid.*, pp. 140–141.

begin with general principles of moral conduct, but would seek to arrive at such principles through the study of human nature itself. Thus, Hutcheson had written, "We must . . . search accurately into the constitution of our nature to see what sort of creatures we are; for what purposes nature has formed us; what character God our Creator requires us to maintain." [68] Like Hutcheson, Witherspoon began his treatment of ethics, the first main division of moral philosophy, with its foundation in the nature of man and with an analysis of man's distinctive powers, senses, and ways of knowing.[69] "It seems a point agreed upon," Witherspoon said, nearly repeating Hutcheson's words, "that the principles of duty and obligation must be drawn from the nature of man. That is to say, if we can discover how his Maker formed him, or for what he intended him, that certainly is what it ought to be." [70]

The concept of the moral sense was the second major theme in Witherspoon's thinking, next in importance to the problem of reason and revelation. With Hutcheson he declared that man has an inherent sense of good and evil, as much a part of his nature as his sense of beauty or any other natural emotion. Witherspoon, however, muted Hutcheson's emphasis upon the close connection between aesthetics and morality, between a sense of beauty and a sense of the good. Instead, he stressed the moral sense in terms of law and obligation. "The various theories upon the principles of beauty," he said, ". . . are of much importance on the subject of taste and criticism, but of very little importance in morals." [71] He did agree with Hutcheson that the moral sense is what all men and the scriptures call "conscience," but he emphasized that conscience is the law which God has written upon man's heart, a law that "both intimates and enforces duty, previous to all reasoning." [72] By interpreting the moral sense as

[68] Francis Hutcheson, *A Short Introduction to Moral Philosophy* (Glasgow: Robert Foulis, 1747), p. 2; referred to henceforth as *Compend*.
[69] Without going into detail, it is possible to indicate how closely Witherspoon followed the Hutchesonian organization of human nature by simply noting the topics covered and the distinctions made by each: the powers of the mind—will and understanding; the external and internal senses; the classes of passions—selfish or benevolent; the conscience or moral sense; the sense of ridicule and sense of shame; etc. Hutcheson, *Compend*, pp. 1–36; Witherspoon, *Moral Philosophy*, pp. 14–35.
[70] Witherspoon, *Moral Philosophy*, p. 4.
[71] *Ibid.*, p. 17.
[72] *Ibid.*, p. 74. Hutcheson also identified the moral sense with conscience. *Compend*, p. 24. In identifying the conscience with the will of God, however, Witherspoon was almost surely following Bishop Butler, who had made this identification one of his basic assumptions in attempting to refute Shaftesbury's notion of beneficence. See the discussions on Butler, in Leslie Stephen, *History of English Thought in*

conscience and an apprehension of God's law, Witherspoon could maintain that all morality worthy of the name is rooted firmly in the divine will.

The Scottish thinkers were all eclectic, but Witherspoon's was an eclecticism with a vengeance. He not only made use of Hutcheson's idea of the moral sense and affirmed the Scottish approach to ethics by the study of human nature, but was also aware of the English rationalists, Wollaston and Clarke, who thought that the subject of morals should be treated by inquiring into the abstract relations of things. Witherspoon did not want to reject either view totally, since, as he feared, "Perhaps neither the one nor the other is wholly right." On the one hand, Witherspoon's view of the moral sense, pointing man to his duty "previous to all reason," squared with the empiricists' emphasis on the primacy of the emotions. On the other hand, his insistence that the law of God is written into the universe as well as the heart, and cannot be altered even by God without "unhinging" our idea of divine excellency itself, put him close to the rationalists' way of thinking.[73] Witherspoon's solution was thoroughly practical: he would have both, and try "to avoid the errors of excess."

This was typical of Witherspoon's entire method in discussing any controversial issue. He would review the major spokesmen on all sides of the question, point out their strong and weak points, and then try to minimize differences by gathering them all together under an all-embracing formulation of his own. Witherspoon tried, for example, to take into account for his students all the various theories in ethics. He named the major representatives of each—Clarke, Hutcheson, Wollaston, Campbell, Smith, Hume, and Edwards—commented on their different analyses, and then summarized by rolling them all up into one:

The result of the whole is that we ought to take the rule of duty from conscience enlightened by reason, experience, and every way in which we can be supposed to learn the will of our Maker, and his intention in creating us such as we are. And we ought to believe that it is as deeply founded as the nature of God himself, being a transcript of his moral excellence, and that it is productive of the highest good.[74]

---

the Eighteenth Century (2 vols.; New York: Harcourt, Brace and World, Inc., 1962, first published, 1871), II, 39–47; and Basil Willey, The Eighteenth Century Background (New York: Columbia University Press, 1941), pp. 84–94.
[73] Witherspoon, Moral Philosophy, pp. 27–28.
[74] Witherspoon, Moral Philosophy, p. 30.

Even if it did result in almost unavoidable inconsistencies accompanied by frequent dogmatic pronouncements, there is still something to be said for Witherspoon's method under the circumstances. Only a dull student would have failed to be stimulated by Witherspoon's spirited discussions of the many positions on one controversial question after another. The whole tone of the lectures, in fact, conveys a sense of the classroom situation in which they were delivered: the overworked professor, eager to introduce his students to the issues of the day and anxious not to confuse them overmuch, simply did not have the leisure to work his way to considered conclusions that were uncomplicated and at the same time intellectually rigorous. In any case, whatever the vagueness of some of his statements, Witherspoon did have a principle of selectivity that could be extremely precise and that had its own kind of intellectual respectability in the eighteenth century. That principle was the test of experience.

A third main characteristic of Witherspoon's thought was its pervasive pragmatic strain. "Reason, conscience, and experience" appeared together in his thinking almost as modalities of the trinity. If the dictates of "conscience, enlightened by reason" fail to give clear guidance, experience itself might provide the key. Witherspoon's Calvinist heritage was showing itself in modern dress. There is in Calvinism traditionally a high appreciation of experience as teacher, and a frequent appeal to nature as guide. Before Locke, Calvinists appealed to "the laws of God, nature, and nations," as known through "perpetual custom, good sense, and right reason." Theodore Beza's rule for seeking illumination and direction from "nature, natural clarity of thought and God himself through the words of St. Paul" bears a remarkable resemblance to Witherspoon's own "reason, conscience, and experience." [75] These slight shifts in vocabulary, however, betokened major transitions in the meaning of the terms.

This inner transformation of concepts is perhaps most apparent in Witherspoon's appeal to "experience." "Experience" often appeared in his writings as meaning that which proves itself useful—eighteenth century "common utility." Witherspoon, indeed, often substituted "common utility" for "experience" freely in his formula.[76] Wither-

---

[75] See Herbert D. Foster, "International Calvinism through Locke and the Revolution of 1688," *American Historical Review*, XXXII (April 1927), 489. J. T. McNeill also has shown that natural law lay at the heart of most Calvinist disquisitions on civil polity and social relationships. J. T. McNeill, "Natural Law in the Teaching of the Reformers," *Journal of Religion*, XXVI (1946), 168–182.

[76] Of natural liberty, for example, he declared that reason teaches it and "common

spoon's attitude toward the world of nature was shaped, for instance, by his appreciation of its usefulness for human purposes. Even in his garden on the farm at Tusculum near Princeton—Witherspoon thought of himself as a "scientific agriculturalist"—he grew only plants useful for food.[77] Witherspoon's comments to his students on theories of beauty aimed to curb excesses of the imagination, and to balance natural beauty with thoughts of order and usefulness:

A wild uncultivated forest, a vast precipice, or steep cataract or water-fall is supposed to be an object more august and striking, than any ornaments produced by human skill. The order and symmetry, however, of architecture and gardening, are highly pleasing, and ought not properly to be compared with the other, as pleasing the imagination in a different degree, so much as in a different kind.[78]

Nature was made for man to use: no thoughts of beauty without adding to them "a reflection on their utility"; no gardens without vegetables.

Witherspoon applied the test of utility to the selection of subjects students should be taught. The study of moral philosophy could be justified, if necessary, by its polemic usefulness alone. History he recommended to his students because the study is "first honorable, being at present in high repute, especially in our country. 2. useful 3. delightful 4. very much connected with and subservient to the interest of religion." [79] The study of composition, taste, and criticism was essential if for no other reason than that no one is so greatly admired, envied, and imitated as "him that has the power of persuasion." Witherspoon did not hesitate to recommend virtue itself for its usefulness, and that of a very material kind: "A good shopkeeper is commonly remarkable for this quality [meekness]. People love to go where they meet with good words and gentle treatment." [80] Utility, for Witherspoon, was never an exclusive, yet always a central and commanding consideration.

This sense of "experience" was especially important for Wither-

---

utility recommends it." On the conduct of war, he said that plans must be devised consistent with "reason, conscience, or common utility." Witherspoon, *Moral Philosophy*, p. 72; "The Druid," *Works*, IX, 234.
[77] Collins, *Witherspoon*, I, 147; II, 185.
[78] Witherspoon, "Lectures on Eloquence," *Works*, VII, 163.
[79] Witherspoon, *Lectures on History*, manuscript, Lecture I.
[80] Witherspoon, "Eloquence," *Works*, VII, 156; Witherspoon, "An Address to the Students of the Senior Class," *Works*, VI, 23.

spoon's theology. For example, his main defense for the doctrine of original sin was that it was a useful description of the way men really behave. "What is the history of the world," he loved to ask rhetorically, "but the history of human guilt." [81] He, likewise, gave greatest attention to those theological doctrines which could be shown to have actual consequences for human conduct. Justification and regeneration—the anthropological rather than the ontological doctrines of the faith—were emphasized because they could be referred to observable behavior—to conversion and obedience.[82]

One of Witherspoon's favorite expressions, "Plain Common Sense," carries the same meaning of "experience" as that which produces useful results. The man who possesses "common sense" is the man gifted by nature with sound judgment; he is judicious in thought and prudent in conduct. He is the man who achieves his goals, best serves society, and is worthy of the highest respect—not the brilliant, who tends to be flighty and unstable; not the erudite, who likely as not will turn pedant; and, not, certainly, the contemplative, who, lovable as he may be, remains merely ineffectual.[83] "Persons of the middle degrees of capacity" are the ones most likely to possess plain common sense, and who "perhaps generally fill the most useful and important stations in life." Men of brilliance whose imaginations are not pruned and shaped by common sense do not deserve unqualified admiration. "A very great genius," he said, "is often like a very fine flower, to be wondered at, but of little service either for food or medicine." [84]

Witherspoon's notion of plain common sense, however, encompassed a meaning of experience that went beyond utility alone. "Common sense" also referred to the time-tested customs, traditions, and values of society—the social virtues which promote settled, orderly human relationships. Witherspoon wrote for his newspaper-reading public:

Let all, therefore, who will or hope to be eminent, remember, that as the height to which you can raise a tower depends upon the size and solidity of its base, so they ought to lay the foundation of their future

[81] Witherspoon, "Divinity," *Works*, VIII, 30, 42, 126.
[82] Witherspoon, "Ministerial Fidelity in declaring the whole counsel of God," *Works*, III, 23.
[83] Witherspoon, "The Druid," *Works*, IX; "Divinity," *Works*, VIII, 18 f.
[84] Witherspoon, "Eloquence," *Works*, VII, 165.

fame deep and strong, in sobriety, prudence, and patient industry, which are the genuine dictates of *plain common sense*.[85]

The dictates of common sense were drawn from the outlook and norms of the surrounding culture. Herein lay both the strength and the danger of common sense.

Witherspoon's common sense view was concerned with action and consequences, with getting things done, for in the end these were the things that mattered. Common sense was capable of producing results on a large scale because it could appeal to the common experience of all men. The strength of common sense was that it gave its adherents a firm grip upon the world about them. The danger in common sense, however, was that it might grip the world too firmly and be unable to let go. Common sense meant not only a way of apprehending and acting upon the world, but also included that which is apprehended, the particular customs and cultural heritage of the immediate society. In most circumstances such a perspective could be expected to have profoundly conservative tendencies. In those situations, however, in which two or more whole social groups were locked in a struggle to determine whose values and goals would prevail—as, perhaps, in the case of the American Revolution—common sense could outfit men for strikingly radical undertakings.

It is in the light of Witherspoon's reliance upon conscience, reason, and experience that his so-called philosophical realism can be accurately appraised. Witherspoon has been credited with having first effectively introduced into America the Scottish philosophical realism initially formulated by Thomas Reid. In his 1753 article for the *Scots Magazine* answering Lord Kames' *Essays on the Principles of Natural and Moral Religion* (1751), Witherspoon put forward certain principles which he later claimed antedated Reid's more elaborate and precise work.[86] Kames, taking off from Hume, had maintained that since man cannot know the external world, and is, therefore, helpless to change it, he cannot be held morally accountable for his actions, but only for his beliefs. Witherspoon's response was basically a simple counter-assertion: man's senses can be trusted; therefore, within acknowledged limits, man is a free moral agent. Witherspoon later incorporated the principle that sense experience is reliable in his

[85] Witherspoon, "The Druid," *Works*, IX, 267.
[86] See Collins, *Witherspoon*, I, 41.

discussions of epistemology in the lectures on moral philosophy.[87]

Witherspoon's epistemological realism was not the product of serious philosophical inquiry. It was essentially a faith affirmation, couched in philosophical terms, that justified what Witherspoon took to be the prerequisites of all discussion and action: conscience, reason, and experience. "That our senses are to be trusted in the information they give use," maintained Witherspoon, "seems to me a first principle, because they are the foundation of all our reasonings." [88]

Most of his critical remarks were not so much directed against the rational skepticism of Hume as against an unsophisticated and caricatured version of Berkeley's idealism, or the "immaterialist system," as Witherspoon called it. He probably shared Reid's conviction that it was in taking Berkeley seriously that Hume first went astray, and it was Berkeley's idealism that he had found Joseph Periam teaching to the undergraduates when he came to the college. His final argument always rested upon the unfortunate consequences of immaterialism for experience and action. Persons who hold such principles, Witherspoon said, "do not deserve to be reasoned with because they do not pretend to communicate knowledge, but to take all knowledge from us." [89] He lost no time in dealing with Periam and the tutors to show that in such cases action took precedence over discussion.

The educational effect of Witherspoon's intellectual outlook can be summarized by looking at the attitude toward learning that it helped to foster. In the first place, Witherspoon's own wide interests and his desire to come to terms with the Enlightenment led him to argue for the importance of wide learning. He expressed this interest concretely through his efforts to expand the curriculum and to strengthen the library. Moreover, his classroom method helped to impress upon his students the same concerns. "The Dr. in his lectures does not go on in the order that System writers generally do," one of his students wrote to a friend, "but chooses out the most important subjects in divinity . . . and treats them in as concise a manner as possible to give us a clear notion of them and gives us the several opinions of the ablest writers." [90]

In the second place, Witherspoon's exaltation of utility provided

[87] Witherspoon, *Moral Philosophy*, pp. 14–15.
[88] *Ibid.*
[89] Witherspoon, *Moral Philosophy*, pp. 14–15.
[90] Quoted in Smith, *The Presbyterian Ministry*, p. 82.

a favorable climate for the sciences and the professions. At the same time, his readiness to dismiss hard intellectual problems and his distaste for specialized knowledge may have discouraged creative scholarship. If Witherspoon's demand for a "pious education" dampened enthusiasm for speculative inquiry, it did enable him, nevertheless, to defend learning as he understood it against its religious despisers. Witherspoon derided any suggestion that learning should not be pursued because it is susceptible to misuse. It may be true, he said, that "learning in general, possessed by a bad man, is unspeakably pernicious," but to rest upon that as an excuse for ignorance is like refusing to bear arms for fear they might fall into enemy hands.[91] He exhorted his graduating classes, therefore, to a life of diligence and application to study, and to the improvement of their talents "as members of society." He recommended that as his students went out into the world they cultivate "the friendship, advice, and assistance of men of learning and worth," as one of the most powerful inducements to their own enterprise and ambition.[92]

IV

The two other areas, in addition to the intellectual, in which Witherspoon exerted great influence upon the college remain to be examined. The first of these was the change he brought about in the conception of the kind of man a liberal education should produce. The second was Witherspoon's application of eighteenth-century political ideas to the social goals of higher education.

The number of eminent public leaders among Witherspoon's alumni, and a decline in the proportion of his students who entered the ministry, have often given rise to the judgment that Witherspoon placed greater emphasis upon training statesmen than he did upon ministerial education.[93] Unfortunately, this explanation has tended to obscure the real nature and depth of the changes that did occur.

If anything, Witherspoon gave ministerial education more atten-

---

[91] Witherspoon, "Eloquence," *Works*, VII, 156.

[92] Witherspoon, "Address to the Senior Class," *Works*, VI, 19.

[93] From 1777 to 1794 only thirty-nine Princeton men became ministers, 13 per cent of the total graduated. From 1766 to 1775, seventy-five or 41 per cent entered the ministry. The decline in percentages of graduates headed for the ministry after the war was somewhat greater at the College of New Jersey than at Harvard and Yale, although it was a general phenomenon. See Bailey B. Burritt, "Professional Distribution of College and University Graduates," United States Bureau of Education, Bulletin 19 (1912).

tion than it had had before, and actually tightened the standards of theological training. The replacement of the classics, basic to ministerial education, in the upper-class years by English composition and moral philosophy did not mean that Witherspoon thought either the classics or the ministry any less important.[94] On the contrary, he considered them so vital that he encouraged every effort to guarantee that students entering the college would already have Greek and Latin well under control. Preparatory language instruction was strengthened in the college grammar school, and entrance examinations continued unabated.

Witherspoon's curriculum emphases can be viewed as having been fashioned with the future minister specifically in mind. The subjects that Witherspoon listed, after divinity, as being particularly important for the minister, because they equipped him both to converse knowledgeably with men of learning and to repel the attacks of adversaries, were precisely those encompassed by his own much celebrated lectures: "1. Languages 2. Moral Philosophy 3. History, sacred and profane 4. Eloquence, including the belles lettres study in general."[95] When attempts were made in the synod in 1783, and again in 1785, to relax the educational requirements for the ministry, it was Witherspoon who headed the successful move to stave them off.[96] If the last resulted in a diminishing of the number of ministers available to meet the growing needs of the church, it was the ironical product of Witherspoon's zeal, not lack of concern, for the ministry as he conceived it.

The really significant change wrought by Witherspoon was in the conception of the ministerial ideal itself. For the New Side, culture had been important for the minister, conversion essential. For Witherspoon it became almost more essential for the minister to be a man of learning and dignity than for him to have had an experience of the new birth. This statement may appear surprising in light of Witherspoon's having chided the Moderates for loving too much the air and manner of fine gentlemen. Indeed, it would have surprised Witherspoon himself had it been put to him as bluntly. Its accuracy, however, can be clearly demonstrated by looking at Witherspoon's own statements about the ministry and the nature of piety.

[94] Recall that Davies and Finley had also emphasized English.
[95] Witherspoon, "Divinity," *Works*, VIII, 24, 18–28.
[96] Trinterud, *Forming of an American Tradition*, p. 266.

In his lectures on eloquence Witherspoon discussed his ideal of the educated man in general and of the minister in particular. These lectures illustrate more completely than any others how much Witherspoon had imbibed the modern spirit during his early years at Edinburgh, and how subtly he had been influenced by his relationship with the Moderates. The lectures on eloquence also show Witherspoon returning again to Scottish sources for his ideas.

As with all his lectures, those on eloquence present a vivid picture of Witherspoon the teacher. The lectures are replete with all manner of subjects pertaining to literary criticism, taste, and effective expression. With the actual demands of pulpit, bar, and assembly in mind, Witherspoon shaped his lectures always with an eye to their future practical applicability. He gave direct advice wherever he deemed it necessary; he compared and contrasted authors, never withholding his own judgment; and he simplified whenever possible. Simplicity for utility's sake was a constantly recurring theme. Witherspoon, for example, dropped the usual and more complicated division of a discourse in favor of the most simple imaginable: "a composition must have a beginning, a middle, and an end." The sound rule for ministers especially was "to avoid all turgid declamation, to keep to experience, and to take things as they really are." [97]

Witherspoon cited name after name from the ancient authors, major and minor, holding them as models that in many areas had never been surpassed. Cautioning his students, however, against thinking that "all the ancient orators had a genius more than human," he paid equal attention to modern writers. Shakespeare, Pope, Addison, Swift, Johnson, Hume, and others were mentioned, critically or admiringly. His treatment of the moderns displayed Witherspoon's essential fairness in its best light, a quality often overshadowed by his readiness for combat. "Dr. Robertson, in History," he said, in reference to his old ecclesiastical archenemy, "has as just a mixture of strength and elegance, as any other author I know in the English language." And, he said, a little grudgingly, of David Hume that, though he was "an infidel in opinion," he was "of great reach and accuracy of judgment in matters of criticism." [98] Witherspoon was willing to give credit where he thought it due.

Witherspoon appears never to have mentioned his old classmate

[97] Witherspoon, "Eloquence," *Works*, VII, 294, 281.
[98] *Ibid.*, pp. 168, 291.

who by that time was the most renowned minister and authority on rhetoric in Scotland, Hugh Blair.[99] The omission is especially interesting because Witherspoon's lectures paralleled Blair's treatment of rhetoric at many points.[100] Perhaps Witherspoon's sense of fairness failed him in his not mentioning Blair, since Blair represented everything in the Moderate minister that Witherspoon had found repugnant. More likely, however, Witherspoon felt that he owed nothing to Blair, that the real debt was to their former teacher at the University of Edinburgh, John Stevenson.

The lectures on eloquence exhibit Witherspoon's Scottish intellectual background; they also reveal something else. The charge that had stung Witherspoon most deeply in his encounters with the Moderates had been that Evangelical ministers were backward and bigoted —uncultured remnants of an uncivilized age. Witherspoon seemed determined to show the Hugh Blairs and William Robertsons of this world that the Evangelical minister, too, could be a gentleman, and without the sacrifice of his Evangelical warmth. Witherspoon also seemed to feel that, in spite of the honor and respect accorded by many in the American church to such persons as Finley, Davies, and Edwards—to the best of the revivalists—ministerial prestige among men of parts and influence was badly in need of repair.

Witherspoon's remedy was simple and twofold: learning and manners. Recommending the study of history to his students, Witherspoon told them, "A clergyman should be a man of liberal knowledge

[99] Blair had been appointed to the chair of logic and rhetoric at Edinburgh as early as 1759. On Blair, see Robert Schmitz, *Hugh Blair* (New York: King's Crown Press, 1948).

[100] Blair and Witherspoon, for example, both had the eighteenth-century fascination with the sublime. They both defined "sublimity" as producing "greatness or elevation of mind," rejected Burke's notion that terror is the sole emotion connected with the sublime, and agreed that sublimity in style consists mainly in simplicity. Witherspoon, "Eloquence," *Works*, VIII, 206; Schmitz, *Blair*, pp. 100–102. Both were interested in style and developed elaborate systems for classifying an author's form of expression. Although the classification system worked out by Witherspoon was not quite as complex as Blair's, they were so similar that, if Witherspoon was not relying on Blair, he was using a common source with him. Schmitz, *Blair*, pp. 106–107; Witherspoon, "Eloquence," pp. 241–245. The Evangelical and Moderate temperaments were nicely contrasted by Witherspoon's and Blair's remarks upon Hervey's *Meditations*, which both used as an example of an ornate style. Witherspoon said Hervey was "elegant"; Blair called him "florid." Blair and Witherspoon showed the same Scottish pride and pleasure in condemning "one modern author of eminence," Samuel Johnson. Johnson, Witherspoon said, "is so stiff and abstracted in his manner, and such a lover of hard words, that he is the worst pattern for young persons that can be named." Witherspoon, "Eloquence," pp. 168–169. Schmitz quotes extensively from Blair's satire of Johnson's style, in *Blair*, pp. 107–108.

and fit for the conversation and society of men of rank and letters. . . ." [101] Though he always maintained a pastoral concern for the common people of the congregations, he was heedful also of the necessity of gaining the respect of those who held the reins of society. "Let no man seek to avoid that reproach which may be his lot, for preaching the truths of the everlasting gospel," on this Witherspoon never surrendered, "but let him always avoid the just reproach of handling them in a mean, slovenly, and indecent manner." [102] Learning was necessary, and, almost equally important, so also was proper etiquette. "It is of considerable consequence," Witherspoon said, "to be accustomed to decency of manners in the best company. This gives an ease of carriage and a sense of delicacy, which is of great use in forming the deportment of an orator." [103] By "orator," Witherspoon made clear that he meant the minister, the lawyer, and the statesman —the very professions, it might be noted, whose potential for leadership in a newly forming society was greatest. The gentlemanly ideal was patently as integral to Witherspoon's picture of the model minister as ever it had been for the Moderates.

It should never be forgotten that, despite the charges of their opponents, the revivalist leaders of the New Side also valued highly the necessity of ministerial propriety and decorum. With Witherspoon, however, a different set of priorities in the relationship between piety and dignity was beginning to take hold. How marked the shift was can be seen best in Witherspoon's own concepts of piety and conversion.

Witherspoon could, and often did, speak the same language as the revivalists in extolling the necessity for a new birth. Witherspoon's description of the regenerating effect of conversion could pass for that of Finley or of Edwards.[104] He could decry the dangers of an unconverted ministry, as had Gilbert Tennent, saying that only a believing preacher would be a probable means of saving others. He did repeat the warning issued to the college students by Samuel Davies not to feel at ease in their studies or their vocations if they had not true religion. Addressing himself to students who had turned from the ministry because they felt no special calling, Witherspoon commended their decision, but cautioned them against the false comfort of thinking they had any less need of a new birth. "Will it not

[101] Witherspoon, "Eloquence," *Works*, VII, 26.
[102] *Ibid.*, p. 4.
[103] *Ibid.*, p. 264.
[104] Witherspoon, "Treatise on Regeneration," *Works*, I, 123, 191.

be a poor consolation, think you," he asked, "in the hour of sickness or death, that you must perish everlastingly, that you go to hell, not as a minister, but a lawyer, or a physician?" There is no reason to suppose that Witherspoon did not mean what he said.[105]

Yet, Witherspoon was inconsistent. By placing conscience and obedience to the law at the heart of his theology, Witherspoon came to stress moral conduct more than conversion itself. There was disagreement among his own students, for example, as to whether he looked upon the disturbances of revivals in the college with much favor at all.[106] He could even counsel his students on occasion, in contradiction to his pronouncements at other times, not to give up the ministry simply because they had doubts about the certainty of their calling. Really, he told them more than once, genuine assurance is "just the grace of hope in lively exercise"; and he comforted them with the thought that, if they made allowance for differing terminology, they would find that most others who had spoken on the subject of assurance meant about the same thing.[107] This was, in any case, a far remove from that piety, the lack of which could bring an unconverted Pharisee-teacher and his flock to perdition.

His emphasis upon right conduct led him to speak of the converting efficacy of the example of virtuous actions themselves—an idea the New Side revivalists would have had considerable difficulty accepting. At times Witherspoon spoke in a way that would have appalled Jonathan Edwards as a gross recommendation of piety for its utility alone. The great advantage of true piety to one destined for the ministry, he told his students, is not merely that it gives "experimental knowledge of religion." "True piety," he said, "will direct a man in the choice of his studies . . . to what may be most profitable to him." It will also be "a powerful motive to diligence in his studies," which are difficult to keep at under any circumstances. Finally, it will give "unspeakable force" to what a minister says: "We see that a man truly pious has often esteem, influence, and success,

---

105 Witherspoon, "Eloquence," *Works*, VIII, 275. Compare Davies: "Unless you secure a happy Immortality, in the few uncertain Years of Life, your Existence, your Reason, your Liberal Education, your religious Advantages, your All, will be your everlasting Curse: And it would be better for you to be Hottentots, or even the most abject and miserable Creatures among the meanest and most noxious of the brutal tribes, than to be the Sons of NASSAU-HALL." Samuel Davies, *Religion and Publick Spirit, A Valedictory Address to the Senior Class* (New York: James Parker & Co., 1761), p. 16.
106 Maclean, *History of the College of New Jersey*, I, 310.
107 Witherspoon, "The Dominion of Providence over the Passions of Men," *Works*, V, 210 ff.; "The Nature and Extent of Visible Religion," *Works*, II, 326–338.

though his parts may be much inferior to others who are more capable, but less conscientious." [108] At this, one thinks more readily perhaps of Poor Richard than of, say, Gilbert Tennent. It is abundantly plain that "piety" did not mean the same thing to Witherspoon that it had meant to the revivalist presidents of the college before him.

Because Witherspoon so often spoke the familiar language of conversion, probably neither he nor his listeners sensed the transformation in meanings that was occurring, and that for this very reason would become all the more complete. This also helps to explain why Witherspoon, whose thought actually had many common elements with that of Old Side Francis Alison, received unquestioning acceptance at the predominantly New Side College of New Jersey.

In emphasizing the moral side of piety, Witherspoon took as his standard of conduct the ideal of the gentleman. He had not emphasized the training of public leaders at the expense of the ministry, but rather had put all the professions upon the same footing. To speak of a gentlemanly ideal, however, would be misleading were it thought to refer to the gentleman of the aristocracy and court. Witherspoon's was the bourgeois gentleman, the man who, not by birth, but by virtue of his prudence, industry, and learning could provide leadership to a burgeoning and aggressive middle class. The Scottish prototype—the Moderate minister and man of letters—was flawed for Witherspoon by strong traces of unorthodoxy and predilections for autocracy. On the American scene, however, the church had been granted a fresh opportunity to erase these defects by casting the mold anew. Witherspoon may have sensed that a relatively fluid society gave the American middle-class gentleman many avenues for influence denied to the Scottish literati by their country's more rigid social organization. Thus, Witherspoon's vision for the college and her graduates was firmly entwined with his hopes for the country itself.

Witherspoon is famous for his energetic participation in the American Revolution. He became a member of New Jersey's Somerset County Committee of Correspondence; led the move to arrest William Franklin, the loyalist Governor of New Jersey; was the only member of the clergy to sign the Declaration of Independence; and served in Congress with few breaks from 1776 through 1782, where he was appointed to more than one hundred committees, including the two vital standing committees on war and foreign affairs. His

[108] Witherspoon, "Eloquence," *Works*, VII, 276.

sermons and published essays were widely read and quoted at home and in Great Britain.[109]

During the entire time, Witherspoon held his post as President of the college, delivering as regularly as possible the lectures in which, long before the actual outbreak of hostilities, he had expounded the political theories justifying the American rebellion. Witherspoon's political theory gave a solid foundation to his own involvement in the Continental Congress and furnished rich resources for his students, such as James Madison, Hugh Henry Breckenridge, John Taylor, and Philip Freneau, to draw upon.[110]

Witherspoon's political theory also provided the basis for his thinking about the social tasks of education. Applying his political principles directly to education, he reformulated the long-standing college goal of education for public leadership in the terms of current eighteenth-century social theory.

Witherspoon's political ideas were based on Protestant-Lockean social contract theory as it was expressed in the works of Francis Hutcheson. It is evident that Witherspoon not only drew upon the same tradition of thought as did Hutcheson, but that in politics he relied directly upon Hutcheson's actual discussions even more than in his treatment of the moral sense. Witherspoon was more critical of Hutcheson than Francis Alison seems to have been, and he rejected or altered Hutcheson whenever it served him to do so.

One of the fundamental principles of both Hutcheson and Witherspoon came from Pufendorf's version of the state of nature as the basis for human society. This was the idea that man possesses in the state of nature certain inherent rights and an intrinsic sociability, which he ought to honor and support in the state of society.[111] Although Hutcheson devoted a special section to man's natural rights, Witherspoon spread his discussion of natural rights under several headings, in particular "our duty to ourselves" and "our duty to others." The threefold scheme—"our duty to God, to ourselves, and to others"—however, was Hutcheson's; and Witherspoon's distribution and description of human rights as "natural and acquired,"

[109] Collins, *Witherspoon*, I, 222–236.
[110] For discussions of Witherspoon's relationship to James Madison, see James H. Smylie, "Madison and Witherspoon," *The Princeton University Library Chronicle*, XXII (Spring 1961), 118–132; and Ralph Ketcham, "James Madison at Princeton," *The Princeton University Library Chronicle*, XXVIII (Autumn 1966), 24–54.
[111] I have relied on Gough's analysis of Pufendorf. John Gough, *The Social Contract: A Critical Study of its Development* (Oxford: The Clarendon Press, 1957), pp. 119 f.

"perfect and imperfect," "alienable and inalienable," were almost word for word from Hutcheson.[112] Where Hutcheson began his section on "Politics" with an analysis of specific social institutions, Witherspoon inserted his discussion of the social contract, probably thinking that this provided a stronger theoretic foundation. When Witherspoon moved on to the particulars, however, his organization was once again the Hutchesonian one, dealing in turn with marriage, parents and children, and masters and servants.[113] Whether he was discussing the acquisition of property, the duties of oaths and contracts, the origin of civil government, or the laws of war, Witherspoon followed Hutcheson closely.

Just as Francis Alison had done, Witherspoon presented to his students the Hutchesonian doctrines of balanced government and the right of resistance. The extent to which Witherspoon was relying upon Hutcheson is illustrated by their discussions of how governments should be organized. To Montesquieu's suggestion of a separation of powers, Witherspoon and Hutcheson, using the same phraseology, including the Latin, both added the idea of a *nexus imperii*, a connection between the branches of government that would make them interdependent.[114] Witherspoon said with Hutcheson that, if the laws of a society turn out to be destructive to the union, the people may break up the old order and begin anew; or that, if the state becomes tyrannical, "the subjects may certainly if in their power, resist and overthrow it." [115] Witherspoon and Hutcheson both agreed that, when pressed, the only final answer to the question, "Who must judge when the government may be resisted?" is "the subjects in general, every one for himself." [116]

The two poles of Witherspoon's social compact theory of government were the beliefs that man is a social creature with a moral sense and that man is a sinner with antisocial tendencies. "Man, made for society, derives his chief advantage of every kind," Witherspoon said, "from the united efforts of many conspiring to the same end." [117] According to Witherspoon the great obstacle to human cooperation, however, is "the humbling and melancholy prospect of sin." Wither-

---

[112] Witherspoon, *Moral Philosophy*, pp. 55–56; Hutcheson, *Compend*, pp. 121–124.
[113] Witherspoon, *Moral Philosophy*, pp. 90–99; Hutcheson, *Compend*, pp. 299 ff.
[114] Witherspoon, *Moral Philosophy*, p. 96; Francis Hutcheson, *A System of Moral Philosophy* (2 vols.; London: Published by his son, 1755), II, 244.
[115] Witherspoon, *Moral Philosophy*, pp. 89, 95–96; Hutcheson, *Compend*, pp. 302–305.
[116] Witherspoon, *Moral Philosophy*, pp. 95–96; Hutcheson, *Compend*, pp. 304–305.
[117] Witherspoon, "Address to the Senior Class," *Works*, VI, 18–19. Compare the similar statement by Hutcheson, *Compend*, p. 118.

spoon did not depart from the orthodox view that sin is a universal malady of mankind. As minister and as moral philosopher, Witherspoon pointed to the testimony of scripture and experience that "all without exception" are prone to do evil from youth, "and that continuously." [118]

The concrete task of the statesman and political theorist was to devise forms of government that would keep man's antisocial tendencies in bounds and allow his social nature some freedom of expression. That this was possible was owing, in Witherspoon's view, to two factors. First, as he explained to his students in divinity, the doctrine of total depravity had never meant that human actions are wholly evil, but that every act is tainted and "essentially defective." There is still a primal goodness in man's heart.[119] Second, God keeps things from getting completely out of hand. "The constant influence and overruling power of divine providence" preserves man from himself.[120] Men could take heart from an awareness of these countervailing forces to human depravity, and exert themselves for the good.

In this light Witherspoon felt governmental systems, in addition to supplying circumstantial proof of human sin, could be explained as a response to it. Governments and laws have always had as their main purpose, he thought, "to bridle the fury of human inclination, and hinder one man from making a prey of another." [121] Witherspoon was obviously relying once again upon the tradition of the social compact. Hutcheson himself had written, "The necessity of civil power . . . must arise either from the imperfections or depravity of men or both." [122]

To explain and underscore the necessity for a complex system of government, Witherspoon called upon a further idea of seventeenth- and eighteenth-century political theory: the principle of counterpoise. The desires and characters of men are such, according to this principle, that each struggles to secure power for himself, so that, if no obstacle is raised, one person or group will sooner or later dominate. "Hence," Witherspoon told his students,

---

[118] See Witherspoon, "Divinity," *Works*, VIII, 122–129; "Man in his Natural State," *Works*, IV, 17; "All Mankind by Nature under Sin," *Works*, II, 9–32.
[119] Witherspoon, "Divinity," *Works*, VIII, 126–127.
[120] Witherspoon, "The Dominion of Providence," *Works*, II, 176–236; "A Sermon delivered at a public Thanksgiving after Peace," *Works*, V, 241.
[121] Witherspoon, "All Mankind by Nature under Sin," *Works*, II, 24.
[122] Hutcheson, *A System of Moral Philosophy*, II, 212.

it appears that every good form of government must be complex, so that the one principle may check the other. It is of consequence to have as much virtue among the particular members of a community as possible; but it is folly to expect that a state should be upheld by integrity in all who have a share in managing it. They must be so balanced that when one draws to his own interest or inclination, there may be an over poise upon the whole.[123]

Arthur O. Lovejoy has shown how the notion of counterpoise, or "over poise" in Witherspoon's phrase, resembled in social theory the popularized celestial mechanics of the Newtonian universe. Just as the planets were held steady in their orbits by the counterbalancing of opposed forces, so too a stable and orderly political society could be constructed on the same principle by balancing opposing social forces.[124]

Witherspoon never supposed, however, that constitutionl arrangements and social mechanics alone could suffice. No system of civil polity could endure indefinitely without virtue and knowledge on the part of its members. "A good form of government," Witherspoon told his congregation, "may hold the rotten materials together for some time, but beyond a certain pitch, even the best constitution will be ineffectual, and slavery must ensue." On the other hand, he added, "when the manners of a nation are pure, when true religion and internal principles maintain their vigour," then nothing can destroy that people.[125]

At this point Witherspoon's political theory became directly applicable to education and the social function of educational agencies. Constitutions furnish the requisite conditions for society, holding conflicting interests in counterpoise and thus creating a little room, a working space, for positive efforts on behalf of the community. Upon such positive efforts the continued well-being of the body politic depends, and such efforts result from the spirit and knowledge provided by religion and education. Every civil society demands the public spirit, integrity, and moral fortitude of its citizens, but in a free society where ultimate control rests with the people a virtuous

[123] Witherspoon, *Moral Philosophy*, 94.
[124] Arthur O. Lovejoy, "The Theory of Human Nature in the American Constitution and the Method of Counterpoise," *Reflections on Human Nature* (Baltimore: The Johns Hopkins Press, 1961), p. 39.
[125] Witherspoon, "Dominion of Providence," *Works*, V, 209.

public is absolutely essential; for in a free state, Witherspoon warned, "if there be a general confusion of manners, there can be nothing but confusion." [126] The church and the college had the political task of making it possible for constitutions to work.

The view held by Witherspoon of the proper relation between church and state further increased the responsibilities of religious and educational institutions within the counterpoise theory. Witherspoon adhered to the position on religious freedom set forth in the Adopting Act of 1729. This Act of the Synod of Philadelphia not only attempted to broaden the rights of individuals to interpret religious doctrine, it also rejected the Westminster Confession's granting of power over the church or over religion in general to civil authorities. The synod specifically stated its refusal to accept those clauses in the Westminster Confession which in any sense "suppose the civil magistrate hath a controlling power over Synods with respect to the exercise of their ministerial authority; or power to persecute any for their religion. . . ." [127]

In his sermons and by his example as a non-separating Evangelical in the Church of Scotland, Witherspoon had expressed his own belief that true faith is only in "the consent and approbation of the heart." His taste of arbitrary civil authority wielded by the Moderates in the patronage controversies strengthened his conviction that true religion wins its way by persuasion, not coercion. "Religious sentiments are very various," Witherspoon said later in his lectures, "and we have given it as one of the perfect rights in natural liberty, and which ought not to be alienated even in society, that every one should judge for himself in matters of religion." [128] When the General Assembly was organized after the war, Article I of the preface to the new Form of Government, drafted under the direction of Witherspoon, committed the church to this same notion of religious freedom based upon principles of theology and natural rights.[129]

---

[126] Witherspoon, "Thanksgiving Sermon," *Works*, V. 266.
[127] Records of the Presbyterian Church, 1729. Quoted in Maurice W. Armstrong, Lefferts A. Loetscher and Charles A. Anderson, eds., *The Presbyterian Enterprise; Sources of American Presbyterian History* (Philadelphia: The Westminster Press, 1956), pp. 30–32.
[128] Witherspoon, *Moral Philosophy*, p. 111.
[129] Trinterud argues, against Collins, that Witherspoon was not as active as others in the reorganization of the church. But Witherspoon is generally thought to have been responsible for the preface to the Form of Government. Trinterud, *Forming of an American Tradition*, pp. 292–293.

For a succinct account of the background and implications of Witherspoon's view of religious freedom, and of its difference from that which prevailed in

Witherspoon's version of religious freedom did not entail complete separation of church and state. The health of society was in a sense the *nexus imperii* binding church and state in a common interest, making one necessary to the other. Although he rejected all systems of established religion, he was aware of the state's need for agencies that would promote morality, public spirit, and a sense of shared values. For Witherspoon, therefore, it was unavoidable, and not the least undesirable that there would be specific points of contact between the civil authorities and the church. These were of two kinds: those which were necessary to preserve the freedom of religious bodies, and those which would enable religious groups to make their contribution to the larger society.

Witherspoon did not feel, for example, that government-sponsored opportunities for public worship would be inconsistent with religious liberty so long as those who dissented were guaranteed their rights.[130] The religious responsibilities of the magistrate included setting an example of piety, punishing vice (and Sabbath-breaking!), and defending the rights of conscience for all.[131] Freedom for religion, not freedom from religion, was Witherspoon's principle. Witherspoon's position fell short of separatism because he insisted upon providing channels for the concrete expression of those social and political obligations he felt were part of a full religious commitment and basic to the welfare of society.

Witherspoon made all religious groups responsible for reciprocating the favor done them by the state in guaranteeing freedom of religion. "By our excellent constitution," he pointed out to his congregation after the war, "they [the churches] are well secured in their religious liberty. The return which is expected of them to the community is, that by the influence of their religious government, their people may be the more regular citizens." [132] Witherspoon linked the demands of the new nation with the requirements of his own political-religious convictions, and drew the church and its colleges directly into the task of nation-building.

Virginia, see James Hastings Nichols, "John Witherspoon on Church and State," in George Hunt, ed., *Calvinism and the Political Order* (Philadelphia: The Westminster Press, 1965), pp. 133 ff.

[130] Witherspoon, "Thanksgiving Sermon," *Works*, V, 268–269; *Moral Philosophy*, p. 112.

[131] Witherspoon, *Moral Philosophy*, p. 113.

[132] Witherspoon favored a more open governmental policy toward Roman Catholics, for example, than was followed in Great Britain. Perhaps Roman Catholics "are never dangerous," he observed, "but when they are oppressed." Witherspoon, *Moral Philosophy*, p. 112.

The church and the college, of course, each had a particular role to perform in this task. The distinctive job of the church was to ensure that morality was firmly grounded in religion; the job of the college was to promote useful knowledge and see that it was put to moral ends. This division of labor was not hard and fast, however, and between the two institutions there was much blurring of functions. Witherspoon could, accordingly, describe the responsibilities of church and college as nearly interchangeable. The church, through its discipline, inculcated morals and manners in the nation. The college helped students to discover that the study of nature led inexorably to considerations of the supernatural and the religious foundations of morality. The result was that, in the context of Witherspoon's thought, the founding of colleges became nearly as important as the planting of churches.

Some measure of Witherspoon's influence can be seen in the new momentum which his students gave to the academy movement. Urging his students to maintain their friendships with each other throughout life for mutual support, Witherspoon observed that "great and eminent men have generally, in every nation, appeared in clusters." [133] He was determined that his students would contribute to the creation of such clusters of influence. Witherspoon suggested where a beginning might be made. "There is no circumstance," he said, "which throws this country so far back in science, as the want of public libraries, where thorough researches might be made, and the small number of learned men to assist in making researches practicable, easy, or complete." [134] His students made an attempt to increase the supply of learned men by founding academies and colleges—a minimum of ten—in Pennsylvania, North and South Carolina, and Virginia.[135]

Witherspoon's impact upon the College of New Jersey and the educational work of the church was many-sided. He introduced his students to some of the most important ideas of the eighteenth century, and in politics, especially, personally demonstrated their usefulness. At a time when the minds of his countrymen were fixed on political concerns, he brought before them his staunch conviction

[133] Witherspoon, "Address to the Senior Class," *Works*, VI, 19.
[134] *Ibid.*, p. 20.
[135] See the list of Witherspoon alumni in Maclean, *History of the College of New Jersey*, I, 358–361. I have counted only those academies founded by students who graduated before 1783. After 1783 the affairs of the college were as much in the hands of Samuel Stanhope Smith as in Witherspoon's, although the Scotsman's name lent its prestige to the college for years.

that the ultimate success of the political venture rested in the beneficent influence of religion and education. By merging piety and civility he shifted the focus of the church's mission away from revivalism toward education. And, finally, he made it possible for the leaders of church and school to see that their traditional Calvinist educational concerns could be defended in current eighteenth-century terms. If the Moderates carried the General Assembly of the Church of Scotland into the Enlightenment, Witherspoon brought the Enlightenment from Scotland to the College of New Jersey and gave it an evangelical baptism.

Before John Witherspoon, leaders of the New Side had viewed with suspicion certain central elements of Scottish Enlightenment thought. After Witherspoon, the full scope of the Scottish Enlightenment began to acquire respectability in the eyes of both the New Side and Old Side leaders. Samuel Stanhope Smith and Benjamin Rush—who both had New Side educational and religious backgrounds—together illustrate the major ways the Scottish example made its impact felt upon late eighteenth-century American higher education.

Chapter V

Education, Progress, and Polygamy:
Samuel Stanhope Smith

John Witherspoon could hardly have wished for a successor more committed to his own religious and educational ideals than was Samuel Stanhope Smith. As the seventh president of the College of New Jersey, Smith continued to broaden and strengthen the college curriculum, to insist upon a modern, well-rounded education for ministers, and to carry on Witherspoon's program of harmonizing religion and Enlightenment rationalism. In the course of his scholarly career Smith pursued the common sense philosophy and other modes of Scottish thought, with greater consistency and breadth than Witherspoon had ever done. Smith was, moreover, as his friend and student Philip Lindsley described him, always "the well-bred, courteous gentleman, every where, at all times, in all companies, on all occasions."[1]

In his own right, and in his own day, Smith enjoyed the reputation of being one of the country's most distinguished educators. It was Smith's fame as an educator, for example, that led George Washington to send his grandson, George Washington Parke Custis, to the College of New Jersey. In 1797 President Washington wrote to Custis advising him to follow Smith's prescribed course conscientiously, and to pay no heed to any contrary suggestions that others might make. Washington assured Custis that "no college has turned out better scholars, or more estimable characters, than Nassau." "Nor," he added, "is there any one whose president is thought more capable to direct a proper system of education than Dr. Smith. . . ."[2] Partly because

---

[1] William Sprague, *Annals of the American Pulpit* (New York: R. Carter and Brothers, 1858), III, 343.
[2] George Washington to George Washington Parke Custis, July 23, 1797, in John C. Fitzpatrick, ed., *The Writings of George Washington* (Washington, D.C.: United States Government Printing Office, 1940), XXXV, 510–511; also see XXXV, 340–341.

of his wide scholarly interests themselves, however, Smith gradually lost the confidence of many of his own trustees and fellow churchmen, and was forced under pressure to resign. When he finally did quit his post, Smith had given the college nearly three decades of outstanding scholarly and administrative leadership.

I

Samuel Stanhope Smith was a member of John Witherspoon's first graduating class at the College of New Jersey in 1769. Smith had entered directly into the junior year at the college at the age of sixteen after having received his early education in his father's famous Pequea Academy. Before his first year at the college was out, Smith had so distinguished himself in mathematics and natural philosophy that the faculty publicly presented him with the complete works of the contemporary mathematics professor at Oxford University. Smith soon became a leader of the coterie of students surrounding the college tutor Joseph Periam, whose version of Berkeleian idealism had captivated the college faculty. For a time he was such an ardent champion of Periam's views that his father feared young Smith's religious principles would be swept away by skepticism and false philosophy. It was probably with no small gratitude and sense of relief that the elder Smith learned of the swift and unrelenting attack launched by the new college president, John Witherspoon, upon the Bishop of Cloyne and his New Jersey disciples. Tutor Periam soon left, and Smith was won completely and permanently to Witherspoon's common sense point of view. On September 27, 1769, as the outstanding graduate, Smith delivered the Latin oration in the first commencement ceremony at which John Witherspoon officiated.[3]

From the time he entered the College of New Jersey, Samuel Stanhope Smith seems to have been committed to the problems and tasks of higher education. After graduation he returned to Pequea, where he studied theology under his father and immersed himself in the classics and modern authors, such as Locke, Warburton, Butler, and Edwards. Here he also began to read Pope, Swift, and Addison and to cultivate his interest in belles lettres, which was to remain

[3] Biographical information on Smith is based upon the memoir, written by Smith's student and friend, Philip Lindsley, in Sprague, *Annals of the American Pulpit*, III, 342–345; the memoir written by another of Smith's students, Frederick Beasley, published as an introduction to Samuel Stanhope Smith, *Sermons of Samuel Stanhope Smith, D.D.*, (2 vols.; Philadelphia: J. Maxwell, 1821), 3–60; and, John Maclean, *History of the College of New Jersey* (2 vols.; Philadelphia: J. B. Lippincott & Sons, 1877), II, 5–146.

throughout his life one of his favorite subjects. Witherspoon called him back to Princeton as a tutor in the classics and belles lettres, but after two years he was ordained by the Presbytery of New Castle and appointed a missionary to the Scotch-Irish settlements in western Virginia. Catechizing and preaching revival sermons, Smith was so well received by the people of Virginia that he was invited to become the first president of Hampden-Sydney College. Before taking charge of the new school, Smith returned to Princeton long enough to marry Witherspoon's eldest daughter, thus connecting himself with his mentor, as Frederick Beasley, one of Smith's students, later put it, "by ties even more intimate and interesting than those which subsist between the professor and pupil." [4]

Although the opening of Hampden-Sydney in 1776 coincided with the outbreak of the war, Smith remained and managed to put the school on such a solid footing that within a year over a hundred students were enrolled and the faculty had been increased to four.[5] Smith introduced essentially the same curriculum that he had known at the College of New Jersey, with perhaps greater emphasis, if his own advertisement of the college was accurate, upon English and science.[6] In 1779, Smith accepted a call from John Witherspoon to become Professor of Moral Philosophy at the College of New Jersey.

Increasingly after 1779 the burden of administering the College of New Jersey fell to Smith. Witherspoon's duties in the Continental Congress after the war, his fund-raising trip to Great Britain in 1783, and his growing physical debility and eventual blindness in the last years of his life placed mounting responsibilities upon Smith. Although Dr. Witherspoon was officially head of the college until he died in 1794, Smith had actually been in charge for almost fifteen years. This observation should not be forgotten when assessing Smith's influence, since many of the graduates of the college during this period were as much students of Smith as of Witherspoon.[7]

---

4 Frederick Beasley, "An Account of the Life and Writings of the Rev. Samuel Stanhope Smith," in Smith, *Sermons*, I, 22.
5 Smith called his brother-in-law David Witherspoon from Princeton, his own brother John Blair Smith, and Samuel Doak to assist him. John Blair Smith succeeded his brother to the presidency of Hampden-Sydney, and Samuel Doak later was the founder of two colleges in Tennessee. A. J. Morrison, *The College of Hampden-Sydney; Calendar of Board Minutes, 1776–1876* (Richmond: The Hermitage Press, 1912).
6 *Ibid.*, pp. 14–15.
7 Among later educators who had graduated from the College of New Jersey between 1779 and 1794 were: Ira Condit (graduated 1784), Vice-President of Queens College, New Jersey; Robert Finley (1787), President of the University of Georgia;

The war had left the college nearly in shambles, physically and financially. Largely through Smith's efforts and leadership, funds were raised—with Smith contributing from his own pocket—the buildings repaired, and classes reorganized. The strain of his duties caused a chronic tubercular condition, from which he suffered most of his life, to hemorrhage so severely that he nearly died. No sooner did he recover than the professorship of theology was added to his other teaching and administrative duties, including his jobs as treasurer of the college and clerk of the Board of Trustees. Finally, in 1786, in something of an official afterthought, the trustees added recognition to the responsibilities they had relentlessly heaped upon him by naming Smith Vice-President of the college. This action came, however, only after Smith's election to the American Philosophical Society and the award of an honorary doctorate from Yale.

The Scottish example, which Witherspoon had personally represented, continued to shape the College of New Jersey under Samuel Stanhope Smith. As Smith worked to modernize the curriculum and to arouse public support for the college, he appears to have very self-consicously taken the Scottish university as his educational model. On at least one occasion, he was quite explicit regarding the institutions of higher education he considered worthy of emulation. In an appeal for funds from the state legislature in 1796, the committee requesting aid, of which Smith was chairman, suggested that it would "not be unbecoming the Legislature of New Jersey to reflect upon the reputation she may acquire, and the influence in the councils of confederated America she may be able to establish, by means of her seat of learning." Then the committee report added:

Athens, that commonwealth of science, of taste, and of art, though subdued by Rome, still continued to govern by instructing her masters. And in the present age, Edinburgh, by her celebrated University, lays both Europe and America under contribution for students.

It was not too much to hope, the committee declared, that the College of New Jersey could become a similar seat of learning, the rival of

Elijah Rattoone (1787), President of Charleston College, South Carolina; Joseph Caldwell (1791), President of the University of North Carolina; Robert Helt Chapman (1789), President of the University of North Carolina after Caldwell; John Henry Hobart (1793), Episcopal Bishop of New York and Professor in the Theological Seminary of New York; and Henry Kollock (1794), Professor of Theology in the College of New Jersey. Although Maclean is fully aware of Smith's important role during this period, he simply lists these men as Witherspoon alumni. Maclean, *History of the College of New Jersey*, I, 358.

any "from the Hudson to Georgia." [8] Smith's ambitions for the college were not small.

Scottish influences upon the college made themselves felt through Smith in three specific areas: in the college curriculum; in the intellectual themes and assumptions that dominated Smith's work as teacher and scholar; and in the social theory of education that Smith developed. Smith's curricular and intellectual contributions will be examined as they affected both the life of the college and Smith's personal fortunes. A concluding analysis of Smith's conception of the social role of education will show how he thought Scottish social theory spoke directly to the American situation.

In 1787 Smith delivered the annual oration before the American Philosophical Society, to which he had been elected only two years earlier. The oration was published the same year with the title *An Essay on the Causes of the Variety of Complexion and Figure in the Human Species*. The following year an Edinburgh edition also appeared.[9] Although its major ideas have long since been abandoned or completely reformulated, the *Essay* stood in the mainstream of the thought of the day. As an introduction to his central interests and the lifelong intellectual tasks Smith set for himself, the *Essay* is invaluable.

As the section appended to the published *Essay* indicates, Smith considered his work to be in part an extended refutation of the views of the Scottish jurist and man of letters, Lord Kames. The various races of mankind, Kames had suggested, were descended from different original pairs of parents, each pair being settled by God after the catastrophe of Babel in the kind of climate for which it was best

---

[8] Report reprinted in Maclean, *History of the College of New Jersey*, II, 13–17.

[9] The full title read: *An Essay on the Causes of the Variety of Complexion and Figure in the Human Species, To Which Are Added Strictures on Lord Kaim's Discourses, on the Original Diversity of Mankind.* The *Essay* was published in Edinburgh under the direction of "a Gentleman of the University of Edinburgh," who, as Winthrop Jordan has pointed out, was actually an American student, Benjamin Smith Barton, later Professor at the University of Pennsylvania and one of America's most prominent naturalists. The editing job by Barton is significant in that it indicates one of the several links Smith had with a whole group of important American educators who had been attracted to the Scottish universities and Scottish scientific achievements. Samuel Stanhope Smith, *An Essay on the Causes of the Variety of Complexion and Figure in the Human Species* (Edinburgh: C. Elliot and T. Kay, 1787). Smith republished the *Essay* in a version twice as large as the original in 1810. The *Essay* has been recently re-edited and published with an extremely useful introduction by Winthrop Jordan. Jordan discusses the historic and continuing interest of Smith's *Essay* for those concerned with current issues of race and society. Samuel Stanhope Smith, *An Essay on the Human Species*, edited by Winthrop Jordan (Cambridge, Mass.: Harvard University Press, 1965). Unless otherwise noted, all references are to the 1787 Edinburgh edition.

suited.[10] Against Kames, Smith rejected what he considered to be "the arbitrary hypothesis that men are originally sprung from different stocks, and are therefore divided by nature into different species."[11] Smith asserted the essential unity of mankind; and the burden of his *Essay* was to demonstrate that racial diversity can be adequately accounted for by the effects of climate and what he called "the state of society" on the one human nature.

In the choice and handling of his topic, Smith was acting as defender of the faith, in much the same spirit as Witherspoon in his effort to reconcile reason and revelation. By arguing that human variations could be explained solely as effects of natural causes, Smith felt he was showing that science supported the Biblical account of man's origins, which Kames' theory had impugned. Smith also insisted that his was the better science since he had had no need for recourse to any "arbitrary hypothesis."[12] In summing up at the end of the *Essay*, Smith expressed his conviction that "the most accurate investigations into the power of nature ever serve to confirm the facts vouchsafed by the authority of revelation." "A just philosophy," he added, "will always be found to be coincident with true theology."[13]

As a first intimation of Smith's immersion in an outlook peculiarly Scottish, the *Essay* was especially revealing. Scotsmen, of course, had no monopoly on the eighteenth-century fascination with primitive peoples.[14] Yet Scottish studies of man were unique in that they were carried out within an intellectual framework marked by a common

[10] Lord Kames, *Sketches of the History of Man* (Edinburgh: W. Creech, 1774). I have relied on Gladys Bryson's discussion of Kames. Gladys Bryson, *Man and Society: The Scottish Inquiry of the Eighteenth Century* (Princeton: Princeton University Press, 1945), especially pp. 64–66.

[11] Smith, *An Essay*, pp. 9–10.

[12] Kames, interestingly enough, appealed to divine intervention in deviating from the Genesis story, while Smith, in striking a blow for revelation, limited himself strictly to natural causes.

[13] Smith, *An Essay*, pp. 163–164.

[14] Many of the best early descriptive studies of the American Indian had come from Scotsmen in America, a reflection perhaps of the early Scottish emphasis on empirical investigation. Smith referred to most of these in his *Essay*, including the influential writings of William Robertson, whom Smith did not hesitate to criticize for his inaccuracies. Scots writers, however, did not by any means constitute a majority of Smith's references, among whom the French naturalist Buffon and, in the 1810 edition of the *Essay*, the German Blumenbach were probably the most important individuals. For Smith on Robertson, see Smith, *Essay*, pp. 103–104. For biographical information on all Smith's references, see Jordan, "A Guide to Smith's References," in Smith, *An Essay on the Human Species* (1965), pp. 253–268.

Roy Harvey Pearce maintains that few were more influential than William Robertson in shaping nineteenth-century American attitudes toward the American Indian. Roy Harvey Pearce, *The Savages of America* (Baltimore: The Johns Hopkins Press, 1953).

method and a set of assumptions about human nature shared by most of the leading Scottish philosophers and social analysts.[15]

Two of Smith's central concerns in the *Essay* show his early affinity with dominant themes in Scottish thought. The first was Smith's interest in discovering general laws of human change and development. Scots moral philosophers were united in their conviction that empirical observations would yield general laws governing human society and behavior, just as they were convinced that the same method in the natural sciences led from particular facts to universal laws.[16] Basic to this methodological assumption was the second concern, belief in the essential uniformity of human nature, which the *Essay* was committed to defend.

It is obvious that Smith's method—the inductive discovery of general laws of nature—rested upon the prior acceptance of the very thing it was trying to prove—the uniformity of human nature. The circularity of his argument, however, would probably not have bothered Smith very much, for he left no doubt about his primary purpose and concern. Without the possibility of scientific generalizations about man, and this demanded the unity of the races, Smith concluded that moral philosophy, scientific theology, political philosophy, and the framing of public policy would all be impossible: "human nature could not be comprehended in any system." In this conviction Smith was at one with his Scottish intellectual contemporaries. The great interest among Scottish thinkers in the origins of human society, its development and continuity through time, and the dynamics of social progress all rested upon belief in the possibility of attaining systematic, general truths about human nature.[17] For Smith, moreover, the system

[15] Bryson, *Man and Society*, pp. 11–29, *passim*.
[16] *Ibid*.
[17] Dugald Stewart later gave summary expression to this common working principle of Scottish analysts: "That the capacities of the human mind have been in all ages the same, and the diversity of phenomena exhibited by our species is the result merely of the different circumstances in which men are placed, has been long received as an incontrovertible logical maxim; or rather, such is the influence of early instruction that we are apt to regard it as one of the most obvious suggestions of common sense. And yet till about the time of Montesquieu, it was by no means so generally recognised by the learned as to have a sensible influence on the fashionable tone of thinking over Europe. The application of this fundamental and leading idea to the natural or *theoretical history* of society in all its various aspects; —to the history of languages, or the arts, of the sciences, of laws, of government, of manners, and of religion,—is the peculiar glory of the latter half of the eighteenth century, and forms a characteristic feature of its philosophy, which even the imagination of Bacon was unable to foresee." Quoted in William C. Lehmann, *John Millar of Glasgow, 1735–1801* (Cambridge: At the University Press, 1960), p. 107.
   Hume gave classic expression to this point of view: "It is universally acknowl-

and order of the universe formed the basis for the harmonious union of his two great interests—science and religion.

Smith's full appropriation of Scottish thought is to be seen in his lectures on moral philosophy, which he published in 1812.[18] James McCosh has maintained that from the date of the publication of Smith's *Lectures* "the Scottish became the most influential philosophy in America."[19] McCosh's appreciation of the importance of Scottish philosophy in America may be in need of some critical revision, but the attention he draws to the pervasiveness of Scottish thought in Smith's *Lectures* is, if anything, understated.

Smith found in the thought of Thomas Reid the philosophical support he needed to show the compatibility between good science and true religion. As will become evident, Smith also had in the common sense philosophy important resources for the clear and convincing presentation of his ideas to his students.

The common sense outlook was first developed by Reid in reaction to the skepticism which he saw as the ultimate result of Hume's consistent Lockean psychology. Reid contended that the very possibility of knowledge and of human communication rests upon certain ultimate principles, or basic assumptions, that simply must be accepted as irreducible constituents of all meaningful experience. These ultimate principles cannot be proved, but neither can they be denied without falling into absurdity.[20]

Among the most important of these ultimate principles were the reality of a world external to the mind, the real identity of the self and its continuity through time, the existence of other minds, and a genuine power of the mind to determine its actions and to judge the validity of ideas. The common sense experience of all mankind attests

---

edged that there is a great uniformity among the actions of men, in all nations and ages, and that human nature remains still the same, in its principles and operations. The same motives always produce the same actions: The same events follow from the same causes." David Hume, *An Enquiry Concerning Human Understanding,* edited by L. A. Selby-Biggs (Oxford: The Clarendon Press, 1902), p. 83.

[18] Samuel Stanhope Smith, *The Lectures, corrected and improved, which have been delivered for a series of years, in the College of New Jersey; on the subjects of moral and political philosophy* (2 vols.; Trenton, N.J.: Daniel Fenton, 1812). Referred to henceforth as *The Lectures.*

[19] James McCosh, *The Scottish Philosophy* (New York: Robert Carter and Brothers, 1875), p. 188.

[20] See especially Thomas Reid, *Essays on the Intellectual Powers of Man,* edited by A. D. Woozley (London: Macmillan and Company, 1941), Essay VI, Chapter 2, "Of Common Sense," and Chapter 5, "The First Principles of Contingent Truths," pp. 329 ff., 372 ff., especially p. 397. Also see McCosh, *The Scottish Philosophy,* pp. 192–227; Bryson, *Man and Society,* pp. 130–136, 143–147; and S. A. Grave, *The Scottish Philosophy of Common Sense* (Oxford: The Clarendon Press, 1960).

to the validity of these principles, thought Reid, and even the structure of all human language has been shaped by them. To doubt these principles in practice was impossible, Reid argued, even for the skeptical philosopher, since to do so would be to deny the very "constitution of our nature."[21]

Educational implications were present in almost every aspect of Smith's philosophical and religious thinking, and it is significant that Smith was aware of them and often made them explicit. He took up Reid's interest in the origin and structure of human languages, for example, and devoted an entire lecture to the subject before proceeding to the epistemological, metaphysical, and ethical issues which occupy the bulk of his first volume in moral philosophy. In so doing he made plain his conviction that philosophy's first concern should be with the practical task of furthering the search for truth and its communication among men. "One of the principle sources of improvement in man, and one of his chief distinctions from the inferior animals," Smith said in this lecture, "is the power of communicating, and recording his thoughts, and increasing and correcting his knowledge by communication."[22] It will not be twisting Smith's own primary concerns, therefore, to try to understand certain of the more important ideas in his philosophic outlook by approaching them through their relevance for education.

In the first place, the Scottish philosophical outlook furnished Smith with a theoretical foundation for his own belief in the importance of education as the deliberate shaping of human personality. Smith developed his philosophy, of course, with broader purposes in mind than education. He did not, however, neglect to draw the educational implications from his thought; nor did he hesitate to fall back on his philosophical principles in promoting his educational views. The two basic elements in Smith's philosophy that gave support to an emphasis upon education were his conception of the relationship between the mind and body, and his notion of the active, integrating power of the mind. Smith derived both ideas primarily from the line of thinking represented by Thomas Reid, but he did not bind himself slavishly to the Scotsman.

In the *Essay* Smith had argued that, while basically uniform, human nature is flexible and subject to an infinite variety of environ-

21 See Reid, *Essays*, pp. 377–385, 406–408.
22 Smith, *The Lectures*, I, 100.

mental influences. Next to climate, the main force affecting human character was the state of society, which, Smith said, comprised the "manner of living" and "passions and ideas of all kinds." [23] Over long periods of time ideas and customs could even alter physical features. "The body and the mind have such reciprocal influence on each other," he said, "that we often see certain peculiar powers or tendencies of the rational faculty intimately connected with certain corporeal forms." [24] It would be interesting, Smith reflected in the *Essay*, to see what could be achieved "by a well-directed care." [25] This conception of the uniformity and flexibility of human nature clearly favored a high valuation of the power of education in its widest sense.

In his lectures on moral philosophy Smith spelled out in greater detail his conception of the mind and its relationship to the world. Here Reid's common sense philosophy was indispensable. As always, of course, Smith did not separate his philosophical and scientific concerns from his theological. In discussing the mind-body relationship, Smith wanted to avoid the danger of both materialism and idealism, which he considered the two religious and philosophical errors of his time. Any idealistic tendencies in his own thinking were checked at the outset by his commitment to common sense realism, but the problem of materialism was more difficult. Smith looked upon materialism as almost synonymous with atheism. The environmentalism of his own *Essay*, however, had come so dangerously close to what appeared to be a form of materialism that he devoted much attention in his *Lectures* to clarifying his position.

Characteristically, he first attacked on scientific grounds the idea that mind is just a function or different appearance of matter. "As far as experiments have ever been made upon it," he said, matter differs fundamentally from mind, and no valid analogy between the nature of spirit and body can be drawn "on true principles of philosophy." The essential difference between them can best be seen in man, he believed, by contrasting the external with the internal senses and the properties of mind with those of matter. Mind, grasped only by the internal senses of consciousness, is self-motivating and undivided; matter, perceived by the external senses, which register such qualities as color, shape, and size, is passive, inert, and divisible into mechanically related parts. In this analysis, mind and matter were distinct in sub-

[23] Smith, *An Essay*, p. 98.
[24] *Ibid.*, p. 193.
[25] *Ibid.*, p. 115; Smith, *The Lectures*, I, 203.

stance and operation and should not be confused.[26] Smith also argued from the theological consequences of materialism. Materialistic interpretations of the mind must be rejected, he was convinced, because they inevitably lead to atheism.[27] Smith would apparently have been willing to accept this as a sufficient argument had there been no other; but, in his view, it had the undeniable corroboration of science and philosophy, which he accordingly emphasized the most.

Smith was aware that this firm distinction between mind and matter posed difficulties for his belief in the mutual interaction of environment and personality. He insisted that there is an inseparable relationship between mind and matter, but felt that philosophy was not advanced enough to explain its workings. Better by far, he thought, to accept a thoroughgoing dualism than to confuse the material and the immaterial.[28]

Smith himself was not quite prepared, however, simply to rest with that. The connections between mind and body were so close, and their effects upon one another played such an important role in all of his thinking, that Smith was willing to conjecture about the nature of the relationship. In this regard he thought that perhaps Hartley's idea of nerve vibration could be helpful. The notion that vibration of the nerves can produce thought seemed to provide a perfectly natural explanation of dreams and so-called supernatural visions.[29] Reid had rejected Hartley's vibration theory, and Smith was fully cognizant of his own deviation from the Scottish philosopher on this score.[30] Smith's use of Hartley illustrates his own speculative and inquisitive nature and his tendency to look for natural causes even of religious phenomena—traits that endeared him less and less to many of his ecclesiastical colleagues.

Reason received an overwhelmingly positive and central role in

---

[26] Smith, *The Lectures*, I, 127, 129–130; also see Lecture VIII, "Of the external senses," and Lecture IX, "Of internal sensation."

[27] *Ibid.*, I, 127 ff.

[28] *Ibid.*, pp. 145–147.

[29] In a long and intriguing footnote Smith relates how he employed his vibratory theory in pastoral counseling, once in persuading a fellow minister that the minister's visions of direct, divine guidance had their origins wholly in the disturbed nervous state of his mind. Smith, *The Lectures*, I, 161 ff.

[30] Letter, Smith to Benjamin Rush, September 27, 1812, photocopy, Princeton University Library, Manuscript Collection, AM 14429.

Bryson writes: "As fantastic as Hartley's theory of vibrations was, it was an attempt to provide a physical basis for an explanation of mental operations. . . . By scorning it, Reid listed himself among those who failed to recognize the more profitable empirical procedures." It was precisely this in Hartley which Smith did recognize. See Bryson, *Man and Society*, p. 145.

Smith's thought. The Scottish tradition of common sense accorded a primary place to the affections as the springs of human action, so that there were certain limitations on what reason could accomplish. Reason could not change man's basic nature; it could not create new affections.[31] In Reid's view, however, reason as the active, integrating power of the mind was also an original principle of consciousness. It was the dual task of reason to analyze and test ideas and to set the goals of conduct and guide the affections in their attainment; happiness and moral conduct both depended upon the governing power of reason.[32] Smith followed Reid closely in emphasizing the active power of reason, especially as it pertained to conduct. Smith defined virtue, for example, as "living according to nature," by which he meant the harmonious functioning of the various components of human nature —the corporeal powers and appetites, the social affections, the intellectual faculties, and the moral sentiments—all under the direction of reason.[33]

Educational implications were always near the surface of Smith's philosophical discussions of the flexibility of human nature and the power of the mind, and he often took pains to bring them out. Again and again Smith uttered words to the effect that man is governed chiefly by reason, and reason, he declared, "is an improvable principle." [34] In discussing the duties of parents, for example, Smith said:

It is education chiefly which makes a man what he is; whether it be well, or ill-conceived. In the idea of education I include not only what is conveyed into the mind by direct and positive instruction, but every impression which is received directly, or incidentally, by precept, example, or intercourse with mankind, which contributes to form the character.[35]

In this sense "education" need not be purposeful, and could be merely another name for experience. By the same token, however, a deliberate education—"direct and positive instruction"—held forth great promise. Education appears in Smith's thought, for example, to have nearly displaced conversion as the most desirable influence in forming human character.[36] Even national characteristics, mental and physical, could be greatly improved, Smith wrote, "by the cultivation of the arts, and

[31] Smith, *The Lectures*, I, 260–262.
[32] Reid, *Essays*, pp. 382, 430.
[33] Smith, *The Lectures*, I, 99; also II, 69 ff.
[34] *Ibid.*
[35] *Ibid.*, II, 45.
[36] Smith comes close to saying this in so many words. *Ibid.*, I, 294–296.

by the refinement of the manners of society." [37] Thus a properly planned and well-executed education became a moral and intellectual responsibility of the first order.

What kind of deliberate education, then, did Smith have in mind? In his philosophical discussions, Smith's high evaluation of the power of "direct and positive instruction" is clear, but the actual details of the type of program he favored remain vague. A partial answer to this question may be found in Smith's own teaching and administrative work at the college. An observation of the method of inquiry and instruction he used, the kind of curriculum he fostered, and the attitudes toward learning he represented and encouraged will help to make Smith's concept of education concrete. A more complete answer, and greater concreteness, will come later in considering Smith's social thought and its educational ramifications.

Smith always carried a full load of classroom responsibilities, and all evidence points to a constant concern on his part for clear and compelling teaching. He did not read his lectures in moral philosophy, but, following the practice for which Scottish professors were noted, required each student to make his own copy of Smith's written lectures. These personal copies from the original then served each student as a text to be studied in preparation for class, which was devoted to questions and discussion. He held a colloquium for his divinity students two evenings each week in which his lecture notes were discussed, with Smith commenting on various topics, directing the course of readings, and suggesting unexplored subjects for written and oral assignments. Smith also met once a week with all of his resident graduate students in a special discussion group—"a kind of philosophical as well as debating society"—where, according to Philip Lindsley, one of the participants, Smith was "the great master—and the liberal umpire in all our wordy battles." [38] With only a few short intermissions Smith taught moral philosophy, divinity, belles lettres, logic, geography, and history during the entire period that he was in full charge of the administration of the college.[39]

In Smith's view his philosophical commitments, teaching methods, and curricular program were all intimately related. The point where they came together—the linchpin—was in Smith's conception of the scientific method, which he took from Scottish thought and developed

[37] Smith, *An Essay*, p. 115; *The Lectures*, I, 303.
[38] Sprague, *Annals of the American Pulpit*, III, 342–345.
[39] *Ibid.*

in considerable detail. In fact Smith began his lectures in moral philosophy with an elaborate discussion of the scientific method.

In Lecture I Smith laid down the basic principles of moral philosophy, the same principles, he emphasized to his students, that governed natural philosophy. He summarized the scientific method in five rules, showing first the movement from particular facts to the elaboration of general laws, and then the proper uses and limitations of these generalizations. Smith's summary of the scientific method reveals some of what is, perhaps, its too simple empirical optimism, but also shows a certain amount of sophistication. Smith's five rules were:

1. "That no law should be admitted on hypothesis, but should rest solely on an induction of facts."
2. "That laws collected from an ample and accurate induction of facts should be deemed universal, till other facts occur to invalidate, or limit the conclusions which have been drawn from them."
3. "That laws founded on a partial induction of facts should not be extended beyond the limits to which they are certainly known to apply."
4. "That similar appearances should, because of the uniformity of nature, be referred, as far as possible to the same causes."
5. "That the testimony of our senses, and of all our simple perceptions, ought to be admitted as true, and no ulterior evidence be required of the reality, or the nature of the facts which they confirm."

The last rule, of course, connected directly with the realist outlook of Thomas Reid.[40]

Although this empirical method was, of course, not unique to Scottish thinkers, it had been developed in systematic detail by them. Moreover, in considering the scientific method as method, and as the only sure avenue to truth in every area of inquiry, Scottish thinkers, more than any others, had been aware of its pedagogical implications.

[40] Reid's discussion of the scientific method as applied to the investigation of the mind was similar to Smith's, though not so systematic. Reid, for example, wrote: "Let us, therefore, lay down this as a fundamental principle in our inquiries into the structure of the mind and its operations—that no regard is due to the conjectures or hypotheses of philosophers, however ancient, however generally received. Let us accustom ourselves to try every opinion by the touchstone of fact and experience. What can fairly be deduced from facts, duly observed or sufficiently attested, is genuine and pure; it is the voice of God and no fiction of human imagination." Besides its unbounded faith in the accessibility of the world through simple observation, this passage reveals the extent to which "hypothesis" had become a scare word to the scientific-minded. Smith, too, held this conception of "hypothesis." Reid, *Essays*, pp. 34–35; Smith, *The Lectures*, I, 19–24.

The results of their efforts were apparent in the field of logic, for example. One of the most important works in logic was *The Elements of Logic* by William Duncan, Professor of Philosophy at Aberdeen University (1752–1760). Duncan's work replaced the *Logick* of Isaac Watts as a text in many of the American colleges in the eighteenth century and was in use at the College of New Jersey when Smith became President.[41] Duncan distinguished between the logic of "analysis" and the logic of "synthesis." "Analysis" described the work of induction from particulars to universals; "synthesis" was the process of organizing and relating general principles and reasoning from them back to the individual facts. The method of synthesis he recommended as particularly suited to communicating and teaching any body of organized knowledge. He thought that it enabled the student to grasp from the outset, without the uncertainties and labor of induction, the most significant results and principles of a subject, from which he could then move to particulars and their relationships to one another in the whole system.

Smith's entire *Lectures* provides an excellent example of a classroom application of Duncan's synthetic method. In lecture after lecture Smith first introduced his students to the central broad ideas underlying the subject being presented, and then, subdividing his topic according to the various principles involved, worked down to specific instances. This method, Smith felt, was especially fitted for the study of moral philosophy, since the subject itself attempted to encompass the whole span of human knowledge and conduct. Thus, he told his students, "The object of the science of moral philosophy . . . is not so much a minute and extensive detail of particular duties . . . as to propose such general *principles* as may enable a rational and reflecting mind to deduce the point of duty for itself, on every case as it arises in practice." The advantages that this method offered the busy classroom teacher, such as Smith, are obvious.

From his undergraduate days to the end of his life Smith was an ardent advocate of eighteenth-century science. In 1784, when plans for the *Essay* may have been taking shape in his mind, Smith expressed his keen scientific interest in other peoples and cultures in correspon-

41 Maclean, *History of the College of New Jersey*, I, 367. Duncan's text was one of the books included in William Smith's 1756 curriculum at the College of Philadelphia. T. H. Montgomery, *A History of the University of Pennsylvania* (Philadelphia: G. W. Jacobs & Co., 1900), p. 236. See Carl Albert Hangartner, S.J., "Movements to Change American College Teaching, 1700–1830" (Ph.D. dissertation, Yale University, 1955), pp. 258 ff. I have relied on Hangartner for my discussion of Duncan's method.

dence with the Scottish minister and future President of Dickinson College, Charles Nisbet.[42] Smith wrote to Nisbet that accurate information about the American Indians was especially sparse. As a remedy Smith proposed that scientific societies should send qualified investigators "to reside among them on a familiar footing; dress and live as they do; and to observe them when they should be under no bias or constraint"—a suggestion with a modern ring to it.[43] Smith's interest in science did not slacken. Questions relating to various scientific issues of the day figured often among the many topics Smith and his physician friend, Benjamin Rush, discussed in the letters they exchanged with each other for more than thirty years.

Smith carried his interest in science over into the college curriculum, which he was determined to make as modern as any in America. Smith was very much aware of the scientific achievements of the Scottish universities and medical schools. When the Scottish-born and Scottish-educated Professor of Mathematics and Natural Philosophy, Walter Minto, died in 1795, Smith replaced him with another Scotsman, John Maclean, a young chemist fresh from the universities of Edinburgh, London, and Paris. Maclean had studied with Joseph Black at Glasgow and Edinburgh, and with Lavoisier in Paris. Smith had Maclean appointed Professor of Chemistry and Natural History, the first American professor of chemistry in a regular arts college outside a medical school.[44]

A year later Smith engaged Samuel Bayard, a future college trustee, to purchase scientific equipment in London.[45] In 1805, Smith secured a natural history cabinet from a man in New York. He wrote to his brother-in-law, the South Carolina physician and historian, David Ramsay, asking for assistance from his Southern friends in procuring items of natural history for the cabinet. "I observe that a rattle snake of great size & age, has lately died, or been killed in the neighborhood of George Town. Would it be possible," Smith asked, "for me to obtain the skeleton and rattlers?" He also requested samples

---

[42] Smith's correspondence with Nisbet, prior to the latter's coming to America, is reprinted in Michael Kraus, "Charles Nisbet and Samuel Stanhope Smith—Two Eighteenth Century Educators," *The Princeton University Library Chronicle*, VI (November 1944), 17–36.

[43] *Ibid.*, pp. 22–23.

[44] Maclean, *History of the College of New Jersey*, II, 10; Theodore Hornberger, *Scientific Thought in the American Colleges, 1638–1800* (Austin: The University of Texas Press, 1945), p. 73.

[45] Letter, Smith to Bayard, December 26, 1796, Princeton University Library, Manuscript Collection.

of the seeds and roots of plants that were typically found in the soil and climate of South Carolina. The entire faculty of the college, Smith said to Ramsay, were behind him "in every exertion of which our finances will admit, for the advancement of science, & of natural science particularly in this institution." [46]

Smith's greatest innovation was to convince the trustees in 1799 to allow special students to study only the scientific part of the curriculum and to by-pass the regular classical studies. Rather than the regular diploma, the trustees awarded a certificate of proficiency to those who completed this course. After ten years, however, the trustees ended the experiment altogether without leaving a record of their reasons.[47] Throughout his career Smith maintained that future ministers should be fully exposed to the study of science, especially natural history. Not only did he think that natural history was a support to revelation, but, he told his divinity students, "I recommend it, likewise, as a study, which contributes peculiarly to purify, exalt and delight the mind. . . ." [48]

Smith endeavored throughout his life to continue Witherspoon's program of harmonizing Enlightenment rationalism and Calvinist doctrine in order to undercut what he discerned as the spreading forces of infidelity. In the process Smith himself was charged by certain leaders in the church with having yielded too much to the other side. Alarmed at what he took to be the progress of infidelity, and probably just as concerned to dispel rumors that he himself was a heretic, Smith felt constrained when he republished his *Essay* in 1810 to emphasize that it had been written as an act of piety. "While others," he wrote ". . . are successfully defending the interior fortresses of religion, and extending her practical sway over the hearts of men, I thought I might render a valuable service to the cause, by cooperating, in some degree, with those who are defending her outworks, and carrying their attacks into the enemy camp." [49]

Smith was far from ever thinking of true science as the enemy, however, and it is difficult to decide which interest was really the

---

[46] Smith to Ramsay, September 29, 1805, Princeton University Library, Manuscript Collection, AM 239 P.H.

[47] Maclean, *History of the College of New Jersey*, II, 29–30.

[48] Samuel Stanhope Smith, *A Comprehensive View of the Leading and Most Important Principles of Natural and Revealed Religion* (New Brunswick, N.J.: Deace & Myer, 1816), pp. 14–15.

[49] Samuel Stanhope Smith, *An Essay on the Causes of the Variety of Complexion and Figure in the Human Species* (New Brunswick, N.J.: J. Simpson & Co., 1810), pp. 4–5.

most natural and fascinating for him, science or religion. His apologetic, consequently, took the form of attempting to demonstrate that true science was religious and that sound theology could have the status and certainty of science. The early conviction that Smith expressed to Benjamin Rush shortly after his election to the American Philosophical Society was one that remained with him throughout life. "Divinity & philosophy when enlightened by the same spirit," wrote Smith, "naturally fall into the same train of thought, & . . . the chair of the philosophical society is as orthodox as the pulpit of Princeton." [50] Rush may have been convinced of the truth of Smith's sentiments, but there were others who were not so sure. Smith's continuing effort to unite science with his own religious principles was eventually to deliver him to his opponents.

Smith attempted to strike a middle position, as he himself said, between "a weak and suspicious scepticism" on the one hand and "a bold and positive dogmatism" on the other. The union he saw between science and common sense philosophy appeared to him to provide the perfect instrument for attaining this aim. Reid, for example, had argued that the belief demanded by common sense empiricism in minds other than our own also entails belief in the existence of the mind of God. Reid had also argued that the common sense rejection of subjectivism implies the acceptance of a moral distinction between right and wrong. Thus, rather than being enemies, science and religion could be shown to support and lead to each other both in matters of faith and of morals.

Smith had little difficulty in adapting his Calvinism to the more man-centered ethic of the Scottish moral philosophers, with their emphasis upon enlightened self-interest and the happiness of benevolence as the measure of individual and social progress.[51] Smith, it is true, did assert repeatedly that the power of sin was too great to hope that reason without revelation would ever reform the world.[52] Despite his own affirmation of orthodoxy, however, the entire drift of Smith's thought moved unmistakably in the opposite direction.

Indeed, it became difficult to see where Smith had left anything essential to revelation in attempting to prop up religion with science

---

[50] Smith to Rush, May 10, 1786, photocopy, Princeton University Library, Manuscript Collection, AM 14429.
[51] See, for example, Smith, The Lectures, II, 82–89. Compare Adam Ferguson, An Essay on the History of Civil Society, edited by Duncan Forbes (Edinburgh: Edinburgh University Press, 1966; first published 1767), pp. 53–57.
[52] Samuel Stanhope Smith, A Comprehensive View of . . . Religion, pp. 73–89.

and philosophy. This tendency in Smith's thought might have gone unnoticed had he, like Witherspoon, always been willing to allow contradictions and uncertainties to stand, side-stepping difficulties by invoking the mystery of the divine sovereignty. His love of speculative inquiry and of system building pushed Smith, however, to entertain views that were, at the very least, novel for a Calvinist divine, and that appeared to many to give infidelity a foothold within the college itself.

In fact, two of Smith's most original applications of Scottish philosophy to doctrinal and ethical problems provoked charges that Smith was heterodox and was exposing his students to dangerous ideas. In an attempt to demonstrate the existence of an absolute moral sensibility underlying the great variety of human customs and practices, he adopted a qualified cultural relativism. Smith said that in judging the merits and virtues of any particular act or social custom it was necessary to take into full consideration revealed religion, natural law, and the differing traditions, laws, tastes, and needs under which various human societies lived, as well as to allow for the possibility of honest error.[53]

From this standpoint Smith even ventured to say that he could see nothing intrinsically wrong in the practice of polygamy, since he could find no evidence that it was contrary to the laws of nature. He stressed that the higher revealed morality of Christianity demanded monogamy, but maintained that the marriage practices of peoples who had not been exposed to Christian teachings had to be judged on other grounds. Because natural law did not provide a universal norm, the morality of monogamy or polygamy was relative to the social and economic contexts in which they were practiced. "I confess," Smith said,

I cannot perceive, from the opinions, and example of the wisest men of antiquity, that the law of nature has prescribed any definite rule upon the subject, and, therefore, where religion has not taken it out of the hands of the legislator, it is to be regarded chiefly as an affair of civil and political regulation.[54]

What must have been exceedingly annoying to those who disagreed with Smith was that he did not stop with this, but devoted several

[53] Smith, *The Lectures*, I, 308–324.
[54] *Ibid.*, II, 120.

pages in *The Lectures* to a detailed critique of natural law arguments against polygamy.[55]

In January 1804, the Reverend William Hill of Virginia wrote to Ashbel Green reporting the rumor he had heard that Smith was undertaking in his lectures "to prove that Polygamy & concubinage are not moral evils" unless "they violate the statutes of the land." Alarmed for the future of the church, Hill concluded, "At any rate it would not do to employ a pupil of Dr. Smiths as a missionary to the Indians where the Dr's plan may be practiced upon without violating either the Laws of God or man." [56] Neither Hill nor Green, however, were willing to press charges against Smith in church court and the matter was dropped, openly at any rate.

Smith's opponents, nevertheless, continued to pick away at his ideas and views as tending toward heresy. Smith had made himself extremely vulnerable to such attacks by boldly proposing a new solution to the highly controversial question of predestination and freedom of the will. The common sense emphasis upon the active power of the mind appeared to Smith to provide a different vantage than had been customary for tackling these old, perplexing problems.

If the concept of the mind as essentially active and self-determining be admitted, Smith argued, the whole sterile dispute between Arminianism and necessitarian doctrines of the will could be circumvented. The will is determined by motives, he said, but the will itself is only one aspect of the mind in operation. The mind, endowed with the powers of "deliberating, judging, comparing, and estimating motives," selects which motives shall move the will. The truth in necessitarian views was that the mind tended to be persuaded by those motives most akin to the present state and disposition of a person's character, but this could always be improved through the cultivation of the individual's moral, aesthetic, and intellectual sensitivities. Moral responsibility was, thus, preserved, as was the incentive to improve the race through education.[57]

The doctrine of predestination could be understood in much the same way: not as God's eternal determination of all events, but as his direct, intuitive foreknowledge of how men would act—the active

55 *Ibid.*, II, 118–127.
56 Hill to Green, January 20, 1804, Princeton University Library, Manuscript Collection, AM 2773.
57 Smith, *The Lectures*, I, 275 ff., 284.

power of the infinite, divine mind in operation.[58] That Smith's solution of the problem, which removed the discussion from the plane of questions about the will to questions about the mind, seemed more semantic than substantial, did not escape his critics.

In April 1808, William Weeks, a student at the college, wrote to his father complaining about the favor which Reid's *Essays* enjoyed at the college under Smith. "Reid is grossly *Arminian,* and advocates a *Self-determining power,* which, if it means anything," said Weeks, "means that the creature is independent of the Creator." [59] The suspicion that Smith was basically Arminian was one that young Weeks shared with more influential figures in the church. The same spring, Smith preached a sermon on baptism which was attacked, again on the grounds that Smith had given higher priority to human faith than to God's granting of unmerited salvation. In a letter to Ashbel Green, who by this time was clearly one of Smith's main antagonists, Smith defended himself by charging that his critics were not making even the first efforts to try to understand what he was really saying. "But there are good men," Smith wrote to Green, "who have learned to think in a set of words; & they cannot easily conceive the idea if the phrase is altered. On the other hand, I have a certain aversion, perhaps ill-founded, to using the same technical language." Then, expressing his contempt for their picayune latching on to details, Smith challenged his critics to come openly to grips with "the *subject* of the sermon itself," which, he added, "in one respect at least, differs considerably from the ordinary representations of the nature of that ordinance." [60]

Many of Smith's difficulties probably stemmed as much from personal antagonisms as from intellectual differences. Indeed, it may be supposed with good reason that many of Smith's opponents were gratified to discover theological irregularities in his thinking which enabled them to vent deeper-lying personal antipathies. Physically handsome, reserved but interesting in conversation, somewhat aristocratic in outlook and bearing, Smith undoubtedly stood in stark contrast to many of his more rustic ministerial colleagues. Archibald

[58] Smith actually prefigured the very formula that was to become famous in the "new divinity" of Nathaniel William Taylor: "certainty without necessity." Smith, *A Comprehensive View . . . of Religion,* pp. 264–267.

[59] William Weeks to Ebenezer Weeks, April 11, 1808, Princeton University Library, Manuscript Collection, AM 11456.

[60] Smith to Green, March 20, 1808, Princeton University Library, Manuscript Collection, AM 9032.

Alexander recounted his own first impression of Smith, when, as a young man, he saw Smith at the 1791 General Assembly. Smith was still Vice-President of the college at the time. "Dr. Witherspoon remained only two or three days," wrote Alexander,

after which Dr. Samuel Stanhope Smith took his place. When he entered the house, I did not observe him, but happening to turn my head I saw a person whom I must still consider the most elegant I ever saw. The beauty of his countenance, the clear and vivid complexion, the symmetry of his form—the exquisite finish of his dress, were such as to strike the beholder at first sight. The thought never occurred to me that he was a clergyman, and I supposed him to be some gentleman of Philadelphia, who had dropped in to hear the debate. I ought to have mentioned that Dr. Witherspoon was as plain an old man as I ever saw, and as free from any assumption of dignity.[61]

In light of Alexander's later involvement with Samuel Miller and Ashbel Green in their opposition to Smith, Alexander's description may have had a double edge to it. Many clearly viewed Smith's "assumption of dignity" as unbefitting his clerical position, and could only have seen Smith's contrast with the plainness of old Dr. Witherspoon as unfortunate. Smith's sermons, for example, were noted for their literary polish and simple but forceful eloquence. Smith himself wrote that in shaping his own style he attempted to combine the fervor of the French preachers with the simplicity and rationality of the English.[62] His pulpit reputation was such as to have him chosen to deliver the eulogy at Trenton on the occasion of Washington's death.[63] It also gave rise to the story that his brother, John Blair Smith, had reproached him with, "Brother Sam, you don't preach Jesus Christ and Him crucified, but Sam Smith and him dignified." Maclean denies that the story was based on fact, but many of Smith's colleagues must have taken some pleasure in thinking it genuine.[64]

---

[61] James W. Alexander, *The Life of Archibald Alexander* (New York: C. Scribner, 1854), p. 99.
[62] Samuel Stanhope Smith, *Sermons* (Newark, N.J.: Jacob Halsey and Co., 1799), "Preface," p. iv.
[63] William Bradbury has done a detailed analysis of Smith's eulogy on Washington, showing how fully it exemplifies the rhetorical principles and practices of Witherspoon's "Lectures on Eloquence." See Samuel Stanhope Smith, *An Oration Upon the Death of General George Washington* (Trenton, N.J.: G. Craft, 1800); William Bradbury, "Adventure in Persuasion" (Ph.D. dissertation, Harvard University, 1966), pp. 129 ff.
[64] Maclean, *History of the College of New Jersey*, II, 133.

Smith, it seems, always gave his enemies plenty of material to work with. For several years after he became Vice-President, Smith carried on a correspondence in the romantic style of late eighteenth-century Europe with his cousin Samuel Blair and his wife, Susan Shippen Blair, and Mrs. Annis Boudinot Stockton. In their letters the men were both referred to as "Cleander," and the two woman as "Fidelia" and "Emilia." The correspondents amused each other with literary and philosophical speculations, tried their hands at poetry, and, above all, declared their personal sentiments and affections for one another in lofty literary fashion. Unfortunately, news of the exchange leaked out. Although it would have been accepted as commonplace in the cultural circles of London and Edinburgh, in eighteenth-century America it became the pretext for a rumor that Smith's relations with his cousin's wife were not altogether savory, and the correspondence had to be dropped for a time.[65] If Smith contrasted vividly with his father-in-law, it was in part because he lived up to Witherspoon's own ideal of the evangelical gentleman and ministerial man of letters with more success than the plain old doctor ever could.

During the last two decades of the century Smith was one of the most prominent Presbyterians in America, and he played an active leadership role in the church. He attended the meetings of the Synods of New York and Philadelphia, and was a member of the crucial committee for organizing the General Assembly and for preparing the new Form of Government.[66] Like Witherspoon, however, Smith had an intense dislike for unnecessary religious disputes, and he pushed much further than did Witherspoon in defending the rights of concience against rigid, doctrinaire orthodoxy. In 1788, Smith's cousin, Samuel Blair, had an invitation to preach in a church at Neshaminy withdrawn because he held the view that all men would eventually be saved. Smith laid the responsibility for his cousin's rejection at the feet of the same persons who had circulated the rumors stemming from Smith's correspondence with Mrs. Blair. Smith's remarks in his letters to Blair about the incident are worth quoting at some length because they reveal his own liberality of mind and his scorn for "such mistaken zealots" who "hate more heartily for God's sake."

[65] Some of the principal letters of the Cleander-Fidelia exchange are reprinted and discussed in David F. Bowers, "The Smith-Blair Correspondence, 1786–1791," *Princeton University Library Chronicle*, IV (June 1943), 123–124. An excellent discussion of this correspondence is provided by Monk, "Samuel Stanhope Smith . . . ," in Thorp, ed., *The Lives of Eighteen from Princeton*, pp. 196–199.

[66] Maclean, *History of the College of New Jersey*, II, 137–138; Leonard J. Trinterud, *The Forming of an American Tradition: A Reexamination of Colonial Presbyterianism* (Philadelphia: Westminster Press, 1949), pp. 284–286.

"These men," Smith wrote to his cousin, "have made you a *heretic*, and me a *rake*. . . ." Although he himself was probably not a universalist in theology, Smith not only assured Blair of his full support, but also encouraged him to publish his views:

As I do not intend to wrap myself in the shroud of orthodoxy with lifeless acquiescence in established systems, I shall be glad to see a question of such moment to mankind candidly, and sensibly discussed. I shall never believe that you are to be rejected from salvation for holding that all other men are to be saved—Therefore your asserting this principle will not provoke any pious rage in me. I will give your argument a fair and cool examination. If I am not convinced, I will represent my objections to you with the same candor—If I cannot answer you I will not grow angry—and that is more than you can say of every Christian Brother— but I have learned long since, not to fight for God as if the devil were in me. If reason and charity cannot promote the cause of truth and piety I cannot see how it should ever flourish under the withering fires of wrath and strife.[67]

Underlying all else, the final source of Smith's intellectual difficulties with many of his Christian brothers was his continuing refusal to be bound unquestioningly to fixed doctrinal formulations. At times, especially when the opposition to Smith was reaching its climax, the issue was posed as one of religion versus science. Preaching before the 1808 General Assembly, Archibald Alexander pled for a seminary separate from the college and devoted exclusively to the training of ministers. Alexander said he doubted whether the course of education pursued in the college was best suited to prepare young men for the ministry. "The great extension of the physical sciences," Alexander explained, "and the taste and fashion of the age, have given such a shape and direction to the academical course that I confess it appears to me to be little adapted to introduce youth to the study of the Sacred Scriptures." [68] No one present who had been privy to the disputes wracking the college could have possibly missed recognizing Smith as the object of this comment.[69] In urging the adoption of

---

[67] Smith to Blair, January 27, 1788, Princeton University Library, Manuscript Collection, AM 12800.

[68] Alexander, *Life of Archibald Alexander*, pp. 314–315.

[69] In opposing a separate theological seminary Smith had said: "The true object of inquiry is, whether, in a state of cultivated society like ours, it is not the duty of those who purpose to devote themselves to the ministry of the gospel, to bestow great pains in the acquisition of literature and science? & whether the rulers of the church ought not to require this qualification in those whom they admit to this holy office?" Samuel Stanhope Smith, "On the Utility and Necessity of Learning

a seminary on these grounds, Alexander was undoubtedly sincere, and was probably assured of a favorable response from many of the ministers present, who did think the question was one of preserving religion against the encroachments of science.[70]

The real issue, however, was much more subtle and complicated, for neither Ashbel Green nor Samuel Miller, associates of Alexander, could be said to have lacked interest in science. Green was a member of the American Philosophical Society and for a time had actually been Professor of Mathematics and Natural Philosophy at the college; Miller's account of eighteenth-century thought, still valuable today, reflects throughout its pages his interest in science.[71] The fundamental point of contention actually concerned the authority of science, and that in turn rested upon what was to be regarded as the source of final authority in matters of faith: the authority of personal conviction, guided by doctrine, or the authority of the creed as normative over all.

Smith's own choice was never in doubt. In 1812 he wrote to Benjamin Rush announcing that he was sending his friend a copy of the first volume of his newly published lectures in moral philosophy. In this letter Smith expressed the attitude toward learning and inquiry that had guided his own writing, teaching, and curriculum-planning in the college. "Some of my opinions," he wrote, "are too philosophical for several of my brethren who are so deadly orthodox, that they cannot find words in the English language, to express their zeal and jealousy upon the subject, & therefore oblige their candidates to swear *ex animo* to all their doctrines. Whether my opinions concur in all things with yours, or not, I know that I address them to a liberal mind which will justly appreciate, and accordingly approve or excuse them." [72]

In opting for their final authority of personal experience and

---

in a Minister of the Gospel," manuscript sermon, n.d., Princeton University Library, Manuscript Collection, AM 12800.

[70] Alexander's interpretation of the issues was probably shared by many. Miller says that his own mentor, Charles Nisbet, President of Dickinson College, was of the opinion that "unless the grace of God produced a different effect, the more intimately men became acquainted with the works of nature, the less mindful were they of their great Author." This was, of course, the direct opposite of Smith's view. Samuel Miller, *Memoir of the Rev. Charles Nisbet, D.D.* (New York: Robert Carter, 1840), pp. 226–227.

[71] Samuel Miller, *A Brief Retrospect of the Eighteenth Century* (2 vols.; New York: T. and J. Swords, 1803).

[72] Smith to Rush, September 27, 1812, Princeton University Library, Manuscript Collection, AM 14429.

conviction, Smith was standing in one long tradition of American Calvinism. On the surface Smith's views appear to have had little connection with his early background as a son and student of his father, one of the acknowledged leaders of the New Side Awakeners. It is possible, however, to see in Smith's conflict with other leaders in the church a perpetuation and climactic eruption of certain unresolved Old Side–New Side tensions. A genuine affinity between Smith's outlook and the Awakening emphasis upon the affections, personal faith, and contemplations of infinity may perhaps be traceable. His use of the Scottish philosophy with its emphasis upon the affections, his own stress upon personal faith and the active powers of the mind, and his descriptions of "the sublimity of science" and its capacity to raise the mind to "conceptions of the vast force and power . . . in the author of nature"—all bear at least a formal relation to aspects of New Side thought, and this may, if nothing else, suggest how Smith so quickly made the switch from Periam to Witherspoon.

Whatever the case may be on these points, however, Smith's refusal to swear *ex animo* to creeds and doctrines comes like an echo from Jonathan Dickinson and the New Side spokesmen in the subscriptionist and revivalist controversies of the 1720's and 1740's. In the earlier disputes the Old Side had twitted the revivalists for their alleged lack of liberal learning and their anti-intellectualism, and had charged that deviation from strict subscription to the creed would open the flood gates to wild and uncontrolled enthusiasms. Now the issues of debate were thoroughly altered and positions ironically reversed. The danger to the heirs of the Old Side seemed to come this time not from uncontrolled emotion, but from unrestrained reason. The one element, nevertheless, which had remained constant in the recurring disputes, from the Adopting Act of 1729 to Smith's resignation of the presidency of the college in 1812, had been the contested authority of personal experience and conviction.

II

Along with his attention to the problems of the College of New Jersey and his own responsibilities there, Smith also gave much thought to the broader role of education in the developing American nation. If Scottish influences shaped his ideas about the college curriculum and his philosophical and theological outlook, Scottish social theory provided the conceptual framework for all his thinking about the role of education in society. Although it would probably be possible to trace a number of specific sources of Smith's ideas, no attempt to do so will be made here. However, certain striking parallels and similarities between the ideas of Smith and those of Adam Ferguson, Professor of Moral Philosophy at the University of Edinburgh (1764–1785), will be pointed out.[73]

The concept of human progress as it was developed by Scottish social theorists furnished Smith with the basis of his understanding of the place of education in society. Smith's own early interest in the idea of progress and his engagement with Scottish thinkers in what Dugald Stewart later termed "conjectural history" are evident in the *Essay*, and continue throughout Smith's writings.[74] From their knowledge of the principles of human nature and the external conditions of human life, the Scots attempted to reconstruct the history of human progress from its simple beginnings to more complex levels of civilization. The central themes of Scottish thinking about human progress

[73] Adam Ferguson graduated (M.A.) from the University of St. Andrews in 1742 and continued his studies in divinity at the University of Edinburgh. During the "Forty-five" and until 1754, he served as Chaplain to the Black Watch. Ferguson was a leading figure among the intellectuals of Scotland, and was especially prominent in the Edinburgh circle. He succeeded Hume as Librarian of the Advocates Library in 1757, and two years later assumed the chair of natural philosophy at Edinburgh. In 1767, three years after his appointment to the chair of pneumatics and moral philosophy, Ferguson brought out the work for which he is most famous, *An Essay on the History of Civil Society*. Ferguson's other main works include *Institutes of Moral Philosophy* (1766, 1769), *The History of the Progress and Termination of the Roman Republic* (1783), and *Principles of Moral and Political Science* (1792). References here are restricted to *An Essay on the History of Civil Society*, edited by Duncan Forbes (Edinburgh: Edinburgh University Press, 1966).

Although Smith mentions Ferguson by name at a few points, there is nothing explicit in Smith's *Lectures* to indicate how closely they reflect the themes of Ferguson's *Essay* and many of the actual positions taken by Ferguson. A reading of the two together leaves no doubt that Smith had read and was impressed by Ferguson's work. I have attempted to show some of the major points of similarity between the two, but a complete awareness of how immersed Smith was in the kind of social analysis undertaken by Ferguson can only be had by looking at the two together.

Useful secondary studies of Ferguson include W. C. Lehmann, *Adam Ferguson and the Beginning of Modern Sociology* (New York: Columbia University Press, 1930), and David Kettler, *The Social and Political Thought of Adam Ferguson* (Columbus: Ohio State University Press, 1965). Bryson also has an excellent treatment of Ferguson. Bryson, *Man and Society*, Chapter II. Also see her article, "The Comparable Interests of the Old Moral Philosophy and the Modern Social Sciences," *Social Forces*, XI (October 1932), 19–27. The importance of Smith's reliance upon Ferguson for purposes of this study is indicated, perhaps, by Bryson's decision to treat Ferguson as "representative of the Scottish group."

[74] Bryson, *Man and Society*, pp. 87–89.

—exemplified by Ferguson's work—were also those that fascinated Smith: the development of society from various stages of "rudeness" to "refinement"; the different conditions that determine the growth and decline of societies and governments; the social effects of environment; and the social importance and interdependence of commerce, custom and manners, and the arts and sciences.

Smith shared the assumption of all the Scottish philosophers that man is by nature a social creature, equipped by his emotional and physical makeup for life in civic society. This view of the social nature of man, with its emphasis upon the primacy of the emotions over reason, had led Scottish writers in the late eighteenth century to a nearly unanimous rejection of popular social contract theories, with their rationalistic interpretation of the origin of government in deliberate human decision. Smith rejected, no less firmly than did his contemporaries in Scotland, the idea that men had ever lived in isolation, or in groups so small that some form of government did not exist. "Mankind," Adam Ferguson wrote, "have always wandered or settled, agreed or quarrelled in troops and companies." Smith took a similar position. The origins of civic society, according to Smith, were familial and rooted in the affections which bind parents to their children—affections "which are the most powerful in the human heart." [75] Life under some form of government, however primitive, was for these thinkers, therefore, simply one aspect of what it means to be human.

Smith, like Ferguson, thought that complex civilization was as natural to man as his original family and tribal life. Refinements in manners, developments in science, and complexity in social organizations were not artificial trappings covering the animal beneath, but were evolved out of the desires and demands inherent in man's nature. Society progresses as does the individual: according to nature, not away from nature.[76]

Smith would have agreed with Ferguson that the idea of the noble savage was nonsense, but Smith did believe that man's original state had been one of a highly advanced civilization. The appearance of savage tribes and primitive nations was for Smith a result of the Fall. Ferguson would have rejected this idea of a primordial golden age as too speculative; however, it did have the effect in Smith's thought of underscoring the view that civilization is natural and that

[75] Ferguson, *Essay*, pp. 16–19; Smith, *The Lectures*, I, 78.
[76] Ferguson, *Essay*, pp. 8–10.

progress is a gradual return to man's true origins. "When man was perfect," wrote Smith to Benjamin Rush, "he inhabited the garden of Eden. When man was fallen he was cast out into a savage forest. And the reciprocal influence of civilization and of piety will probably tend to bring on that final and happy order of ages which religion hath predicted." [77] Thus education, in so far as it contributed to human progress and civilization, shared with religion the high aim of enabling man to recapture his own best and most natural self.

The high value Smith placed upon education as essential to the future progress of America became evident when Smith turned to the specific conditions determining social progress. The growth and decline of nations, as well as the variations observable in history among the many forms of known government, he thought could be attributed to three causes: the vicissitudes of fortune, national character, and differing national goals and policies.[78] With allowance made for the accidents of chance, and the influences and limitations of environment, it was important, therefore, to focus on those factors wherein human nature and human goals were fully operative. The task of "the philosopher and of the legislator," Smith said, was to try to discover those institutional arrangements which most effectually contributed to the welfare of society, so as "to render the earth that beautiful and comfortable habitation which seems to have been the ultimate design of the creator in its formation." [79] The millennium had not become completely secularized in Smith's thought, but men were certainly to have a large hand in ushering it in.[80]

In Smith's view, the essential requisite of any society was the capacity to propagate and maintain the species. For advances in civilization to take place, population had to be multiplied and held at the highest optimum level. In his deliberation on the best population balance, Smith expressed himself in Malthusian terms although he was

---

[77] Smith to Rush, May 10, 1786, Princeton University Library, Manuscript Collection, AM 14429; see Ferguson, *Essay*, p. 242.
[78] Smith, *The Lectures*, I, 77–78; see Ferguson, *Essay*, pp. 210–214.
[79] Smith, *The Lectures*, I, 58.
[80] Ernest Tuveson has suggested that many of the important origins of the idea of progress are to be found in Christian apocalyptic and millennial theorists of the seventeenth century. Ernest Lee Tuveson, *Millennium and Utopia: A Study of the Background of the Idea of Progress* (Berkeley: University of California Press, 1949). Also see Perry Miller, "The End of the World," *Errand into the Wilderness* (New York: Harper Torchbooks, 1956), pp. 217–240. On the importance of the idea of progress in nineteenth-century America, see Arthur A. Ekirch, Jr., *The Idea of Progress in America, 1815–1860* (New York: Columbia University Press, 1944).

probably relying upon Ferguson, who had anticipated the formula of Malthus. "The maximum population," said Smith, "can never exceed the maximum of the provision raised within the country, or introduced into it by commerce." [81] He added that the standard of living of any people depends upon their values, desires, and living habits. If a nation is careless or addicted to luxury, they will inevitably impair their population and with it their future potential and prospects.

Finding themselves participants in a new order of affluence, the Scots philosophers devoted much attention to trying to determine the right balance between luxurious living and social progress. Smith, also, thought that Americans should consider very carefully the question of what constitutes too much civilized refinement, and he never tired of reminding his students that national decline is linked inseparably with "the corruption and disorder of the public manners." [82] The two most important subjects to which persons concerned with national progress should address themselves were, accordingly, the promotion of useful learning and the cultivation of virtuous character. Both were primary concerns of the educator.

Early in his career Smith expressed great hopes for the American nation. All the necessary ingredients for a bright future were at hand, if only Americans would make a full and enlightened use of them: a growing population, ample land and natural resources, and the beginnings of a government with the potential for maintaining a right balance between security and freedom.[83] Smith, however, did not hold to an optimistic view of inevitable progress, nor did he think that progress could be forced. Attempts of a society or elements within it to leap ahead suddenly without passing through the necessary stages of development could only cause upheavals that would result in a reversion to a worsened state of affairs. Smith condemned slavery, for

---

[81] Smith, *The Lectures*, I, 55–56. Ferguson had written, "Men will crowd where the situation is tempting, and, in a few generations will people every country to the measure of its means of subsistence." Ferguson, *Essay*, p. 141.

[82] Smith, *The Lectures*, I, 55–56; II, 111. Smith's whole discussion of the relation between population, forms of government, learning and national wealth, and morals closely resembles the thought of Ferguson. From almost exactly the same position taken by Ferguson, for example, Smith argued, against Benjamin Rush, that all war should not be condemned as an unmitigated evil, since war often led to useful scientific discoveries and the martial spirit often produced that vigor and discipline necessary to strong national character. Letter, Smith to Rush, February 19, 1790, Princeton University Library, Manuscript Collection, AM 14429. See Ferguson, *Essay*, pp. 24, 101.

[83] See the letter from Smith to Rush, April 10, 1787, Princeton University Library, Manuscript Collection, AM 14429.

example, as a terrible evil that had to be ended. He was convinced, however, that the end of slavery would have to be realized by degrees. Although his own form of gradualism was extremely liberal by many contemporary standards, involving as it did large grants of land in the West to former slaves and plans for deliberate intermarriage, full emancipation, Smith felt, would only be achieved through a skillful combination of public education and law.[84]

Above all, every step in the progress of a nation depended on the firmness of the citizens in upholding sound moral and religious principles and their zeal in furthering the pursuit of knowledge and learning. Smith's theory of gradual social change gave intellectual support and justification to his emphasis upon education as one of the chief means for guiding social change. Education would actually serve as a check upon the kind of violent and sudden change Smith feared, while yet ensuring constant movement forward.

Over the years Smith grew increasingly alarmed at the spread of attitudes and behavior he considered dangerous. Despite his basically optimistic temperament, Smith grew more and more uneasy in his hopes for the progress of America. As he assessed the attitudes of his fellow countrymen and observed the unrest and turbulence in the new nation, not the least of which was being felt within the college itself, he sensed a breakdown in the ordered social relationships that in his view made a stable society possible. Smith's social outlook was unabashedly hierarchical. Public manners and public virtues meant for him, among other things, the recognition of rank, respect for one's superiors, and conduct in keeping with one's assigned place in the social order.

In fact, individual and social virtue in Smith's thought were two sides of the same coin: an eighteenth-century vision of system with each part subordinated to the whole. Individual virtue, "living according to nature," as already noted, meant for Smith the harmonious operation of the principles of human nature, each in their proper place, the pleasures and faculties of the body being "the lowest in the scale, and the moral sentiments the highest." [85] A smoothly functioning and virtuous society was, likewise, one in which each member duly strove to fulfill the responsibilities and manner of life commensurate with his rank in the social scale. At the top of Smith's social scale

[84] See Smith, *The Lectures*, I, 169–178.
[85] See Smith, *The Lectures*, II, 72. See also Ferguson's discussion of the "History of Subordination," *Essay*, pp. 121–135, 184–187.

stood the civil authorities, property holders, and, of course, men of learning. Smith was careful to point out to his students that authority of scholars, too, along with that of property holders and civic officials, was essential to "the peace and prosperity of the state." Scholars, he said, had often directly and indirectly influenced the laws of nations and their roles in international affairs.[86]

Samuel Stanhope Smith, for all of his respect for the individual, was no lover of the masses. Unbounded political and economic equality, he thought, could only be hurtful to society. In a republican form of government too much democracy was a bad thing, for it would weaken and corrupt respect for authority and encourage the release of unrestrained popular passions. "Universal suffrage," Smith said, "is always dangerous," and he proposed that strict property requirements limit the privilege of voting. At the same time he wanted to avoid the "rocks of aristocracy" by including in the electorate as many citizens concerned with the real interests of the country as possible. He thought that this could best be accomplished by taking land—"the basis of the republic"—as the standard of property, rather than money, which he feared could be manipulated more easily and secretly by a powerful few than could land. Smith sensed, however, somewhat inconsistently perhaps with his own conception of the relation between progress and population growth, that the future stability of the country appeared increasingly uncertain. As the population multiplied, the clamor and pressures from the masses for a hand in the government would also increase, and the effects, Smith said, were to be feared. The dual safeguard that he envisioned was to continue to restrict the number of electors while making every effort to inform and educate the populace.[87]

As always, then, Smith's thought returned to education. In the 1796 petition to the New Jersey legislature Smith had written about the need to educate all the people. "The poor," he wrote, "ought to have access to the fountains of knowledge as well as the wealthy; they have equal talents from nature, and are equally capable of becoming enlightened patriots, legislators, and instructors." [88] When he published his lectures on moral philosophy, he continued to call for universal education, but this time he took special pains to specify exactly what kind of education he had in mind.

[86] Smith, *The Lectures*, II, 309–310, 355 ff.
[87] *Ibid.*, pp. 295–297.
[88] Maclean, *History of the College of New Jersey*, II, 17.

In his *Lectures* Smith called for two kinds of education. Every state legislature, he said, should take steps to provide all citizens with instruction in their moral and civic responsibilities and in the rudiments necessary for "transacting their ordinary affairs with promptness and intelligence." Such an education would help to improve public morals and lower the crime rate. In addition special provisions should also be made for instructing future leaders of society in the liberal arts and higher branches of science. Colleges and universities, Smith declared, "might be regarded as so many elementary schools for training a constant succession of wise and enlightened statesmen for the republic." Graduates of the higher institutions, even if they never actually participated in the administration of government itself, would, nevertheless, raise the political and moral tone of the country by their very presence.[89]

A gentleman in outlook and demeanor, a Federalist in politics, Smith was also something of an elitist in education. However, his educational elitism, if it may justly be called that, was qualified in certain respects. In the first place, the higher branches of learning would be open to all "who have the inclination and leisure to pursue them." Although in practice this would restrict a college education to the wealthy, it did not in principle rule out provisions which might conceivably be made for private philanthropy or state scholarship aid. In the second place, the principles of civic instruction that Smith desired for the populace were to be exactly the same as those he demanded for the nation's leaders.

The American constitution was to be the backbone of all civic instruction and was to be interpreted by a reading of the *Federalist*. "The principles of our government, and, if possible, a summary of our legal institutions . . . ," he told his students, "ought to join essential objects in the education of every American Scholar." (He then blithely ended page 329 of his *Lectures* with the instructions: "Here the federal constitution is to be committed to memory.") He suggested that an elementary textbook be compiled, based upon the laws and constitution of the land, for use in primary schools, and that its principles form the basis for civic instruction "from the highest to the lowest order of schools in the state." [90] In political education, at least, there was to be no difference in kind, regardless of the levels of education otherwise available to the different classes of society.

[89] Smith, *The Lectures*, II, 227–228.
[90] *Ibid.*, pp. 306–307.

Like the Scots, Smith feared the enervating effect of too much luxury upon society, and he extolled the social benefits of simplicity and frugality. As befit an eighteenth-century gentleman cleric who would have felt almost as much at home in the Select Society of Edinburgh as in the synod meeting at Philadelphia, Smith did not, however, reject all the physical and social niceties of life out of hand. "Ignorant rudeness," he felt, was just as dangerous as a "vicious and sickly refinement." "A certain taste, on the contrary, for the conveniences and elegancies of art," he said, "not only adds to the comfort of living, but, by creating new demands on industry, and furnishing new incentives both to ingenuity and exertion, becomes also a productive source of population." [91] As early as 1790 Smith was criticizing the tendency he thought he discerned among many of his fellow Americans to be neither refined nor simple in their tastes, but crudely materialistic. The parents of many of his students, Smith wrote to Benjamin Rush, "consider education as nothing more than a subordinate art to getting money. And they aim at no other scholarship than that that will *soonest* put them in a way of turning the penny. So much are the reproaches of foreigners verified that we are a nation of little dealers, and shifty sharpers, without any dignity, without any enlargement of idea, without taste, without a sense of national honor, and intent only on profit." As a consequence students were coming to the college "the most unmatriculated creatures in nature." [92]

Education itself, he thought, could provide the needed remedy. Although Smith was a leader in urging the study of English and modern scientific subjects, he did not in any way denigrate the value of the classical languages. The way to make curricular innovations at the college level possible, Smith felt, was not to throw out the ancient languages, but to raise the standards of college preparatory education. "We want a great reform," he wrote Rush, "in the elementary parts of education that may be extended over the whole country." [93] Whether institutions of education could be improved in accordance with his ideals without popular respect for learning, the very thing Smith saw as lacking, was not a question he appears to have considered.

Some have suggested that Smith's tragedy was that in an "age

[91] *Ibid.*, I, 74.
[92] Smith to Rush, February 25, 1790, Princeton University Library, Manuscript Collection, AM 14429.
[93] *Ibid.*

of transition" he clung to an older hierarchical view of society no longer tenable given the changing realities of the nineteenth century. This is undoubtedly true, but Smith also wanted to rely upon persuasion—rather than the arbitrary exercise of authority—to bring persons to accept their rank and place in the social order. Unfortunately, he could count less and less upon this kind of voluntary compliance—in the college especially. The students entering the college in the late eighteenth and early nineteenth centuries, in an era of social and intellectual unrest, were not disposed to submit passively to the discipline thrust upon them by the faculty and trustees.

Student disturbances and overt acts of disobedience occurred with increasing frequency. Smith's emphasis upon tact and reasoned persuasion put him at a disadvantage both with the students who were discharging their emotions and with the trustees who were demanding a greater show of authority. Even at Yale, Smith's fellow president, Timothy Dwight, was being forced to cope with his student problems by adopting the religious revival as a means of channeling his students' emotions in desirable directions.[94] Smith appears never to have entertained this option; indeed, he seems to have ruled it out long before. As much as Dwight, however, Smith considered the general student unrest a result of infidelity and immorality.

In 1802 Nassau Hall burned to the ground. Smith suspected arson. In a letter to Jedediah Morse, who himself was raising the cry that a Jacobinic plot was afoot in the land, Smith charged that the fire was "one effect of those irreligious and demoralizing principles which are tearing the bands of society asunder." [95] Because of his reputation as an educator, Smith had little difficulty raising money to rebuild the college, and a year later was already complaining to Ashbel Green that the faculty was too small to care adequately for the large number of students.[96]

Discipline problems continued unabated however. In 1807 the college erupted in a riot which ended with the trustees dismissing about 125 students. Within two years students were again causing trouble. Throughout the entire period Smith was caught, as Wertenbaker has commented, in a bind between the students' demands for

---

[94] See Charles E. Cuningham, *Timothy Dwight, 1752–1817* (New York: The Macmillan Company, 1942), pp. 263–264, 303–304.
[95] Smith to Morse, March 10, 1802, Princeton University Library, Manuscript Collection, AM 2164.
[96] Smith to Green, November 26, 1803, Princeton University Library, Manuscript Collection, AM 2166.

more freedom and the trustees' insistence upon tighter discipline and a heavier authoritarian hand from the faculty. Smith's earliest biographers all assert that Smith himself never lost the respect of the students, and imply that, had it not been for the trustees' constant meddling in disciplinary affairs, Smith, with his sense of tact and reason, might have been able to deal with the students with much greater success.[97]

The disciplinary problems, however, appear to have added force to the growing suspicion that Smith's intellectual and theological ideas were not reliable. The determination of such persons as Green, Miller, and Alexander to guarantee a sound ministerial education, which they were positive the college was not providing under the suspect President, also increased the pressure on Smith. Smith's insistence that ministers required a well-rounded education in the arts and physical sciences, and his opposition to the movement for a seminary, as early as 1806, when he drew up a memorandum declaring that the college was fully equipped to provide needed theological preparation without a separate seminary, did not help his position.[98]

Finally, in August 1812, the trustees appointed Green and Miller as a committee to establish a seminary and elected a vice-president with the clear intention of changing the administration of the college in the fall. John Maclean, Smith's friend, resigned in protest on August 13, and Smith, claiming ill health as his reason, handed in his resignation the following day.[99]

Smith's resignation and the subsequent control of the college by persons opposed to him have made it difficult for some historians to view him as representing anything other than a kind of interesting interlude in the development of Princeton. A recent historian of Presbyterianism in American culture has listed "the first five of the Princeton tradition" as consisting of Witherspoon, Green, Alexander,

[97] Philip Lindsley wrote in 1848: "The dignity of his bearing, though not repulsive or oppressive, was uniform and imposing. His very presence would rebuke, overawe, and silence the most turbulent assemblage of youth that ever met for sport or riot,—during my time at least." Lindsley's time at the college began right after the fire of 1802. "We regarded the Doctor," Lindsley added, "as a firm, resolute, fearless, decided man,—who would not wink at crime or folly,—but, who, nevertheless, cherished towards us the most kindly and paternal feelings. My present deliberate opinion is, that he was one of the ablest and most successful diciplinarians of any age." Sprague, *Annals of the American Pulpit*, III, 343. See especially Beasley, "An Account of the Life and Writings of the Rev. Samuel Stanhope Smith," pp. 50–52. Also Maclean, *History of the College of New Jersey*, II, 135, 146.
[98] Maclean, *History of the College of New Jersey*, II, 105–106.
[99] *Ibid.*, pp. 98–99.

Miller, and Hodge.[100] This was certainly one line of tradition that
began with Witherspoon, but was it the only one? Witherspoon's
own thought was so loose-knit that it could be developed in various
directions by those who came after him. The question is whether
Smith's educational influence and his own particular elaboration of
Witherspoon's bequest ended with his resignation, or had a more
significant impact than his eclipse at the college by Green, Miller, and
Alexander might suggest.

The fond and admiring accounts of Smith given by some of his
former students would indicate that he did have a lasting influence
upon them at least. While President of the University of Nashville,
Philip Lindsley, formerly a student and intimate friend of Smith,
wrote:

From our childhood, we (the students) had never heard the Doctor's name
pronounced but with praise. We came to the College, therefore, prepared
to look upon him as the great man of the age. His superior talents and
accomplishments, as a preacher, scholar, philosopher, and writer, were
every where spoken of and acknowledged. And we never doubted that
he possessed all the attributes and graces which could dignify and adorn
the high station which he filled. Such were our prepossessions in his
favour at the outset. And there was no subsequent reaction. He daily
grew in our esteem.[101]

This was elegy, to be sure, but its trustworthiness is strengthened by
Lindsley's known reluctance to praise fellow college presidents indiscriminately.[102] Although no attempt will be made here to trace and assess the
long-range influence of Smith, two points should be noted which
suggest that Smith's attitude toward learning and his own educational
emphases were not without an important lasting effect. In the first
place, one cannot read the list of men who were students of Smith
without being struck by the diversity of theological and philosophical
positions which they later represented. A wide spectrum of outlook
came to be represented in such persons as John Henry Hobart, Bishop

---

[100] Elwyn Allen Smith, The Presbyterian Ministry in American Culture (Philadelphia:
The Westminster Press, 1962), p. 132.
[101] Sprague, Annals of the American Pulpit, III, 342.
[102] Expressions of admiration for Smith, similar to those of Lindsley and Beasley,
came also from Robert Finley. See Isaac Brown, Memoirs of the Rev. Robert
Finley, D.D. . . . with Brief Sketches of some of his Contemporaries (New Brunswick, N.J.: Terhune & Letson, 1819), p. 25.

of the Episcopal Church; Theodore Frelinghuysen, Chancellor of the University of New York City and President of Rutgers; William Meade, Bishop of the Episcopal Church and President of the Theological School of the Episcopal Church in Virginia; Frederick Beasley, President of the University of Pennsylvania; Joseph Caldwell, President of the University of North Carolina; and, of course, Philip Lindsley, President of the University of Nashville. Hobart, Caldwell, Lindsley, and Beasley all served under Smith as tutors at the college for at least two years. The apparent ease with which Smith's students adopted a variety of theological positions, as suggested by this list, may reflect Smith's relatively tolerant attitude toward religious differences and freedom of philosophical inquiry. If so, it also indicates that from their point of view stricter Presbyterians had good reason to harbor suspicions against his influence.

In the second place, certain of Smith's students who became college presidents appear to have instituted courses of study that were directly in keeping with Smith's own desire to combine a solid liberal arts course with scientific and professional training. Robert Finley, student of both Witherspoon and Smith, head of the Baskingridge Academy, and President-elect of the University of Georgia before his death, favored instruction in agricultural science in addition to the regular liberal arts.[103] At the University of North Carolina, Joseph Caldwell, a staunch Presbyterian, worked to establish a broad classical and scientific curriculum. Caldwell himself taught mathematics, traveled to Europe to purchase scientific books and equipment, and helped to build from his own funds one of the earliest observatories connected with an American college.[104] The student of Smith who was probably most famous for his innovations in higher education was Philip Lindsley. At the University of Nashville, Lindsley attempted to erect a modern university of well-developed faculties, uniting a solid liberal arts course with instruction in agriculture, the mechanical trades, and business. Lindsley was also an outspoken opponent of sectarian influences in college founding and control.[105]

[103] The Reverend Isaac Brown, Robert Finley's biographer and also a student and tutor under Smith, attached to his 1819 account of Finley's life a proposal for Presbyterian education that, likewise, called for the inclusion of agricultural science as a priority subject in the regular curriculum. Brown, *Memoirs of the Rev. Robert Finley*.

[104] See the article on Joseph Caldwell in the *Dictionary of American Biography*. Also see Donald Come, "The Influence of Princeton on Higher Education in the South before 1825," *William and Mary Quarterly*, 3rd ser., II (1945), 384-385.

[105] Lack of community support eventually brought about the failure of Lindsley's

Outlines of a pattern of influence extending from Smith to Lindsley do appear, and they are strengthened further by the unreserved admiration that Lindsley, and men such as Frederick Beasley and Robert Finley, expressed for Smith.

For purposes of this study, however, Smith is important in his own right, for he illustrated many of the ways in which Scottish thought and practice could be adapted to a variety of American educational needs and purposes in the late eighteenth century. Smith's very faith in the power of education to shape the individual and society received strong support from Scottish thought. As long as Smith spoke of education in general, however, he was noticeably vague in specifying what kind of education he thought best. There was little in Smith's broad definition of education as any impression on the mind "which is received directly, or incidentally" that would suggest guidelines or criteria for spelling out a purposive educational program. When he did become concrete in developing the college curriculum, in shaping course content, in helping his students deal with pressing intellectual problems, even in formulating a social theory to undergird his demands for adequate civic instruction, Smith time and again drew upon Scottish resources.

The threat of infidelity and immorality was as much a concern to Smith as to his opponents in the church. Smith, however, was convinced that the threat could be combated and overcome on its own grounds through reasoned persuasion and argument. In this Samuel Stanhope Smith was, indeed, the epitome of eighteenth-century gentility and rationality. As the forces of an aggressive Protestantism gathered in the early years of the new century, Smith found himself standing more and more alone, the representative of an earlier time. In 1817, two years before his death, Smith presented the college with his published works, remarking: "I have served, since the year 1779, with a zeal, diligence, and fidelity which now in the closing moments of life, I can look back upon with entire self-approbation." [106] So, in the end, Samuel Stanhope Smith was not a tragic figure; but then the eighteenth century was not a tragic age.

---

plans. See Lindsley's various writings on education and the account of his life in *The Works of Philip Lindsley, D.D.*, edited by LeRoy J. Halsey (3 vols.; Philadelphia: J. B. Lippincott, 1866). Frederick Rudolph discusses Lindsley as one of a handful of important early nineteenth-century reformers in higher education. Frederick Rudolph, *The American College and University* (New York: Vintage Books, 1965), pp. 116–118.

[106] Quoted in Monk, "Samuel Stanhope Smith," in Thorp, ed., *The Lives of Eighteen from Princeton*, p. 107.

From Nottingham Academy
to the "Edinburgh of America":
Benjamin Rush

A few weeks after the death of Benjamin Rush in 1813, John Adams wrote to Thomas Jefferson: "I lament with you the loss of Rush. I know of no Character living or dead, who has done more real good in America." [1] Adams had known Benjamin Rush as an intimate friend and correspondent for years. The rest of the country had known Rush as a leading Philadelphia physician, an active and outspoken social and educational reformer, and the nation's foremost medical educator.

Benjamin Rush was an alumnus of a Presbyterian academy and of the College of New Jersey; and his ties to the college did not end with his graduation. As a young medical student at Edinburgh, Benjamin Rush performed his first major service for American education in helping to persuade Mrs. Witherspoon to leave Paisley so that her husband could accept the new job that had been offered him at Princeton.[2] Rush was also the personal physician of Samuel Stanhope Smith, with whom he corresponded for years, testing and sharing ideas; at one point Rush received valuable encouragement and help from Smith for one of his favorite educational projects. Many of Rush's main interests, however, were different from those of John Witherspoon and Samuel Stanhope Smith. His career, therefore, provides further insight into the relationships that developed between the

---

[1] Quoted in John A. Schutz and Douglass Adair, eds., *The Spur of Fame; Dialogues of John Adams and Benjamin Rush, 1805–1813* (San Marino, Calif.: The Huntington Library, 1966), p. 283.

[2] The full story of Rush's part in bringing Witherspoon to America is told in L. H. Butterfield, *John Witherspoon Comes to America* (Princeton: Princeton University Press, 1953).

academy and Princeton traditions and other major movements in American higher education.

Benjamin Rush is especially important for purposes of this study in that he reveals the wider pattern of Scottish influences in American education, of which Witherspoon and Smith were only a part. By mid-eighteenth century the different contacts between American and Scottish higher education had begun to coalesce. The establishment of the Presbyterian academies, the presence in America of Scottish-trained educators such as Alison and Witherspoon, an increasing appropriation of Scottish thought, and a rising stream of American students to Scotland were all, by 1765, interrelated. Nowhere do these interrelationships appear with more clarity than in the life of Benjamin Rush.

Three sides of Rush's educational career are here examined: his participation in the movement by American medical students to acquire professional training in Scottish universities; his promotion of educational schemes for the new nation; and his work as a medical educator.

I

Benjamin Rush received his early schooling at the academy conducted by his uncle, Samuel Finley, at West Nottingham, Maryland. Rush, whose father had died when he was a boy of six, became closely attached to Finley, and remained so until the latter's death.[3] In later life Rush wrote that Finley's "mode of teaching" first "inspired me with a love of knowledge."[4] It was also Finley who persuaded Rush, after his graduation from the College of New Jersey in 1760, to become a physician. Samuel Davies had suggested to Rush that he enter law, but the uncle's advice prevailed.[5]

Rush apprenticed himself to Dr. John Redman in Philadelphia, with whom he remained as a pupil for nearly six years. In 1766, Rush decided, as his preceptor Redman had done before him, to pursue his medical studies at the University of Edinburgh. On November 3, 1766, Benjamin Rush arrived in Edinburgh with another American

---

[3] *Letters of Benjamin Rush,* edited by L. H. Butterfield (2 vols.; Princeton: Princeton University Press, 1951), I, 4–5; *The Autobiography of Benjamin Rush,* edited by George Corner (Princeton: Princeton University Press, 1948), pp. 35–36. These works are henceforth referred to as Rush, *Letters,* and Rush, *Autobiography.*
[4] Rush describes his years at the Nottingham Academy and College of New Jersey in his *Autobiography,* pp. 32–37.
[5] Rush, *Autobiography,* pp. 36–37.

student, Jonathan Potts, bearing letters of introduction from John Morgan in Philadelphia to the Edinburgh medical faculty. Benjamin Franklin in London also forwarded letters to his Edinburgh friends recommending the two young Americans to their care and hospitality.[6]

In sailing for Edinburgh, Rush was following a practice that was already well established and growing among colonial medical students. At the beginning of the eighteenth century, since there were no medical schools in the colonies, aspiring physicians usually received their advanced medical training as apprentices to experienced and practicing doctors, who were often European-trained immigrants. Around 1720, however, young American physicians with the interest and means began to go abroad after their apprenticeship to complete their medical education at a European university. The first stimulus for study abroad may have come from the London-educated Dr. John Kearsley, a British immigrant and Philadelphia's leading physician during the first half of the century. In the 1720's several of Kearsley's students—Lloyd Zachary, Thomas Cadwallader, Thomas Bond, and others—left for Europe to pursue their studies, thus setting a pattern many were to follow.[7]

At first Americans went to Paris, Leyden, and London; but after the death of Boerhaave at Leydon in 1738, Edinburgh's rising star began to shine, and American students turned increasingly toward Scotland. In 1748, Dr. John Redman, also one of Kearsley's students, returned to Philadelphia from a year of study at Edinburgh, followed by a year at Leyden, where he had received his M.D. degree. Redman can be seen as marking a turning point, for after him the Edinburgh degree itself became the most coveted.

Even those Americans studying first in London under the Scottish-trained doctors who dominated London's medical practice and education—John Fothergill, John Pringle, Colin McKenzie, and the Hunter brothers—were urged by their teachers not to return home without a stint at Edinburgh. Frequently with an able assist from Franklin, in the case of Americans, the London professors sent their own surgical and anatomical students north for a grounding in medical theory. Thus, the central figures in the founding of America's first three medical schools—William Shippen, Jr., John Morgan, Benjamin

---

[6] *Ibid.*, pp. 39–40; see Rush, *Letters*, I, 27.
[7] See George W. Corner, *Two Centuries of Medicine* (Philadelphia: J. B. Lippincott & Co., 1965), pp. 3, 6; Elizabeth H. Thomson, "Thomas Bond, First Professor of Clinical Medicine in the American Colonies," *Journal of Medical Education*, XXXIII (September 1958), 616.

Waterhouse, and Samuel Bard—all went to Edinburgh with the encouragement of Fothergill and the Hunters.[8] The London doctors understandably wanted their students "to lay a foundation in practice" —that is in anatomy and classical instruction, their own forte—before entering upon the theoretical approach in which Edinburgh excelled. The practice that came to prevail with American students, however, was actually the opposite one of capping their initial and major studies at Edinburgh with a year in the London hospitals "walking the wards."

In fact it seems that at times Americans, especially those who did not avail themselves of the Hunters' brilliant lectures, tended to look down upon the practical London experience as somewhat inferior to the more "profound" theoretical approach of the Edinburgh faculty. Having spent two months in the London hospitals between sessions at Edinburgh, John Ravenscroft from Virginia, for example, wrote home in 1768 that "in respect of Medical knowledge Edinburgh is a much fitter place but then the Name of having been in London etc. has its advantages too." [9] Rush expressed a similar approval of the Edinburgh emphasis when, about to leave Scotland for the south, he wrote that he did not expect to learn much in London "from the random prescriptions of the London hospital physicians." Once in London, however, he was forced to revise his opinion of what the London doctors had to teach him, despite their lack of "philosophical principles." [10]

Whitfield J. Bell, Jr., has pointed out that between 1755 and 1766 more than twice as many Americans studied at Edinburgh as received degrees, and that most of those who did not receive degrees were in Edinburgh for as long as one to four years.[11] In 1772 Thomas Parke of Pennsylvania, while at Edinburgh, wrote that almost every Philadelphia doctor had studied there.[12] From Virginia alone, between

[8] Betsy Copping Corner, *William Shippen, Jr., Pioneer in American Medical Education* (Philadelphia: American Philosophical Society, 1951), pp. 82, 89, 93; John Blake, "Benjamin Waterhouse, Harvard's First Professor of Physic," *Journal of Medical Education*, XXXIII (November 1958), 771; Claude Edwin Heaton, "Samuel Bard, 1742–1821," *Journal of Medical Education*, XXXIII (October 1958), 717; Whitfield J. Bell, Jr., *John Morgan, Continental Doctor* (Philadelphia: University of Pennsylvania Press, 1965), pp. 46 ff.

[9] D. M. Lyon, "A Student of 1765–70," *Edinburgh Medical Journal*, XLVIII (1951), 194.

[10] Rush, *Letters*, I, 61, 66.

[11] Whitfield J. Bell, Jr., "Some American Students of 'That Shining Oracle of Physic,' Dr. William Cullen of Edinburgh, 1755–1766," *Proceedings of the American Philosophical Society*, XCIV (June 1950), 279.

[12] Whitfield J. Bell, Jr., "Thomas Parke's Life in England and Scotland," *The Pennsylvania Magazine of History and Biography* (July 1951), p. 246.

1760 and 1790 twenty-seven physicians received Edinburgh degrees and at least eighteen others studied at Edinburgh.[13] From 1765 to the end of the century, 113 Americans are known to have received the M.D. degree from Edinburgh, and an almost equal number probably studied there without completing a thesis.[14]

Certain Presbyterian academies were more than casually linked with this movement. The alumni of Samuel Finley's academy who became outstanding members of the medical profession are especially noteworthy. Finley guided John Morgan and William Shippen, Jr., as well as Rush, through their college preparatory studies at Nottingham. Finley, who had lent his encouragement to Rush's choice of a medical career, may well have done the same for Morgan and Shippen. Morgan, like Rush, certainly held Finley in high esteem. More than fifteen years after he had left Nottingham, Morgan thought Finley interested enough in his ideas to send the minister a copy of his *Discourse on the Institution of Medical Schools in America.* The respect was mutual, and Finley put his own son under Morgan as a medical apprentice.[15] All three Nottingham alumni—Rush, Morgan, and Shippen—received medical degrees from Edinburgh and became members of the faculty of the first medical school in America. Other prominent physicians who studied with Finley at Nottingham and attended Edinburgh University included Gerardus Clarkson, one of the founders and a president of the Philadelphia College of Physicians, and Thomas Ruston, Philadelphia physician and author of works on smallpox and yellow fever. Another physician, who, though he did not go to Edinburgh, studied with Rush at Nottingham and the College of New Jersey, was John Archer, founder of the Medical and Chirurgical Faculty of Maryland.[16]

---

[13] See Wyndham B. Blanton, *Medicine in Virginia in the Eighteenth Century* (Richmond: Garrett & Massie, 1931), p. 87.

[14] See the list of American names taken from the Edinburgh University matriculation rolls by Samuel Lewis and published in the *New England Historical and Genealogical Register*, XLII (1888), 159–165. Also see Bell, "Some American Students of . . . Dr. William Cullen," p. 279; J. Gordon Wilson, "The Influence of Edinburgh on American Medicine in the Eighteenth Century," *Institute of Medicine of Chicago*, VII (January 1929), 134. One of the first to examine the close relationship between American and Scottish medicine was Francis R. Packard in "How London and Edinburgh Influenced Medicine in Philadelphia in the Eighteenth Century," *Annals of Medical History*, New Series, IV (1932), 219–244.

[15] Bell, *John Morgan*, pp. 25, 154.

[16] Rush, *Autobiography*, pp. 34–35, 189–190. To the list of outstanding physicians who received their early education at Nottingham under Samuel Finley the name of Dr. James Tilton should be added. Tilton became a member of the first graduating class of the medical school at Philadelphia and was offered a professorship. James Thacher, *American Medical Biography* (2 vols.; Boston: Richardson & Lord and Cotton & Barnard, 1828), II, 129–131.

Rush, Morgan, and Archer, moreover, served their own medical apprenticeships under John Redman, an alumnus of William Tennent's Log College. Redman became a fairly important figure in his own right in the institutionalization of medical and scientific pursuits. A consultant to the Pennsylvania Hospital (appointed 1752), a lifelong member of the American Philosophical Society, a trustee of both the College of Philadelphia and the College of New Jersey, Redman was the first president of the College of Physicians of Philadelphia (1787).[17]

In a sense John Redman represented the completion of the full circle from William Tennent and the Log College, back to Edinburgh, and from thence to new developments in American higher education. The Presbyterian academies were not, of course, the only or even the most important influences in encouraging American students to pursue their medical studies in Scotland. The academies, however, did join and help to undergird the movement; and they furnished some key personnel in the efforts to bring the benefits of this overseas training to full realization on the American scene.

Rush and the other Americans at Edinburgh entered completely into the life of the university. The student organizations that flourished along with the other discussion and drinking clubs of Scottish society extended also to the medical school. The most important of these was the Royal Medical Society, which met once a week to consider papers presented by its members. Several months after his arrival Rush proudly wrote home that he had been elected to the Society.[18] Over fifty Americans were elected to membership in the Royal Medical Society before 1776, and several of them served as the Society's annual president.[19] Students from Virginia at Edinburgh in 1760–61 formed their own Virginia Club, and bound themselves to follow, after returning home, the Edinburgh practice of refusing to mingle the trades of apothecary and surgeon with the pure duties of the physician.[20] It was in student groups such as these that Morgan,

[17] Accounts of Redman may be found in William S. Middleton, "John Redman," *Annals of Medical History,* VIII (Autumn 1926), 213–223; and Whitfield J. Bell, Jr., "John Redman (1722–1808): Medical Preceptor of Philadelphia," *Transactions and Studies of the College of Physicians of Philadelphia,* 4th ser., XXV (1957–58), 103–111.
[18] Rush, *Letters,* I, 40.
[19] See Alvin R. Riggs, "The Colonial American Medical Student at Edinburgh," *University of Edinburgh Journal,* XX (1961), 147; Bell, "American Medical Students of . . . William Cullen," *Proceedings of the American Philosophical Society,* XCIV (June 1950), 279.
[20] Blanton, *Medicine in Virginia in the Eighteenth Century,* p. 93.

Shippen, the Virginians Arthur Lee and Theodorick Bland, Jr., and other colonials at Edinburgh first began to lay plans for an American medical school, even deciding what subjects each should teach.[21]

Edinburgh society also gave the Americans a warm welcome. Upon his arrival Rush found himself ushered almost immediately into the highest intellectual and social circles of the city. Dining at the home of Sir Alexander Dick, to whom he had been introduced by Franklin, Rush met David Hume a few weeks after his arrival. At the home of one of his medical professors, Dr. Gregory, Rush met William Robertson, Principal of the university, and already widely known for his *History of Scotland*. The poets Thomas Blacklock and Dugald Buchanan were also among Rush's many acquaintances in Edinburgh. Rush struck up a particularly warm friendship with the family of the Earl of Leven, a leader in the Church of Scotland. He even became infatuated with the Earl's daughter, Lady Jane. Rush was strongly religious, and his New Side background led him naturally into the Evangelical circles of the Church of Scotland, where he met John Witherspoon and became a close friend of the Reverend John Erskine, the correspondent of many Americans. Rush also renewed his acquaintance with George Whitefield, whom he had met as a boy in America, visiting with Whitefield several times in Edinburgh and London.[22]

These social contacts undoubtedly provided welcome respite from the medical course, which most Americans seem to have found demanding. Edinburgh appears to have been the first British university to insist on testing all candidates for a medical degree. After 1767, furthermore, every candidate for the examination was required to complete the whole course of medical science, including botany, materia medica, anatomy and surgery, chemistry, theory of physic, practice of physic, and clinical lectures.[23] The rigor of the course was reflected in repeated complaints by many American students about a certain amount of drudgery. Theodorick Bland, Jr., wrote to his father in 1761:

My usual hours of attending the college are at least seven daily, which scarce afford time for necessary refreshments; add to these the night taken

[21] See Bell, *John Morgan*, pp. 72–73.
[22] Rush, *Autobiography*, pp. 42–52.
[23] See Lyon, "A Student of 1765–70," p. 196; also, Letter, Thomas Tucker to his brother, St. George Tucker, January 10, 1768, quoted in Blanton, *Medicine in Virginia in the Eighteenth Century*, p. 90.

up in revising and recapitulating the work of the preceding day, and I am convinced you will not require an apology for my silence.[24]

In his second year, John Ravenscroft wrote to his father still more forcefully, "I have worked like a Jack Ass since I came to town." [25]

The candidate for the M.D. was required to have his thesis—usually written first in English, then translated into Latin—read, corrected, and approved by one of the professors. After submitting the first English draft of his thesis to his adviser, John Ravenscroft was unable to suppress the perennial cry of the graduate student. "I'm like to greet [weep] about my thesis," he declared,

for Dr. Gregory to whom I had shown what I had wrote has set me to work so that I will be obliged to do it all over afresh and writing two or three times over 15 folio pages is na sma Drink—It was so provoking when he was reading it over—he would hum and hah at every line and say 'My Dear this is not English.' 'This I don't understand' two or three times on every page, when I thought the sense clear enough and the meaning as plain as the Nose on his face—I heartily wish the month of June was come. I am tired of my present work.[26]

These little pictures of hardship were probably drawn as vividly as possible to impress the folks at home with their son's diligence and application while abroad. But, at the least, study in Edinburgh was not simply part of a European Grand Tour for gentlemen.

The main incentive for the Americans to work hard came from the reputation of the university and its faculty. When Rush arrived in Edinburgh the renown of the university, and especially of its medical school, was at its height. For two years he attended the lectures of Alexander Munro *secundus* in anatomy, Joseph Black in chemistry, James Russell in natural philosophy, and William Cullen in the institutes of medicine. In the second year, besides repeating these courses, he also went to the lectures of John Gregory in the practice of physic and of John Hope in materia medica.[27] This was as distinguished a group of scientists and teachers as Rush could have wished for. So inspired was he by the intellectual climate he found

[24] Quoted in Blanton, *Medicine in Virginia in the Eighteenth Century*, p. 89. Similar complaints from other Americans may be found in Heaton, "Samuel Bard, 1742–1821," pp. 717–718; and Bell, *John Morgan*, p. 70.

[25] Quoted in Lyon, "A Student of 1765–70," p. 191.

[26] Quoted in *ibid.*, p. 197.

[27] Rush, *Autobiography*, p. 42.

about him that in a letter to a Philadelphia friend he wrote, "Tis now in the zenith of its glory. The whole world I believe does not afford a set of greater men than are at present united in the College of Edinburgh." [28] Contemplating the new medical school in Philadelphia, Rush exclaimed to John Morgan in a flush of enthusiasm, "Methinks I see the place of my nativity becoming the *Edinburgh of America.*" [29]

Of all his professors, Rush was most attracted to William Cullen and Joseph Black. Rush had been advised by John Morgan to devote himself especially to the study of chemistry so that he could teach the subject in the medical school at Philadelphia when he returned. The abilities of Black so impressed Rush that he felt he would be doing Black a dishonor if, after leaving Edinburgh, he attended the chemistry lectures of anyone else in Great Britain.[30] Rush's greatest admiration, however, was for William Cullen—"Dr. Cullen, the great, the unrivalled Dr. Cullen," Rush described him to Morgan.[31]

Cullen was esteemed for his skill in the classroom, his wide reading, and his personal concern for his students. Rush was not alone in experiencing Cullen's especially warm acceptance of Americans, nor in voicing deep admiration for the Scotsman.[32] Samuel Bard, soon to become founder of the medical school at King's College (New York), wrote that he thought nothing could exceed Cullen's manner of teaching: "Being so entertaining as well as instructive, that I could listen to him with pleasure for three hours, instead of one." [33] Indeed, it was as teacher that Cullen made his deepest impact upon Rush. Even after Rush had begun to break away from Cullen's system, the Scotsman remained Rush's ideal of what a great teacher and scientist should be. In the *Eulogium* he delivered before his colleagues at Philadelphia, most of whom had also studied under Cullen, Rush said:

You will recollect, with me, how agreeably he accommodated himself to our different capacities and tempers; how kindly he dissipated our youthful blushes, by inviting us to ask him questions; and how much he taught us, by his inquiries, of the nature of the soil, climate, products, and diseases of even our own country.

[28] Rush, *Letters*, I, 41.
[29] *Ibid.*, p. 29.
[30] *Ibid.*, p. 61.
[31] *Ibid.*, p. 62.
[32] See Bell, "Some American Students of . . . William Cullen," pp. 275–281.
[33] Quoted in Riggs, "The Colonial American Medical Student at Edinburgh," p. 146.

Rush commented in the same speech that Cullen had taught the professors at Philadelphia "the art of teaching others," and had thereby "conveyed the benefits of his discoveries into every part of the United States." [34]

In 1800 Rush touched upon his own excessive tendency "to hold great men in veneration, and no one in greater than my master Dr. Cullen." [35] As L. H. Butterfield has observed, Rush's writings, his conduct in the classroom and at the sickbed, and his views of the social uses of medicine and science always reflected the influence of William Cullen. [36]

With his thesis completed, Rush left Edinburgh in September 1768, to spend eight months in London and to make a brief visit to Paris. In London he took in as much of the great city's culture as possible. Through Benjamin Franklin he met Sir John Fothergill and John Coakley Lettsom, with whom he corresponded the rest of his life. He also met Sir John Pringle, the physician, attended the lectures and dissections of Dr. William Hunter, dined with Samuel Johnson, and visited John Wilkes in prison. [37]

Only a few weeks after returning home to Philadelphia, Rush was appointed to the chair of chemistry in the medical school at Philadelphia. Rush always cherished the memory of his studies in Edinburgh. "The two years I spent in Edinburgh," Rush wrote in the summer of 1800, "I consider as the most important in their influence upon my character and conduct of any period of my life." [38] Rush may have underestimated in this statement the importance of other influences in his life—he never could curb his inclination to exaggerate. The Scottish inspiration was, nevertheless, to be of central importance in Rush's contributions to American education.

II

Rush soon became caught up in the events leading to the break with England. He wrote in his autobiography that he had first been converted to republican principles by John Bostock, a young Englishman and fellow medical student at Edinburgh, who introduced him

[34] Benjamin Rush, *An Eulogium in honor of the late Dr. William Cullen* (Philadelphia: Dobson, 1790), reprinted in Benjamin Rush, *Essays, Literary, Moral and Philosophical* (Philadelphia: Thomas & Samuel F. Bradford, 1798), p. 337. Referred to henceforth as Rush, *Eulogium on Cullen*, and Rush, *Essays*, respectively.
[35] Rush, *Autobiography*, p. 88.
[36] Rush, *Letters*, I, 30, n. 1.
[37] Rush, *Autobiography*, pp. 52 ff.
[38] *Ibid.*, p. 43.

to the views of Algernon Sidney, the Commonwealth rebel executed by Charles II.[39] It has been pointed out, however, that Rush had expressed opposition to the Stamp Act even before leaving Philadelphia, so he was ripe for Bostock's opinions.[40] The significance of Bostock's influence was probably that it provided Rush with the intellectual justification he needed for the direction his political thinking was already taking. In any case once hostilities broke out between the colonies and England Rush entered the fray as an active and ardent patriot.

Rush was responsible for the name and publication of Thomas Paine's pamphlet *Common Sense* and, as a member of the Continental Congress in 1776, he was the only physician to sign the Declaration of Independence. At the beginning of the war he was appointed Physician General of the Middle Department of the Continental Army. Shocked by conditions in the American military hospitals, Rush was quickly embroiled in a quarrel with William Shippen, Jr., Director-General of the army medical department. The dispute soon led to a falling out between Rush and General Washington, and Rush resigned from the army in 1777. At the end of the war Rush was, nevertheless, once again active in politics. He publicly and successfully called for the repeal of the Pennsylvania Test Law, and as a member of the state ratification convention fought for the adoption of the federal constitution. Finally, in 1790 he helped to bring about the adoption of a new state constitution for Pennsylvania.[41]

At the close of the war Rush lamented that many people felt the Revolution itself was over. "This is so far from being the case," he wrote in 1786, "that we have only finished the first act of the great drama. We have changed our forms of government, but it remains yet to effect a revolution in our principles, opinions, and manners so as to accommodate them to the forms of government we have adopted." [42] He probably read with much approval the conviction expressed to him the following year by Samuel Stanhope Smith that American scholarship would eventually rival and surpass that of Europe.[43] Rush had long harbored even greater hopes for his

[39] *Ibid.*, pp. 46, 89.
[40] *Ibid.*, p. 46, n. 19.
[41] Rush's political activities are described in detail by Nathan G. Goodman in *Benjamin Rush: Physician and Citizen, 1746–1813* (Philadelphia: University of Pennsylvania Press, 1934), especially Chapter IV.
[42] Rush, *Letters*, I, 388.
[43] Smith to Rush, April 10, 1787, Princeton University Library, Manuscript Collection, AM 14429.

country, and in 1788 he wrote to John Adams: "America has ever
appeared to me to be the theater on which human nature will reach its
greatest civil, literary, and religious honors. *Now* is the time to sow
the seeds of each of them." [44] Rush had lost no time in turning his
attention to the real revolution waiting to be fulfilled.

Remarkably versatile and possessed of almost incredible funds
of energy, Benjamin Rush threw himself into the promotion of one
cause after another in what L. H. Butterfield has aptly called Rush's
"one-man crusade to remake America." Rush became the outspoken
advocate of most of the social reforms that were first to acquire
importance in the nineteenth century. He helped organize the first
antislavery society in America, championed humane treatment of the
mentally ill, fought capital punishment, and instigated the beginnings
of an American temperance movement. Almost every type of educational problem exercised his concern and attention. He promoted
the extension of educational opportunities at every level: he was the
principal founder of Dickinson College in western Pennsylvania;
he helped to establish the Philadelphia Sunday School Society, another
first of its kind in America; and he was a leading spokesman for a
system of free schools in the state. He battled to introduce curricular
reforms from elementary through higher education, and he drew up
one of the earliest plans for a national university. All of this activity
was carried on, it should be remembered, while Rush was himself
practicing medicine, writing medical treatises and textbooks, and
holding down his own teaching posts in medicine at the College of
Philadelphia and University of Pennsylvania.[45]

The picture in Rush's mind of the America he hoped for was
large and many-sided. "I long to see," he wrote, "an asylum prepared
for the persecuted and oppressed of all countries, and a door opened
for the progress of knowledge, literature, the arts, and the gospel of
Jesus Christ to the ends of the earth." [46] This vision of America combined Rush's political principles and his deep religious convictions.

Rush had been raised within the fold of New Side Calvinism, and

[44] Rush, *Letters*, I, 468–469.
[45] Rush's teaching posts included: Professor of Chemistry in the College of Philadelphia—elected, 1760; Professor of Theory and Practice of Medicine, College of
Philadelphia—elected, 1789; Professor of the Institutes of Medicine, University of
Pennsylvania—elected, 1792; Professor of the Practice of Physic, University
of Pennsylvania—elected, 1796.
[46] Rush, *Letters*, I, 221.

religious concerns remained central to his thinking throughout life.[47] Finding sectarian doctrine too narrow, however, and judging the "aristocracy of Presbyterianism" contrary to a free and humanitarian society, Rush became convinced of the universalist belief that all men would eventually be saved.[48] His turn to universalism was, nevertheless, more than a negative rejection of sectarianism, and was never a sign of religious indifference. For Rush, religion offered the only sure foundation for a good society and universalism was the most all-embracing and compelling form of religion. Repeatedly Rush said that he found the strongest motivation for public service and the true source of republican forms of government in God's benevolence and the universal salvation of mankind.[49]

Rush's universalism can, perhaps, best be understood as a combination of an Enlightenment faith in order, harmony, and divine benevolence with the outlook of his early New Side Calvinism. Rush himself frequently chose to explain his religious viewpoint in such terms, and with good reason.[50] Although Rush once described his beliefs as "a compound of the orthodoxy and heterodoxy of most of our Christian churches," there did exist a clear continuity between Rush's New Side background and many of his political, social, and religious convictions. As a student Rush could not have helped being exposed by Finley and Davies to the New Side stress upon the religious imperatives of public service and patriotism. The traditional New Side distrust of sectarian and doctrinaire encapsulations of the truth seems, moreover, to have had a natural tendency at times toward rational liberalism and theological universalism, as Samuel Stanhope Smith and his cousin Samuel Blair illustrate.[51] Finally, Rush's republican Christ-

---

[47] Rush has too often been placed without qualification in the camp of eighteenth-century American deism. The deep religious strain in Rush has been noted by L. H. Butterfield, and needs to be emphasized if either Rush or his times are to be understood adequately. See L. H. Butterfield, "Introduction," *Letters of Benjamin Rush*, I, lxix. For treatments of Rush that tend to ignore or miscast his religious side, see David Tyack, "Forming the National Character," *Harvard Educational Review*, XXXVI (1966), 29–41, and Daniel Boorstin, *The Lost World of Thomas Jefferson* (New York: H. Holt, 1948).

[48] Rush, *Letters*, I, 490, 600; also see Rush, *Autobiography*, pp. 163–166, 334–345.

[49] Rush, *Letters*, I, 583–584, 419; Rush, *Autobiography*, pp. 226, 333–335. Rush's move to universalism was no doubt hastened and confirmed by his own personal and political difficulties with certain Presbyterians, especially John Ewing. See, for example, Rush, *Letters*, I, 338–339, 379–380, 409, 433–434.

[50] Rush, *Letters*, I, 371, 419.

[51] Rush himself noted the similarity between Blair's case and the hostility his own universalism engendered. *Ibid.*, p. 433.

ianity and social millennialism had much in common with New Side millennialism and its hope for a new social order and the appearance of technological wonders.[52] Rush provides another instance, and a better understanding, of the ways in which the Enlightenment and evangelical Christianity could be considered compatible and mutually supporting.[53]

In the end the blend did not work for Rush, and it is interesting that in his case it was the religious element that won out. From the beginning the universalist convictions of Rush were as much the product of his evangelical Christianity as they were of his Enlightenment optimism. Rush always relied most heavily in arguing for universalism upon the inner logic of certain orthodox doctrines of the Christian faith. He called whenever possible, of course, upon the support and corroboration of science, even, for example, recommending a Bible commentary to Jefferson in 1811 because its author "professes uncommon qualifications for such a work. He is a naturalist, a philosopher, a chemist, an anatomist, well read in geography and travels, and a profound oriental scholar." [54] The most telling arguments for Rush were, nevertheless, those from scripture and doctrine itself. The unity of the race in original sin—a conviction which Rush emphasized more and more—implied a universal atonement and the unity of all mankind in salvation. "For if Christ died for *all*, as Mr. Wesley always taught, it will soon appear," Rush wrote, "a necessary consequence that *all* shall be saved." [55] Rush grew increasingly conservative in religious matters, placing greater stress on the authority of scripture and revelation and even denying the value of natural theology—at one point going so far as to reject deism in the same breath with paganism and atheism.[56] His New Side Calvinism had made it possible for Rush to shape a religious understanding that supported the Enlightenment aims and outlooks he so ardently championed. His final disillusionment was not so much with science and modern philosophy as with their pursuit apart from a religious grounding. When, therefore, he ultimately felt constrained to make a choice, it was for the religious.[57]

[52] See, for example, *ibid.*, II, 834, 837.
[53] *Ibid.*, I, 611–612.
[54] *Ibid.*, II, 1079.
[55] *Ibid.*, I, 611.
[56] *Ibid.*, II, 799, 936; Rush, *Autobiography*, p. 334; also see *Letters*, II, 919, 1171.
[57] If this interpretation is correct, it shows Rush to have been less a religious "weather-cock," to use L. H. Butterfield's phrase, than he otherwise appears. The irony

For all of his talk about revolution and a new era in human affairs, Rush was never a radical revolutionary. His opposition to the unicameral legislature established under the first Pennsylvania constitution was motivated by his fear that too much unrestrained democracy was bound to degenerate into "licentiousness" and "mobocracy."[58] In his social reforms Rush expressly rejected the charge that his programs were "utopian schemes." They were "utopian," he admitted, if by that was meant visionary and innovative; but they were not utopian, he insisted, in the sense of being unrealizable within the present state of American society.[59]

Rush's faith in the power of education provided him with the assurance that his vision for America was a real possibility. Rush hoped for a society in which, to employ one of his favorite phrases, "liberty, learning, and the Gospel" would flourish. Not only learning, but liberty and the Gospel as well, depended for their realization, in Rush's view, upon education. He assigned to education, therefore, a threefold task related to the political, social and religious dimensions of his national ideal: to instill republican principles of government, to spread and promote useful knowledge, and to inspire religious commitment and a love of virtue.

The reliance that Rush placed upon education at every level as the chief instrument of social and political progress underscores how little he was the radical and how much the progressive. Even as a social reformer Rush was primarily an educator in the broadest sense. As his many pamphlets and newspaper articles and his support of Philadelphia's scientific and service organizations attest, Rush pinned most of his hopes for the success of his causes upon the power of persuasion. Although Rush's conception of education was not limited to formal educational institutions—schools, colleges, and learned societies—as his own publishing and propaganda efforts show, institutionalized education was of prime importance. In this regard, while

was that the essentially liberal Rush can be seen in his later years as an early spokesman for a resurgent Protestantism that in the nineteenth century came to represent some of the very sectarianism Rush had opposed. Irony is compounded when it is remembered that Samuel Stanhope Smith, whom Rush had chided on occasion for his conservatism, was one of the last to hold out against a dogmatic pietism.

58 Rush, *Letters*, I, 114, 240, 244. Writing to John Adams in 1805, Rush described the political parties in Pennsylvania as four: old Tories, honest Federalists, violent Democrats, and moderate Republicans. In these terms Rush was a moderate Republican in politics and a moderate progressive in social reform. Rush, *Letters*, II, 900.

59 Benjamin Rush, *Thoughts Upon Amusements and Punishments Which Are Proper for Schools* (Philadelphia: Dobson, 1790), reprinted in Rush, *Essays*, pp. 57-74.

his confidence in the power of education may itself have been utopian, his educational plans and proposals were concrete and specific.

In formulating his educational schemes, Rush drew often from his Scottish experience, sometimes directly, sometimes implicitly. Scottish thinkers and Scottish institutions served Rush in two ways: they provided an important source of inspiration for the shaping of Rush's educational ideals; and they also provided the substance of many of Rush's specific educational views and recommendations. The appeal of the Scottish example was natural to Rush and it lent itself handily to his purposes. Rush had been impressed by the caliber of his Edinburgh teachers and their international reputations. He had seen for himself how the intellectual life of Scotland was centered in the universities and fostered by their presence. Finally, he had admired the leading work of Scottish professors in applying their scientific discoveries to the development of Scottish industry and agriculture.

Rush drew sustenance for his views from French and English, as well as Scottish sources, but the last remained primary. His belief that schools and colleges were the most important agents of social progress found confirmation in the close connection between Scottish educational institutions and the cultural life of Scotland. In Scotland, Rush had a model, imperfect as it might be, for his own ideals of republican education—a concrete example that his educational schemes were not utopian dreams unrelated to anything in reality. To be sure, he thought that he could improve on the Scottish example, and he hoped that America would eventually surpass anything Europe could offer. He had his model, nevertheless, and Rush did not hesitate either to appeal to it or to draw from it as the occasion demanded.

The first facet of the educational task was political—to implant in the citizens of the new nation the patriotic devotion and competence required to maintain the principles and institutions of a republican government. Rush's basic conception of republican education was really no different from that held by many of his fellow Americans. Although differing at points in details, it was in essentials the understanding seen already in Samuel Stanhope Smith, and was one shared by persons of such otherwise disparate political orientations as Thomas Jefferson and Noah Webster. The aims of republican education as conceived by Rush and others were to enlighten the general populace through a broad diffusion of knowledge, train up leaders for the state, and prevent the clash of factions by shaping a uniform, homogeneous American character.[60] Although Rush was not original or alone in his view of republican education, his was perhaps the most complete enunciation of the theory, and his efforts to put the theory into practice were equaled by few.

Recent critiques of republican educational theory have made much of the danger implicit in the emphasis upon creating a uniform national character, as though this were a precursor of latter-day totalitarianism.[61] Rush, it is true, in proposing a system of free schools for Pennsylvania, presented one of the most extreme statements of this goal.[62] He spoke of converting men into "republican machines" and of "producing one general, and uniform system of education" which would "render the mass of the people more homogenous, and thereby fit them more easily for uniform and peaceable government." [63] Rush's conception of homogeneity, however, was much more complex—or much less totalitarian, as some would have it—than these statements might indicate.

To appreciate fully what Rush had in mind, his "Thoughts upon the Mode of Education Proper in a Republic" should be read alongside his "Proposal of a German College," printed in the *Pennsylvania Gazette* a year earlier.[64] As L. H. Butterfield has pointed out, Rush was one of the earliest non-German friends and backers of the

[60] Recent discussions of the aims of republican education include Rush Welter, *Popular Education and Democratic Thought in America* (New York: Columbia University Press, 1962), pp. 23–44; David Tyack, "Forming the National Character," *Harvard Educational Review*, XXXVI (1966), 29–41; Allen O. Hansen, *Liberalism and American Education in the Eighteenth Century* (New York: The Macmillan Company, 1926). Hansen analyzes a number of eighteenth-century writings on republican education, though much of Hansen's interpretation needs reassessment.
[61] Tyack takes this position in "Forming the National Character." Although Tyack is helpful in uncovering some of the inconsistencies in a homogenizing education that is both democratic and directed, his analysis, complete with a quotation from Bertolt Brecht, of totalitarian tendencies in republican education is somewhat overdrawn. If anachronisms are to be avoided, Benjamin Rush's stress upon creating "republican machines," for example, needs to be read in the light of Newtonian mechanics, not Orwellian apocalyptics.
[62] Benjamin Rush, *A Plan for the Establishment of Public Schools and the Diffusion of Knowledge in Pennsylvania: To Which Are Added Thoughts Upon the Mode of Education, Proper in a Republic. Addressed to the Legislature and Citizens of the State* (Philadelphia: Thomas Dobson, 1786), reprinted as the first two selections in Rush, *Essays*, pp. 1–5, 6–20. The first is referred to henceforth as "A Plan for Public Schools in Pennsylvania," and the second as "Mode of Education Proper in a Republic."
Also see Benjamin Rush, "To the Citizens of Philadelphia: A Plan for Free Schools," *The Independent Gazeteer* (Philadelphia), March 28, 1787; reprinted in Rush, *Letters*, I, 412–415.
[63] Rush, "Mode of Education Proper in a Republic," *Essays*, pp. 6–20.
[64] Benjamin Rush, "To the Citizens of Pennsylvania of German Birth and Extraction: Proposal of a German College," *Pennsylvania Gazette*, August 31, 1785, in *Letters*, I, 365–368.

Pennsylvania Germans, a student of their language and admirer of their culture.[65] In his *Gazette* article Rush dealt with two conflicting objections to a German college: that it would either isolate the Germans or would undermine their distinctive way of life. Rush affirmed the value of the German language and culture and denied that they would be lost even if the German college included instruction in English, which he devoutly hoped it would. He proclaimed that society needed the riches each national and religious group had to offer. A system which made a uniform education available to all, he argued, would open the doors to every social group and be precisely the means by which each could bring its distinctive contributions into the mainstream of American life. What Rush loved to call "one homogeneous mass of people" was, thus, not utterly simplistic in its conception.[66] If history has proven Rush too sanguine in his hopes for the achievement of diversity amidst unity, that would seem to be a question of a different order.

Most proponents of republican education tended to distinguish, as Jefferson and Samuel Stanhope Smith did, between lower education for the common people and higher learning for the nation's leaders. On this issue Rush appears to have vacillated somewhat, but eventually to have come down on the side of the orthodox. In the mid-eighties he was writing that higher learning should be available to all, if "aristocratic juntos" were to be destroyed, and that only narrow-minded men would fear having too many colleges and too many learned men.[67] His utterances on common education, however, always stressed the need for an enlightened populace in order that the nation's leaders would be able "to carry the people with them," and to avoid those situations which threatened to destroy republican governments "where the common people are ignorant and vicious." [68]

In 1788, when he drafted one of the first proposals for a national university, Rush made the distinction between the two kinds of education unmistakable by suggesting that only graduates of the federal university should be allowed to hold office in the government. Although Rush apparently abandoned this particular requirement for public office—he at least did not push for it—he does seem to have continued to hold to the view that higher learning should be restricted to public leaders. Late in his life (1810) he favored a raise

---

[65] See Rush, *Letters*, I, 368, n. 1.
[66] *Ibid.*, p. 366.
[67] See *ibid.*, pp. 368, 427.
[68] *Ibid.*

in the tuition at Dickinson College as a means of holding down the number of the learned in proportion to the laboring population. Should learning become universal, he wrote, "it would be as destructive to civilization as universal barbarism." [69] It is not clear from his own words, however, whether Rush disapproved of universal higher education out of a distrust of the common man or a profound disillusionment with the upper and professional classes. Rush insisted to the end, nevertheless, that reading, writing, and arithmetic should be "as common and cheap as air"—"a kind of sixth or civil sense" possessed by every citizen in the Republic. [70]

If the first facet of the educational task, in Rush's opinion was to further republican government, the second was to promote useful knowledge. In his reports to John Morgan while he was a student in Edinburgh, Rush took the liberty of suggesting the need for the establishment of a "literary and physical" society in Philadelphia after the pattern of the Edinburgh Philosophical Society. [71] The advice was gratuitous since Morgan, immediately after his own return from Edinburgh, had already taken the lead in the formation in 1766 of the American Society Held in Philadelphia for the Promotion of Useful Knowledge. Two years later Morgan helped to engineer the union of this group with the rival American Philosophical Society. Rush had been elected to the American Society while in Edinburgh, and he, therefore, automatically became a member of the American Philosophical Society in 1769.

The preface to the first volume of *Transactions* of the new society, published two years later, stated the aims of the group with the declaration: "Knowledge is of little use, when confined to mere speculation." The preface went on to relate the determination of the members "to confine their disquisitions, principally, to such subjects as tend to the improvement of their country, and advancement of its interest and prosperity." [72] Rush threw himself wholeheartedly into the life of the Society and the pursuit of its aims. [73]

The general eighteenth-century enthusiasm for seeking social

[69] *Ibid.*, II, 1053.
[70] See, *ibid.*
[71] *Ibid.*, I, 49, 51.
[72] *Transactions of the American Philosophical Society*, Vol. I, 1771. Quoted in L. H. Butterfield, "Benjamin Rush as a Promoter of Useful Knowledge," *Proceedings of the American Philosophical Society*, XCII (1948), 28. This is an excellent article for an idea of the full scope of Rush's activity in this area.
[73] Between 1770 and 1797 Rush delivered fifteen papers before the Society. For a full listing of titles and dates of publication, see Butterfield, "Benjamin Rush as a Promoter of Useful Knowledge," pp. 35–36.

progress through applied science gained added impetus in America after the Revolution.[74] Rush was eloquent in tying the promotion of useful knowledge to the duties of patriotism. In his sixth oration before the Philosophical Society he exclaimed, "What may we not expect from this harmony between the sciences and government!"[75] The curricular program Rush presented for republican education made the connection between his national hopes and the advancement of practical knowledge explicit. The central studies which he felt should shape the complete school and college curriculum included: the modern languages—French, German, and, above all, English; the science of government; commerce, agriculture, and industry; chemistry, natural history, and mathematics, especially in their practical application; ancient and modern history; and because a productive nation must be a healthy nation, athletics.[76]

None of his educational reforms were more vital to Rush than the abolition of the classical languages—to him always the "dead languages"—from the center of the school and college curriculum. Useful knowledge, free government, and religion and morals all suffered because of the inordinate amount of time spent in the teaching of Latin and Greek. Rush himself had not been able to master the ancient languages at his uncle's school, he had been embarrassed in early attempts to correspond in Latin, and his efforts to brush up on his Latin were never very successful.[77] His delight and relief must have been immense, therefore, when he arrived at the University of Edinburgh to find that William Cullen had inaugurated, for the first time anywhere, the practice of delivering medical lectures in English rather than Latin.[78] From this time on any doubts he may have had about his own scholarly abilities in the ancient tongues must have given way completely to the conviction that emphasis on Latin and Greek

[74] For several examples of the effect of patriotic fervor on the pursuit of science in Philadelphia, see Whitfield J. Bell, Jr., "The Scientific Environment of Philadelphia, 1775–1790," *Proceedings of the American Philosophical Society*, XCII (1948), 13.
[75] Benjamin Rush, *Medicine Among the Indians In North America* (Philadelphia: Crukshank, 1774), reprinted in Dagobert Runes, ed., *The Selected Writings of Benjamin Rush* (New York: Philosophical Library, 1947), p. 291.
[76] Rush, "Mode of Education Proper in a Republic," *Essays;* Benjamin Rush, "Sermon on Exercise," in Runes, ed., *Selected Writings*, pp. 358–372; Benjamin Rush, "Observations upon the Study of the Latin and Greek languages, as a branch of liberal Education, with hints of a plan of liberal Instruction, without them, accommodated to the present state of society, manners and government in the United States," *American Museum* (June 1789), reprinted in Rush, *Essays*, pp. 21–56.
[77] Rush, *Letters*, I, 18, 524; Rush, *Autobiography*, p. 42.
[78] See Douglas Guthrie, *A History of Medicine* (Philadelphia: J. B. Lippincott, 1946), p. 222.

was itself wrong. Throughout his life he never allowed an opportunity to attack the classical curriculum to pass.[79]

Rush's obsession with the classical languages stemmed in large measure from his conviction that his hopes for national progress were doomed if the time spent on Latin and Greek were not spent studying English and science instead. "The nation which shall first shake off the fetters of those ancient languages," he wrote, "will advance further in knowledge, and in happiness, in twenty years, than any nation in Europe has done, in a hundred." [80] The standard of universal education that he considered essential to republican government also demanded the elimination of Latin and Greek as prerequisites to higher learning and study of the sciences. Furthermore, the prejudices of the common people against schools and colleges as nests of the idle and the rich would be removed, he argued, with the elimination of Latin and Greek.[81] Finally, he thought the religion and morals of the country would be raised if schoolboys had less exposure to heathen mythology.[82]

At times his vituperation of the classics was ferocious: "The human intellects are brutalized by being stuffed in early life with such offal learning," he wrote. He was not surprised that the classics had been revived in France by none other than the tyrannical Napoleon; and he did not shrink even from placing the evils of the classical curriculum in the same category as those visited upon mankind by war, slavery, and drunkenness.[83] Too much attention to Latin and Greek harmed rather than helped the development of a good English style—much better, he thought, to study Swift and Hume, Rush's own favorite stylists.[84]

Many of Rush's concrete proposals, however, were moderate and made good sense. He allowed that students might need to acquire a reading knowledge of the classics. Ministers would need a reading knowledge of the Greek testament, but would be well-advised to devote most of their energies to Hebrew.[85] Rush did not feel that classical studies should be ignored altogether, but he did think they

---

[79] For example, see Rush's friendly but earnest disagreement with John Adams in 1810 over the value of Greek and Latin. Schutz and Adair, eds., *The Spur of Fame,* pp. 166–179.
[80] Rush, "Observations . . . upon Latin and Greek," *Essays,* p. 43.
[81] *Ibid.,* pp. 25, 43; Rush, *Letters,* I, 522.
[82] Rush, *Autobiography,* p. 345; *Letters,* II, 946.
[83] Rush, *Letters,* I, 518, 525.
[84] *Ibid.,* I, 524.
[85] *Ibid.,* I, 946; II, 1060.

should be left in the hands of specialists—linguists, whose translations would be of genuine and widespread use.[86]

Rush had two favorite authorities for the support of his position on Latin and Greek: Benjamin Franklin and William Cullen. Franklin's reputation and well-known views on English instruction provided Rush with powerful ammunition in popularizing his curricular reforms and in arguing with unconvinced fellow Americans.[87] Cullen was of more importance to Rush personally, however, in providing him with indisputable evidence of the rightness of his convictions. Rush gave Cullen most of the credit for introducing English as "the vehicle of instruction in the University of Edinburgh" and for "delivering medicine from the fetters of Latin." Cullen's own scientific renown and the advance of British medicine in general, Rush suggested, could perhaps best be ascribed "to the present fashionable custom of communicating medical knowledge in the English language.[88]

The support that Rush's Scottish experience gave to his promotion of useful knowledge is especially apparent in another of his pet curricular emphases: the study of chemistry. When Rush arrived in Edinburgh, Black had just succeeded his teacher, Cullen, to the chair of chemistry in the university. Black was by far the better chemist, but Rush always rated him a step below Cullen. Rush probably tended to think of Black as still only a brilliant student of the master, Cullen himself. Black was perhaps more theoretically oriented than Cullen, but he cannot be said to have lacked interest in the practical applications of his subject. Rush acknowledged the importance of Black's discovery of carbon dioxide, but he never really understood Black's theories of latent heat, although he seems to have been vaguely aware of their importance.[89] Under the combined influence of Cullen and Black, however, Rush became thoroughly convinced of the practical uses of chemistry.

Rush subsequently included chemistry in all of his curricular schemes. Chemistry, he declared, had a direct application to medicine, to agriculture and industry, and to the kitchen. For Rush the study

[86] Rush, "Observations . . . on Latin and Greek," Essays, p. 41.
[87] Rush, Letters, I, 520; II, 1080; Rush, "Observations . . . on Latin and Greek," Essays, pp. 21–22.
[88] Rush, Eulogium on Cullen, p. 371.
[89] See Josiah Charles Trent, "Benjamin Rush in Edinburgh, 1766–1768," in E. Ashworth Underwood, ed., Science, Medicine, and History (London: Oxford University Press, 1953), II, 179–186. See especially p. 183, where Trent quotes from his private manuscript copy of Rush's 1771 lectures on chemistry.

of chemistry even had aesthetic and political ramifications. It "en-
larges one's acquaintance with the wonders of nature and the
mysteries of art"; and, he suggested, chemical operations furnish
an analogy for the construction of durable government through
the skillfull combination of powers.[90]

Rush strove to impress upon his audiences the importance of
chemistry for agriculture. At the beginning of the eighteenth century Scottish farming was notorious for its backwardness and low
productivity. By the end of the century many Scottish farms had
achieved an international reputation for their progressiveness, and
Scottish agriculturists were in demand in all parts of Europe. Rush
frequently cited the chemical and agricultural research of Cullen,
Black, and Francis Home as being responsible for many of the advances in British farming.[91] In the middle of the eighteenth century
Lord Kames had, in fact, induced William Cullen to give lectures at
the university on the science of agriculture. These were expanded
over the years, and, in 1790, the University of Edinburgh inaugurated
what was probably the first chair of agriculture established at any
university.[92] It may be no accident that Rush was the first to suggest,
in 1809, the founding of a professorship of rural economy at the
University of Pennsylvania.[93] He certainly felt that Scotland excelled
in the study of agriculture and "agricultural science."

The emphasis Rush placed upon agriculture furnishes an excellent
illustration of the role played by the Scottish example in Rush's
own promotion of useful knowledge. What impressed Rush was the
function of the Scottish university as the organizing and directing
center of the forces of improvement. In promoting "agricultural
science" and useful knowledge in general, Rush was giving expression to an almost universal eighteenth-century ideal. The Scottish

[90] See Rush, "Mode of Education Proper in a Republic," *Essays,* pp. 17–18; Rush,
"Observations . . . on Latin and Greek," *Essays,* p. 47. Also see L. H. Butterfield,
"Introduction," *Syllabus of a Course of Lectures* by Benjamin Rush (Philadelphia:
Friends of the University of Pennsylvania Library, 1954, A Facsimile Reprint of
the 1770 Edition), pp. 5–13.

[91] Benjamin Rush, "The Vices and Virtues of Physicians," *Sixteen Introductory Lectures upon the Institutes and Practice of Medicine* (Philadelphia: Bradford and
Inskeep, 1811), reprinted in Runes, ed., *Selected Writings,* p. 308; Rush, *Eulogium
on Cullen,* pp. 326–327.

[92] Alexander Grant, *The Story of the University of Edinburgh* (London: Longmans,
Green, and Co., 1884), I, 344–347.

[93] Nothing came of his proposal at the time. There is no direct evidence that this
proposal was inspired by the example of Edinburgh, although in suggesting it Rush
did allude to the example of the "European universities," and he made known his
admiration for Scottish agricultural research. See Rush, *Letters,* II, 1023.

example served Rush by showing concretely that educational institutions devoted to the promotion of useful knowledge could
actually be the foremost agents of social progress.

The third task of republican education as conceived by Benjamin Rush was to instill religious conviction in the youth and
future citizens of the new nation. Rush often declared that without
the pervasive influence of Christian principles free government was
doomed. John Witherspoon had said that civil liberty is necessary
for the protection of religious liberty. Rush sometimes spoke in
similar fashion, and at other times he argued, in a more Jeffersonian
vein, that religious liberty is the safeguard of civil liberty. His own
basic position, though, was actually different from that of either
Witherspoon or Jefferson. In Rush's view civil and religious liberty
alike had their roots in Christian principles. Christian principles meant
to Rush, of course, the principles of universal Christianity. "A belief
in God's universal love to all his creatures," he wrote ". . . is a *polar*
truth. It leads to truths upon all subjects, more especially upon the
subject of government." [94]

The Bible should be taught in schools, he insisted, because it
above all other books "favours that equality among mankind, that
respect for just laws, and all those sober and frugal virtues, which
constitute the soul of republicanism." [95] He rejected moral philosophy
as unequal to this task because he thought it had cut morality loose
from the religious grounding that alone could sustain the social
virtues.[96]

The free school plan Rush placed before the public called for
parochial schools supported by public funds. This would ensure the
religious training of children. Referring to one of his favorite examples, Rush said that the moral and enlightened character of the
people of Scotland and New England was the direct result of just
such a system of schools as he was proposing.[97]

[94] Rush, *Letters*, II, 584; also see Rush, "Thoughts upon Education," *Essays*, p. 2.
[95] Rush, "A Defense of the Bible as a School Book," *Essays*, p. 113.
[96] With approval, Rush attributed to Jonathan Edwards the saying that moral
philosophy is "infidelity systematized." In a sense this attitude represented a throw-
back to an earlier tradition. It is interesting that the clerics, Witherspoon and
Smith, were arguing for moral philosophy from just the opposite direction. Rush's
attitude played into the hands of Smith's opponents in the College of New Jersey,
and he came to support Ashbel Green's plan, *contra* Smith, for a seminary detached
from the liberal arts college. Rush, *Letters*, II, 946–947; Rush, "Observations . . .
on Latin and Greek," *Essays*, pp. 49–50.
[97] Rush, "A Defense of the Bible as a School Book," *Essays*, p. 100.

Rush saw no contradictions between his universalism and permitting each denomination to maintain its own schools. In order to be taught, religion required systematic presentation, and each system would, therefore, express the belief of a particular religious group. His solution to the threat of sectarianism was similar to his thinking about the place of ethnic groups in American society. Each religious group, like each ethnic group, had its contribution to make, but no one group had more than a partial grasp of the truth. By enabling every denomination to have its schools, religious instruction would be guaranteed, each group would make its contribution, and the combined influence of all would check and cancel out the errors and excesses of any particular one. The counterpoise theory had its ethnic and religious as well as political applications.[98] In Rush's conception of republican education the religious task encompassed the others. "A Christian," he wrote, "cannot fail of being a republican," and, he added, "A Christian cannot fail of being useful to the republic. . . ."[99]

In his concrete educational undertakings Rush devoted his main energies to higher education. His efforts on behalf of Dickinson and Franklin colleges produced the most important and substantial results of his institutional proposals. The immediate impulse for the idea of establishing Dickinson College, in Carlisle, Pennsylvania, was Rush's dismay over the dismantling and reconstruction of the College of Philadelphia as a state university in 1779 by the radical Pennsylvania legislature. Rush looked upon the action of the legislature as tyrannical and motivated by narrow sectarian and political interests—interests, in other words, opposed to his own. Moreover, he personally disliked John Ewing, Provost of the new university and an Old Side Presbyterian.[100] Dickinson College was Rush's personal and political answer to both Ewing and the legislature.

Although Rush had to whip up support for his projected college beyond the Susquehanna, he received early and strong encouragement from at least one respected member of the American academic community. In 1783 Samuel Stanhope Smith wrote to Rush:

I do not think that at present you have it in your power to render a greater service to your country, than by contributing to establish such an

---

98 Rush, *Autobiography*, pp. 339–340; also see Rush, *Letters*, I, 294–295.
99 Rush, "Mode of Education Proper in a Republic," *Essays*, pp. 8–9.
100 Rush, *Letters*, I, 335–339.

institution, & thereby making learning more cheap & easily attainable by
the remoter parts of Pennsylvania, & several other states. The diffusion
of knowledge is the diffusion of virtue and freedom. The more equally
science is spread over the country, the more equally will its interests, and
liberties be understood & enjoyed.[101]

Indefatigably and almost single-handedly Rush gathered a board of
trustees from the republican leaders of Carlisle and Philadelphia;
argued, wheedled, and lured them into full support for the college;
and managed to secure a college charter in 1783. For nearly twenty
years Rush and John Montgomery, the leading member of the board
of trustees, were responsible for the life of the college.[102]

That Rush was a political moderate is nowhere better illustrated
than in his action to found Dickinson. Rush saw the radical west-
erners and Philadelphia artisans, who controlled the legislature and
who were responsible for the state constitution, as a threat to stable
government and to the respect for learning necessary for national
progress.[103] The anti-intellectual outbursts that greeted the establishment of Dickinson College attest that the frontier settlers as well as
Rush linked higher education with a certain degree of social distinction. To the radical this link was a manifestation of the forces of
conservatism and aristocracy; to Rush it was a necessary concom-
itant of representative and progressive government. Rush, who became a firm Jeffersonian, was himself sincerely convinced that
Dickinson would be a means for improving the manners and morals
of the settlers, and also a bulwark against the very aristocratic and
conservative elements the settlers feared.

Rush wanted Dickinson, and after it Franklin College, which he
regarded as a younger sister of Dickinson, to become part of his
master plan for a state-wide educational system.[104] This plan called
for a free school system and a network of four colleges located in

[101] Smith to Rush, July 20, 1783, Princeton University Library, Manuscript Collection,
AM 14429.
[102] See James Bonar, "Benjamin Rush and the Theory and Practice of Republican
Education in Pennsylvania" (Ph.D. dissertation, Johns Hopkins University, 1965).
This is a good treatment of Rush's educational views, and especially of his college-
founding activity. It supplements the earlier pioneering work of Harry G. Good,
Benjamin Rush and His Services to American Education (Berne, Indiana: Witness
Press, 1918).
[103] L. H. Butterfield, "Benjamin Rush and the Beginnings of 'John and Mary's College'
Over Susquehanna," *Bulwark of Liberty*, The Boyd Lee Spahr Lectures in Americana (Carlisle, Pa.: Fleming H. Revell Company, 1950), pp. 32 ff.
[104] Rush, "A Plan for Public Schools in Pennsylvania," *Essays*, pp. 3–4.

major towns across the state. Dickinson and Franklin would be the outposts of civilization and the American constitution in the west. "From these two colleges," he wrote, "we hope will issue rays of knowledge which shall finally reform our constitution and laws, and humanize even the half-civilized inhabitants of the western counties of Pennsylvania." [105] Rush clung to his ambition for the college. And, in 1802, in the midst of financial and disciplinary problems at Dickinson, Rush was trying to bolster his own spirits and those of the trusteees with the even more expansive thought that the college would be the source of "light and knowledge" to the whole western United States.[106]

Rush said he would never be satisfied until his colleges were equal to European universities, and by "European" it is obvious that he meant above all the Scottish universities. The Scottish example not only gave support to his ideal of the college as a generator of social stability and progress, but it also contributed important particulars to his specific educational plans. The very notion of four colleges spread across the state was suggested to him by the four university towns of Scotland and the benevolent influence that he, at least, supposed emanated from them. The two English universities, Oxford and Cambridge, were larger, and Rush looked upon them as "seats of dissipation." He also recommended the practice he had experienced in Edinburgh of boarding students in private homes, in preference to college dormitories, which he thought conducive to bad morals and poor discipline.[107]

The whole tenor of Rush's thought, together with the fame that John Witherspoon had brought to the College of New Jersey, made it only natural that Rush would look to Scotland for a president for Dickinson College.[108] The man selected was the Scottish minister, Charles Nisbet, whom Witherspoon years before had recommended for the College of New Jersey rather than himself. Nisbet had serious doubts about leaving Scotland, however, and again Samuel Stanhope Smith came to Rush's aid, this time by establishing a correspondence

---

[105] Rush, *Letters*, I, 416; also, 316.
[106] See Rush to John Montgomery, July 3, 1802, quoted in Whitfield J. Bell, Jr., "The Other Man on Bingham's Porch," *John and Mary's College*, The Boyd Lee Spahr Lectures in Americana (Carlisle, Pa.: Fleming H. Revell Company, 1956), p. 34.
[107] Rush, "Mode of Education Proper in a Republic," *Essays*, p. 14. In 1802, therefore, he opposed the building of a dormitory at Dickinson. Rush, *Letters*, II, 866.
[108] See Samuel Miller, *Memoirs of the Rev. Charles Nisbet, D.D.* (New York: Robert Carter, 1840), pp. 109, 290–291.

with Nisbet. Smith took great pains to answer in detail the Scotsman's many questions about America.[109] Finally persuaded, Nisbet accepted the offer and moved with his family to America in 1785 to take charge of the new college.

Rush himself was responsible for planning the curriculum of the college. His course of study demonstrated a sense of realism and an ability to compromise by combining his own favorite innovations with traditional subjects. French, German, and English were to be taught, but so too were Latin, Greek, and Hebrew. Geography and, of course, chemistry were to be included in the mathematics and natural philosophy course. In addition the students would study logic and metaphysics, divinity, moral philosophy, and rhetoric in all their branches. Rush hoped to have a faculty of five and several teachers in the attached preparatory grammar school.[110]

Unfortunately the course of study drawn up by Rush immediately encountered serious obstacles. Financial difficulties made it impossible to support the full complement of faculty desired by Rush, and for twenty years Nisbet, two other professors, and the grammar school master carried the entire teaching load. The students rebelled against the faculty requirement of a three-to-four-year degree course. Although Nisbet attempted to hold the line against lowering the standard, the trustees gave in to the students' demands that they be granted a degree after one year of study. Not until 1802 was the course extended to two years.[111] Less serious, but cause for chagrin, Robert Tait, the English teacher whom Rush himself had secured for the college from Scotland, was forced to give up his post within the first year because of his heavy Scots brogue.[112]

To complicate matters, Rush and Nisbet had difficulty getting along. The two men found each other mutually irritating—Rush could not abide Nisbet's sarcasm, and Nisbet distrusted Rush's enthusiasms; they differed in politics—the one a Jeffersonian and the other a Federalist; they clashed over the curriculum—Nisbet was a classical scholar and Rush an opponent of the dead languages; and they could not agree on religion—Rush thought Nisbet a narrow

[109] The correspondence is reprinted in Michael Kraus, "Charles Nisbet and Samuel Stanhope Smith—Two Eighteenth Century Educators," *The Princeton University Library Chronicle*, IV (November 1944), 17–36. Rush may very well have initiated the correspondence between Smith and Nisbet. See Rush, *Letters*, I, 324.
[110] James Bonar, "Benjamin Rush and . . . Republican Education in Pennsylvania," pp. 106–108.
[111] *Ibid.*, pp. 114–116.
[112] Rush, *Letters*, I, 378.

Presbyterian and Nisbet described Rush as an "Everythingarian." [113] Despite stormy relations between the founder, the President, the trustees, the students, and the community, Dickinson College managed to keep going. Futhermore, compared to some other new colleges of the same period, Dickinson appears to have done a creditable job.[114] By 1811 Rush was able to note with pride, "The College at Carlisle . . . is a flourishing institution." [115]

In formulating his many educational ideals and proposals, Rush had received inspiration, guidance, and confirmation from his Scottish experience. It is true that the example of no single country could monopolize the mind of so wide-ranging a thinker as Benjamin Rush. He gathered ideas from every available source, and exchanged letters with Englishmen, as well as Scotsmen.[116] Rush was a child of his age, and many of his educational views were common currency of the Enlightenment and of American nationalism. At a basic level, however, the Scottish example was of decisive importance. When he looked for the model university, Rush thought of Edinburgh; when he described the model chemist, Rush pointed to Cullen and Black; when he described the model teacher, Rush held up the example of Cullen. That is to say, when Rush looked for guidance, when he felt the need to justify his ideas or allude to precedents, he first thought of Scotland.

III

Benjamin Rush was America's only important systematic writer on medical subjects in the late eighteenth century, and one of the country's leading medical educators. Although Rush's interest and activity in other fields had its starts and stops, his work as a practitioner and teacher of medicine never ceased. While historians of education have made much of Rush as a spokesman for nationalist

---

[113] See Goodman, *Benjamin Rush*, pp. 329–338. After his experiences with Tait and Nisbet, Rush could not help voicing some rueful thoughts about his "Scottish speculations." Rush, *Letters*, I, 378.

[114] James Bonar points out that, although it was unequal to the standards of the older colleges, the two- and three-year courses of study, when adopted, did compare favorably with other newer colleges, such as Jefferson College, Washington College, Transylvania University, and even the University of Pennsylvania. Bonar, "Benjamin Rush and . . . Republican Education in Pennsylvania," p. 118.

[115] Rush, *Letters*, II, 1116.

[116] It should be noted again, perhaps, that two of his most important correspondents in England—Lettsom and Fothergill—were Scottish-educated, a circumstance that did not go unobserved by Rush himself.

education, they have virtually ignored his role as a central figure in the early history of American academic science.

Not surprisingly, medicine became for Rush a vehicle for his many other concerns and interests. Political forms and public health, Rush stressed, had a reciprocal influence upon one another. "There is an indissoluble union," Rush wrote, "between moral, political, and physical happiness." Elective and representative governments, he said, are not only the most favorable to public and individual happiness, they are also the most productive of physical health and vigor.[117] Rush also pointed out with some pride that by the same token American diseases are stronger. When Americans are sick, they are really sick, and require much more potent medical treatment than do the inhabitants of exhausted, senescent Europe. With his bleedings and purges Rush had the heroic treatment made to order.[118] Rush's medical views also took on quasi-religious tones from his millennialist hopes as he described that coming day when all diseases would be curable and "when old age shall be the only outlet of human life." [119] And, since medicine was for Rush demonstrably the most useful of all the branches of knowledge, he urged the popularization of medicine by making it a part of every school and college education.[120]

Rush returned from Scotland with definite ideas about how scientific inquiry should proceed. The scientific method as Rush conceived it was somewhat different from that set forth by Samuel Stanhope Smith, though both methods had important Scottish roots. The version adhered to by Smith was already the more orthodox, and exerted its hold over scientists well into the nineteenth century. Scottish philosophers had taken up and very nearly canonized the so-called Newtonian or Baconian method of induction. According to this view, it will be recalled, science, and moral philosophy as well, advanced by induction from observation to general laws. The epistemology of Scottish common sense seemed to lend further validity and simplicity to the inductive method in the insistence that the testimony of the senses is to be trusted. It has already been seen

[117] Benjamin Rush, *Three Lectures Upon Animal Life* (Philadelphia: Dobson, 1799), in Runes, ed., *Selected Writings*, p. 168.
[118] See Bell, "Scientific Environment in Philadelphia," *Proceedings of the American Philosophical Society*, XCII (1948), 13.
[119] Rush, *Eulogium on Cullen*, pp. 342–343.
[120] Benjamin Rush, "A Lecture on the Progress of Medicine," reprinted in Runes, ed., *Selected Writings*, pp. 237–238.

how Smith explicitly anchored his own formulation of the inductive method in the common sense rule that "the information of the senses are intended to be ultimate." [121] From this point of view simple observation and classification were themselves ultimate, and there could be no good reason why they would not yield up the desired laws of nature. As long as the accumulation of empirical data remained meager or did not appear to contradict accepted interpretations, the inductive method could serve as a spur and guide to further research. Yet in the nineteenth century, when these simple "laws of nature" began to be lost under a mountain of unassimilated factual observations, the weaknesses of the Scottish method became evident.

Against this empirical and inductive emphasis, Rush's conception of the scientific method was much more rationalistic and deductive. A brief look at the state of nineteenth-century American science will help to throw Rush's own scientific method into perspective. Two problems became especially perplexing in the early nineteenth century. One difficulty had to do with the nature of the scientific procedure itself. How was the scientist to know what to make of his collection of facts? What principles of discrimination was he to employ to separate the important from the trivial, and how was he to determine the new directions his inquiries should take? Simple observation offered little guidance and scientists groped for solutions. Some turned to analogy as a means of probing the unobservable, or abandoned induction to embrace explanations of nature that they thought could be rationally deduced. The results in both cases at times became extremely farfetched. Others clung to induction still more tenaciously. As George Daniels has shown, the methodological difficulties of nineteenth-century science were a long time being settled.[122]

The second problem, though slightly different, was related. No one scientist could hope to master all the details being rapidly amassed even in his own field. By the 1820's specialization was being urged by many as the only real solution to the growing complexity

[121] Samuel Stanhope Smith, *The Lectures, corrected and improved, which have been delivered for a series of years, in the College of New Jersey; on the subjects of moral and political philosophy* (2 vols.; Trenton, N.J.: Daniel Fenton, 1812), I, 23 f.

[122] George Daniels analyzes in detail the state of American science in the first half of the nineteenth century. In this and the following paragraph I rely upon his discussion. George H. Daniels, *American Science in the Age of Jackson* (New York: Columbia University Press, 1968).

of science. However, a few, mostly amateur scientists, in an unsuccessful rearguard action, continued to fight the movement toward specialization.

Even Benjamin Silliman at Yale, as late as 1839, resisted the division of his own subject, chemistry, into specialized areas, and proposed an alternate solution. His idea is interesting because it was almost a direct application to chemistry of what Smith had suggested for the teaching of moral philosophy. Silliman admitted that the body of facts was so extensive that if they were all to be taught chemistry would perforce have to be broken down into specialties. He thought the time would soon be at hand, however, when it would be possible to teach chemistry under a few general principles, "with no more facts than are necessary to illustrate the principles . . . without compelling the professor to lead, and the pupil to follow, through every maze of the vast labyrinth." [123] Silliman's hope, destined even then to frustration, also reveals how intimately connected research and pedagogical concerns were at the time. Smith's pedagogical orientation has already been pointed out, and Rush's thinking also had such an orientation.

The problems of both method and specialization were involved in Rush's understanding of scientific advance. In Scotland, Cullen had impressed Rush with the importance of introducing order and system into the study of medicine by developing theoretical principles to guide observation and practice. Although Cullen gave lip service to the necessity of avoiding the extremes of either "dogmatism" or "empiricism," as Rush himself did on numerous occasions, Cullen's own emphasis was decidedly systematic and rational. Rush firmly believed that the greatest danger to the progress of medical science came from empiricism, "observation without principles." [124] "To observe is to think," Rush told his students, "and to think is to reason in medicine." Bare facts were worse than useless to the physician because they could confuse and lead him astray. The physician who possessed a solid, systematic theoretical grounding would know what to make of his observations and could boldly apply himself to new cases without being needlessly tied to previous experience. So con-

---

[123] Quoted in Daniels, *American Science in the Age of Jackson*, pp. 27–28. Smith had said that in moral philosophy the object was "to propose such general principles as may enable a rational and reflecting mind to deduce the point of duty for itself, on every case as it arises in practice." Smith, *The Lectures*, I, p. 24.

[124] Rush, "The Progress of Medicine," in Runes, ed., *Selected Writings*, p. 243; Rush, "Observations and Reasoning in Medicine," *ibid.*, p. 245.

vinced was Rush of the need to combine theory and observation that he anticipated a future day when there would arise "a complete system of principles in medicine." [125]

To this point little exists in Rush's emphasis upon system to set his method apart from the usual insistence at the time on drawing general laws from particular facts. Rush, however, gave his method a dynamism that was lacking in the other. Rush was not content with mere passive induction. No progress was possible and no new areas of inquiry would appear unless the scientist actively entertained conjecture, hypothesis, even the "effusions of the imagination" as "the germs of future discovery." [126] In an obvious swipe at the methodologically orthodox of his day, who took Newton's disavowal of hypothesis literally, Rush said that Newton had founded an empire in science upon hypothesis, "for most of his discoveries were the result of preconceived hypotheses." [127] There was also a certain dynamism, and more than a touch of eighteenth-century optimism, in Rush's conception of one system's supplanting another in a dialectical movement toward perfection. He admitted that his system, too, would be altered and pass away "in the progress of science"; but he always seemed more ready to recognize when the last moments had arrived for the systems of other eighteenth-century medical theorists, such as Boerhaave, Stahl, Cullen, and Brown, than for the system of Benjamin Rush[128].

The merits and shortcomings of Rush's scientific method can perhaps best be seen in his theories of physical and mental illness.[129] Rush returned from Scotland an enthusiastic champion of Cullen's medical theories as well as of his method. Most of the trained Philadelphia doctors, such as John Redman, had followed the more eclectic theories and practices of Boerhaave, and were not initially receptive

---

[125] Rush, "The Progress of Medicine," in Runes, *Selected Writings*, p. 243; Rush, "Observations and Reasoning in Medicine," in Runes, ed., *Selected Writings*, p. 245.
[126] Rush, "Lectures on Animal Life," in Runes, *Selected Writings*, p. 161.
[127] Rush, *Eulogium on Cullen*, p. 328.
[128] Rush, *Letters*, II, 916, 1140–1; also Rush, "Observations and Reasoning in Medicine," in Runes, ed., *Selected Writings*, pp. 250 ff.
[129] Excellent discussions of Rush's medical theories and their place in eighteenth-century medicine include: George W. Corner, "Rush's Medical Theories," in Rush, *Autobiography*, Appendix I; Richard H. Shryock, *Medicine and Society in America, 1660–1860* (New York: New York University Press, 1960), pp. 67–76; Richard H. Shryock, "Benjamin Rush from the Perspective of the Twentieth Century," *Transactions and Studies of the College of Physicians of Philadelphia*, XIV (April 1946), 113–120; Lester S. King, *The Medical World of the Eighteenth Century* (Chicago: University of Chicago Press, 1958), pp. 139–150.

to the newest ideas from Edinburgh. Cullen described disease primarily as a malfunctioning of the nervous system leading to spasms and fever, and eventually to general debility. He thought fever was the result of "spasms in the extreme arteries" or capillaries.

Rush grew gradually dissatisfied with Cullen's theories. Rejecting Cullen's complex nosologies as too cumbersome and confusing with their classification of more than 1,300 different diseases, Rush sought a unitary theory of all disease—and found one. John Brown, another Scot and fellow student with Rush under Cullen, had simplified Cullen still further by making debility the basic disease state. Taking his start from Brown and retaining Cullen's theory of fever, Rush decided that debility was not disease but its "predisposing" or proximate cause, and as such, inaccessible. The disease state itself was fever; that is, irregular convulsive excitement of the vascular system. This, then, was what demanded treatment. The crux of Rush's theory was that, whatever the cause of disease, the body was capable of only the one reaction of vascular tension and convulsion. "Be not startled, gentlemen," he told students in 1791, "follow me and I will say there is but one disease in the world." [130] There was, likewise, but one treatment: induce relaxation and abolish convulsion—bleed and purge.

During and after the great yellow fever epidemics of 1793 and 1797, through which Rush labored with great risk of his own life, he followed the leadings of his own theory with a vengeance. Recommending that, if necessary, four-fifths of the body's blood supply could be drained away, Rush claimed that seldom did more than one in twenty yellow fever patients die when given the benefit of his treatment.[131] Not everyone was convinced. In the epidemic of 1797 criticism of Rush mounted to such a degree that his reputation was damaged. William Cobbett, the Philadelphia journalist, launched the most vicious attack, incurring in the process a libel suit, which he lost. Cobbett described Rush's treatment as "one of those great discoveries which are made from time to time for the depopulation of the earth." [132] Although Rush had many followers, controversy dogged him until after his death, and by the 1820's his theories were being abandoned wholesale.

When Rush turned to the study of mental illness, his results

---

[130] Benjamin Rush, *Lectures on the Practice of Physic,* quoted in Shryock, "Benjamin Rush from the Perspective of the Twentieth Century," p. 70.
[131] See Goodman, *Benjamin Rush,* pp. 224, 250.
[132] Quoted in Shryock, *Medicine and Society in America,* p. 70.

were of more lasting value and the investigatory potential of his method of inquiry more apparent. Rush had long been interested in the care and treatment of the insane. Humanitarian that he was, Rush insisted that the insane should be treated with kindness and respect, and it was largely through his efforts that the state legislature in 1792 appropriated money for the construction of a special ward for the mentally ill in the Pennsylvania Hospital. Rush's interest in the nature of mental illness led to his publishing some of the most significant American writings in the field to appear prior to the Civil War.[133]

Rush brought to the study of mental illness his own understanding and reformulation of the psychology developed by Scottish philosophers, with their emphasis upon the emotions and faculties of the mind. In so doing, however, Rush was not uncritical of Scottish philosophy. It is interesting that Rush at one point presented the entire catalog of his reform views in the context of a criticism of Thomas Reid's notion of common sense. As others had, Rush picked up the ambiguity in the term "common sense," which he thought rendered it useless and misleading. He said that common sense and truth do not necessarily coincide, for "common sense" is only another term for socially accepted customs and opinions and varies in different ages and countries.[134] Rush distinguished between reason and common sense, a distinction that had been made in the writings of another Scotsman whom Rush deeply admired, James Beattie, Professor of Moral Philosophy at Marischal College, Aberdeen.[135] The business of reason, Rush said, "is to correct the evidence of our senses." In

[133] The major published works by Rush on mental illness are his earlier *Enquiry into the Influences of Physical Causes upon the Moral Faculty*, delivered before the American Philosophical Society in 1786, and his major text, *Medical Inquiries and Observations upon the Diseases of the Mind* (Philadelphia: Kimber & Richardson, 1812). The latter has been reprinted in a facsimile edition by the New York Academy of Medicine (New York, 1962). All references to the *Medical Inquiries and Observations upon the Diseases of the Mind* are to the 1962 edition.

[134] Rush said, for example, that it is common sense, not truth, that supports outmoded medical practice, monarchies, capital punishment, sectarianism, and the teaching of Latin and Greek! Rush, "Thoughts on Common Sense," *Essays*, pp. 249–256.

[135] Rush had Beattie elected to the American Philosophical Society in 1786. Beattie's major philosophical work, *Essay on the Nature and Immutability of Truth*, was a popularization of the common sense philosophy of Reid. Much of Rush's admiration for Beattie came from his belief that Beattie had refuted Hume's skepticism. As a matter of fact, Beattie simply by-passed Hume's main arguments. See Gladys Bryson, *Man and Society: The Scottish Inquiry of the Eighteenth Century* (Princeton: Princeton University Press, 1945), p. 134; James McCosh, *The Scottish Philosophy* (New York: Robert Carter and Brothers, 1875), pp. 230–238; Rush, *Letters*, I, 394; II, 746–748.

this regard Rush did not hold to the Scottish realist philosophy. This did not prevent him, however, from taking up concepts from Scottish philosophy and psychology.

Rush utilized the Scottish philosophical distinction and analogy between the external senses of the body and the internal senses of the mind. The internal senses, or mental faculties, according to Rush, were nine in number: understanding, memory, imagination, passions, the principle of faith, will, the moral faculty, conscience, and the sense of deity.[136] The internal senses were for Rush, as for the Scots philosophers, innate, part of the given equipment of the human person. He stressed, however, more in line with strict Lockean and perhaps with French sensationalist views, that the innate senses respond only to stimuli conveyed by the external senses—though he was not always consistent in this. Thus, he was able to apply his theory of physical disease to the problem of mental illness. "The cause of madness," he wrote, "is seated primarily in the blood-vessels of the brain, and . . . it depends upon the same kind of morbid and irregular actions that constitute other arterial diseases." [137] The result was a malfunctioning of the faculties of the mind located in those areas of the brain affected by the vascular disturbance.

Rush was content merely to describe the interworking of the blood vessels and the mind, since he did not feel that scientific knowledge was enough advanced to explain the precise nature of the relationship between the two. Attempts to read complete consistency into Rush bog down, but the main lines of his theory are clear enough. While the immediate state of mental illness was to be attributed to fever in the brain, this could be brought on by any number of predisposing causes. Some of these causes were purely physical, such as tumor, diseases in other parts of the body, climate, and diet. Others, such as fear, shock, feelings of guilt and religious opinions, sorrow and, social custom were more psychological, or mental. Rush concluded that most cases of insanity were the result of mental, rather than corporeal causes. Because the mental faculties were not discrete entities, but thoroughly interrelated, disorders in one could bring about derangement in others.

Using faculty psychology Rush was able to describe and clarify many different types of mental disease, including several which were not usually thought of in terms of illness at all. Rush described

---

[136] Rush, *Medical Inquiries . . . upon the Diseases of the Mind*, p. 10.
[137] *Ibid.*, p. 17.

various kinds of intellectual derangement, to which he gave names according to the symptoms produced. His discussion of the diseases of the moral faculties is, however, by far the most interesting. He thought this part of the mind was the same as the "moral sense" of Francis Hutcheson, the "sympathy" of Adam Smith, or the "moral instinct" of Rousseau; but Rush himself preferred the term "moral faculties" used by James Beattie.[138]

In his later writing Rush described two major types of illness arising from disorder of the moral faculty. The most common is when the moral faculty simply does not operate and leaves the will at the mercy of the emotions and passions. The second type is when the three moral faculties—the moral sense, the conscience, and the sense of deity—are all disturbed.[139] Moral derangement, resulting in lying, kleptomania, drunkenness, suicide, murder, and even disruption of the understanding, could again have both physical and mental causes. The moral faculties especially, but the others as well, depended for their proper development and stability upon the influences of education, form of government, and the state of society.

Here it was that Rush found medical confirmation for his social, religious, and political convictions. Representative governments and free presses, he said, "serve, like chimneys in a house, to conduct from the individual and public mind, all the discontent, vexation, and resentment, which have been generated in the passions by real or supposed evils. . . ." [140] The right kind of moral and religious education early in life was as essential for the proper formation of character and intellect as early language instruction was for correct pronunciation.

The results of Rush's scientific method are easy to criticize from the perspective of the present, but the weakness in the method itself is not so easy to locate. It can be maintained that in his search for a theoretical system Rush overemphasized the rational and deductive at the expense of observation and empirical data. There is some truth in this. Certainly the results of medical research did not justify the dogmatic assurance with which Rush held to his monistic theory of disease. Rush, furthermore, resorted to analogy with abandon whenever it served the purposes of his theory. He claimed

---

138 Rush, "The Influence of Physical Causes upon the Moral Faculty," in Runes, ed., *Selected Writings*, p. 182.
139 Rush, *Medical Inquiries . . . upon the Diseases of the Mind*, pp. 259 ff., 357 ff.
140 *Ibid.*, p. 68.

that despite the many manifestations of disease, its underlying unity was as actual as that of water, dew, and snow; and the proliferation of disease description was to be regarded in science with the same disdain as was polytheism in religion.[141]

Rush possessed considerable skill, nevertheless, in collecting empirical data, as his descriptions of yellow fever and mental illness amply demonstrate. In certain respects, also, his belief that scientific investigation advanced by means of projected hypotheses was more subtle, and perhaps closer to present understanding of the methods of science, than some later nineteenth-century attempts to stick purely to observation and induction. Many nineteenth-century scientists, even with more observational data at hand, found themselves, when they tried to move ahead methodologically, falling back on the use of analogy.

It might be more accurate and helpful to suggest that Rush's main difficulty was not so much that his method was too rational, but rather that his categories of analysis were too imprecise. Analogy was too loose and all-embracing, and the state of medical science could not yet provide him with the conceptual tools necessary for the formulation of sharp, analytic hypotheses. When Rush did borrow diagnostic and analytic categories from other fields, however, his method produced useful results. Incorporating the concepts of Scottish mental philosophy into his medical theories enabled Rush to move ahead of his colleagues in the study of insanity. In fact, he may have taken the clinical implications of faculty psychology just about as far as they could go. Without the aid of more precise analytic tools Rush was unable to exploit the full potential of his own rather farsighted view of the scientific method. Under the heavy pressures of teaching and practice, moreover, the appeal of a unitary theory of disease must have been immense, especially when its rudiments could be included in the ordinary school curriculum. It may have also seemed that both methodological perplexities and conditions driving toward specialization could be avoided by such a theory.

In bringing medical rather than theological categories to bear upon the study of moral—or personality—disorder, Rush has been described as being quite ahead of his time. It should be pointed out, however, without denying Rush's originality, that he was in fact

[141] See Goodman, *Benjamin Rush*, p. 235.

making use of certain advanced currents of thought of his own day. To realize this, one has only to recall the close connection drawn between the mind and the body by Samuel Stanhope Smith in his 1786 *Essay*. Smith himself touched upon the medical implications of his moral philosophy. "The skillful physician," Smith wrote, "will frequently have occasion to vary his remedies according as he apprehends the seat of a disease to reside chiefly in the body, or the mind." And Smith added, in characteristic fashion, that the minister, likewise, might be spared much embarrassment if he understood the human economy well enough to distinguish true piety from nervous disorders.[142] Perhaps the friends, Smith and Rush, had some mutual influence upon one another. Rush himself, by combining the categories of Scottish psychology with his many and frequently very astute clinical observations, was able to bring the full scope of mental illness within the framework of medical theory and to give its study some real semblance of scientific precision.

Benjamin Rush was one of the most active advocates of American nationalist aspirations in the early years of the Republic. His writings and his life gave forceful expression to the hopes held by many of his fellow countrymen about the power of science to transform American society and the power of education to form the national character. When Rush attempted to give content and concrete shape to his educational ideals, he, too, turned as often as not to Scotland for guidance and examples. He found in Scottish thought, Scottish institutions, and Scottish teachers the models that appeared to him peculiarly suited for adaptation to the American scene.

The confidence of Benjamin Rush in the benefits that Edinburgh, especially, had to confer upon America remained undiminished. Time and again he encouraged his own students to seek further training in Scotland and equipped them with letters of introduction to his friends on the Edinburgh faculty. Such important figures in early American science as Benjamin Smith Barton and Nathaniel Chapman departed for Edinburgh with Rush's blessings and letters of recommendation.[143]

In 1810, more than fifty years after his father had made the journey, young James Rush sailed for Edinburgh to complete his

[142] Smith, *The Lectures*, I, 141–142.
[143] Barton became Professor of Materia Medica and Botany at the University of Pennsylvania and Chapman the first president of the American Medical Association. See Rush, *Letters*, II, 838–839. Chapman returned from Edinburgh with a special gift for Rush from the Earl of Buchan. Rush, *Letters*, II, 929–931.

studies in medicine. "Perhaps there is at present no spot upon the earth," the old doctor wrote to his son in Edinburgh, "where religion, science, and literature combine more to produce moral and intellectual pleasures than in the metropolis of Scotland." [144] Apparently even his own "Edinburgh of America" had yet to outstrip the glories of its parent. Benjamin Rush did not recognize that at the time he was writing to his son the attraction of Edinburgh was beginning to be challenged by other European centers of learning and culture. Already the young Benjamin Barton had rounded off his years at Edinburgh with some time at Goettingen, and Adam Seybert, Barton's friend, had started for Edinburgh only to turn south toward Germany. That, however, is the beginning of another story.

[144] Rush, *Letters*, II, 1038.

Chapter VII

Science, Society, and the Curriculum: Conclusions

This study has been concerned with those Scottish educational influences in eighteenth-century America associated primarily with the Presbyterian academies and the College of New Jersey. A larger pattern of Scottish influences on American higher education, however, has also been glimpsed from time to time. Although it would fall outside the scope of this study to appraise the full impact of Scotland upon the American college, the major configurations of this larger pattern can be drawn. The task that remains, therefore, is to relate the early Princeton traditions to some of the wider issues and developments in eighteenth-century American higher education.

Four areas are especially worthy of attention: First, the late eighteenth century saw the emergence in American higher education of a genuine academic scientific community. Second, the American college became one of the central arenas in which the conflicting claims of the Enlightenment and of traditional religious points of view were mediated. Third, major efforts were made toward enunciating a social theory of education appropriate to the specific situation and needs of the new American nation. Finally, American educators applied themselves self-consciously, and often with considerable success, to the task of constructing a modern college curriculum. In all four areas Americans concerned with education found themselves frequently guided and informed by Scottish ideas and examples.

I

One strand in the wider network of Scottish influences on American higher education, which this study has touched upon in the career of Benjamin Rush, deserves a few pages of special attention. This was the appearance in late eighteenth-century America of an embryonic community of professional, academic scientists. Two major sources of Scottish scientific thought in the American college must be considered: the Scottish scientists and physicians who immigrated to America, especially during the first half of the century; and the American students who returned from their medical studies in Scotland during the latter half of the century.

Scottish intellectuals and university-educated persons came to America for a variety of reasons in the eighteenth century. Many able Scotsmen found opportunities in the colonies for political service and advancement that they would not have found open to them in Scotland; hence, they were often readier to live abroad than their fellow Englishmen, who enjoyed ample opportunities for themselves at home. In their comparison of the similar provincial status of Scotland and America, Bernard Bailyn and John Clive have stressed the crucial role in America of the royal officials and agents of the British government. They point out that the colonial agents of British imperialism were frequently the social leaders in the major towns, "cultural go-betweens" with immense influence on the fashions, styles, and thought in the provinces.[1] America and Scotland were much alike in this regard. There was, however, one essential difference between the two. Clive and Bailyn neglect to point out that many of the royal officials and government agents in the American colonies were themselves Scotsmen. During the eighteenth century there was a total of about thirty Scottish-born governors and lieutenant governors in charge of American colonial affairs. In many instances these officials were surrounded and supported by strong Scots factions which enjoyed considerable political and financial influence.[2] Even English army units serving in America often found themselves placed under

---

[1] John Clive and Bernard Bailyn, "England's Cultural Provinces: Scotland and America," *The William and Mary Quarterly*, 3rd ser., XI (April 1954), 208.

[2] Opportunities for trade also attracted many Scots businessmen and merchants to the colonies. By mid-century nearly every American port of any importance had its Scots business community of merchants, clerks, and shopkeepers. Scottish business influence, while not negligible in the nothern coastal cities, was, of course, strongest in the South, where representatives of Glasgow shipping firms dominated the Chesapeake tobacco trade. The factors, or agents, of the great Glasgow firms set up stores and trading posts in the back country where they became not only the chief engrossers of American tobacco, but also extended credit to the planters, and, by 1775, controlled the distribution of imports in Maryland and Virginia. Ian Cargill Graham, *Colonists from Scotland: Emigration to North America, 1707-1783* (Ithaca: Cornell University Press, 1956), pp. 117, 142.

Scots officers, much to the discontent of the troops; and many of the military doctors were Edinburgh-trained Scotsmen.[3]

As might be expected, the activities of Scots creditors and royal agents in the colonies did not always inspire good feelings toward Scotsmen, particularly during the last years before the Revolution. Nevertheless, the intellectual and educational contributions of Scottish colonial officials, frequently men of learning, should be noted. Probably the most famous of these men was Cadwallader Colden, a leading figure in colonial intellectual circles, and author of important scientific and philosophic treatises. A graduate of the University of Edinburgh and a trained physician, Colden was Lieutenant Governor of New York from 1760 to 1775. In North Carolina, Governor Gabriel Johnstone, a zealous protector of royal interests, displayed a concern with colonial education. Born in Dundee, Johnstone was a graduate of the University of St. Andrews, where he had studied medicine and oriental languages. As Governor he repeatedly enjoined the North Carolina Assembly to set up a comprehensive system of schools. Even in Virginia the Presbyterians received some early crucial assistance from Scottish-born officials. The Synod of Philadelphia in 1738 was encouraged by Governor William Gooch, also a Scot, to begin its educational and missionary activities in the Great Valley of Virginia. And, when Samuel Davies arrived in Scotland in 1753 to raise funds for the College of New Jersey, he was pleasantly surprised to discover that the way had been smoothed for him by letters of recommendation to the Provost and other leaders of Glasgow from the Scottish-born Governor of Virginia, Robert Dinwiddie.[4]

Most striking, however, in the first two thirds of the century, were the scientific and intellectual contributions made by Scottish physicians in the colonies. Several names stand out. In Boston there

---

[3] See James Hayes, "Scottish Officers in the British Army, 1714–63," *Scottish Historical Review*, XXXVII (1958), 23–33. Army doctors provided some of the most important early links between the colonies and the Scottish universities. Many Scottish physicians came into the colonies as military men in the French and Indian Wars, and then decided to stay. For example, Dr. Hugh Mercer (M.D. Aberdeen), a practicing physician in Pennsylvania and Virginia, who later died fighting the British, and Dr. James Craik (M.D. Edinburgh), raised to physician-general of the army under Washington, both initially came to the colonies as members of Braddocks' expedition. See Theodore Diller, "Pioneer Medicine in Western Pennsylvania," *Annals of Medical History*, VIII (1926), 141–155.

[4] Peter Ross, *The Scot in America* (New York: The Raeburn Book Co., 1896), p. 82; Carl Bridenbaugh, *Mitre and Sceptre* (New York: Oxford University Press, 1962), p. 131; W. H. Foote, *Sketches of Virginia* (2 vols.; Philadelphia: William S. Martien, 1850–55), I, 263.

was William Douglass; in Annapolis, Alexander Hamilton; in Charleston, John Lining, Alexander Garden, and Lionel Chalmers; in Urbana, Virginia, John Mitchell; in Philadelphia, and later New York, Adam Thomson; and also in New York, Peter Middleton and, of course, Cadwallader Colden. All of these men, trained physicians, settled in the colonies before 1750, most had been born in Scotland, and all had received the whole or a major part of their higher education at Scottish universities.[5]

Three things about these men were especially significant. First, they were instrumental in helping to form the beginnings of an inter-

---

[5] These individuals were included in the innermost circles of American intellectual life. Most of them were outstanding in at least one field; several were prolific writers in a wide range of subjects. William Douglass, educated at Edinburgh and Leyden, settled in Boston in 1718, and discovered that he was the only physician in that city with an M.D. degree. Notorious for his controversy with Cotton Mather over smallpox inoculation, Douglass is more favorably remembered for his work, *A Summary, Historical and Political . . . of the British Settlements in North America* (1760), as well as for his careful descriptions of scarlet fever. See Brook Hindle, *The Pursuit of Science in Revolutionary America, 1735–1789* (Chapel Hill: The University of North Carolina Press, 1956), pp. 38, 48–50, 58–61.

In 1750, in what Carl Bridenbaugh says may have been the first public medical lecture in this country, Adam Thomson presented his method of preparing the body for inoculation. Thomson's system, which was defended in print by Dr. Alexander Hamilton, was widely adopted in Europe, where it was known as "the American method." Carl Bridenbaugh, *Cities in Revolt* (New York: Alfred A. Knopf, 1965), pp. 200–201.

Dr. Peter Middleton, another Edinburgh-trained Scotsman, settled in New York in 1730. Together with John Bard, also Edinburgh-trained, Middleton performed the first dissection before students in America, and, with Samuel Bard, helped in 1767 to set up the medical school at King's College in New York. James Thacher, *American Medical Biography* (2 vols.; Boston: Richardson and Lord and Cotton and Barnard, 1828), I, 384.

In South Carolina, Lionel Chalmers practiced medicine, sent papers on various subjects to the old American Society at Philadelphia, and in 1776 published his *Essays on the Weather and Diseases of South Carolina*, one of the finest general medical works in the colonies. Bridenbaugh, *Cities in Revolt*, p. 410. John Lining of Charleston wrote on botanical and meteorological subjects, but his influential *History of the Yellow Fever* was his most important work. F. C. Bing, "John Lining, An Early American Scientist," *Scientific Monthly*, XXVI (1928), 249–252. Also see Hindle, *The Pursuit of Science in Revolutionary America*, pp. 50–51.

Cadwallader Colden, John Mitchell, and Alexander Garden did especially important work in natural history, and were among the first in the colonies to grasp and apply the Linnaean system of classification. Colden and Mitchell were known for their publications on a variety of other subjects as well. Mitchell's "Map of North America" and Colden's *History of the Five Indian Nations*, for example, were considered authoritative works on both sides of the Atlantic for many years. Lewis Leonard Gitin, "Cadwallader Colden," *New York History*, XVI (1935), 169–177. Hindle, *The Pursuit of Science in Revolutionary America*, pp. 50–58; Wyndham B. Blanton, *Medicine in Virginia in the Eighteenth Century* (Richmond: Garrett & Massie, 1931, *passim*; also see John C. Greene, "American Science Comes of Age, 1780–1820," *The Journal of American History*, LV (June 1968), 22–28.

colonial community of intellectuals. Together with such other leading American scientists as Franklin, James Logan, and John Bartram, they corresponded regularly among themselves, exchanging ideas, proposing new schemes, and offering their comments and criticisms of one another's work. The Scots were early identified in the colonies as a group. The editors of the *American Medical and Philosophical Register* later in the century, for example, expressed recognition that the contributions of these men were related. Referring to John Mitchell, the editors wrote that "with Chalmers and Lining of South Carolina and Alexander and Colden of New York he has done much for the advancement of medical and physical science on this side of the Atlantic." [6] Early impetus to organize colonial science and scientists also came from the Scots. According to Brook Hindle, it was Colden who, writing to William Douglass in 1728, first made the suggestion for a colonial scientific academy; and eight years later Douglass communicated to Colden news of the formation of a medical society in Boston.[7]

The naturalists, furthermore, were especially active in establishing close and early links with major European thinkers. It was with the encouragement of Peter Collinson, one of Franklin's favorite London correspondents, that Colden completed and published his treatise on the Indians. Both John Mitchell and Alexander Garden, as well as Colden, maintained a long-standing and intimate correspondence with Gronovius in Holland and Linnaeus in Upsala, sending them new specimens from America for investigation and classification.[8]

Second, the academic background of these Scottish physicians set them apart from most of their fellow American scientists. Whereas the majority of American scientists—like John Bartram and Benjamin Franklin—were exceptionally gifted, but basically amateurs, the Scots were university-trained, and, what is more, aware of the difference. For example, as Hindle points out, Colden and Garden were in agreement that John Bartram was doing pioneer work in natural history, but they also felt that Bartram was seriously hindered by a weak command of the systematic principles of botany.[9]

Finally, these physician-scientists consciously maintained their

---

[6] Quoted in Blanton, *Medicine in Virginia in the Eighteenth Century*, p. 139.
[7] Hindle, *The Pursuit of Science in Revolutionary America*, pp. 60–61.
[8] *Ibid.*, pp. 38–43; Blanton, *Medicine in Virginia in the Eighteenth Century*, pp. 137–141.
[9] Hindle, *The Pursuit of Science in Revolutionary America*, p. 26.

identity as Scotsmen. All were active members of the St. Andrew's Societies or other Scottish charitable organizations which existed in most of the larger cities. Adam Thomson was, in fact, a founding member of the St. Andrew's Societies in both New York and Philadelphia; William Douglass and Alexander Hamilton both wrote descriptions of the Societies in their cities, Boston and Annapolis respectively.[10] More important, however, than the patriotic and charitable sentiments involved in their promotion of the Scottish Societies was the strong sense displayed, especially by Garden, Colden, Lining, and Mitchell, of the intellectual debt they owed to their Scottish professors. All appear to have kept in close touch with their former professors at Edinburgh.[11]

The presence in the colonies of these outstanding Scottish physicians probably encouraged Americans to seek professional medical training in Scotland, as growing numbers did. The most immediate effect of American study at Edinburgh was, of course, the founding of the first American medical schools by Edinburgh graduates: at Philadelphia in 1765, at New York in 1767, and at Boston in 1782. The short-lived attempt of James McClurg (Edinburgh M.D., 1770), to establish a medical department at William and Mary, where he taught as Professor of Anatomy and Medicine from 1779 to 1783, should also be included in this list.[12]

The story of the founding of the first medical schools in America has been told often, and need not be repeated. It is sufficient here merely to underscore the importance of the Edinburgh institutional ideal as the pattern for the American schools. The plan for an American medical school began to take concrete shape in the circle of colonial students at Edinburgh.[13] John Morgan, who had been a mem-

[10] See Graham, *Colonists from Scotland*, pp. 131–133.

[11] John Lining, for example, published on botanical subjects in the *Edinburgh Essays* and the *Edinburgh Medical Journal* and exchanged letters with his former teachers at the university, Robert Whytt and Charles Alston. Bridenbaugh, *Cities in Revolt*, p. 200.

On the close relationship which Colden, Lining, Mitchell, and Garden maintained with Alston and Whytt, also see Hindle, *The Pursuit of Science in Revolutionary America*, pp. 26, 46–47, 51–52; Blanton, *Medicine in Virginia in the Eighteenth Century*, p. 127; J. Gordon Wilson, "The Influence of Edinburgh on American Medicine in the Eighteenth Century," *Institute of Medicine of Chicago*, VII (January 15, 1929), 135.

[12] Blanton, *Medicine in Virginia in the Eighteenth Century*, p. 330.

[13] As already noted, Morgan and Shippen, and the Virginians, Arthur Lee and Theodorick Bland Jr., along with other colonial students at Edinburgh, often discussed the need for an American medical school. Whitfield J. Bell, Jr., *John Morgan, Continental Doctor* (Philadelphia: University of Pennsylvania Press, 1965), pp. 72–73.

ber of this Edinburgh group, presented the idea of putting science and medicine on a firm institutional footing at the 1765 commencement services of the College of Philadelphia. The scheme for a medical faculty, which Morgan, with William Smith's help, succeeded in persuading the College of Philadelphia to adopt, was based upon the Scottish tradition of a school connected with an arts college, rather than the London form of a hospital-school.[14] The medical school at King's College, New York, also was modeled closely after the Edinburgh school, with even a stone hospital, "after the plan of the Royal Infirmary of Edinburgh," to provide clinical lectures.[15]

The impact of medical study in Edinburgh on American higher education extended far beyond the inspiration to found medical schools, however. For one thing, the study of medicine fostered the development of many of the specialized sciences such as chemistry, botany, paleontology, and geology. For another, medicine led the way in the early academic institutionalization of science.

These developments were interrelated, and were directly encouraged by the experience of American medical students at Edinburgh. In the first place, Americans there had every incentive to view medicine as a subject to be studied within the context of the total university curriculum. This incentive derived only in part from the traditional connection between the Edinburgh medical school and the university. It came also from the exposure of American students

---

Samuel Bard could hardly contain his disappointment at being too young to be included in the plans for the first school. "I own I feel a little jealous of the Philadelphians," Bard wrote to his father, "and should be glad to see the College of New York at least upon an equality with theirs." Carl Bridenbaugh, *Cities in Revolt*, p. 230. Bard lost no time and his medical school at King's College, New York, opened in 1767 with a six-member faculty, five of whom were also Edinburgh graduates.

14 John Morgan, *A Discourse Upon the Institution of Medical Schools in America* (Philadelphia: University of Pennsylvania Facsimile Reprint, 1965; first published 1765), pp. 29, 36. Also see Richard Shryock, *Medicine and Society in America, 1660–1860* (New York: New York University Press, 1960), p. 24. Edinburgh also appears to have supplied the model for the founding of the Pennsylvania Hospital a few years earlier. In 1760 Benjamin Franklin wrote to his friend, Sir Alexander Dick in Edinburgh: "I inclose you one of our Philadelphia Newspapers, supposing that it may give you and my good Lord Provost some Pleasure, to see that we have imitated the Edinburgh Institution in that remote Part of the world." *Writings of Benjamin Franklin*, edited by Albert Henry Smyth (10 vols.; New York: The Macmillan Company, 1902), IV, 1–2. The plan of examination for degree candidates at Philadelphia was also the same as that used at Edinburgh. The Edinburgh procedure is described in full by Samuel Bard in a letter to his father, May 15, 1765, reprinted in B. C. Corner, *William Shippen, Jr., Pioneer in American Medical Education* (Philadelphia: American Philosophical Society, 1951), p. 152.

15 Bridenbaugh, *Cities in Revolt*, p. 280.

to a range of intellectual stimulation beyond that of their medical studies through their contacts with other intellectuals in the university and city. Besides his work in medicine, John Morgan, for example, made a point of sitting in on the lectures on rhetoric and belles lettres delivered by Hugh Blair in the university. "Thou won't be satisfied," Morgan's friend Professor William Hewson chided him from London, "without being a Physiologist, Chemist, Physician, & Rhetorician. Mercy upon us, where will you end." [16] Future American academicians were making acquaintance with Scottish intellectual life at the very moment of its full bloom, and seeing it as an integrally related whole. In the second place, the Edinburgh requirement that students pass through the entire medical program also meant that future American professors of medicine would return home ready to offer instruction in a wide spectrum of scientific subjects. Finally, the achievements of their university professors impressed the Americans with the importance of the sciences' having strong institutional support.

In his 1765 *Discourse Upon the Institution of Medical Schools in America*, John Morgan wrote: "Private schemes for propagating knowledge are unstable in their nature, and the cultivation of useful learning can only be effectively promoted under those who are patrons of science, and under the authority and direction of men incorporated for the improvement of literature." Morgan also presented as one of the compelling reasons for the establishment of a medical school the advances it would bring in other fields of science, especially those connected with natural history.[17] Morgan himself insisted that medical students should be accepted only after they had received a thorough grounding in the general arts and sciences. Although the College of Philadelphia dropped Morgan's premedical requirements in 1787, and though many of his ideas about the professional standards of physicians were either never realized or severely compromised, Morgan had given expression to two trends that would continue. After the Revolution specialized scientific studies previously connected with medicine continued to develop on their own, and became increasingly implanted in academic institutions.

The outstanding work in natural history, theretofore mainly the province of American amateurs, was more and more carried out by professors of materia medica. Benjamin Waterhouse in Boston, Samuel

16 Quoted in Bell, *John Morgan*, p. 67.
17 Morgan, *Discourse*, pp. 29, 36, 52–54, 58–59.

Latham Mitchill in New York, Benjamin Smith Barton in Philadelphia, and Henry Muhlenberg at Franklin College dominated the field. Chemistry was also entering a new phase. Benjamin Rush, his pupil James Woodhouse, Samuel Latham Mitchill again, and John Maclean at Princeton were leading the way in America. All of these men were, incidentally, known to Rush, and all, with the exception of Muhlenberg and Woodhouse, had studied at Edinburgh.

The developments taking place in natural history are well illustrated by the career of Benjamin Smith Barton. Brook Hindle has contrasted the world of difference that separated the academic work of Barton from his predecessors, the gentlemen naturalists, John and William Bartram.[18] Barton graduated from the College of Philadelphia, going from there to two years of study at Edinburgh in 1786, followed by a year at Goettingen. The letter of introduction which Barton carried with him from Rush to William Cullen flatteringly informed Cullen of Barton's desire to graduate from Edinburgh "where (unfortunately for all the other universities in the world) degrees have a kind of exclusive preeminence." [19] Barton found Edinburgh congenial, and in his letters to his brother, Barton frequently spoke with admiration of Joseph Black. He distinguished himself by winning the coveted Harveian prize for his dissertation in materia medica. As a student he also published in Edinburgh Part One of his *Observations on Some Parts of Natural History*, and edited the Edinburgh version of Samuel Stanhope Smith's *Essay*.[20]

Returning from Europe in 1789, Barton was asked to teach botany and the first American course in natural history.[21] For twenty

18 Hindle, *The Pursuit of Science in Revolutionary America*, pp. 308–311.
19 Benjamin Rush, *Letters of Benjamin Rush*, edited by L. H. Butterfield (2 vols.; Princeton: Princeton University Press, 1951), I, 392.
20 An important article on Barton is Francis Pennell's "Benjamin Smith Barton as Naturalist," *Proceedings of the American Philosophical Society*, LXXXVI (1942), 108–122. Also see Edgar Fahs Smith, "Benjamin Smith Barton, 1766–1815," Lancaster County (Pa.) Historical Society, *Papers*, XXVIII (1924), 59–66.
21 The development of natural history itself into systematic and specialized fields of study is well illustrated by the work of Caspar Wistar in anatomy. Wistar, a graduate of the College of Philadelphia, received an M.D. from the University of Edinburgh in 1786. While a student at Edinburgh, Wistar was a favorite of Professors Charles Stewart and William Cullen. He served as President of the Royal Medical Society in Edinburgh for two successive years, and dedicated his Edinburgh M.D. thesis to Benjamin Franklin and William Cullen. Thacher, *American Medical Biography*, II, 207–208. Three years after his graduation from Edinburgh he succeeded Rush to the chair of chemistry in the newly reopened College of Philadelphia—Rush having been appointed Professor of the Theory and Practice of Medicine. In 1792 Wistar took over the chair of anatomy, surgery, and midwifery

years (1795–1815), Barton held the chair of materia medica, referring to himself as "Professor of Materia Medica, Natural History, and Botany." Barton was as instrumental as anyone in putting the study of natural history upon a systematic basis. He authored numerous works and in 1803 brought out the first American textbook in botany, his *Elements of Botany or Outlines of the Natural History of Vegetables*. In 1813, two years before his own death, he added to his teaching duties the professorship of the "practice of Physic," left vacant by the death of Benjamin Rush.[22]

In the field of chemistry the beginnings of a real community of scientists in the late eighteenth century were even more strikingly apparent than in natural history. The study of combustion and the use of the balance were bringing about a genuine revolution in the subject of chemistry. For Americans the 1794 arrival in Philadelphia of Joseph Priestley, famed for his attainments as divine, educator, and scientist, was a great event. An outstanding and imaginative chemist, Priestley was the leading spokesman in the defense of phlogiston against "Old Oxygen." That American chemistry was already acquiring the characteristics of a mature science is shown by the fact that there were a number of chemists who, despite their respect for Priestley, were ready to challenge his theories.

Most of those who led in arguing the theories of Lavoisier against

---

in the medical faculty of the University of Pennsylvania. As with Barton and so many of Rush's colleagues, Rush's initial friendship with Wistar dissolved in a quarrel in the 1793 yellow fever epidemic when Wistar failed to give public support to Rush's cures.

Wistar is perhaps best known as the author of the first American *System of Anatomy* (1811), but his pioneer work in the field later to be known as vertebrate paleontology was also significant. One of the earliest in America to become interested in the study of fossils was George Croghan, Scotch-Irish immigrant and one of the foremost Indian agents in America. Croghan collected specimens from the Big Bone Lick on the Ohio River in 1766, and sent them to Lord Shelburne, Franklin, and others in London. Croghan's specimens created a stir of excitement in scientific circles, and during the rest of the century the Big Bone Lick continued to attract the attention of others, including Caspar Wistar. The difference between the gifted amateur and the academic specialist is vivid in the contrast between Croghan and Wistar. According to George Gaylord Simpson, the papers written by Wistar, though only two in number, were the first technical studies of paleontology of professional quality to be done in America. Much of the credit for fossil study that has been given to Jefferson, Simpson says, should rightfully go to Wistar, as Jefferson himself urged. See G. G. Simpson, "The Beginnings of Vertebrate Paleontology in North America," *Proceedings of the American Philosophical Society*, LXXXVI (1942), pp. 13–188.

22 Despite Rush's original sponsorship of Barton, the two were seldom on friendly terms, mainly because Rush took offence at Barton's membership in the circle of professors surrounding William Shippen. See Rush, *Letters*, II, 225.

Priestley had been trained, like Rush, under Joseph Black in Scotland, and several were protégés of Rush himself. One of the first, according to Edgar Fahs Smith, to actually use the terminology of Lavoisier was Samuel Latham Mitchill. Mitchill was not a student of Rush but he had studied under Black at Edinburgh. Appointed to the chair of chemistry at Columbia in 1792, Mitchill came to dominate scientific circles in New York. A fascinating man, Mitchill is worth mentioning here, if for no other reason than to indicate another of the important academic and scientific ties with Scotland in the early years of the Republic.[23]

Benjamin Rush, of course, enjoyed a special place among American chemists as the first professor of the subject. Both Rush and Black were slow in coming round to a full acceptance of the French theories, but Rush must have been cognizant of them and sympathetic, since his own students quickly took up the new ideas of combustion, respiration, and oxidation.

James Woodhouse, Rush's student and his candidate for the chair of chemistry at Philadelphia, performed several important tasks for the future of the science. Woodhouse led in the founding of the Chemical Society of Philadelphia in 1792, and through his careful experiments and published papers helped to bring about the final defeat of the doctrine of phlogiston in America, all the while remaining on friendly terms with Priestley. Like Rush, Woodhouse was immensely interested in applied chemistry and laboratory methods of instruction. His laboratory achievements were such as to gain the admiration of many, including Thomas Cooper, then the professor of chemistry at Dickinson College. Woodhouse was also the teacher of both Robert Hare, one of the most imaginative American scientists in the early nineteenth century, and Benjamin Silliman of Yale.[24] As Morgan, Rush, and others had envisaged, medical education was, indeed, encouraging advances in other subjects.

Rush, it will be remembered, was also the first to alert Samuel Stanhope Smith to the qualifications of John Maclean and to advise

23 Edgar Fahs Smith, *Samuel Latham Mitchill—A Father in American Chemistry* (New York: Columbia University Press, 1922), p. 11. Also see Courtney Robert Hall, *A Scientist in the Early Republic: Samuel Latham Mitchill, 1764–1831* (New York: Columbia University Press, 1934), especially pp. 19, 47–48.
24 On Benjamin Rush, James Woodhouse, and their connections, see Edgar Fahs Smith, *Chemistry in Old Philadelphia* (Philadelphia: J. B. Lippincott Company, 1919). Also see Edgar Fahs Smith, *Chemistry in America* (New York: Appleton & Company, 1914).

Maclean to settle at Princeton. Maclean, shortly thereafter, joined the faculty at the College of New Jersey and immediately entered the lists against the doctrine of phlogiston.[25] The far-reaching implications of the spreading network of Scottish scientific influences during this period is vividly illustrated in the relationship between John Maclean and Benjamin Silliman. As Professor of Chemistry at Yale, editor of *The American Journal of Science and Arts*, and a founder of the Sheffield Scientific Institute, Benjamin Silliman was to exert immense influence on American science before the Civil War.

As a young man Silliman received his first real introduction to chemistry in correspondence and talks with John Maclean at Princeton. "Dr. Maclean," Silliman later wrote,

was a man of brilliant mind, with all the acumen of his native Scotland; and a sprinkling of wit gave variety to his conversation. I regard him as my earliest master of chemistry, and Princeton as my first starting-point in that pursuit; although I had not an opportunity to attend any lectures there.[26]

Silliman then studied under James Woodhouse at Philadelphia, and finally went to Edinburgh for two years. Later Silliman and Maclean collaborated in bringing out the first American edition of William Henry's *An Epitome of Chemistry*.[27]

Although natural philosophy and the scientific subjects associated with it were firmly established in the American college curriculum by 1740, the pursuit of science in America throughout the eighteenth century, and into the nineteenth, was also much dependent upon the work of amateurs. By 1802, however, all of the twenty-one full-time jobs in science in America were in academic institutions, including medical schools. There were only about sixteen colleges of any real importance in America at the time; yet the number of professional scientists was still relatively small.[28] It reflected the growing trend, nevertheless, away from the amateur pursuit of science toward its academic and professional development.

---

[25] See John Maclean, *A Memoir of John Maclean, M.D.* (Princeton: at the "Press" office, 1876), p. 18.
[26] From a letter quoted in John F. Fulton and Elizabeth H. Thompson, *Benjamin Silliman, 1779–1864* (New York: Henry Schuman, 1947), pp. 30–31.
[27] Maclean, *A Memoir of John Maclean, M.D.*, p. 53.
[28] See Theodore Hornberger, *Scientific Thought in the American Colleges, 1638–1800* (Austin: University of Texas Press, 1945), pp. 6–15; also George H. Daniels, *American Science in the Age of Jackson* (New York: Columbia University Press, 1968), pp. 34–35. The amateur status of much science in colonial America is admirably treated by Hindle, *The Pursuit of Science in Revolutionary America*.

It would take nearly another half century for a true scientific community to appear, but a skeletal framework was being raised in the late eighteenth century. In this early phase of development the Scottish university made direct and decisive contributions: First, the Scottish university provided important intellectual substance. Sometimes, as in the case of Cullen's theories, the results left much to be desired; in other instances, as with Black's chemistry and Hope's materia medica, the contributions were invaluable. Futhermore, the Scottish university furnished strong support and inspiration for the institutional ideal of the systematic pursuit of science in close connection with the liberal arts and with the colleges of the nation. And finally, it should be stressed again, the Scottish university offered confirmation and example to the Enlightenment and Republican faith in the college as an active agent of social progress and as more than a guardian of tradition.

II

Before the arrival of John Witherspoon both the Old Side and New Side Presbyterians had established important links with Scotland. Each, however, drew upon those Scottish traditions which, across the distance of the Atlantic, appeared most congenial to their own outlooks and interests. Edwards, Davies, and the Tennents corresponded with Evangelical, revival-minded Scottish ministers; Alison and his Old Side colleagues sought help from Hutcheson and other Moderate leaders in the Church of Scotland. From the beginning these transatlantic contacts helped to bring the new American colleges into an international intellectual community and to prevent them from being locked too tightly into the provincialism of their own religious and social antagonisms. William Smith and Francis Alison, for example, fought intensely over the religious control of the colonies and the College of Philadelphia; but they shared similar intellectual interests and backgrounds, and remained together on the faculty of a college that continued to grow under their leadership. The leaders of the College of New Jersey differed in outlook from both Smith and Alison on many points; but they too were members of a larger international community that opened to them still wider horizons in the person of John Witherspoon.

Witherspoon's blending of the Scottish Enlightenment with the viewpoints of both the Old Side and the New Side ushered in an entirely new situation. After Witherspoon, the full intellectual resources of the Scottish Enlightenment became increasingly available to Presbyterians of every stripe. The old theological distinctions no longer seemed to govern what was to be selected from Scottish thought. Witherspoon had helped to show that the very achievements of the Moderate literati could be put to the service of true religion. Americans soon seemed to forget that the culture-loving Scottish ministers had at one time been suspect to the devout.

At least three characteristics of Scottish thought, as it was introduced by Witherspoon, made this change possible. In the first place, the eclecticism of his own outlook was broad and flexible enough that it could be made to include a wide spectrum of viewpoints. Moreover, Scottish thought itself was broad and inclusive, and could be put to various uses. Both Old Side and New Side, for example, were able to tap aspects of Scottish thought that appeared to support or to follow logically from their own concerns and convictions. Finally, the Scottish Enlightenment never severed its roots in its religious past. The close alliance between the Church of Scotland and the representatives of culture also eventually gave to Scottish thought an added element of religious respectability. As religious issues in America shifted increasingly from conflicts among the faithful to a growing need to reconcile belief itself with modern science and philosophy, Scottish thought appeared all the more attractive.

Purportedly rational and scientific, yet rejecting skepticism and affirming the reality of the world and the evidences of a divine creator, Scottish common sense realism, for example, could commend itself to a wide range of theological views. By the beginning of the nineteenth century, as Sydney Ahlstrom has shown, the apologetic resources proffered by common sense philosophy had been recognized and taken up by American theologians and churchmen as varied as William Ellery Channing, Bishop William White of the Episcopal Church, and Timothy Dwight and Nathaniel Taylor of Yale, as well as by the Old School Calvinists of Princeton Theological Seminary and others.[29] Years before, however, John Witherspoon had demonstrated the potential in Scottish thought for effecting the needed reconciliation between religion and the modern spirit. The different

---

[29] See Sydney E. Ahlstrom, "The Scottish Philosophy and American Theology," *Church History*, XXIV (1955), 257–272. Even Thomas Jefferson, an admirer of the writings of Lord Kames, combined the Scottish realism of Dugald Stewart with the ideology of Destutt de Tracy in his own thought. See Adrienne Koch, *The Philosophy of Thomas Jefferson* (Gloucester, Mass.: Peter Smith, 1957), pp. 17, 49–53.

forms this reconciliation could take were illustrated by Samuel Stanhope Smith, who sought to reveal the transcendent dimensions of science, and by Benjamin Rush, who appealed to the testimony of the moral faculty and the sense of deity as scientific justification for his religious progressivism.

There was also no reason why Scottish natural science, and Scottish scientists, should not find favor among Americans of varying persuasions. Scottish science and psychology, for example, carried neither the stigma of atheism, frequently associated with the French materialists, nor even the stain of religious heterodoxy of such Englishmen as Joseph Priestley and David Hartley. This was especially important in the American colleges where churches were strongly represented, if not in complete control. At the same time the genuine abilities and accomplishments of Scottish scientists could satisfy any demands for scientific competence.

By way of illustration, both sides of Scottish science were exemplified in Walter Minto, Professor of Mathematics and Natural Philosophy at the College of New Jersey from 1787 to 1796. As a youth Minto attended the University of Edinburgh under Ferguson, Robertson, and Blair, and , after a period of theological studies, took up his lifelong career in mathematics. When he came to Princeton, he had already achieved an outstanding reputation in Scotland as a mathematician, was a recipient of an honorary degree of Doctor of Law from Aberdeen University, and was the co-author with the Earl of Buchan of a biography of John Napier, the inventor of logarithms. A friend of Franklin and Rush, Minto was elected to the American Philosophical Society in 1789. At the college commencement in September 1788, Minto delivered the inaugural oration, "On the Progress and Importance of the Mathematical Sciences." Minto's oration closed with a prayer for America addressed to the "Father of truth and reason and of everything that lives." Minto's successor at the college, John Maclean, was no less accomplished in his own field of chemistry, and was perhaps even more devout.[30]

American scientists in the nineteenth century almost unanimously took the position that science was a true handmaiden to theology. In doing so, they too relied upon Scottish realism. According to George H. Daniels, one explanation for the concern of nine-

[30] Maclean, *Memoirs of John Maclean,* pp. 56–57. Luther P. Eisenhart, "Walter Minto and the Earl of Buchan," *Proceedings of the American Philosophical Society,* XCIV (June 1950), 282–294.

teenth-century American scientists to affirm that their work complemented theology rather than competed with it was the need of a growing scientific community to avoid conflict with its chief rival profession, the Protestant clergy.[31] Whatever the merits of this sociological explanation, the scientists were using basic arguments already sketched in the eighteenth century by the theologians—the sublimity of science celebrated by Samuel Stanhope Smith being a case in point. The ultimate results, however, appear to have been beneficial neither to science nor to theology, and to have robbed both of a needed inner dynamic and self-direction.[32]

The socially and intellectually conservative uses to which Scottish common sense realism seems to have been put in the nineteenth century have encouraged similar interpretations of the introduction of the philosophy in the eighteenth century.[33] In this light the initial welcome accorded to common sense is then also seen as a reactionary attempt on the part of the orthodox to neutralize the corroding acids of science and critical philosophy. There is enough truth in this interpretation to make it especially tempting.

It is only part of the truth, however, and its anachronistic simplification produces unfortunate results, particularly for the historian of education. In the first place, the role played by Scottish realism in the early Princeton tradition seems to defy the neat application of the conservative-liberal categories. Witherspoon, Smith, and, for that matter, Rush were all in their ways certainly conservative enough, and their reliance upon Scottish thought had its full quota of reaction. At the same time, Witherspoon mediated many of the values dear to his Moderate opponents; Smith incurred charges of heresy and infidelity; and Rush produced a rather unorthodox combination out of the medical theories of Cullen, the Scottish faculty psychology, his political republicanism, and his New Side Calvinist background. By no stretch of the imagination did any of the three speak disparagingly or grudgingly of science and the scientific temper.

[31] See Daniels, *American Science in the Age of Jackson*, p. 51. Daniels points repeatedly to the important part played by Scottish realism in the outlook and method of many nineteenth-century American scientists.

[32] See the judgments of Ahlstrom and Daniels regarding the final effect of the Scottish philosophy upon theology and science respectively. Ahlstrom, "The Scottish Philosophy and American Theology," pp. 268–269; Daniels, *American Science in the Age of Jackson*, pp. 100–101.

[33] The classic statement is that of J. Woodbridge Riley, who described the movement of Scottish realism into the Middle and Southern states as "a kind of intellectual glacier" and its triumph as "the glacial age in American thought." J. Woodbridge Riley, *American Philosophy; The Early Schools* (New York: Dodd, Mead, & Company, 1907), p. 478.

Even when the conservative characteristics of each are duly acknowledged, the use of Scottish thought by Smith and Rush, especially, can be viewed as a somewhat adventuresome attempt—"bold" would perhaps be too strong a word—not merely to buttress religious faith, but also to move it into the mainstream of what were taken to be the most progressive currents of the age. Scottish philosophy in the eighteenth century had both liberal and conservative components. If the conservative did, indeed, later come to predominate, the earlier picture at any rate seems to have been much more complex.

Another, still more important problem is involved in appraising Scottish influences upon education in the eighteenth century, as distinct from the nineteenth century. In the latter period, it was apparently Scottish realism itself—the so-called Scottish school of Reid, Stewart, Hamilton, and Brown—that was of prime importance to Americans. Philosophical realism in the earlier period, however, was only one among several Scottish offerings that Americans found attractive.

Scottish social thought was at least as important to eighteenth-century Americans as Scottish epistemology. American educators who turned their attention after the Revolution to the problems of the new nation confronted the task of reconciling the need for social change and the need for stability. The new science, the new politics, even a new and changing population, held the promise of great progress; yet, at the same time, each posed a potential threat to social order. Just as Scottish philosophy had offered a means of reconciling religious concerns and secular learning, so, too, Scottish social thought presented a concept of progress that appeared to strike a balance between change and order, and between the needs of the individual and the needs of society.

In the first place, Scotsmen, such as Ferguson, tended to see progress in terms of the interaction between the individual and the larger community. The appeal of the alternative French emphasis, as represented by Condorcet, for example, upon the individual and his discoveries as the primary forces of progress was weakened and discredited in the eyes of many Americans by the events of the French Revolution.[34] In the second place, the Scottish view of the pliability of human nature within the limits of the social and natural environment made a special place for education, but accorded it both a pro-

[34] I have relied upon the discussion of Condorcet in Kingsley Martin, *The Rise of French Liberal Thought* (New York: New York University Press, 1954), pp. 289–292.

gressive and a conserving function. Finally, in addition to this broad—even vague—notion of education, which in itself could serve as a source of motivation and needed rhetoric, Scotland offered concrete examples and models: a system of feeder schools, progressive universities, learned professors, and modern pedagogy.

It is particularly interesting that Scottish social and educational theory was broad enough that Americans could make of it what they needed for their own situation. Furthermore, in the variety of Scottish educational practices, Americans of differing persuasions could find examples to meet their own liking and demands. So it was that the Federalist, liberal-conservative Samuel Stanhope Smith, and the Jeffersonian, conservative-liberal Benjamin Rush, could both draw upon Scottish thought and practice. Even concerning the point on which they differed most, the priorities in republican education, both could appeal to Scotland for support: Smith emphasizing the stabilizing classical tradition fundamental to Scottish philosophy; Rush promoting the utility of the modern languages made respectable by Scottish teachers.

The range of Scottish influences has been most apparent in this study in American attempts to build a modern college curriculum. Scottish educators in the eighteenth century were already seeking solutions to three of the most perplexing problems in modern higher education. The first problem was the rapid expansion of knowledge that was beginning to press upon institutions of higher education. In response to the mounting specialization in nearly every field of inquiry and the proliferation of new subject areas, the Scottish universities were among the first to abolish regenting and to introduce the specialized professorship. The Scottish emphasis upon system and method, no less present in moral philosophy than in medicine, also reflected the concern of Scotsmen to find some integrating and unifying framework or principles that would relate the different disciplines to each other.

The second problem had to do with the relevancy of knowledge and its application to the realities of life and society. Here, especially, Scotsmen appeared to have provided some clear answers. Their scientists had excelled in relating theory to Scottish social and economic needs, and their philosophers were engaged in analyzing human nature and society. The development of the common sense philosophy itself rested upon the pragmatic orientation of Scottish thought and the fear that Hume's philosophy would dissolve the grounds for practical action. Hume himself, of course, pursued his inquiry into the human mind out of a similar concern "to free learning" from "abstruse philosophy and metaphysical jargon"—and "such airy sciences." [35]

Scotsmen, finally, devoted much attention to the moral uses of knowledge. Learning should be promoted because of its morally beneficient effect alone, if for no other reason. "It is certain," Hume said, voicing a common conviction, "that a serious attention to the sciences and liberal arts, softens and humanizes the temper, and cherishes those fine emotions, in which true virtue and honour consists." [36] The significance of moral philosophy was precisely that it promised to uncover natural ethical laws that would enable men in all circumstances to decide how they ought to act and to what purposes they should apply their knowledge.

Indeed, one explanation, perhaps, for the importance attached to moral philosophy, both in Scotland and America, was that it touched squarely upon all three educational problems. Not only was moral philosophy by its nature concerned with the relevance and moral uses of knowledge, but, as developed by the Scotsmen, it seemed to solve the problem of integrating knowledge. Included within the compass of moral philosophy were the nascent social sciences of economics, political science, and psychology, which Scotsmen took an early lead in developing.[37] In applying to each of these subject areas the inductive, scientific method, Scottish moral philosophy suggested that an integrating principle of knowledge was at hand.

The inductive method of attempting to move from particular to general laws was extended from science and moral philosophy to the entire curriculum. Both in the teaching of individual subjects and in the structure of the overall course of study the desire to follow the

---

[35] David Hume, *Enquiries Concerning the Human Understanding and Concerning the Principles of Morals*, edited by L. A. Selby-Biggs (Oxford: The Clarendon Press, 1902), p. 12.

[36] Quoted in John Stewart, *The Moral and Political Philosophy of David Hume* (New York: Columbia University Press, 1963), p. 357, n. 31.

[37] Gladys Bryson calls moral philosophy, in relation to the subjects which emerged from its subdivisions, "the matrix discipline." See Gladys Bryson, *Man and Society: The Scottish Inquiry of the Eighteenth Century* (Princeton: Princeton University Press, 1945), pp. 239–245. Also see three articles by Gladys Bryson: "The Emergence of the Social Sciences from Moral Philosophy," *International Journal of Ethics*, XLII (April 1932), 304–323; "The Comparable Interests of the Old Moral Philosophy and the Modern Social Sciences," *Social Forces*, XI (October 1932), 19–27; and "Sociology Considered as Moral Philosophy," *Sociological Review*, XXIV (January 1932), 26–36.

inductive method provided an underlying unity in the development of the eighteenth-century Scottish university. The Aberdeen reforms, it will be recalled, deliberately tried to arrange the curriculum so that students would be introduced to concrete, factual studies in their early years, and ascend gradually to the more abstract and general philosophical courses in their last years. The same principle was applied in the organizing and teaching of individual subjects, such as logic and literature and rhetoric, as well as science and moral philosophy.

The attempt to apply a general scientific method to all courses has already been observed in the moral philosophy lectures of Alison, Witherspoon, and Smith, and in the use of the logic of William Duncan at the Colleges of New Jersey and Philadelphia, and elsewhere. Witherspoon's lectures on eloquence also seem to have been based upon the procedure of deriving systematic literary categories from the examination of specific authors, then using those categories as basic critical tools for further literary analysis. This method was highly developed, though in somewhat different ways, by Lord Kames in his *Elements of Criticism* (1762) and by Hugh Blair in his *Lectures on Rhetoric and Belles Lettres* (1783). Both Kames and Blair insisted that their critical method was one of ascending from observation and experience to general principles. After Witherspoon, the works of Kames and Blair were both used fairly extensively in the American colleges.[38] It is the judgment of Carl Albert Hangartner that the influence of the method of Kames and Blair, with all of its shortcomings, "appears to have been one of the factors which raised the study of English literature to the status of a separate area of study and teaching and prepared the way for the establishment of departments in the colleges in the nineteenth century." [39]

The introduction of modern courses into the curriculum, which has been observed at Princeton, Philadelphia, and Dickinson, was general in most American colleges by the end of the century.[40] Cur-

[38] At Yale Kames was in use as early as 1777 and Blair as early as 1785. See Carl Albert Hangartner, "Movements to Change American College Teaching, 1700–1830," (Ph.D. dissertation, Yale University, 1955), p. 193. Blair was in use at Harvard in 1788, at Columbia in 1792, at Princeton in 1800, and at Brown in 1803. See Louis F. Snow, *The College Curriculum in the United States* (New York: Printed for the author, 1907), pp. 83, 97, 116, 113.

[39] Hangartner, "Movements to Change American College Teaching, 1700–1830," p. 192. For an assessment of the importance of Scottish literary criticism in the early nineteenth century in America, see William Charvat, *The Origins of American Critical Thought 1810–1835* (Philadelphia: University of Pennsylvania Press, 1936).

[40] See Snow, *The College Curriculum in the United States*, pp. 82–140.

riculum expansion, however, was only a part of the story, for this expansion does not appear to have taken place haphazardly or by mere accretion. Eighteenth-century Scottish educators thought they possessed in the inductive scientific method a guiding principle both for teaching individual courses and for relating courses to one another in the curriculum as a whole. It is possible to see the eighteenth-century fascination with system in the Aberdeen-type of curriculum that was repeated with variations at Philadelphia and Princeton. The macrocosmic structure of the large curriculum was replicated in the microcosm of the teaching and organization of individual subjects. Although the ideal was seldom realized in full in the American colleges, partly because of limited resources and partly because the ideal itself was not without its own problems, a definite model, nevertheless, did exist.

Snow sees Harvard, Yale, Brown, and Columbia all following a curriculum pattern by 1825 similar to the one introduced at Philadelphia in 1756.[41] Although Snow's claims for the direct influence of the ideas of William Smith seem extravagant, the organizing principles were, nevertheless, essentially the ones first instituted at Aberdeen University. If by 1825, as is sometimes maintained, this curricular scheme had lost its innovative character and had hardened into a kind of inflexible educational orthodoxy,[42] the causes are probably to be sought as much in changing expectations for the colleges as in the inherent limitations of the system itself.[43]

It remains for someone to undertake a careful examination of the relationships among the early American colleges, and of their mutual influence upon one another.[44] One especially intriguing question, for example, concerns the possible influence of the Aberdeen model on Thomas Jefferson's 1779 curricular reform proposals for the College

41 *The College Curriculum in the United States*, pp. 96, 123. Also compare the Dartmouth curriculum; see Herbert D. Foster, "Webster and Choate in College: Dartmouth under the Curriculum of 1796–1819," in *The Collected Papers of Herbert D. Foster* (Privately printed, 1929), pp. 213–249.
42 This is the position assumed by Snow, for example. Snow, *The College Curriculum*, pp. 141 ff.
43 If these speculations are at all accurate, the similarity between the development of the college curriculum and the interpretation of the changing function of Scottish realism suggested above is obvious.
44 To cite one example of the kind of data needing analysis: Rhode Island College (founded 1764) reproduced Samuel Finley's Princeton curriculum under its first president, James Manning, who graduated from the College of New Jersey under Finley. Texts in use at Rhode Island in 1783 included Kames' *Elements of Criticism*, Hutcheson's *Moral Philosophy*, Duncan's *Logic*, and several Scottish mathematical works. Snow, *The College Curriculum*, pp. 108–109.

of William and Mary.[45] Although there appears to be no evidence linking the influence of William Smith to William and Mary, another close personal connection between Jefferson and Aberdeen has attracted the notice of historians.

In 1758, William Small, a graduate of Marischal College (1755), subscribed his oath as Professor of Natural Philosophy at William and Mary. For six years Small taught mathematics and natural philosophy at the college. At the end of this time, perhaps because he was disappointed about not being made president of the college, he returned to Great Britain, where he was associated with the Lunar Society of Birmingham, a prominent group of leading British educational and scientific figures. Upon his return to Great Britain Small carried out a commission to purchase scientific equipment for the college.[46]

Among the little extant information regarding Small's influence at William and Mary, the most important comes from Thomas Jefferson himself. Jefferson, Small's student from 1760 until 1762, included a well-known tribute to his Scottish teacher in his account of his college years:

It was my great good fortune, and what probably fixed the destinies of my life, that Dr. William Small of Scotland, was then Professor of Mathematics, a man profound in most of the useful branches of science, with a happy talent of communication, correct and gentlemanly manners, and an enlarged and liberal mind. He, most happily for me, became soon attached to me, and made me his daily companion when not engaged in the school; and from his conversation I got my first views of the expansion of science, and of the system of things in which we are placed. Fortunately, the philosophical chair became vacant soon after my arrival at college, and he was appointed to fill it *per interim:* and he was the first who ever gave, in that college, regular lectures in Ethics, Rhetoric, and Belles Lettres.[47]

[45] A chair of medicine was established at Marischal in 1700; wide-ranging reforms in natural philosophy were attempted in 1726, but were not successfully instituted until 1753; a chair of Oriental languages was established in 1741; and history, natural and civil, belles lettres, ethics, jurisprudence, and politics were also included in the 1753 curriculum. Jefferson's plan of 1779 contained all of these emphases in one form or another. For Jefferson, see Roy J. Honeywell, *The Educational Work of Thomas Jefferson* (Cambridge: Harvard University Press, 1931), pp. 110–111.

[46] See Herbert L. Ganter, "William Small, Jefferson's Beloved Teacher," *William and Mary Quarterly*, 3rd ser. (1947), 505–507; also "Portion of Physical Apparatus, Purchased by Dr. William Small in 1767," *William and Mary Quarterly*, XVI (1907–8), 166–168.

[47] Andrew A. Lipscomb, ed., *The Writings of Thomas Jefferson* (Washington, D.C.: The Thomas Jefferson Memorial Associates, 1903), I, 3. A few years earlier Jeffer-

The extent to which Jefferson may have obtained specific ideas for his 1779 curriculum from William Small remains a tantalizing question. Jefferson's proposals, however, were not unlike other American college programs that had similar links to the Scottish universities.

By the end of the eighteenth century, Americans were asserting their own cultural, as well as political, integrity. The many plans put forth in the years of the early Republic for national systems of education and for a federal university reflected American desires to keep abreast, and wherever possible, ahead of European cultural achievements. These educational schemes told much, to be sure, about American hopes, fears, and fantasies at the beginning of the nineteenth century. In higher education, however, the stillborn proposals for a federal university were much less significant than the changes that had actually been taking place at more fundamental levels: in the curriculum, in teaching, in the founding of new colleges, in American intellectual concerns and outlooks. Whatever indigenous qualities had come to characterize the eighteenth-century American, they had not developed in isolation from a genuine transatlantic community that extended from beyond the Susquehanna to the Thames—and, in education, to the Firth of Forth and above the River Tay.

---

son had written that Dr. Small was "to me as a father. To his enlightened and affectionate guidance of my studies while at college, I am indebted for everything. . . . He first introduced into both schools [of philosophy and mathematics] rational and elevated courses of study, and, from an extraordinary conjunction of eloquence and logic, was enabled to communicate them to the students with great effect" (*ibid.*, XIV, 231).

⟩⟩⟩ Bibliography ⟨⟨⟨

Several of the standard works on American higher education allude to the importance of Scottish influences in the colonial colleges, but do not provide enough information or analysis for a comprehensive appraisal. In his *History of Higher Education in America* (1900), published over fifty years ago, Charles F. Thwing detected two strains of British influence in the colonial college, one strictly English, represented by Harvard, and the other Scottish, represented by William and Mary. The value of Thwing's brief and general comments was limited, however, and lay chiefly in suggesting the need for further research on the subject. More recently, two other historians, John Brubacher and Willis Rudy in *Higher Education in Transition* (1958), have made even stronger claims for the importance of Scottish influences, asserting that in the American colonial colleges all major deviations from the English norm "were due mainly to Scottish influence." The granting of unauthorized degrees, as in the early years at Harvard; the incorporation of both a university and a degree-granting college by a single letters patent, as at William and Mary; the institution of lay control and the emergence of the strong college president; and the spread of science in the eighteenth-century college curriculum were all developments that were deeply influenced by Scottish practices, according to Brubacher and Rudy. Because their book was essentially a survey, Brubacher and Rudy did not explore some of the more problematic aspects of their assertions, but they did provide forceful evidence of the need for further study.

Similar brief references to a Scottish impact upon American higher education appear in Frederick Rudolph: *The American College and University* (1962). Evidence for Scottish influences upon seventeenth-century Harvard and William and Mary are discussed in Samuel Eliot Morison: *The Founding of Harvard University* (1935), and Richard Hofstadter and Walter P. Metzger: *The Development of Academic Freedom in the*

United States (1955). P. J. Anderson: "Aberdeen Influence on American Universities," *Aberdeen University Review*, V (1917–18), 27–31, is too vague to permit any definite conclusions. A. Bailey Cutts points to one possible source of Scottish influence in "The Educational Influence of Aberdeen in Seventeenth Century Virginia," *William and Mary Quarterly*, 2nd. ser., XV (July 1935), 229–249; but the difficulty of weighing the comparative importance of various transatlantic influences apart from more thorough studies can be seen by reading Cutts' article alongside Courtlandt Canby: "A Note on the Influence of Oxford upon William and Mary College in the Eighteenth Century," *William and Mary Quarterly*, 2nd ser., XXI (July 1941), 243–247. Carl Albert Hangartner provides an extremely useful analysis of changes in the curriculum and teaching methods of the colonial colleges, many of which he thinks were inspired by Scottish university practices, in "Movements to Change American College Teaching, 1700–1830" (Ph.D. dissertation, Yale University, 1955).

The only author who has addressed himself specifically to the question, "Whether, and to what extent, the five Scottish universities made their impact felt upon the early American colleges," is the Scottish historian George S. Pryde. In a short monograph entitled *The Scottish Universities and the Colleges of Colonial America* (1957), Pryde looks for evidence of important interrelationships between the Scottish universities and the nine colonial colleges. The areas surveyed by Pryde include: the founding of Harvard and William and Mary; the work of Scottish-born educators in America, particularly William Smith at the College of Philadelphia, James Blair at William and Mary, and John Witherspoon at Princeton; the founding of American medical schools; and miscellaneous other topics, such as Scottish influence upon French studies in America, college fund-raising in Scotland, academic dress, and lesser academic personalities. The very brevity of Pryde's work (55 pages), however, imposes severe limitations on the depth of his analysis. Problems of interpretation are also neglected because Pryde tends toward an over-institutional conception of his subject. It is important to know, for example, not only that moral philosophy was included in the college curriculum, but also what was actually taught in the moral philosophy lectures. It is interesting to discover that Scotsmen were read by American educators; it is still more intriguing to ask why they were read and what use was made of them. Pryde accords these kinds of questions scant attention. Pryde's is a pioneering exploration, nevertheless, and will remain the beginning point for subsequent studies of the subject.

To date there appears to be no comprehensive treatment of Scottish cultural influences in nineteenth-century America, although the existing works on individual topics indicate the need for such a study. Sydney Ahlstrom demonstrates the importance of Scottish philosophy for eighteenth- and nineteenth-century American theology, and provides extensive references, in "The Scottish Philosophy and American Theology," *Church History*, XXIV (1955), 257–272. The importance of Scottish intellectual influences in nineteenth-century American political economy, literary criticism, and historical and cultural attitudes respectively are discussed in Michael O'Connor: *Origins of Academic Economics in the United States* (1944); William Charvat: *The Origins of American Critical Thought, 1810–1835;* and Roy Harvey Pearce, *The Savages of America* (1953).

Chapter I: The Scottish Universities in the Enlightenment

One of the most useful general histories of Scottish education, in both its scope and its detail, is John Kerr: *Scottish Education: School and University from Early Times to 1908* (1910). H. M. Knox: *Two Hundred and Fifty Years of Scottish Education, 1696–1946* (1953), while a helpful survey, is of less value than Kerr. Particularly helpful because it treats the development of Scottish education at all levels in its social and cultural context is Alexander Morgan: *Rise and Progress of Scottish Education* (1927). Still the definitive study of Scottish municipal education is James Grant: *History of the Burgh Schools of Scotland* (1876).

Among the older histories of the Scottish universities which remain indispensable despite the appearance of more recent works are Robert S. Rait: *The University of Aberdeen: A History* (1895); James M. Anderson: *The University of St. Andrews: An Historical Sketch* (1878); James Coutts: *A History of the University of Glasgow from its Foundations in 1451 to 1909* (1909); and Alexander Grant: *The Story of the University of Edinburgh* (2 vols.; 1884). *Notes on the Evolution of the Arts Curriculum in the Universities of Aberdeen* (1908) contains useful, brief selections from the university records.

More recent works include histories of the Scottish universities and studies of special topics in Scottish higher education. G. D. Henderson: *The Founding of Marischal College Aberdeen* (1947) is an admirable treatment, not only of the origins of Marischal, but also of the educational, cultural, and religious forces that helped to shape the college. Isabel Kenrick has discussed the progressive educational forces at work in seventeenth- and early eighteenth-century Edinburgh University in "The University of Edinburgh, 1660–1715; A Study in the Transformation of Teaching Methods and Curriculum" (Ph.D. dissertation, Bryn Mawr College, 1956). R. G. Cant: *The University of St. Andrews* (1946) is brief, but especially useful for the eighteenth century. J. D. Mackie: *The University of Glasgow, 1451–1951* (1954), although covering a long time span, is strong on the earlier periods and contains much detailed information and analysis regarding faculty, curriculum, and university government in the eighteenth century. Alexander Morgan: *Scottish University Studies* (1933) is an especially useful examination of crucial developments in the constitution, curriculum, and faculties of the universities in both the medieval and modern periods.

Some of the important educational proposals of the Scottish reformers can be found in *The Scots Confession* and *The First Book of Discipline* in John Knox: *History of the Reformation*, edited by W. Croft Dickinson (1949). The reformers and their educational ideas are discussed in J. H. S. Burleigh: *A Church History of Scotland* (1960). Several dimensions of the relationship between religious and educational concerns in Scotland are illuminated in the outstanding study by G. D. Henderson: *Religious Life in Seventeenth Century Scotland* (1937). Henderson also provides a useful, brief discussion of parish schooling in *The Scottish Ruling Elder* (1935). D. J. Withrington: "The S.P.C.K. and Highland Schools in Mid-Eighteenth Century," *The Scottish Historical Review*, XLI (1962), 89–99, explores aspects of the effectiveness and strength of the church's continuing concern for elementary education into the eighteenth century. The essays by G. D. Henderson collected in *The Burning Bush, Studies in Scottish Church History* (1957) provide many insights into the relationships between learning and religion in seventeenth- and eighteenth-century Scotland.

The authoritative history of Scotland is still P. Hume Brown: *History of Scotland* (3 vols.; 1899). Brown discusses the eighteenth-century Scottish renaissance rather uncritically, but, as always, interestingly, in his article, "Scotland in the Eighteenth Century," *The Scottish Historical Review*, VI (1909), 343–356. George S. Pryde: *Scotland from 1603 to the Present Day* (1962) is useful as a general history, though the chapter "The Dawn of the Scottish Enlightenment" is little more than an introduction to main features of the Scottish Enlightenment. William Croft Dickinson: *A Source Book of Scottish History* (3 vols.; 1952–53) makes available many important documents.

William Law Mathieson, in *Scotland and the Union: A History of Scotland from 1695–1747* (1905) and in its sequel, *The Awakening of Scotland: A History from 1767–1797* (1910), presents invaluable accounts of the political, religious, and intellectual history of Scotland during the eighteenth century. Henry Grey Graham: *The Social Life of Scotland in the Eighteenth Century* (1899) is comprehensive and always interesting, although Graham tends to underestimate the degree of intellectual ferment in the late seventeenth and early eighteenth century, and his treatment of pre-Moderate Presbyterianism is almost altogether unsympathetic. H. W. Meikle: *Some Aspects of 17th Century Scotland* (1947) is a good corrective to Graham's version of the earlier period.

A brief discussion of eighteenth-century Scottish society appears in George S. Pryde: "Social Life in Scotland since 1707," *Historical Association Pamphlet*, No. 98 (1934). Laurence James Saunders: *Scottish Democracy, 1815–1840* (1950) is devoted to the nineteenth century, but contains valuable background information, particularly on education and politics.

Henry Hamilton: *An Economic History of Scotland in the Eighteenth Century* (1963) will remain the standard work on the subject for some time, and is a veritable source book of information on eighteenth-century Scottish agriculture, industry, communications, and commerce. A brief treatment of the Scottish economy during the period is Hamilton's earlier article, "The Economic Evolution of Scotland in the 18th and 19th Centuries," *Historical Association Leaflet*, No. 19 (1933). R. H. Campbell: *Scotland since 1707: The Rise of an Industrial Society* (1964) is more analytical and explanatory than Hamilton, and almost as comprehensive. Archibald Clow and Nan L. Clow, in *The Chemical Revolution* (1952), point out the crucial leadership of Scotland in the Industrial Revolution. Agnes Mure Mackenzie: *Scotland in Modern Times* (1921) also discusses the relationship between the economic and cultural awakening of eighteenth-century Scotland.

The Scottish literati and intelligentsia of the eighteenth century have been studied from various perspectives. Henry Grey Graham: *Scottish Men of Letters in the Eighteenth Century* (1901) is an entertaining treatment of the Scottish literati, anecdotal, but particularly valuable in depicting the many personal relationships that bound the Scottish intellectuals together. Gladys Bryson: *Man and Society: The Scottish Inquiry of the Eighteenth Century* (1945) is an extremely illuminating examination of the social thought of the major Scottish philosophers. Bryson also includes in her work a bibliography of the major works of the Scottish thinkers. The older, commendatory discussion of the philosophical work of a host of Scottish writers is James McCosh: *The Scottish Philosophy* (1875), which is especially valuable for its treatment of early eighteenth-century university professors.

Several biographies of individual Scottish thinkers have appeared in recent years that treat the development of their thought in its social and cultural context. Among these are: John B. Stewart: *The Moral and Political Philosophy of David Hume* (1963); David Kettler, *The Social and Political Thought of Adam Ferguson* (1965); William C. Lehmann: *John Millar of Glasgow, 1735–1801* (1960); and C. R. Fay: *Adam Smith and the Scotland of His Day* (1956). John Hermann Randall, Jr.: *The Career of Philosophy* (2 vols.; 1962, 1965) contains perceptive treatments of Scottish philosophy, and points out some of the many relationships between Scottish and Continental intellectuals. Harold Thompson:

A Scottish Man of Feeling (1931) portrays Edinburgh literary society in the late eighteenth and early nineteenth centuries, and contains some information on the university. Extracts from Carlo Deanina's "Essay on the Progress of Learning among the Scots" are reprinted with comments in Henry Meikle: "The Learning of the Scots in the Eighteenth Century," *The Scottish Historical Review*, VII (1910), 289–293. The unresolved tension in eighteenth-century Scotland between English and indigenous Scottish culture is suggestively explored in David Daiches: *The Paradox of Scottish Culture: The Eighteenth Century Experience* (1964).

Important information, especially with respect to the role of the Moderate clergy in Scottish intellectual life, is contained in the older "Biographical Memoirs of Adam Smith, William Robertson, and Thomas Reid," by Dugald Stewart. These have been reprinted from the *Collected Works of Dugald Stewart*, edited by Sir William Hamilton (1858), in Dugald Stewart: *Biographical Memoir of Adam Smith* (1966). The development of Moderatism is discussed in detail in the two works mentioned above by William Mathieson. Although he is concerned mainly with the Moderate clergy, William Nelson Hawley draws together much information in a master's thesis, "The Intellectual Development of the Scottish Clergy in the Eighteenth Century" (University of Chicago Divinity School, 1937). The theological issues in the struggle between the Moderate and Evangelical parties in the Church of Scotland are analyzed in John Macleod: *Scottish Theology in Relation to Church History since the Reformation* (1943) and Henry F. Henderson: *The Religious Controversies of Scotland* (1905). The *Autobiography* of Alexander Carlyle (1861), a leading Moderate minister, is indispensable for the light it sheds upon the church, the universities, and Scottish social life. H. M. B. Reid: *The Divinity Professors in the University of Glasgow, 1640–1903* (1923) is a series of biographies containing much valuable information on the life of the church, the teaching of theology in the university, and the major theological controversies of the period. Most of Reid's work is devoted to the seventeenth and eighteenth centuries.

Information on the progressive curriculum and pedagogy of the Scottish universities can be gleaned from a number of sources, in addition to the histories and explicit studies of Scottish higher education and biographies of individuals. In her article, " 'When It Is That Colonies May Turn Independent': An Analysis of the Environment and Politics of Francis Hutcheson (1694–1746)," *William and Mary Quarterly*, 3rd ser., XI (April 1954), 214–251, Caroline Robbins cites the names of several Scottish professors who led in classroom and curricular reform, as does McCosh in *The Scottish Philosophy*. The literature on the development of the Scottish medical schools and of academic science is voluminous.

Some of the more recent writings include: J. D. Comrie: *History of Scottish Medicine* (2 vols.; 1932); Douglas Guthrie, "The Rise and Progress of Medical Education in Scotland," *Bulletin of the New York Academy of Medicine*, XXV (1949), 521–527; Douglas Guthrie: *A History of Medicine* (1945); H. P. Tait: "Medical Education at the Scottish Universities to the Close of the Eighteenth Century," in *The Evolution of Medical Education in Britain*, edited by F. N. L. Poynter (1966), pp. 53–68. Special topics in Scottish medical education during the period are treated in Douglas Guthrie: "The Influence of the Leyden School upon Scottish Medicine," *Medical History*, III (April 1959), 108–122; Douglas Guthrie: "The Three Alexander Munros and the Foundation of the Edinburgh Medical School," *Journal of the Royal College of Surgeons of Edinburgh*, II (September 1956), 24–34; G. A. G. Mitchell: "The Medical History of Aberdeen and its Universities," *Aberdeen University Review*, XXXVII (1958), 225–238; and Douglas Guthrie: *Extramural Medical Education in Edinburgh* (1965).

There is no comprehensive treatment of Scottish and American cultural relationships in the eighteenth century. Some of the early literature is seriously limited by chauvinism and lack of discrimination, although with careful sifting it can be made to yield helpful information. Such works include: Peter Ross: *The Scot in America* (1896); Donald MacDougall: *Scots and Scots' Descendents in America* (1917); George Fraser Black: *Scotland's Mark on America* (1921); and Whitlaw Reid: *The Scot in America and the Ulster Scot* (1911). Works of this type and other major types of literature dealing with Scottish-American relationships are assayed, and areas needing further research are pointed out, in George Shepperson: "Writings in Scottish-American History: A Brief Survey," *William and Mary Quarterly*, 3rd ser., XI (April 1954), 163–178.

The entire issue of the *William and Mary Quarterly* containing Shepperson's article is devoted to an examination of the cultural, political, and commercial links between eighteenth-century Scotland and America. John Clive and Bernard Bailyn, in "England's Cultural Provinces: Scotland and America" (pp. 200–213), point out the similarities in the status of Scotland and America in relation to England, but they do not explore the existence of special relationships between Scotland and America. Political and commercial influences of Scotland upon America are examined by Caroline Robbins: " 'When It Is That Colonies May Turn Independent': An Analysis of the Environment and Politics of Francis Hutcheson" (pp. 214–251); by Dalphy I. Fagerstrom: "Scottish Opinion and the American Revolution" (pp. 252–275); and by Jacob M. Price: "The Rise of Glasgow in the Chesapeake Tobacco Trade, 1707–1775" (pp. 179–199).

Several diverse works indicate the variety of Scottish cultural and intellectual relationships with America. J. Bennett Nolan: *Benjamin Franklin in Scotland and Ireland* (1938) documents one influential American's friendships with Scottish intellectuals. The names and activities of many Scottish immigrants in colonial America may be discovered in Carl Bridenbaugh: *Cities in Revolt* (1959). Certain aspects of early American medical study in Scotland are treated in Whitfield J. Bell, Jr.: "Some American Students of 'That Shining Oracle of Physic,' Dr. William Cullen of Edinburgh, 1755–1766," *Proceedings of the American Philosophical Society*, XCIV (June 1950), 275–281, and J. Gordon Wilson: "The Influence of Edinburgh on American Medicine in the Eighteenth Century," *Institute of Medicine of Chicago*, VII (January 1929), 129–138. Finally, J. A. V. Butler: *Early Scientific Links Between Scotland and America* (offprint from eighteenth-century Lectureship in Chemistry, n.d.) briefly discusses the advances of Scottish science and its influence upon America.

Chapter II: The Presbyterian Academy

Works dealing with the various immigrant groups from Scotland and Ulster are discussed in George Shepperson: "Writings in Scottish-American History: A Brief Survey," *William and Mary Quarterly*, 3rd ser., XI (April 1954), 163–178. Although many of the older treatments are uncritical and often confused, H. J. Ford: *The Scotch-Irish in America* (1915) is a valuable exception. Charles A. Hanna: *The Scotch-Irish, or the Scot in North Britain, North Ireland, and North America* (2 vols.; 1902) is useful at times as a collection of source materials. Recent scholarship has distinguished between the Highland and Island Scots, the Lowland Scots, and the Scotch-Irish, and has focused upon each group separately. An excellent study by Ian Cargill Graham, *Colonists from Scotland* (1956), examines the reasons for eighteenth-century emigration from Scotland itself, the settlement and occupation patterns of the immigrants in the colonies, and the available estimates of the numbers of immigrants. James G. Leyburn: *The Scotch-Irish* (1962), while not as probing as Graham's study and of limited value on the Ulster background of the immigrants, presents, nevertheless, a comprehensive picture of the Scotch-Irish in America. R. J. Dickson: *Ulster Emigration to Colonial America, 1718–1775* (1966) complements Leyburn's work with its concentration upon conditions in Ulster and its careful analysis of the records of ships leaving Irish ports in the eighteenth century; but Dickson, in turn, virtually ignores the American side of the Atlantic and the pull factors of Ulster emigration. Leyburn on immigration and Dickson on emigration need to be read together. Two works dealing with specific areas and distinct immigrant groups are Duane Meyer: *The Highland*

Scots of North Carolina, 1732–1776 (1961), and Wayland F. Dunaway: *The Scotch-Irish of Colonial Pennsylvania* (1944). The conclusions of Dunaway's somewhat earlier study have in the main been confirmed in the later works.

J. S. Reid: *History of the Presbyterian Church in Ireland* (3 vols.; 1867), though old and with its own distinct bias, is detailed and comprehensive. Particularly useful for locating many of the Ulster Presbyterian academies is Thomas Witherow: *Historical and Literary Memorials of Presbyterianism in Ireland, 1623–1731* (1879). A penetrating modern study that sheds light upon the role of education in the Irish Presbyterian church is J. C. Beckett: *Protestant Dissent in Ireland, 1687–1780* (1948). W. R. Scott: *Francis Hutcheson* (1900) describes Francis Hutcheson's academy at Dublin and that of Hutcheson's teacher, the Reverend McAlpin, at Killyleagh. The works on Scotch-Irish immigration also contain much useful information on the Presbyterian Church in Ireland.

Leonard J. Trinterud: *The Forming of an American Tradition: A Reexamination of Colonial Presbyterianism* (1949) is carefully researched and always informative—even provocative—in its interpretations of theological and ecclesiological issues in early American Presbyterianism. Guy S. Klett: *Presbyterians in Colonial Pennsylvania* (1937) is a history of one area of special Presbyterian strength in colonial America. Chapters in Gaius J. Slosser, ed.: *They Seek a Country: The American Presbyterians* (1955) provide helpful general information on the colonial period. Ernest Thompson: *Presbyterians in the South, 1607–1861* (1963) is a comprehensive history of the Presbyterian church in one section of the country, and is especially useful in identifying many academy founders and teachers by name and location. Elwyn Allen Smith examines the intellectual and theological outlooks of the colonial church in the first seven chapters of *The Presbyterian Ministry in American Culture: A Study in Changing Concepts, 1700–1900* (1962). Still useful, and containing references to Presbyterian education, are the older Charles A. Briggs: *American Presbyterianism* (1885) and E. H. Gillett: *History of the Presbyterian Church in the United States*, I (1864). Richard Webster: *A History of the Presbyterian Church in America* (1857) contains brief biographies of scores of early Presbyterian ministers. Valuable selections from primary documents are printed in Maurice W. Armstrong, Lefferts A. Loetscher, and Charles A. Anderson, eds.: *The Presbyterian Enterprise: Sources of American Presbyterian History* (1956).

The biographies of individual Presbyterian ministers in volumes three and four of William B. Sprague's *Annals of the American Pulpit* (1858) contain a wealth of primary material not otherwise available. W. H. Foote's two volume *Sketches of Virginia* (1850 and 1855) and his *Sketches of North Carolina* (1846) are filled with detail and charming to read, and also present primary material in quotations from letters, journals, and church documents.

Three works are particularly valuable for an understanding of Presbyterianism in the total context of colonial American religious and cultural history. William Warren Sweet: *Religion in Colonial America* (1951) presents a broad sweep of the religious history of the period, but with much illuminating detail. Sidney Mead: *The Lively Experiment* (1963) contains probing analyses of the relationship between the central religious, cultural, and intellectual issues of colonial and early nineteenth-century America. An integrated picture of American religious history from 1630 to 1820 emerges from the combination of primary documents with introductory and interpretive commentary in H. Shelton Smith, Robert T. Handy, and Lefferts A. Loetscher: *American Christianity: An Interpretation with Representative Documents*, I (1960).

After more than two centuries, interpretations of the Great Awakening still excite controversy. Although the Awakening was an inter-colonial phenomenon, most of the standard works deal with specific sections of the country. Charles Hartshorne Maxson: *The Great Awakening in the Middle Colonies* (1920) discusses the course of the revivals in that section of the country, and devotes some attention to their effect on educational institutions. Still a useful treatment of the revivals in New England, with material on the reactions of the Harvard and Yale faculties, is Joseph Tracy: *The Great Awakening: History of the Revival of Religion in the Time of Edwards and Whitefield* (1842). A new examination of the same area by Edwin Scott Gaustad in *The Great Awakening in New England* (1957) attempts a classification of the major parties involved that is helpful for an understanding of revivalist and anti-revivalist attitudes toward learning. Wesley M. Gewehr: *The Great Awakening in Virginia, 1740–1790* (1930) treats the Awakening in Virginia as having developed in three distinct phases—Presbyterian, Baptist, and Methodist —suggesting that all revivalists of the eighteenth century are not to be grouped together indiscriminately. C. C. Goen: *Revivalism and Separatism in New England, 1740–1800* (1962) also suggests that even the attitudes toward learning of the radical Separatists were more complex than is sometimes supposed. L. J. Trinterud: *The Forming of an American Tradition* explores many of the theological, educational, and social attitudes of New Side Presbyterianism, and sees them as having had a decisive impact on the development of the early church. Alan Heimert: *Religion and the American Mind* (1966), a major revisionist effort stressing the formative influence of revivalist Calvinism on American social and political attitudes in the late eighteenth century, demands reconsideration of revivalist and anti-revivalist commitments to education.

Information on individual New Side leaders appears in several published primary materials and some excellent secondary studies. Important sermons and writings of various leading figures in the revival controversies are reprinted in Alan Heimert, ed.: *The Great Awakening* (1967), and Heimert's "Introduction" to this anthology provides further reassessment of the revivals. Perry Miller: "The Rhetoric of Sensation," *Errand into the Wilderness* (1956) is an imaginative analysis of Edwards' preaching. In his doctoral dissertation, "Conversion and Revivalism" (University of Chicago, 1962), John Opie, Jr., studies major revivalists from the Great Awakening into the early nineteenth century, providing new insights into the complexity of the thought of the Awakening leaders. Important sermons by the Tennents, Robert Smith, Samuel Finley, and others are collected in Samuel Davies Alexander: *Sermons and Essays by the Tennents and their Contemporaries* (1855). An illuminating study of Samuel Davies is George William Pilcher: "Preacher of the New Light, Samuel Davies, 1724–1761" (unpublished Ph.D. dissertation, University of Illinois, 1963). Davies' *Journal* is reprinted in W. H. Foote: *Sketches of Virginia*, I (1850). Valuable insights into Davies' educational concerns are provided in his own published sermon, *Religion and Public Spirit, A Valedictory Address to the Senior Class, Delivered in Nassau Hall* (1761). Davies' impressive classical scholarship is discussed in Richard Gummere: "Samuel Davies: Classical Champion of Religious Freedom," *Journal of Presbyterian History*, XL (1962), 67–74. Edwards' sermons and treatises are collected in various editions of his works. Selections from Jonathan Edwards' major writings and an extensive bibliography of his works, together with an interpretive introduction, are in Clarence Faust and Thomas Johnson, eds.: *Jonathan Edwards, Selections* (1935). Jonathan Edwards: *Religious Affections*, edited by John Smith (1959), is his mature work on conversion. The *American Bibliography* of Charles Evans provides a listing of many of the published works of the revivalists and an index to the microtext of the American Antiquarian Society.

The founders and alumni of the principle New Side academies are usually mentioned in most histories of the Presbyterian church. The only attempt, however, to present a comprehensive picture of the academy movement appears in the early article of Henry D. Funk: "The Influence of the Presbyterian Church in Early American History," *Journal of the Presbyterian Historical Society*, XII (1924–27), 152–189. Funk's list of Presbyterian academies (pp. 184–185) provided the inspiration and the core for my own list, which I have compiled from various sources (see Appendix). Nelson R. Burr: *Education in New Jersey, 1630–1871* (1942) recognizes the importance of the Presbyterian academy movement in New Jersey, and identifies several of the lesser-known academies of that state.

Because of its role in the Awakening and the leadership of its graduates in the missionary and educational work of the church, the Log College of William Tennent, Sr., has received the most attention from church historians. Many primary materials from a variety of sources are collected in Thomas C. Pears, Jr., and Guy Klett, compilers: *A Documentary History of William Tennent and the Log College* (1940). Archibald Alexander: *Biographical Sketches of the Founder and Principal Alumni of the Log College* (1840) has provided the basis for many later accounts, and is valuable for its presentation of much contemporary material. Two articles of limited usefulness bearing upon the relation between the Log College and Princeton are George H. Ingram: "The Story of the Log College," *Journal of the Presbyterian Historical Society*, XII (1924–27), 487–511, and E. R. Craven: "The Log College of Neshaminy and Princeton University," *Journal of the Presbyterian Historical Society*, I (1901–02), 308–314. Also see George H. Ingram: "Biographies of the Alumni of the Log College," *Journal of the Presbyterian Historical Society*, XIV (March 1930), 1–27, for brief, but relatively detailed, biographies of the Log College alumni. A brief biography of Samuel Blair, founder of Fagg's Manor Academy, is J. D. Edmiston Turner: "Reverend Samuel Blair, 1712–1751," *Journal of the Presbyterian Historical Society*, XXIX (1951), 227–236.

There are several sources that make it possible to reconstruct a picture of the curriculum, teaching methods, and student life in other academies besides the Log College. Franklin B. Dwight describes the academies of Jonathan Dickinson and Aaron Burr in "The Early History of the Educational Institutions of New Jersey, The Newark Academy," *Proceedings of the New Jersey Historical Society*, III (1898–1900), IV (1901–1905). Frederick Beasley describes his student days at the Pequea Academy of Robert Smith in his "Preface" to Samuel Stanhope Smith, *Sermons* (2 vols.; 1821). A more recent study which draws upon and adds to Beasley's account is Jacob Newton Beam: "Dr. Robert Smith's Academy at Pequea, Pennsylvania," *Journal of the Presbyterian Historical Society*, VIII (December 1915), 145–161. Benjamin Rush's description of his years at the Nottingham Academy of his uncle, Samuel Finley, is in *The Autobiography of Benjamin Rush*, edited by George W. Corner (1948), pp. 28–35. The Old Side academy at Newark, Delaware, is the subject of George H. Ryden: "The Relation of the Newark Academy of Delaware to the Presbyterian Church and to Higher Education in the American Colonies," *Delaware Notes*, 9th ser. (1935), 7–42. E. W. Caruthers: *A Sketch of the Life and Character of the Reverend David Caldwell, D.D.* (1842) devotes some pages to Caldwell's important academy in North Carolina. James D. Moffat: *Pioneer Educators in Washington County, Pa.* (1896) looks at the early Presbyterian academies that preceded Jefferson College, as does James I. Brownson: "The Educational History of Presbyterianism in Western Pennsylvania and

Adjacent Regions," *Centenary Memorial of the Planting and Growth of Presbyterianism in Western Pa. and Parts Adjacent* (n.d.). The academy of Joseph McMillan, which was chartered as Jefferson College in 1802, is discussed in Dwight R. Guthrie: *John McMillan, The Apostle of Presbyterianism in the West* (1952). John Opie, Jr.: "James McGready: Theologian of Frontier Revivalism," *Church History*, XXXIV (December 1965), 445–456, is a study of one of McMillan's most important students. The long tradition of obtaining strictly theological training in the homes of ministers, as distinct from the broader instruction of the academies, is studied in detail in Mary L. Gambrell: *Ministerial Training in Eighteenth Century New England* (1937), and in William O. Shewmaker: "The Training of the Protestant Ministry in the United States of America, before the Establishment of Theological Seminaries," *Papers of the American Society of Church History*, 2nd ser., VI (1921), 71–197.

A fund of information—in many ways unsurpassed—and the basis for all subsequent histories of Princeton University is John Maclean: *History of the College of New Jersey* (2 vols.; 1877). Thomas Jefferson Wertenbaker: *Princeton, 1746–1896* (1946) is the now standard history of the university. Francis L. Broderick: "Pulpit, Physics, and Politics: The Curriculum of the College of New Jersey, 1746–1794," *William and Mary Quarterly*, 3rd ser., VI (1949), 42–60, is a careful study of the early development of the Princeton curriculum with reference to its social and political setting. Louis Franklin Snow: *The College Curriculum in the United States* (1907) makes it possible to compare the curriculum of the College of New Jersey with that of other American colleges in the eighteenth century. Extremely helpful in locating many of the important Presbyterian academies and in examining their relationship to the College of New Jersey is Donald Robert Come: "The Influence of Princeton in Higher Education in the South Before 1825," *William and Mary Quarterly*, 3rd ser., II (1945), 359–396. A general study is needed of the contributions of Presbyterian academy alumni to American intellectual and cultural life in the Revolutionary period, since many academy graduates were outstanding in the writing of history, in politics and law, and in medicine and science, as well as in theology.

The influence of the English dissenting academies on American higher education in the eighteenth century has not been studied in any depth. Samuel Eliot Morison: *Harvard College in the Seventeenth Century* (2 vols.; 1936) describes the important work of Charles Morton, the founder of Newington Green Academy near London, as Vice-President of Harvard in the last decade of the seventeenth century. In examining the early relationships between the College of New Jersey, the English dissenting academies, and the Scottish universities, I have found three studies of the dissenting academies indispensable. Irene

Parker: *Dissenting Academies in England* (1914) is a pioneering work that treats three types of academies as they developed in three chronological phases. Of much more value because they analyze in detail the curricula, teaching methods, and lives of individual tutors in over seventy English dissenting academies are H. McLachlan: *English Education under the Test Acts* (1931) and J. W. Ashley Smith: *The Birth of Modern Education* (1954). McLachlan and Smith complement each other in that McLachlan organizes his work according to those academies which were primarily for ministerial training and those which were broader in purpose, and Smith organizes his study on the basis of the tutors' educational backgrounds and the sources of their educational ideas. Olive Griffiths: *Religion and Learning* (1935) is a thorough and highly illuminating analysis of the relationship between theology and attitudes toward learning among English and Scottish Presbyterians. A similar study of American education in the colonial period is badly needed.

Two articles on Jonathan Edwards which document his relationships with Scottish churchmen are G. D. Henderson: "Jonathan Edwards and Scotland," *The Burning Bush* (1957), pp. 151–162, and Ralph G. Turnbull: "Jonathan Edwards and Great Britain," *The Evangelical Quarterly*, XXX (1958), 68–74.

Chapter III: Francis Alison

Primary sources on Francis Alison, while sparse and somewhat scattered, do exist. A group of valuable letters from Alison to Ezra Stiles is reprinted in *Extracts from the Itineraries . . . of Ezra Stiles, 1755–1794,* edited by Franklin B. Dexter (1916); and frequent references to Alison appear in *The Literary Diary of Ezra Stiles,* edited by Franklin B. Dexter (3 vols.; 1901). Some manuscript materials are also available. The library of the Presbyterian Historical Society in Philadelphia has a small collection of Alison papers, the most important of which are a number of sermons in Alison's own hand. Notes taken in Alison's course in moral philosophy and metaphysics at the College of Philadelphia by his students Jasper Yeates and Samuel Jones are in the library of the University of Pennsylvania. Alison's only published sermon is his *Peace and Union Recommended, A Sermon Preached before the Reverend Synod of Philadelphia and the Reverend Commission of the Synod of New York at Philadelphia, May 24, 1758.*

There is no biography of Alison. Two articles written by Thomas C. Pears, Jr. shortly before his death, in preparation for a biography, remain the best treatments of Alison's career. Thomas C. Pears, Jr.: "Francis Alison, Colonial Educator," *Delaware Notes,* 17th ser. (1944), 9–22, and "Francis Alison," *Journal of the Presbyterian Historical Society,* XXVIII

(1950), 213–225, reconstruct Alison's life from a number of scattered sources and are particularly valuable for the primary materials they assemble in quotations from letters, newspaper articles, and church records. Many of the details of Alison's work at the Newark Academy and the College of Philadelphia are presented in George H. Ryden: "The Relation of the Newark Academy of Delaware to the Presbyterian Church and to Higher Education in the American Colonies," *Delaware Notes*, 9th ser. (1935), 7–42. Thomas C. Montgomery: *A History of the University of Pennsylvania, 1740–1770* (1900) also reprints many source materials on Alison, although Montgomery's own account of the university must be read with some caution. L. J. Trinterud: *The Forming of an American Tradition* (1949) interprets Alison's work as the leader of the Old Side Presbyterians.

Insights into Alison's educational background in Scotland can be drawn from various descriptions of his Scottish university professors. Appraisals of Professor John Stevenson at the University of Edinburgh by a number of important Scottish intellectuals may be found in John Veitch: "Memoir of Dugald Stewart," in Dugald Stewart, *Biographical Memoir of Adam Smith*, edited by William Hamilton (1966; first published 1858); in Alexander Carlyle: *Autobiography* (1861); and in James McCosh "John Stevenson, 1694–1775," *The Scottish Philosophy* (1875), p. 109. Francis Hutcheson's teaching at the University of Glasgow is described in William Robert Scott: *Francis Hutcheson* (1900). Descriptions of the work of Alison's students and insights into his own educational influence are found in David Hosack: "Biographical Memoirs of Hugh Williamson," *Collections of the New York Historical Society for the Year 1821*, III (1821), 125–180; in the article on John Ewing by Samuel Miller, in William B. Sprague: *Annals of the American Pulpit*, III (1858), 216–219; and in James Edwin Hendricks: "Charles Thomson and the American Enlightenment" (Ph.D. dissertation, University of Virginia, 1961).

Carl Bridenbaugh and Jessica Bridenbaugh: *Rebels and Gentlemen* (1942) contains important information on Alison, and is especially useful in depicting his influence on the creation of the Philadelphia Academy. Albert Frank Gegenheimer: *William Smith, Educator and Churchman, 1727–1803* (1943) is the best biography of William Smith. Gegenheimer discusses Smith's *College of Mirania*, his background at Aberdeen University, and his curriculum at the College of Philadelphia. The full curriculum at the College of Philadelphia is reprinted in Thomas Montgomery: *A History of the University of Pennsylvania, 1740–1770* (1900), pp. 236–239. Theodore Hornberger: *Scientific Thought in the American Colleges, 1638–1800* (1945) assesses the scientific aspects of Smith's curriculum. Theodore Hornberger: "A Note on the Probable Source of

Provost Smith's Famous Curriculum for the College of Philadelphia,"
Pennsylvania Magazine of History, LVIII (1934), 370–376, dissents from
the view that Aberdeen University was the source. Information pertinent
to the question may also be found in Dale Randall: "Dodsley's *Preceptor*
—A Window into the Eighteenth Century," *Journal of the Rutger's
University Library*, XXII (December 1958), 10–27; and James McCosh:
"David Fordyce, 1711–1751," and "William Duncan, 1717–1782," in
The Scottish Philosophy (1875), pp. 106–107. Major statements from the
1753 Aberdeen reform plans are printed in *Notes on the Evolution of the
Arts Curriculum in the Universities of Aberdeen* (1908), pp. 8–9. Francis
Alison's turbulent relationship with William Smith and his intercolonial
leadership of anti-episcopal forces are described in Carl Bridenbaugh:
Mitre and Sceptre (1962).

Francis Hutcheson: *A Short Introduction to Moral Philosophy*
(1747) and Francis Hutcheson: *A System of Moral Philosophy* (2 vols.;
1755) contain the content of his university lectures. Gladys Bryson: *Man
and Society* presents the social and philosophical thought of Francis
Hutcheson, and shows his important influence upon most of the other
major Scottish thinkers of the eighteenth century. W. R. Scott: *Francis
Hutcheson* (1900) is a thorough analysis of Hutcheson's philosophy. Extracts from letters of Hutcheson describing his work and aims in the
Scottish church and university are reprinted in the Appendix of McCosh's
The Scottish Philosophy. Hutcheson's political thought and its influence
upon America is examined by Caroline Robbins in the previously mentioned article, " 'When It Is That Colonies May Turn Independent:'
An Analysis of the Environment and Politics of Francis Hutcheson."
Useful for relating Hutcheson's thought to other major schools of British
philosophy are chapters in Sir Leslie Stephen: *History of English
Thought in the Eighteenth Century* (1962; first published 1876), as are
the "Introduction" and readings in L. A. Selby-Bigge, ed.: *British Moralists*
(1897).

Alison's reliance upon the thought of Francis Hutcheson is clearly
evident in the manuscript notes of his lectures. Jasper Yeates: "Moral
Philosophy in Three Books . . . To Which is subjoined Communis
Ethical Compendium: or A Compend of Ethics, in Latin, 1759"; Samuel
Jones: "His Book of Practical Philosophy, viz. Ethics and the Law of
Nature: begun 7th Anno Dom. 1760, at the College of Philadelphia under
the Direction and Tuition of the Reverend Mr. Francis Alison, D.D.";
and Jasper Yeates: "Metaphysics in Three Parts . . . Read in the College
of Philadelphia under the Tuition and Direction of Francis Alison, 1760,"
are all three in the library of the University of Pennsylvania. Thomas
Pears, Jr.: "Presbyterians and American Freedom," *Journal of the Presbyterian Historical Society*, XXIX (June 1951), 77–95, contains important

quotations from different Alison manuscripts, and adds evidence that the strain of political thought represented by Hutcheson was strong in American Presbyterianism.

Several works are particularly valuable for an understanding of the bearing of Calvinist political traditions upon the thought of Francis Hutcheson and Francis Alison. John T. McNeill: *The History and Character of Calvinism* (1954) is an excellent general history. Herbert D. Foster: "International Calvinism through Locke and the Revolution of 1688," *American Historical Review*, XXXII (April 1927), 475–499, is still the basis of many later studies. Various facets of Calvinist political thought are explored in the essays in George Hunt, ed.: *Calvinism and the Political Order* (1965). The Calvinist origins of liberal democracy are analyzed in James Hastings Nichols: *Democracy and the Churches* (1951). Nichols also has an extensive bibliography of the voluminous literature on the subject. A central theme of Calvinist political theory is treated in J. T. McNeill: "Natural Law in the Teachings of the Reformers," *Journal of Religion*, XXVI (1946), 168–182. G. D. Henderson: *Religious Life in Seventeenth-Century Scotland* (1937) documents the influence of continental political theorists upon the teaching and thinking of Scottish university professors in both the seventeenth and eighteenth centuries. Caroline Robbins: *The Eighteenth-Century Commonwealthman* (1961) is a comprehensive study of the Commonwealth tradition, containing some specific references to its Presbyterian representatives in America.

The basic ideas of Hutcheson's philosophy that engaged the attention of Jonathan Edwards appear in Francis Hutcheson: *An Inquiry into the Original of Our Ideas of Beauty and Virtue; In Two Treatises* (1726). Edwards' major refutation of Hutcheson's views is his treatise, *The Nature of True Virtue*, in *The Works of Jonathan Edwards*, III, edited by Sereno E. Dwight (1829–30). For Edwards' appropriation of Scottish empirical psychology, see Jonathan Edwards: *Religious Affections*, edited by John Smith (1959). Useful analyses of Edwards' argument with Hutcheson are A. O. Aldridge: "Edwards and Hutcheson," *The Harvard Theological Review*, XLIV (1951), 35–53, and the "Introduction" in Clarence Faust and Thomas Johnson, eds.: *Jonathan Edwards, Selections* (1935), pp. lxcc–xciii.

Chapter IV: John Witherspoon

A four-volume edition of the *Works of John Witherspoon* was published in Philadelphia in 1800 under the supervision of Ashbel Green. A nine-volume edition of the *Works of John Witherspoon* was published in Edinburgh in 1804–5. I have used the nine-volume Edinburgh edition, and references to Witherspoon's *Works* in the following comments are to this edition. The only critical edition of Witherspoon's writings is the *Lectures on Moral Philosophy* edited by Varnum Lansing Collins (1912). The Witherspoon Collection in the Princeton University Library is fully cataloged. Among the important unpublished manuscript items in the Princeton University Library are forty pages of notes from Witherspoon's "Lectures on History," copied by his student Abel Johnson, and a list of "Titles of Volumes Once Belonging to President Witherspoon and bought by the College from President Smith."

Varnum Lansing Collins: *President Witherspoon* (2 vols.; 1925) is the most scholarly full-length biography of Witherspoon. Collins' study contains an inclusive bibliography of Witherspoon's sermons, treatises, and other writings. An "Account of the Life of John Witherspoon" by the Reverend John Rodgers constitutes the preface to the first volume of the Edinburgh edition of Witherspoon's *Works*. Valuable biographical information on Witherspoon, particularly with reference to his administration of the College of New Jersey, is presented in the first volume of John Maclean: *History of the College of New Jersey* (1877), pp. 300–414. Delightful and suggestive are the pages on Witherspoon in Moses Coit Tyler: *The Literary History of the American Revolution, 1763-83* (2 vols.; 1897), pp. 319-330. Brief, but also useful, is Thomas Jefferson Wertenbaker: "John Witherspoon (1723-1794), Father of American Presbyterianism; Maker of Statesmen," in Willard Thorp, ed.: *The Lives of Eighteen from Princeton* (1946). Wayne William Witte: "John Witherspoon: An Exposition and Interpretation of his Theological Views as the Motivation of his Ecclesiastical, Educational, and Political Career in Scotland and America" (Ph.D. dissertation, Princeton Theological Seminary, 1953) is more useful for its exposition than for its interpretation. L. H. Butterfield: *John Witherspoon Comes to America* (1953) is an account of the negotiations between Witherspoon in Scotland and the trustees of the College of New Jersey, with much of the extant correspondence reprinted in full. Witherspoon's "Address to the Inhabitants of Jamaica, and other West India Islands, in behalf of the College of New Jersey," in *Works*, VIII, 308-330, stating Witherspoon's college ideals, should be read in conjunction with the treatments already cited dealing with the history and curriculum of the college. The College of New Jersey: *A General Account of the Rise and State of the College Lately Established in the Province of New-Jersey in America . . . for the Information of the Friends of Learning and Piety in Great Britain* (1752, 1754) was written by Gilbert Tennent and Samuel Davies, and is essential for comparing the original educational ideals of the college with those of Witherspoon. Bailey B. Burritt: "Professional Distribution of College and University Graduates," United States Bureau of Education, Bulletin

19 (1912), presents data on the professions entered by American college graduates before and after the Revolution.

George Eugene Rich: "John Witherspoon: His Scottish Intellectual Background" (Ph.D. dissertation, Syracuse University, 1964), is thorough, and draws upon materials available only in the collections of the University of Edinburgh and records of the Church of Scotland. Rich reprints in two appendices Witherspoon's early grappling with philosophical problems: his master's thesis, "A Philosophical Disputation: Concerning the Immortality of the Mind" (1739) and his article, "Remarks on an Essay on Human Liberty," from the *Scots Magazine* (1753). The contacts established by Samuel Davies and Gilbert Tennent with Scottish church leaders, including Witherspoon, are described by Samuel Davies in his *Journal*, reprinted in W. H. Foote: *Sketches of Virginia*, I (1850).

The works on Scottish church history mentioned in the section of biographical notes on Chapter I are all helpful in understanding Witherspoon's role in the Church of Scotland and in the controversies between the Evangelical and Moderate parties. Among the sermons and theological writings in Witherspoon's *Works* that give expression to his religious views during his years in Scotland, the most important are the "Essay on the Connection between the Doctrine of Justification by the Imputed Righteousness of Christ" and "A Practical Treatise on Regeneration," *Works*, I, 36–104, 107–331. Witherspoon's major satiric attack on the Moderate clergy in 1753 is presented in his *Ecclesiastical Characteristics; or the Arcana of Church Policy—being a humble attempt to open up the Mystery of Moderation, Works*, VI, 153–222. Witherspoon's *A Serious Inquiry into the Nature and Affects of the Stage, Works*, VI, 34–128, contains his attack upon the Moderates in the *Douglas* controversy of 1757.

The major systematic expositions of Witherspoon's theological and philosophical views at the College of New Jersey are his "Lectures on Divinity," *Works*, VIII, 9–164, and *Lectures on Moral Philosophy*, edited by Varnum Lansing Collins (1912). Other writings and sermons by Witherspoon that are particularly useful for the insights they provide into his philosophical, educational, and political thought include "The Druid" articles, *Works*, IX, 224–291; "The Dominion of Providence over the Passions of Men," *Works*, V, 172–236; "The Nature and Extent of Visible Religion," *Works*, II, 326–338; "All Mankind by Nature under Sin," *Works*, II, 9–32; "Man in his Natural State," *Works*, IV, 9–22; "A Sermon delivered at a public Thanksgiving after Peace," *Works*, V, 237–271; "Address to the Students of the Senior Class," *Works*, VI, 9–33; and "Ministerial Fidelity in declaring the whole counsel of God," *Works*, III, 258–318.

Many of Witherspoon's educational ideals are expressed in his "Lectures on Eloquence," *Works*, VII, 155–317. The manuscript notes of

Witherspoon's "Lectures on History," copied by Abel Johnson, and in the Princeton University Library, are also useful. Francis Hutcheson: *A Short Introduction to Moral Philosophy* (1747) and *A System of Moral Philosophy* (2 vols.; 1755) are the primary sources for tracing Scottish influences in Witherspoon's philosophical and political theories. Robert Schmitz: *Hugh Blair* (1946) is a careful analysis of the literary theories of Hugh Blair, to which Witherspoon's own literary theories bear a close resemblance.

Much work is still needed on the relationship between the teaching of moral philosophy in the American colleges and the attitudes of American political and social leaders in the Revolutionary and early national periods. With respect to Witherspoon, I have found several articles on specific aspects of his thought and work particularly helpful. Arthur O. Lovejoy's important essay, "The Theory of Human Nature in the American Constitution and the Method of Counterpoise," in his *Reflections on Human Nature* (1961), pp. 37–66, is extremely useful in considering the intriguing relationship between the college lectures of such men as Witherspoon and Alison and the thought of many early American political and cultural leaders. James H. Smylie: "Madison and Witherspoon," *The Princeton University Library Chronicle*, XXII (Spring 1961), 118–132; and Ralph Ketcham: "James Madison at Princeton," *The Princeton University Library Chronicle*, XXVIII (Autumn 1966), 24–54, both explore the influence of Witherspoon upon the political theories of his student James Madison. John Stewart: "Madison and Wilson: An Interrupted Philosophy," *The Princeton University Library Chronicle*, XXIII (Spring 1962), 91–108, also notes the similarities between Witherspoon's and Madison's thought. All three articles remain somewhat inconclusive, however, when they attempt to move from pointing out similarities to tracing actual, identifiable influences. One possible direction future research might take would be to analyze the thought and careers of graduates of those academies where Witherspoon's moral philosophy lectures are known to have been used, such as at Liberty Hall, Virginia, under William Graham, at Hampden-Sidney under Samuel Stanhope Smith, and at David Caldwell's academy in North Carolina.

James Hastings Nichols: "John Witherspoon on Church and State," in *Calvinism and the Political Order*, edited by George Hunt (1965), is a succinct analysis of Witherspoon's view of religious freedom. James L. McAllister: "John Witherspoon: Academic Advocate for American Freedom," in *A Miscellany of American Christianity*, edited by Stuart C. Henry (1963), pp. 183–224, is a solid exposition of Witherspoon's moral philosophy, though it tends to portray Witherspoon's sense of public service as something new at the College of New Jersey.

Among the general works that are especially helpful in relating

Witherspoon's thought to the major intellectual issues of the eighteenth century are Basil Willey: *The Eighteenth Century Background* (1941); John Hermann Randall, Jr.: *The Role of Knowledge in Western Religion* (1958); Leslie Stephen: *History of English Thought in the Eighteenth Century* (2 vols.; 1962; first published 1871); and, John Gough: *The Social Contract: A Critical Study of its Development* (1957).

Chapter V: Samuel Stanhope Smith

Smith manuscript materials are scarce. The largest group is in the Samuel Stanhope Smith Collection of the Princeton University Library. These are mostly letters, catalogs of Smith's library, a few documents relating to the administration of the college, and some lecture notes. The Princeton library also has photocopies of an extremely valuable collection of the original correspondence between Smith and Benjamin Rush that is in the Benjamin Rush Collection of the Library Company of Philadelphia.

There is no full-length biography of Samuel Stanhope Smith. Biographical data is available from several sources, a few of them nearly primary in status. Philip Lindsley has provided a long, admiring letter on Smith, his teacher and friend, for William B. Sprague: *Annals of the American Pulpit* (1858) III, 342–345. Frederick Beasley, another of his students, prefaced his edition of the *Sermons of Samuel Stanhope Smith* (2 vols.; 1821) with a long memoir of Smith. John Maclean, whose father taught chemistry at the college under Smith, devoted two long chapters to an account of Smith's life and administration of the college in his *History of the College of New Jersey* (1877), II, 5–146. Two first-rate, recent articles dealing with the life and thought of Smith are Samuel Holt Monk: "Samuel Stanhope Smith (1751–1819): Friend of Rational Liberty," in Willard Thorp, ed.: *The Lives of Eighteen from Princeton* (1946), pp. 86–110, and William Hudnut, III: "Samuel Stanhope Smith: Enlightened Conservative," *Journal of the History of Ideas*, XVII (1956), 540–552. Chapters on Samuel Stanhope Smith that help to show John Witherspoon's influence upon his thinking appear in William Bradbury: "Adventure in Persuasion" (unpublished Ph.D. dissertation, Harvard University, 1966). Some useful information on Smith's work at Hampden-Sydney College is contained in two books by A. J. Morrison: *The College of Hampden-Sidney; Calendar of Board Minutes, 1776–1876* (1912) and *College of Hampden-Sidney; Dictionary of Biography, 1776–1825* (1921).

Samuel Stanhope Smith: *An Essay on the Causes of the Variety of Complexion and Figure in the Human Species, To Which Are Added Strictures on Lord Kaim's Discourses, on the Original Diversity of Mankind* was published in America in 1786, in Edinburgh in 1787, and again in an enlarged edition in this country in 1810. Of all Smith's works the *Essay* has been of most enduring interest. A modern critical edition titled *An Essay on the Human Species*, edited by Winthrop Jordan (1966), has an excellent introduction and "A Guide to Smith's References" that effectively demonstrates Smith's immersion in the leading thought of his day and assesses the *Essay's* lasting significance. Again, of much help in elucidating the key assumptions of Scottish social thought, many of which Smith shared, is Gladys Bryson: *Man and Society*. William C. Lehmann: *John Millar of Glasgow, 1735–1801* (1960) contains an analysis of Scottish "theoretical history."

To my knowledge, the only attempt at a comprehensive examination of Scottish philosophy in eighteenth- and nineteenth-century American colleges is the doctoral dissertation of Richard J. Petersen: "Scottish Common Sense in America, 1768–1850: An Evaluation of Its Influence" (The American University, 1963). Petersen's work, however, is narrower in scope than the title suggests, and constitutes only a beginning for a much larger and much needed study. The major themes in the thought of Thomas Reid, whose epistemology is basic to Smith's philosophy, have been made conveniently accessible in Reid's *Essays on the Intellectual Powers of Man*, edited by A. D. Woozley (1941), with an illuminating introductory discussion by Woozley. In addition to Bryson and the older study by McCosh, S. A. Grave: *The Scottish Philosophy of Common Sense* (1960) is helpful—and more critical than McCosh. Smith published two volumes of his own lectures in moral philosophy, in which long sections show the influence of Reid, as *The Lectures, corrected and improved, which have been delivered for a series of years, in the College of New Jersey; on the subjects of moral and political philosophy* (1812).

Several works provide insights into Smith's influence on the curriculum of the College of New Jersey. Maclean's chapters on Smith's administration of the college are indispensable. Carl Albert Hangartner, S.J.: "Movements to Change American College Teaching, 1700–1830" (Ph.D. dissertation, Yale University, 1955) elucidates William Duncan's method of logic, which Smith's teaching illustrates. The breadth of Smith's scientific interests is clear in the letters and commentary in Michael Kraus: "Charles Nisbet and Samuel Stanhope Smith—Two Eighteenth Century Educators," *The Princeton University Library Chronicle*, VI (November 1944), 17–36. Also illustrative of Smith's desire to combine science and religion are sections in his published lectures on religion, including *Lectures on the Evidences of the Christian Religion* (1809), and *A Comprehensive View of the Leading and Most Important Principles of Natural and Revealed Religion* (1816). The most explicit statement of his insistence that ministerial education rest on a broad liberal arts and science foundation is an undated manuscript sermon in the Princeton University

Library entitled "On the Utility and Necessity of Learning in a Minister of the Gospel." Smith's published eulogy, "An Oration Upon the Death of General George Washington" (1800), is a prime example of his mature rhetoric.

A most important notebook containing transcripts of the letters from the Blair-Smith correspondence is in the Princeton University Library. Several of these letters are reprinted with commentary in David F. Bowers: "The Smith-Blair Correspondence, 1786–1791," *Princeton University Library Chronicle*, IV (June 1943), 123–134. The best discussion of this correspondence, however, is that of Samuel Holt Monk in the article cited earlier. Although these letters shed light upon Smith's difficulties with other leaders in the church, the intricacies of the controversy and details of the political maneuvering that must surely have been involved remain hidden. Relevant to the religious and educational attitudes of Smith's chief opponents are passages in James W. Alexander: *The Life of Archibald Alexander* (1854), and Samuel Miller: *Memoir of the Rev. Charles Nisbet, D.D.* (1840). Charles E. Cuningham: *Timothy Dwight, 1752–1817* (1942) presents a picture of a contemporary American college president.

Scottish common sense philosophy was only one facet of Scottish thought that Americans found useful. Equally important, if not more important, to Americans in the eighteenth century were the assumptions of Scottish social analysis. Adam Ferguson: *An Essay on the History of Civil Society*, edited by Duncan Forbes (1966) expresses the major themes that dominate the political philosophy sections of Smith's *Lectures*. Works useful for an understanding of Ferguson include, as always, Gladys Bryson: *Man and Society;* W. C. Lehmann: *Adam Ferguson and the Beginning of Modern Sociology* (1930); and David Kettler: *The Social and Political Thought of Adam Ferguson* (1965). The importance of Scottish social thought in Smith's own social theory of education suggests a whole area of inquiry that, with a few exceptions, has been ignored. How important were the assumptions of Scottish thought in providing an ideology for the founding of schools and colleges in the growing nation before the Civil War? Did shared assumptions derived from Scottish moral philosophy, for example, help to undergird the Presbyterian and Congregational Plan of Union of 1801 and the very active joint promotion by those two churches of college founding during the first decades of the nineteenth centuries? Gladys Bryson: "The Comparable Interests of the Old Moral Philosophy and the Modern Social Sciences," *Social Forces*, XI (October 1932), 19–27, is an exploratory article, concluding that "by way of the Scottish morality, chiefly, there came into the curricula of American colleges and universities a certain pattern of thought concerning human relations and institutions," and indicating that perhaps such questions are warranted. Smith certainly provides one point of departure for determining the lineaments of such a pattern.

The relationship between the concept of social progress in Smith and later theories may be examined with the use of Arthur A. Ekirsh, Jr.: *The Idea of Progress in America, 1815–1860* (1944). Ernest Lee Tuveson: *Millennium and Utopia: A Study of the Background of the Idea of Progress* (1949) studies the origins of the idea of progress in Christian apocalyptic and millennial theorists of the seventeenth century. In this connection, also see Perry Miller: "The End of the World," *Errand into the Wilderness* (1956), 217–239. Samuel Stanhope Smith represents a perfect latter-day subject for continuing the kind of study undertaken by Tuveson.

That an assessment of the long-range influence of Smith, or of the educational attitudes and concerns he represented, might prove fruitful is suggested by passages in *The Works of Philip Lindsley, D.D.*, edited by Leroy J. Halsey (3 vols.; 1866); "Joseph Caldwell," *Dictionary of American Biography;* Donald Come: "The Influence of Princeton on Higher Education in the South before 1825," *William and Mary Quarterly*, 3rd ser., II (1945), 384–385; and Isaac V. Brown: *Memoirs of the Rev. Robert Finley, D.D. . . . with Brief Sketches of some of his contemporaries* (1812).

Chapter VI: Benjamin Rush

Recent Rush scholarship has resulted in the publication of a variety of manuscripts and letters that are immeasurably valuable as primary sources for understanding both Benjamin Rush and his times. *The Autobiography of Benjamin Rush,* edited by George W. Corner (1948), is the definitive edition of Rush's own account of his life, together with his "Commonplace Book" for 1789–1813. Its usefulness is enhanced by Corner's many scholarly notes and appendices. L. H. Butterfield has published almost half of the known Rush letters from more than sixty different sources in two volumes of *Letters of Benjamin Rush* (1951). Butterfield's extensive and detailed notes, cross-references, introductory comments, and other scholarly apparatus, including an exhaustive index, make these two volumes a veritable mine of information on nearly every conceivable subject related to Rush's life. John A. Schutz and Douglass Adair, eds.: *The Spur of Fame; Dialogues of John Adams and Benjamin Rush, 1805–1813* (1966) reprints, with commentaries, the important Rush-Adams correspondence. L. H. Butterfield: *John Witherspoon Comes to America* (1953) also includes letters of Benjamin Rush and tells the story of his part in bringing John Witherspoon to the College of New Jersey. Butterfield's "A Survey of the Benjamin Rush Papers," *Pennsylvania Magazine of History and Biography*, LXX (January 1946), 78–111, is a guide to existing Rush manuscripts.

Rush's own major published works are less readily accessible. Many of his most important writings, particularly those expressing his views on education, are collected in Benjamin Rush: *Essays, Literary, Moral, and Philosophical* (1789). Rush's *Medical Inquiries and Observations upon the Diseases of the Mind* (1812) has been reprinted in a facsimile edition (1962) by the New York Academy of Medicine. Dagobert Runes, ed.: *The Selected Writings of Benjamin Rush* (1947) contains a number of Rush's writings from the *Essays*, and from two of his main medical works, *Sixteen Introductory Lectures, to courses of lectures upon the institutes and practice of medicine* (1811), and the multivolume *Medical Inquiries and Observations* (five editions, 1789–1819). Runes makes several of Rush's writings easily accessible, but unfortunately his selections are uneven in quality, and he has provided very few critical aids; therefore, the reader must go to the originals or other guides for sources and dates of publication. A scholarly edition of selections from Rush's major writings would be a welcome complement to the work of Butterfield, Corner, and Schutz and Adair.

Articles and books on various specific aspects of Rush's thought and life abound. However, the only good general biography is Nathan Goodman: *Benjamin Rush: Physician and Citizen, 1746–1813* (1934). Goodman includes an extensive bibliography of Rush's manuscripts and published writings, of contemporary sources, and of secondary writings up to 1934. Most other biographies of Rush have focused upon one or another facet of his many-sided career. Two recent biographies of Rush as a physician are Winthrop Neilson and Frances Neilson: *Verdict for the Doctor— The Case of Benjamin Rush* (1958), which concentrates upon the Cobbett-Rush controversy, and Carl Binger: *Revolutionary Doctor, Benjamin Rush, 1746–1813* (1966). A careful and illuminating treatment of Rush's educational views, and especially of his college-founding activity, is James Bonar, "Benjamin Rush and the Theory and Practice of Republican Education in Pennsylvania," (Ph.D. dissertation, Johns Hopkins University, 1965). Bonar supplements the earlier pioneering work of Harry G. Good: *Benjamin Rush and His Services to American Education* (1918). Donald John D'Elia: "Benjamin Rush: An Intellectual Biography" (Ph.D. dissertation, Pennsylvania State University, 1965) is a good discussion of Rush's thought and its development, and notes the lasting influence upon Rush of his Scottish teachers.

Rush has been treated in this study as a link between Scottish education, the Princeton tradition, and other major developments in eighteenth-century higher education. It has been my contention not only that American medical study in Scotland was one of these important developments, but also that Rush's Edinburgh experience was crucial in shaping his own educational ideas and proposals. General medical histories providing background information on eighteenth-century medicine and medical education include Douglas Guthrie: *A History of Medicine* (1946); the first chapters in George W. Corner: *Two Centuries of Medicine* (1965); Lester S. King: *The Medical World of the Eighteenth Century* (1958); and John D. Comrie: *History of Scottish Medicine to 1860* (1927). Richard H. Shryock: *Medicine and Society in America, 1660–1860* (1960) is a model treatment of ideas in their social context.

Estimates of the magnitude of American study at Edinburgh can begin with the "List of American Graduates in Medicine in the University of Edinburgh" taken from the university matriculation rolls by Samuel Lewis, and published in the *New England Historical and Genealogical Register*, XLII (1888), 159–165. Among the first attempts to appraise transatlantic influences upon American medical study were J. Gordon Wilson: "The Influence of Edinburgh on American Medicine in the Eighteenth Century," *Institute of Medicine of Chicago*, VII (January 15, 1929), 129–138; and Francis R. Packard: "How London and Edinburgh Influenced Medicine in Philadelphia in the Eighteenth Century," *Annals of Medical History*, n.s., IV (1932), 219–244. Whitfield J. Bell, Jr.: "Some American Students of 'That Shining Oracle of Physic,' Dr. William Cullen of Edinburgh, 1755–1766," *Proceedings of the American Philosophical Society*, XCIV (June 1950), 275–281, discusses the first large wave of American students at Edinburgh between 1755 and 1766, with special attention to the important influence of William Cullen. Alvin R. Riggs, "The Colonial American Medical Student at Edinburgh," *University of Edinburgh Journal*, XX (1961), 141–150, drawing partly upon records in the University of Edinburgh, interestingly portrays the life led by the American students in Edinburgh. Wyndham B. Blanton: *Medicine in Virginia in the Eighteenth Century* (1931) identifies many Virginians who studied in Edinburgh and reprints portions from the letters sent home by such students as Thomas Tudor Tucker and Theodorick Bland. D. M. Lyon: "A Student of 1765–70—A Glimpse of Eighteenth Century Medicine," *Edinburgh Medical Journal*, XLVIII (January–December 1941), 185–208, uses the student experiences of John Ravenscroft of Virginia as a basis for discussing the nature of Edinburgh medical education during the period. Benjamin Rush's own description of his years abroad appears in Corner's edition of Rush's *Autobiography*, pp. 38–78. Josiah Charles Trent: "Benjamin Rush in Edinburgh, 1766–1768," in *Science, Medicine, and History*, edited by E. Ashworth (1953), II, 179–186, discusses Rush's experience, drawing upon Rush manuscripts in Trent's own private collection. Rush refers to the influence William

Cullen had upon him repeatedly in various writings, but see especially his "An Eulogium upon Dr. William Cullen," in his *Essays*, pp. 321–343.

Useful treatments of the founders of American medical schools who studied at Edinburgh include Betsy Copping Corner: *William Shippen, Jr., Pioneer in American Medical Education* (1951); Whitfield J. Bell, Jr.: *John Morgan, Continental Doctor* (1965); Claude Edwin Heaton: "Samuel Bard, 1742–1841," *Journal of Medical Education*, XXXIII (October 1958), 717–720; John Blake: "Benjamin Waterhouse, Harvard's First Professor of Physics," *Journal of Medical Education*, XXXIII (November 1958), 771–782; and Elizabeth H. Thompson: "Thomas Bond, First Professor of Clinical Medicine in the American Colonies," *Journal of Medical Education*, XXXIII (September 1958), 614–624. An interesting article could be written, and none exists, on Samuel Finley's influence upon the many students of his who became leading early American medical educators: Benjamin Rush, William Shippen, Jr., John Morgan, John Archer, and James Tilton. Two interesting discussions of John Redman are William S. Middleton: "John Redman," *Annals of Medical History*, VIII (Autumn 1926), 213–223; and, Whitfield J. Bell, Jr.: "John Redman (1722–1808): Medical Preceptor of Philadelphia," *Transactions and Studies of the College of Physicians of Philadelphia*, 4th ser., XXV (1957–58), 103–111. Much valuable data on early American physicians is contained in the two volumes of James Thacher: *American Medical Biography* (1828).

George W. Corner and L. H. Butterfield have been among the first to begin to underscore the need to view the religious, political, educational, and medical sides of Rush's thought and activity as an interrelated whole. Many of Rush's views on republican education, and his proposals for putting them into effect, are published in the *Essays*. Benjamin Rush: *A Plan for the Establishment of Public Schools and the Diffusion of Knowledge in Pennsylvania; To Which Are Added Thoughts Upon the Mode of Education, Proper in a Republic. Addressed to the Legislature and Citizens of the State* (1786) is reprinted as the first two selections in the *Essays*, pp. 1–5, 6–20. Similar plans are put forward in Rush's proposals "To the Citizens of Philadelphia: A Plan for Free Schools" (1787), reprinted in the *Letters*, I, 412–415, and in his first public promotion of the plan that eventually culminated in the founding of Franklin College, "To the Citizens of Pennsylvania of German Birth and Extraction: Proposal of a German College," (1783), *Letters*, I, 365–368. Also see Benjamin Rush: "Thoughts upon Female Education, Accommodated to the Present State of Society, Manners and Government, in the United States," *Essays*, pp. 75–92, and, Benjamin Rush: "Thoughts upon the Amusements and Punishments Which Are Proper in School," *Essays*, pp. 57–74. The article which appeared in the *Federal Gazette*, October 29, 1788, and in the *American Museum*, IV (November 1788), "To Friends of the Federal Government: A Plan for a Federal University," has been attributed to Rush by L. H. Butterfield, who reprints it in Rush's *Letters*, I, 491–496.

Rush's writings, in addition to those already cited and passages in the *Letters*, that bear directly upon his ideas of what the ideal school and college curriculum should be include his "Observations upon the Study of the Latin and Greek languages, as a branch of liberal Education, with hints of a plan of liberal instruction, without them, accommodated to the present state of society, manners, and government in the United States," *Essays*, pp. 21–56, and his "A Defense of the use of the Bible as a School Book, Addressed to the Reverend Jeremy Belknap of Boston," *Essays*, pp. 93–113. Specific emphases in his adaptation of the school and college curriculum to the promotion of useful knowledge are also seen in the following works by Rush: "Medicine Among the Indians of North America" (1774), in Runes, ed.: *Selected Writings of Benjamin Rush*, pp. 254–292; "The Vices and Virtues of Physicians," *Sixteen Introductory Lectures upon the Institutes and Practice of Medicine* (1811) in Runes, ed.: *Selected Writings*, pp. 293–307; and "An Eulogium upon Dr. William Cullen," *Essays*, pp. 321–343. For a vivid illustration of Rush's practical view of science, see the facsimile reprint of Rush's 1770 *Syllabus of a Course of Lectures on Chemistry* (1954) and the "Introduction" by L. H. Butterfield. Butterfield's "Benjamin Rush as a Promoter of Useful Knowledge," *Proceedings of the American Philosophical Society*, XCII (1948), 26–36, presents an excellent view of Rush's activity in this area, and cites the relevant writings of Rush himself. Whitfield J. Bell, Jr.: "The Scientific Environment of Philadelphia, 1775–1790," in the same issue of the *Proceedings of the American Philosophical Society*, pp. 6–14, portrays the climate in which Rush's ideas were nourished.

The dissertation by James Bonar: "Benjamin Rush and the Theory and Practice of Republican Education in Pennsylvania," cited above, is the most careful treatment of Rush's activity in establishing Dickinson College. L. H. Butterfield: "Benjamin Rush and the Beginnings of 'John and Mary's College' over Susquehanna," *Bulwark of Liberty* (1950), and Whitfield J. Bell, Jr.: "The Other Man on Bingham's Porch," *John and Mary's College* (1956), both in the Boyd Lee Spahr Lectures in Americana, are accounts of the initial undertaking to found Dickinson College. Samuel Miller: *Memoir of the Rev. Charles Nisbet, D.D.* (1840) is a biography of the first president of Dickinson College by one of his own theology students. The best recent study of Charles Nisbet is Jean Lowe: "An Inquiry into the Life and Ideas of Charles Nisbet" (master's thesis, Columbia University, 1944).

Historians of education, except as they have been specifically historians of medical education, have tended to overlook the importance of medicine in the development of the American college curriculum. I have tried to treat Rush's medical theories, not for their own sake, but for the insights they provide into attempts of late eighteenth-century Americans to come to grips with the theoretical and pedagogical problems of an expanding scientific curriculum, and into the ways in which Scottish science supplied them with both solutions and difficulties. Thomas S. Kuhn: *The Structure of Scientific Revolutions* (1962) and George H. Daniels: *American Science in the Age of Jackson* (1968) have stressed the view that scientific ideas must be understood within the thought patterns of their own time, and not within a developmental framework that tends to assess them from the standpoint of the present. This historiographical approach has seemed to me to do justice, not only to Rush's theories and methods, which otherwise often appear naive, if not absurd, but also to the general situation faced by the teachers and doers of science in early American higher education.

Excellent discussions of Rush's medical theories and their place in eighteenth-century medicine include George W. Corner: "Appendix I," *Autobiography of Benjamin Rush* (1948); Richard H. Shryock: *Medicine and Society in America, 1660–1860* (1960); Richard H. Shryock: "Benjamin Rush from the Perspective of the Twentieth Century," *Transactions and Studies of the College of Physicians of Philadelphia*, XIV (April 1946), 113–120; and Lester S. King: *The Medical World of the Eighteenth Century* (1958), pp. 139–150. Rush's own writings that are also particularly useful are "The Progress of Medicine," "Lectures on Animal Life," and "Observations and Reasoning in Medicine," all in Runes, ed., *Selected Writings*, pp. 227–244, 133–180, 245–253.

Useful discussions of Rush's theories of mental illness include Eric T. Carlson and Meribeth M. Simpson: "The Definition of Mental Illness: Benjamin Rush," *The American Journal of Psychiatry*, CXXI (September 1964), 209–214; Eric T. Carlson and Meribeth M. Simpson: "Benjamin Rush's Use of the Moral Faculty," *Bulletin of the History of Medicine*, XXXIX (January–February 1965), 22–33; and Fritz Wittels: "The Contribution of Benjamin Rush to Psychiatry," *Bulletin of the Theory of Medicine*, XX (1946), 157–166. The major published works by Rush on mental illness are his earlier *Enquiry into the Influences of Physical Causes upon the Moral Faculty*, delivered before the American Philosophical Society in 1786, and his major text, *Medical Inquiries and Observations upon the Diseases of the Mind* (1812; facsimile ed., 1962). Rush also dealt with the moral sense in his 1810 lecture, "On the Study of Medical Jurisprudence," *Sixteen Introductory Lectures to Courses of Lectures upon the Institutes and Practice of Medicine* (1811), and in "The Influence of Physical Causes upon the Moral Faculty," in Runes, ed., *Selected Writings*, pp. 181–211. Rush's critique of common sense appears in "Thoughts on Common Sense," *Essays*, pp. 249–256.

Chapter VII: Science, Society, and the Curriculum: Conclusions

I have pointed to the importance of Scottish influences in four major areas of eighteenth-century American higher education: the development of academic science, the relationship between religion and learning, the need to formulate a social theory of education, and the growth of the college curriculum. A great need exists, however, for general and specific studies of these and other topics in American higher education during the national period. This was a time that was marked also by intense activity in the founding of colleges, frequently with interdenominational cooperation; considerable exchange of ideas and personnel among many of the colleges; continuing transatlantic cultural exchange; the growth of student societies; and widespread student discontent. In looking at Scottish educational influences, I have touched upon some of these wider topics, and have virtually ignored others. We need to know much more than we do about the colleges during this period, particularly about their place and function within the wider American culture.

Directly relevant to the history of education, and a model for further studies of the interaction between persons, ideas, and institutions is Brook Hindle: *The Pursuit of Science in Revolutionary America, 1735–1789* (1956). Hindle recognizes the Scottish background of many of America's important early scientists, as does John C. Greene: "American Science Comes of Age, 1780–1820," *The Journal of American History*, LV (June 1968), 22–41. Other general information about early Scots scientists in America appears in such secondary works as: Carl Bridenbaugh: *Cities in Revolt* (1965); Ian Cargill Graham: *Colonists from Scotland* (1956); Wyndham B. Blanton: *Medicine in Virginia in the Eighteenth Century* (1931); Theodore Hornberger: *Scientific Thought in the American Colleges, 1638–1800* (1945); and J. Gordon Wilson: "The Influence of Edinburgh on American Medicine in the Eighteenth Century," *Institutes of Medicine of Chicago*, VII (January 15, 1929), 129-138. The natural history work of some of these early Scots is discussed in M. L. Fernald: "Some Early Botanists of the American Philosophical Society," *Proceedings of the American Philosophical Society*, LXXXVI (1942), 63–71. Useful treatments of individuals include F. C. Bing: "John Lining, An Early American Scientist," *Scientific Monthly*, XXVI (1928), 249–252; Herbert Thatcher: "Dr. Mitchell, M.D., F.R.S., of Virginia," *Virginia Magazine of History and Biography*, XXXIX (1931), 126–135; and Lewis L. Gitin: "Cadwallader Colden, as Scientist and Philosopher," *New York History*, XVI

(1935), 169–177. Aspects of other Scottish-American relationships which were conducive to bringing individual Scotsmen to America are explored in Theodore Diller: "Pioneer Medicine in Western Pennsylvania," *Annals of Medical History*, VIII (1926), 141–155, and James Hayes: "Scottish Officers in the British Army, 1714–63," *Scottish Historical Review*, XXXVII (1958), 23–33.

John Morgan: *A Discourse Upon the Institution of Medical Schools in America* (1765; facsimile edition 1965) provides perhaps the best place to begin for a glimpse of the relationship between medical education and the academic institutionalization of science. Richard H. Shryock: *Medicine and Society in America, 1660–1860* (1960), as well as the works already alluded to by Brook Hindle, George H. Daniels, and Theodore Hornberger, discuss various aspects of the institutionalization of science in the eighteenth and nineteenth centuries.

There are some good articles and full-length biographies on different individual American scientists in the national period. Some of these include Whitfield J. Bell, Jr.: *John Morgan, Continental Doctor* (1965); Betsy Copping Corner: *William Shippen, Jr.* (1951); Francis Pennell: "Benjamin Smith Barton as Naturalist," *Proceedings of the American Philosophical Society*, LXXXVI (1942), 108–122; Courtney Robert Hall: *A Scientist in the Early Republic, Samuel Latham Mitchill* (1934); Edgar Fahs Smith: "Samuel Latham Mitchill—A Father of American Chemistry," *The Chandler Lectures* (1922); John Maclean: *A Memoir of John Maclean* (1876); and John F. Fulton and Elizabeth H. Thompson: *Benjamin Silliman, 1779–1864* (1967). G. G. Simpson: "The Beginnings of Vertebrate Paleontology in North America," *Proceedings of the American Philosophical Society*, LXXXVI (1942), 130–198, discusses the contributions of Caspar Wistar to that field. Edgar Fahs Smith discusses early American chemists and chemistry in *Chemistry in Old Philadelphia* (1919) and *Chemistry in America* (1914).

Scottish realism found a variety of uses at the hands of Americans in the nineteenth century, as the works alluded to in the section of bibliographical notes on Chapter I indicate. The function of the broader political and social ideas of Scottish moral philosophy in eighteenth-century American thought has not, however, been adequately studied. Gladys Bryson: *Man and Society* is, again, indispensable for background. Kingsley Martin: *The Rise of French Liberal Thought* (1954) is one source for comparing the themes of Scottish social thought with those of the French. Bryson herself also begins to point out the relationship between moral philosophy and the later social sciences in three articles, "The Emergence of the Social Sciences from Moral Philosophy," *International Journal of Ethics*, XLII (April 1932), 304–323; "The Comparable Interests of the Old Moral Philosophy and the Modern Social Sciences," *Social Forces*,

XI (October 1932) 19–27; and "Sociology Considered as Moral Philosophy," *Sociological Review*, XXIV (January 1932), 26–36.

Louis F. Snow: *The College Curriculum in the United States* (1907) is still the best single source for comparative data on courses in the American colonial college, but the subject needs to be studied anew. Carl Albert Hangartner: "Movements to Change American College Teaching, 1700–1830" (Ph.D. dissertation, Yale University, 1955) moves beyond the mere listing of courses to an analysis of teaching method and textbook content. Herbert D. Foster: "Webster and Choate in College: Dartmouth under the Curriculum of 1796–1819," *The Collected Papers of Herbert D. Foster* (1929), pp. 213–249, illustrates one way in which studies of the college curriculum can be related to understanding the careers of outstanding individuals.

Adrienne Koch: *The Philosophy of Thomas Jefferson* (1957) contains the best analysis of the influence of Scottish and French thought upon Thomas Jefferson. Essential for an understanding of Jefferson's educational work is Roy J. Honeywell: *The Educational Work of Thomas Jefferson* (1931). Herbert L. Ganter discusses what is known about William Small at William and Mary in "William Small, Jefferson's Beloved Teacher," *William and Mary Quarterly*, 3rd ser., IV (1947), 505–507. A partial list of the scientific equipment bought by Small for the college in England is published in "Portion of Physical Apparatus, Purchased by Dr. William Small in 1767," *William and Mary Quarterly*, XVI (1907-8), 166–168. Jefferson's tributes to Small and his influence are published in Andrew A. Lipscomb, ed.: *The Writings of Thomas Jefferson* (1903), I, 3; XIV, 231.

Presbyterian Academies

Founding Date	Minister	Name	Location
			New Jersey
1740	Aaron Burr		Newark
1740	Jonathan Dickinson		Elizabethtown
1743	Eliab Byram		Mendham
1752	Samuel Kennedy		Baskingridge
1766	Charles McKnight, William Tennent, Jr., Alexander Mitchell		Lower Freehold
1767	Francis Barber, John Wright		Hackensack
ca. 1770	Ebenezer Pemberton, Joseph Periam, Tapping Reeve		Elizabethtown
ca. 1778	John Woodhull	Freehold Academy	Monmouth
ca. 1787	Robert Finley		Baskingridge
			Maryland
1723	Thomas Evans		Pencader
1743	Francis Alison		New London
1756	James Hunt		Rockville
1763 incorporated	(not identified)		Frederick

Founding Date	*Minister*	*Name*	*Location*
			Pennsylvania
1728	William Tennent	Log College	Neshaminy
1739	Samuel Blair	Fagg's Manor	Londonderry
ca. 1739	Hugh Stevenson		Philadelphia
1741	John Roan		Neshaminy
1744	Samuel Finley		Nottingham
1750	Robert Smith		Pequea
1751	John Todd		Providence
1753	Sampson Smith		Chestnut Level
ca. 1759	George Duffield		Carlisle
1761	John King		Conococheaque Settlement
1771	James Latta		Chestnut Level
1775	Colin McFarquhar		Donegal
1779	(not identified)		Upper Octorora
ca. 1780	Henry McKinley		Carlisle
1782	Alexander Dobin		Gettysburg
1782	Thaddeus Dod		Ten Mile
1782	John McMillan		Chartiers
1783	Joseph Smith		Buffalo
1783	(not identified)		Bath
			Virginia
ca. 1739	John Craig		Augusta Co.
1751	John Todd		Providence
1753	John Brown		near Providence
ca. 1766	Hezekiah Balch		Fauquier Co.
ca. 1770	Adam Goodlet		Culpepper
1773	Christopher Macrae		Littleton Parish
1763	James Waddell		Northern Neck
ca. 1776	Daniel McCalla	Washington Henry	Hanover Co.
1775	Samuel Stanhope Smith	Prince Edward (became Hampden-Sydney)	Prince Edward Co.

Founding Date	Minister	Name	Location
			North Carolina*
1760	James Tate		Wilmington
1760	David Ker		Crowfield
1767	David Caldwell		Guilford Co.
1768	Joseph Alexander	Queens Museum	Sugar Creek
ca. 1774	John Barr		Rowan Co.
1774	James Hall	Clio's Nursery	Bethany
			South Carolina
1769	Hugh Alison		Charleston
1776	Joseph Alexander		Waxhaw
ca. 1780	Joseph Alexander		Bullock's Creek
1781	(not identified)		Fairforest
1781	(not identified)	Bethel	York District
1784	Thomas Harris McCaule		Winnsborough
1785	John Springer		Ninety-Six
1797	(not identified)		Spartanburg
			Tennessee
1785	Hezekiah Balch		Greenville
1785	Samuel Doak	Martin's Academy	Washington Co.
1785	Thomas Craighead	Davidson Academy	Davidson Co.
1794	Samuel Carrick		Knoxville
			Kentucky
1785	David Rice	Transylvania Seminary	Danville
1797	(not identified)		Pisgah
			Georgia
1793	Moses Waddell		Columbia Co.

* W. H. Foote says there were also academies under Presbyterian ministers in Edenton, Newborn, Onslow, Burke, Centre, and Buffalo. William Henry Foote, *Sketches of North Carolina* (New York: Robert Carter, 1846), pp. 513, 517, 543.

Founding Date	Minister	Name	Location
			New York
1743	Samuel Dunlop		Cherry Valley
1795	Samuel Buell		Easthampton, L.I.

Based on: Harry D. Funk, "The Influence of the Presbyterian Church in Early American History," *Journal of the Presbyterian Historical Society*, XII (1924–1927), 26–63, 152–189, 193–246, 281–316; Donald Robert Come, "The Influence of Princeton on Higher Education in the South before 1825," *William and Mary Quarterly*, 3rd ser., II (1945), 359–396; William Henry Foote, *Sketches of Virginia* (2 vols.; Philadelphia: William S. Martien, 1850–1855); William Henry Foote, *Sketches of North Carolina* (New York: Robert Carter, 1846); William B. Sprague, *Annals of the American Pulpit* (New York: R. Carter and Brothers, 1858), III; Richard Webster, *History of the Presbyterian Church in America* (Philadelphia: Joseph Wilson, 1857); Guy Klett, *Presbyterians in Colonial Pennsylvania* (Philadelphia: University of Pennsylvania Press, 1937); Wayland F. Dunaway, *The Scotch-Irish of Colonial Pennsylvania* (Chapel Hill: University of North Carolina Press, 1944); Henry Jones Ford, *The Scotch-Irish in America* (Princeton: Princeton University Press, 1915); Nelson R. Burr, *Education in New Jersey, 1630–1871* (Princeton: Princeton University Press, 1942); C. L. Raper, *The Church and Private Schools of North Carolina* (Greensboro, N.C.: J. J. Stone, 1898); Ernest Thompson, *Presbyterians in the South, 1607–1861* (Richmond, Va.: John Knox Press, 1963); A. J. Morrison, *College of Hampden-Sidney, Dictionary of Biography 1776–1825* (Hampden-Sidney, Va.: Hampden-Sidney College, n.d.); Wesley M. Gewehr, *The Great Awakening in Virginia, 1740–1790* (Durham, N.C.: Duke University Press, 1930); George W. Corner, ed., *The Autobiography of Benjamin Rush* (Princeton: Princeton University Press, for the American Philosophical Society, 1948); Varnum Lansing Collins, *President Witherspoon* (2 vols.; Princeton: Princeton University Press, 1925).

Index

Aberdeen Doctors, 22

Academies, English dissenting, 65–70

Academies, Presbyterian, 36–72, *passim;* in Ulster, 39–40, 65, 75; in America, 39; New Side, 55–56, 58; Old Side, 57–58, 73–75, 77; and College of New Jersey, 59; curriculum and student life of, 60–63, 73–75; education of non-ministerial students in, 60; influence on American medicine, 189–190

Academy of Design (Glasgow), 30

Act of Toleration (1689), 66

Adair, Douglas, 272

Adams, John, 185, 196, 199n

Addison, Joseph, 50, 133, 147

Adopting Act (1729), 43, 44, 142, 171

Agriculture, Scottish, 4–5, 207

Agriculture, study of, 83, 183, 204, 207

Ahlstrom, Sydney, 238, 240n, 250

Aiken, John, 69

Aldridge, A. O., 99n, 265

Alexander, Archibald, 166–170, 181, 182, 260

Alexander, James W., 271

Alexander, Samuel Davies, 259

Alison, Francis, 73–102, *passim;* New London Academy (Pa.), 57–58, 77–80; criticism of New Side scholarship, 73–74; background and education, 75–77; influence of Scottish professors on, 76–77; outstanding students of, 61n, 77–80; promotion of learning and practical science, 80–81; Newark Academy (Del.), 80–82; Rector of Philadelphia Academy, 80, 82; friendship with Benjamin Franklin, 82; Vice-Provost and Professor at College of Philadelphia, 83–84; relationship with William Smith, 85–86; friendship with Ezra Stiles, 73–74, 86–87; moral philosophy course, 88–

95; influence of Francis Hutcheson on, 88–95, 97–98; moral philosophy and public action of, 91–95; spokesman for Commonwealth political theory, 92–93; opposition to Anglicanism, 93–94; opposition to Stamp Act, 94; relationship to Scottish Moderates, 95–98; Old Side convictions of, 97–99; *Peace and Union Recommended*, 97n; contributions to American higher education, 73–75, 77–82, 86–95; cited, 57, 60, 103, 114, 122, 138, 186, 237, 244, 262–265

Alston, Charles, 230n

American Journal of Science and Arts, 236

American Medical and Philosophical Register, 229

American Philosophical Society, 79, 80, 149, 150, 163, 170, 190, 203, 219n, 239

American Revolution, 7, 36, 93–95, 129, 137–138, 148–149, 193–196, 241

American Society Held in Philadelphia for the Promotion of Useful Knowledge, 203

Analogy, scientific method of, 221

Analysis, method of logical, 160. *See also* Logic

Anatomy, 27, 233n

Anderson, Charles A., 257

Anderson, James M., 251

Anderson, John, 30n

Anderson, P. J., 21n, 250

Anti-intellectualism: New Side responses to charges of, 44–45, 59, 64, 74–75; of New England Separates, 48; of Old Side, 53; of revivalists assessed, 47–55; of John Witherspoon, 120–121, 125–126, 129–131

Antrim Philosophical and Theological School, 40